OXFORD-WARBURG STUDIES

General Editors

IAN MACLEAN *and* BILL SHERMAN

Oxford–Warburg Studies comprise works of original research on the intellectual and cultural history of Europe, with particular reference to the transmission and reception of ideas and images originating in the ancient world. The emphasis of the series is on elite rather than popular culture, and the underlying aim is to foster an interdisciplinary approach based on primary sources, which may be visual as well as written, and may extend to materials in a wide range of vernaculars and ancient languages. The authors of the series have addressed in particular the relationship between classical scholarship and the Christian tradition, the influence of modes of transmission on the uptake of ideas, the contributions of great scholars to the learning of their day, and the study of the Italian and Northern manifestations of humanism and their aftermath.

Former Series Editors

CHARLES HOPE
T. S. R. BOASE
J. B. TRAPP
DENYS HAY

OXFORD-WARBURG STUDIES

The Invention of
Papal History

*Onofrio Panvinio between Renaissance
and Catholic Reform*

STEFAN BAUER

OXFORD
UNIVERSITY PRESS

OXFORD
UNIVERSITY PRESS

Great Clarendon Street, Oxford, OX2 6DP,
United Kingdom

Oxford University Press is a department of the University of Oxford.
It furthers the University's objective of excellence in research, scholarship,
and education by publishing worldwide. Oxford is a registered trade mark of
Oxford University Press in the UK and in certain other countries

First Edition published in 2020

Impression: 1

Published in the United States of America by Oxford University Press
198 Madison Avenue, New York, NY 10016, United States of America

British Library Cataloguing in Publication Data
Data available

Library of Congress Control Number: 2019944769

ISBN 978-0-19-880700-1

DOI: 10.1093/oso/9780198807001.001.0001

Printed and bound by
CPI Group (UK) Ltd, Croydon, CR0 4YY

Acknowledgements

Institutions from several countries have made my work possible. These range from the library and archives of the Vatican, as well as other libraries in Rome and London, to institutions that provided generous financial support. My research began when I was a postdoctoral research associate at the German Historical Institute in Rome. It continued thanks to research grants from the Gerda Henkel Foundation and the Holcim Foundation. I finished several sections during my time as a *chargé de cours* in Fribourg, Switzerland. My work was also supported by the Italian-German Historical Institute in Trent, where I worked on the collaborative research project 'Transitions'. The last sections were completed during my time as a lecturer at the University of York. A longer version of this text was accepted as a habilitation thesis by the University of Fribourg in 2018; the reports of the committee provided helpful advice. Individuals who have helped and encouraged me are too numerous to mention. I would like to single out Alexander Koller (Rome), Volker Reinhardt (Fribourg), Simon Ditchfield (York), Jill Kraye, Martin Davies, and David Chambers (London), Karl Gersbach OSA (Chicago), Will Stenhouse (New York), Ingo Herklotz (Marburg), Markus Völkel (Berlin), Carlo Taviani (Rome), Giuseppe Guazzelli (Palermo), Ann Giletti (Oxford), Juan Acevedo (Cambridge), Anthony Grafton (Princeton), and my parents for their continued and unstinting support. My thanks also go to Ian Maclean and Charles Hope for accepting this book into the series and to the readers of the Press for their valuable suggestions. I hope that others who helped will forgive me for not making this list unfeasibly long. They can also be assured of my gratitude. This book is dedicated to my wife, Elisabetta.

Contents

List of Figures and Table

Figures

Table

Abbreviations and Conventions

AAug	*Analecta Augustiniana*
ACDF	Archivio della Congregazione per la dottrina della fede, Vatican City
ASV	Archivio Segreto Vaticano
BAM	Biblioteca Ambrosiana, Milan
BAV	Biblioteca Apostolica Vaticana
BNF	Bibliothèque nationale de France, Paris
Clm	Bayerische Staatsbibliothek, Munich, Codex Latinus Monacensis
Concilium	Görres-Gesellschaft (ed.): *Concilium Tridentinum: diariorum,*
Tridentinum	*actorum, epistularum, tractatuum nova collectio*, 13 vols (Freiburg im Breisgau, 1901–2001)
DBI	*Dizionario biografico degli italiani* (Rome, 1960–)
DVC-III	Onofrio Panvinio, *De varia creatione Romani pontificis*, version in 3 books
DVC-X	*De varia creatione*, version in 10 books
ILS	'Index librorum scriptorum bibliothecae Fratris Onophrii Veronensis', Vat. lat. 3451.ii, fos 1ʳ–29ʳ (autograph catalogue of manuscripts and printed books in Panvinio's possession, *c*.1564–7)
MS	manuscript
QFIAB	*Quellen und Forschungen aus italienischen Archiven und Bibliotheken*
SR	A. Mai (ed.): *Spicilegium Romanum*, 10 vols (Rome, 1839–44)
Vat. lat.	Biblioteca Apostolica Vaticana, Codice Vaticano latino

In my citations from documents, I expand abbreviations, repunctuate, add accents, modernize the capitalization, change 'u' to 'v' and vice versa (to distinguish the vowel from the consonant) and change 'j' to 'i' where necessary, but without otherwise modernizing the spelling. The numbers of popes are always changed to Roman numerals (e.g., Pius II). Names, numbers, and dates of popes are taken from J. N. D. Kelly, *The Oxford Dictionary of Popes* (Oxford, 1986). Translations are my own unless otherwise indicated.

Introduction

On Christmas Day 1567, Cardinal Alessandro Farnese wrote a letter introducing Onofrio Panvinio (1530–68) to a relative residing at the Spanish court in Madrid: 'Today he has the first place among all historians of our time and especially in ecclesiastical history, as is proved by his many printed works which pass through the hands of the learned men all over Europe.' His *Church History* (*Historia ecclesiastica*), which Panvinio hoped to publish with the help of King Philip II, would add to his fame.[1] A few weeks later, while the first manuscript volume of this work may have been travelling to Madrid, Panvinio set out on a fateful voyage to accompany Cardinal Farnese from Rome to Sicily. He was thirty-eight years old when he died in Palermo in April 1568.

The cardinal's judgement about Panvinio's pre-eminence among the historians of his time was surely a rhetorical device, and Panvinio may even have drafted his own letter for the cardinal's signature—a practice still regularly observed for letters of recommendation in Italy today. His peers, such as Carlo Sigonio (*c.*1522–84) and Cesare Baronio (1538–1607), lived much longer and died in their sixties, but Panvinio's writing career was particularly intense from an early age. As a friar belonging to a great mendicant order (the Hermits of St Augustine), Panvinio was certainly adept at finding patrons. These included Cardinal Marcello Cervini, who became Pope Marcellus II; Alessandro Farnese, the Roman Church's wealthiest cardinal; Pope Pius IV; Hans Jakob Fugger, a rich bibliophile from a German merchant family; Emperors Ferdinand I and Maximilian II; and—although he was somewhat reluctant—King Philip II, ruler of the first empire on which the sun never set. Panvinio's productivity was also prodigious. In fact, it

---

[1] A. Farnese to Francesco Maria II della Rovere, 25 December 1567, MS Vatican City, Biblioteca Apostolica Vaticana (hereafter BAV), Vat. lat. 6412, fo. 353^r, ed. D. A. Perini, *Onofrio Panvinio e le sue opere* (Rome, 1899), 244–5: 'Frate Honofrio Panvino…hoggidì tiene il primo luogo tra tutti gli historici del nostro tempo et spetialmente nell'historia ecclesiastica, come fanno fede molte sue opere già impresse che vanno per le mani degli huomini letterati di tutta l'Europa, ma più espressamente ne farà fede una che egli è per mandar fuora al presente, intitulata *Historia ecclesiastica*, che sarà distinta in sette tomi'.

The Invention of Papal History: Onofrio Panvinio between Renaissance and Catholic Reform. Stefan Bauer, Oxford University Press (2020). © Stefan Bauer.
DOI: 10.1093/oso/9780198807001.001.0001

would be hard to find another historian who had amassed such a large amount of material and written so many historical texts, on such a broad variety of subjects, by the age of thirty-eight.

History-writing in early modern Rome before Cesare Baronio's *Ecclesiastical Annals* (1588–1607) is a surprisingly underexplored subject, with major open questions. How was the history of post-classical Rome and of the Church written in the Catholic Reformation? Scholarship has neglected this question. Historical texts composed in papal Rome at this time have been considered secondary to relation to the city's significance for the history of art. As is well known, the Curia employed art to legitimate its own power and engage with various publics. For example, the fresco 'The Donation of Constantine' in Raphael's *Stanze* in the Vatican justified papal temporal rule for an audience of curial officials and visiting diplomats, whilst the frescoes in the church of Santo Stefano Rotondo (showing the torture of early Christian martyrs) incited young Jesuit seminarians to go on dangerous missions.[2] Yet, this book corrects the distorting emphasis in scholarship on the visual arts and shows how history-writing became part of a comprehensive formation of the image and self-perception of the papacy. Taking the example of Onofrio Panvinio, it shows that history-writing and its implications were a central concern of Rome's ruling elite. It also demonstrates that this historiography by no means consisted entirely of commissioned works written for patrons; rather, a creative interplay existed between, on the one hand, the endeavours of authors to explore the past and, on the other hand, the constraints of patronage and ideology placed on them.

In Chapters 1 and 2, the study provides, for the first time since Davide Aurelio Perini's monograph of 1899,[3] an up-to-date intellectual biography of Panvinio, which shows that he was much more than the antiquarian and historian of Ancient Rome whom existing scholarship has generally presumed him to be. His wide range of historical interests is investigated and

---

[2] On history painting and other forms of visual propaganda in Rome see V. Reinhardt, *Rom: Kunst und Geschichte 1480–1650* (Freiburg im Breisgau, 1992); M. Firpo and F. Biferali, 'Navicula Petri': l'arte dei papi nel Cinquecento, 1527–1571 (Bari, 2009); J. L. de Jong, *The Power and the Glorification: Papal Pretensions and the Art of Propaganda in the Fifteenth and Sixteenth Centuries* (University Park, PA, 2013). On the relationship between the visual arts and historiography see S. Bauer, 'Quod adhuc extat: le relazioni tra testo e monumento nella biografia papale del Rinascimento', *Quellen und Forschungen aus italienischen Archiven und Bibliotheken* (hereafter *QFIAB*), 91 (2011), 217–48.

[3] Perini, *Panvinio*. See also id., *Bibliographia Augustiniana*, 4 vols (Florence, 1929–38), iii. 53–65.

explained within a biographical context. The first chapter begins with a discussion of his date of birth and his family background in Verona. I dispel myths about his mother's family being part of the nobility, drawing on a manuscript collection of documents about Panvinio's life assembled in the eighteenth century by Bartolomeo Campagnola, a scholar from Verona; these documents have not previously been used by historians. I discuss Panvinio's schooling in Verona (that he attended the well-known cathedral school has been overlooked) and fill in the historical background of Sant'Eufemia, his Augustinian house in Verona. Panvinio's relations with the general of the order, Girolamo Seripando, are then discussed, as are his studies in Naples and Rome on the basis of all available archival documents. With the help of an inventory of his books, which he compiled at the age of nineteen, I reconstruct his early interests, which focused on chronology and Roman antiquity. I then consider Panvinio's first work: the Chronicle of the Augustinian Order (1551). He found another patron in Cardinal Marcello Cervini (elected pope in 1555), who encouraged him to study ecclesiastical history as well as Roman antiquity. The first fruit of this new approach was Panvinio's treatise on papal primacy (*De primatu Petri*, 1553).

I next turn to the earliest series of historical accounts Panvinio wrote: the histories of several Roman noble families of his time. I discuss how Panvinio applied his method of historical research to create genealogies from Late Antiquity and the Middle Ages to the fifteenth century. This section deals with Panvinio's histories of the Frangipane, Savelli, Massimo, Mattei, and other families. In the rich and remarkably reliable historical documentation which he assembled, Panvinio also made small but decisive interventions, resorting to forgery to prove his points. For instance, the Savelli expected Panvinio to prove that Pope Honorius III (r. 1216–27) had been a family member; to support this argument, Panvinio falsified a papal bull by adding the words 'de Sabello' to the text. In the section about the Cibo family, I explain how the descendants of Pope Innocent VIII (Giovanni Battista Cibo, r. 1484–92) threatened Panvinio with physical harm when he wrote that this pope had come from a modest background. After sustained pressure, he changed the text and stated that Innocent's father had been a knight.

Cardinal Alessandro Farnese (1520–89) became Panvinio's most important patron, giving him access to a significant learned circle. From 1557 to 1559, Panvinio went into exile from Rome with Farnese, spending two years in Parma and Venice. Both Farnese and Panvinio had reasons to avoid the zealous Pope Paul IV; Farnese left for political reasons, while Panvinio had to leave because, despite his being a friar, he lived outside his Augustinian house—a privilege Paul IV outlawed. In 1557–8, Panvinio published the *Fasti* (lists of ancient Roman magistrates), to which he appended a detailed commentary. It was one of the first editions of the fragments of these lists which had been discovered in the Roman Forum ten years earlier. The *Fasti* raises interesting questions regarding epigraphy and forgery. I argue it should come as no surprise that humanist culture was prone to forgeries. After all, humanists prided themselves on imitating classical Latin literature as closely as possible. By inventing or altering inscriptions, scholars not only wanted to show their ability to emulate antiquity, but also sometimes had commercial motives; though the market for inscribed tablets was smaller than that for ancient sculptures, such tablets were regularly sold. There were other aims, too: to 'bewilder the ignorant and test the learned' (a scholar's game) and to satisfy local or family pride. Panvinio's unpublished collections of inscriptions, therefore, came into disrepute. His other works on Roman antiquity were companion volumes to the *Fasti*: the *Commentaries on the Roman Republic* and the *Roman Emperors*. In these works, Panvinio was innovative in various ways. In his *Fasti*, he reconciled the Varronian numbering of years with that on the *Fasti* tablets. In his *Commentaries on the Roman Republic*, he attempted to combine static antiquarian methods with historico-chronological narrative, using not only literary sources, but also evidence deriving from epigraphy, numismatics, and archaeology. Finally, his approach included a pioneering interest in 'scholarly illustrations' as a means of enhancing the reader's knowledge of the ancient world; he employed artists to produce exact representations of ancient scenes. In general, scholarly research about pagan Rome remained largely free from confessional constraints. As Protestants accused the Renaissance Church of paganizing tendencies, Catholics tended to emphasize the rupture between Christian and pagan Rome.[4]

Chapter 2 begins with Panvinio's journey to Germany in the summer of 1559. After his return to Rome in September 1559, in time for the conclave in which Pius IV was elected, Panvinio started publishing only works on sacred matters, although he continued to produce unpublished studies on Roman antiquity. In 1565, he was given a position in the Vatican Library; but he held on to it for less than a year because the next pope, Pius V, did not renew it for financial reasons. In this period Panvinio also found new,

---

[4] I. Herklotz, 'Antike Denkmäler Roms in Streit der Konfessionen', in C. Stiegemann (ed.), *Wunder Roms im Blick des Nordens von der Antike bis zur Gegenwart* (Petersberg, 2017), 212–25.

important patrons in Germany and Spain: Hans Jakob Fugger, Cardinal Otto Truchsess von Waldburg (prince-bishop of Augsburg), and, among royalty, the Habsburgs Maximilian II and Philip II. During this phase of his career, Panvinio employed several scribes—and the more he had to pay the scribes, the more funding he needed from patrons. This, in turn, meant that he had to produce yet more manuscripts. His feverish productivity was halted only by his untimely death. This chapter ends with a discussion of the fate of Panvinio's manuscripts, the publication of which after his death in 1568 was held up by an order of Pius V as well as by the Congregations of the Index of Prohibited Books and the Inquisition.

Chapter 3 deals with Panvinio's history of papal elections (*De varia creatione Romani pontificis*). He was the first author to write such a work, and he succeeded in putting together an extensive range of relevant historical material to cover 1500 years of history. In this work, Panvinio felt particularly free to criticize past popes for their 'lust' for power, while at the same time defending papal primacy. Panvinio stated in his preface that he wanted to demonstrate two things: first, that there had been several different forms of election from the time of St Peter to his own day; and second, that no variation in the electoral process had taken place without the authority and consent of the popes themselves. The chapter begins with Panvinio's composition of his work from 1558 onwards and discusses its relationship to Angelo Massarelli's *Modes or Forms Observed at Various Times in the Elections of Popes* (1554). Next, the differences between Panvinio's shorter three-book version of *De varia creatione* and the comprehensive ten-book version are explored. After a summary of our current state of knowledge about the history of papal elections, which has been made topical by Benedict XVI's resignation and the election of the first non-European pope, I examine the ten-book version in detail and analyse Panvinio's manner of working. I lay out his synoptical method of presenting orthodox and non-orthodox sources. One of the key issues is his presentation of change, discord, and diversity in the Church's past.[5] Panvinio stated 'What I have written will not please the Christian reader', and he included some hard-hitting criticism of the papacy's growing bid for secular power from Gregory VII (1073–85) onwards. A substantial section is devoted to Panvinio's treatment of Gregory, which he inserted as a biography into the

---

[5] On the explosive potential of this idea in the Catholic context see, e.g., E. Cameron, *Interpreting Christian History: The Challenge of the Churches' Past* (Oxford, 2005), 142; and below, 94, 142, 210–211.

history of papal elections. It is significant that Panvinio did not attempt to publish the full version of *De varia creatione*, but instead presented an abridgement—which still contained much criticism of the Church's past—to Pius IV and his nephew, Cardinal Carlo Borromeo. The significance of the work is attested to by the spread of its manuscript copies through several European countries.

Chapter 4 ('Church History, Censorship, and Confessionalization') begins by considering the interrelationship of history and theology. From the Reformation onwards, church history presented a challenge to each confession in its own right. I review how Protestants re-invented the prevailing models of church history and how Catholics responded by underlining the uninterrupted continuity of the apostolic traditions. In the second section, I concentrate on the genre of papal biography, reviewing the various contemporary authors who wrote on the subject, from Giannozzo Manetti in the fifteenth century to Andrea Nicoletti in the seventeenth. I then focus on Panvinio's continuation of Bartolomeo Platina's *Lives of the Popes* with lives from Sixtus IV to Pius V. By editing and continuing the humanist Platina's standard papal biographies from the fifteenth century, Panvinio put himself in the position of being considered the most important authority on papal history.[6] In a third section, the question of the censorship of historical works by Catholic theologians is discussed by comparing the cases of other important authors including Carlo Sigonio. Censorship of Panvinio's short history of popes and cardinals (*Romani pontifices et cardinales*, 1557) is discussed as an example. In the next section, I investigate the question of the extent to which Panvinio could be considered a 'voice' of the papacy and to what extent his unpublished *Church History* was an expression of the confessionalization of historiography. Confessionalization is understood here as a process by which historiography was shaped by, and contributed to, confession-building.[7] Panvinio's premature death prevented him from completing a large and definitive Catholic *Church History* (*Historia ecclesiastica*)—a task which would later be taken up successfully by another author, the Oratorian Cesare Baronio. Panvinio left only a manuscript version of this work, the first volume of which was censored by Robert Bellarmine.

---

[6]   On Platina see S. Bauer, *The Censorship and Fortuna of Platina's Lives of the Popes in the Sixteenth Century* (Turnhout, 2006).

[7]   For a general discussion of this term see U. Lotz-Heumann, 'Confessionalization', in A. Bamji, G. H. Janssen, and M. Laven (eds), *The Ashgate Research Companion to the Counter-Reformation* (Farnham, 2013), 33–53. See also N. Hardy and D. Levitin (eds), *Confessionalisation and Erudition in Early Modern Europe: An Episode in the History of the Humanities* (Oxford, forthcoming).

As is illustrated by the censorships of Panvinio's *Historia ecclesiastica*, *De primatu Petri*, *De varia creatione*, and papal biographies, Catholic ecclesiastical history became more thoroughly confessionalized from the 1580s onwards.[8] The last section of this book deals with two interventions of censorship in Panvinio's history of papal elections. A commission met in 1592 to decide what should be done with all Panvinio's manuscripts. The papers of this commission, which catalogued and censored Panvinio's works, are analysed here in detail. I argue that one of its members, the Spanish jurist Francisco Peña, must have also authored the commission's censorship. The focus of Peña's censorship was on four areas: Panvinio's belief that emperors exerted power over popes for centuries; his idea that it was not beneficial to the Church for this relationship to be inverted from Gregory VII onwards; his use of unorthodox sources; and his disapproval of the behaviour of clerics. A second case of censorship of *De varia creatione* came in the form of an annotated edition created by the German Jesuit Jakob Gretser in 1609. Gretser published Panvinio's account of Gregory VII from Fugger's manuscripts. He warned his readers that Panvinio had used several authors who were critical of the Church. Panvinio was defended by Gretser's Swiss adversary, Melchior Goldast, who commended him for his 'unrestrained voice, constant spirit, truthful pen and bold style'.[9] According to the Protestant church historian Johann Matthias Schröckh (d. 1808), Panvinio's work on Gregory VII was the most moderate and useful of all available biographies of this pope because it did not seem to lean towards either side.

Panvinio has received both praise from contemporaries and recognition from modern scholars. The philologist and historian Joseph Scaliger (1540–1609) was impressed during his meeting with Panvinio (together with Marc-Antoine Muret), which occurred on a rainy day at the Orsini palace on Monte Giordano in Rome in October 1565. Scaliger, who did not know Panvinio, guessed who he was after exchanging only a few words with him. He added that he recognized Panvinio even though he did not look like a friar because of the long robe and hat (*galerus*) which protected him from the heavy rain.[10] He later referred to Panvinio repeatedly as the 'father of

---

[8] For a parallel development in Christian archaeology—that is, the confessionalization of research on catacombs from the 1580s—see I. Herklotz, 'Chi era Priscilla? Baronio e le ricerche sulla Roma sotterranea', in G. A. Guazzelli, R. Michetti, and F. Scorza Barcellona (eds), *Cesare Baronio tra santità e scrittura storica* (Rome, 2012), 425–44.

[9] See below, 205.

[10] J. J. Scaliger, *Confutatio fabulae Burdonum*, in D. Heinsius, *Hercules tuam fidem* (Leiden, 1608), 366–7: 'obvolutus enim erat longa et talari penula, galero autem tectus propter imbrem illius diei, qui multus fuerat, ita ut nullum vestigium monachi appareret'. The humanist Muret

history' ('pater historiae').[11] Scaliger, whom both Baronio and Isaac Casaubon considered the greatest scholar of his time, influenced learned opinion. Justus Lipsius echoed Scaliger's judgement in 1600, stating that Panvinio was 'the true and principal father of history and chronology'.[12] Even the leading Catholic theologian Robert Bellarmine, who had doubts about Panvinio's orthodoxy, listed him in 1613 as the most important Italian scholar of chronology of the second half of the sixteenth century. Panvinio was succeeded in this role—in Bellarmine's view—by himself.[13]

Nineteenth-century scholars endorsed these positive judgements. Hermann Grauert, a German Catholic historian, held in 1890 that Panvinio 'stands out like a *heros* on the field of the historical and antiquarian disciplines of the mid-sixteenth century. He was essentially the father of modern historical research'.[14] The pioneer of Christian archaeology, Giovanni Battista De Rossi, in his *Roma sotterranea* (1864), referred to Panvinio's studies of church history. He argued that Panvinio had 'opened the way for Cesare Baronio and had lighted the holy flame of the science of Christian antiquity, which was later never extinguished again'.[15] The Swiss Jesuit theologian Hugo Hurter listed Panvinio, in his *Nomenclator*, as the most distinguished ('omnium celebrior') writer of church history for the period 1564–80.[16] The German Catholic theologian Heinrich Schrörs planned to write a biography of Panvinio (though it was never completed); he thought that Panvinio was 'a

---

was a member of the household of Cardinal Ippolito d'Este, a patron of the arts, who had rented the palace. On this meeting see also A. Grafton, *Joseph Scaliger: A Study in the History of Classical Scholarship*, 2 vols (Oxford, 1983–93), i. 119.

[11] J. J. Scaliger, *De emendatione temporum* (Paris, 1583), 248: 'amicus noster Onufrius Panvinius, optimus vir et in cuius obitu omnes numeri historiae collacrumarunt'; ibid. 264: 'Onufrius Panvinius pater historiae'. See also Grafton, *Scaliger*, i. 1.

[12] J. Lipsius, *Dissertatiuncula apud principes; item C. Plini Panegyricus* (Antwerp, 1600), 23: 'Onufrius, verus pater principalis historiae et fastorum'.

[13] R. Bellarmine, *De scriptoribus ecclesiasticis* (Rome, 1613), Appendix, 'Index chronologorum' (not paginated). See also below, 177.

[14] H. Grauert, Review of F. X. Kraus, *Über das Studium der Theologie sonst und jetzt*, *Historisches Jahrbuch*, 11 (1890), 816–17: 'Er ragt Mitte des 16. Jahrhunderts wie ein Heros auf dem Gebiete der historischen und antiquarischen Disziplinen hervor. Im Grunde genommen ist er der Vater der modernen kritischen Geschichtsforschung.'

[15] G. B. De Rossi, *La Roma sotterranea cristiana*, 3 vols (Rome, 1864–77), i. 9: 'aperse la via al Baronio ed accese la sacra fiamma, dipoi mai più spenta, della scienza antiquaria cristiana'. See also G. A. Guazzelli, 'Roman Antiquities and Christian Archaeology', in P. M. Jones, B. Wisch, and S. Ditchfield (eds), *A Companion to Early Modern Rome, 1492–1692* (Leiden, 2019), 530–45.

[16] H. Hurter, *Nomenclator literarius theologiae catholicae*, 3rd edn, 5 vols (Innsbruck, 1903–13), iii, col. 91: 'Pauci fuerunt, qui hac epocha in illustranda historia ecclesiastica versati sint. Omnium celebrior est Onuphrius Panvini.'

truly great talent in the field of church history'.[17] In 1927 Paul Maria Baumgarten, a historian and priest who worked in Rome, praised Panvinio's 'exceptionally sound criticism' as well as his 'ingenious use of sources'. Panvinio was, in sum, a 'tremendously brilliant scholar'.[18]

In 1933 Hubert Jedin noted Panvinio's 'great importance' and pointed out the lamentable lack of a satisfactory biography of him.[19] The only general study on Panvinio remained the book from 1899 by the Augustinian Perini. Perini offered a short biography, then dealt with both Panvinio's works on ancient Rome and his studies of medieval and ecclesiastical history. This book was uncritical and erroneous. Panvinio is still best known for his works on Roman antiquity, which were analysed by Jean-Louis Ferrary in a monograph in 1996.[20] Individual aspects of Panvinio's life and the *fortuna* of some of his works have been studied in meticulous fashion by Karl Gersbach.[21] One of the aims of the present study is to correct the previous focus on Panvinio's antiquarian research and to give equal weight to his works on ecclesiastical history.[22]

Both historiography in Rome before Baronio and the interrelationship of history and theology have been awaiting a profound re-examination. Pontianus Polman (1897–1968) showed how controversial literature helped create historical research in the sixteenth century. In 2003 Irena Backus updated Polman's work, with special attention given to the study of the Church Fathers in the sixteenth century.[23] Neither Polman nor Backus focused on Rome before *c*.1580. Catholic responses to the most important Protestant *Church History* (the *Magdeburg Centuries*, 1559–74) have been

[17] G. Klapczynski, *Katholischer Historismus? Zum historischen Denken in der deutschsprachigen Kirchengeschichte um 1900* (Stuttgart, 2013), 75.

[18] P. M. Baumgarten, *Hispanica IV: spanische Versuche der Widerlegung der Centuriae Magdeburgenses* (Krumbach, 1927), 7, 30: 'ungemein gesunde Kritik, geniale Quellenverwertung'; 'ungemein genialer Gelehrter'.

[19] H. Jedin, Review of P. Polman, *L'élément historique*, *Theologische Revue*, 8 (1933), cols 305–11, at col. 311.

[20] J.-L. Ferrary, *Onofrio Panvinio et les antiquités romaines* (Rome, 1996). See also W. Stenhouse, *Reading Inscriptions and Writing Ancient History: Historical Scholarship in the Late Renaissance* (London, 2005), *ad indicem*.

[21] References to Gersbach's articles are given in the chapters below.

[22] See also my biographical outline 'Panvinio, Onofrio', in *Dizionario biografico degli italiani* (Rome, 1960–) (hereafter *DBI*), lxxxi. 36–9.

[23] P. Polman, *L'élément historique dans la controverse religieuse du XVIᵉ siècle* (Gembloux, 1932); I. Backus, *Historical Method and Confessional Identity in the Era of the Reformation (1378–1615)* (Leiden, 2003). See also S. Bauer, 'Pontianus Polman Re-imagined: How (Not) to Write a History of Religious Polemics', *Renaissance Studies* (forthcoming).

studied in some detail regarding Spain—but, again, not with sufficient precision in the treatment of sources and secondary literature.[24]

The case of Panvinio enables us to trace changes in the approach to history-writing across the epochs of the Renaissance and the Catholic Reformation. To do this, we must look at Panvinio's treatment of sources and his presentation of narrative. The inclusion of original sources which interrupted the main narrative was a traditional feature of church history, already used by Eusebius of Caesarea in the fourth century. Eusebius invented this method to document the history of the early Church.[25] Humanist historians of the early Renaissance, by contrast, tended to avoid inserting original documents into their polished accounts of history: they sought to emulate the historians of classical antiquity prior to Eusebius, and eschewed what they saw as a medieval practice.[26] In this respect, Panvinio distanced himself from humanist historiography by continuing the documentary method of Eusebius and his medieval followers. Examples of this approach are Panvinio's *Church History*, as well as his histories of papal elections and Roman families.

His use of language was not humanist, either. In a treatise on the vice-chancellor of the Roman Church, Panvinio apologized to Cardinal Farnese for writing 'in a plain style, certainly, and as the subject requires in scholastic terminology better suited to a monk than a man of letters'.[27] He returned to the problem of rhetoric at the end of his *Commentaries on the Roman Republic*, where it appears he attacked superficial humanist eloquence. After conceding his own lack of rhetorical brilliance, Panvinio affirmed that conveying an understanding of both antiquity and other disciplines did not rest on the splendour of words but rather on the truth of the described deeds.[28] This was a literary *topos* (which, to be sure, always contained an element of

---

[24] M. Flacius et al., *Ecclesiastica historia* (also known as the *Magdeburg Centuries*), 13 vols (Basel, 1559–74); J. L. Orella y Unzué, *Respuestas católicas a las Centurias de Magdeburgo (1559–1588)* (Madrid, 1976).

[25] A. Momigliano, *The Classical Foundations of Modern Historiography* (Berkeley, CA, 1990), 132–52; A. Grafton, 'Church History in Early Modern Europe: Tradition and Innovation', in K. Van Liere, S. Ditchfield, and H. Louthan (eds), *Sacred History: Uses of the Christian Past in the Renaissance World* (Oxford, 2012), 3–26, at pp. 17–18; id., 'Past Belief: The Fall and Rise of Ecclesiastical History in Early Modern Europe', in P. Nord, K. Guenther, and M. Weiss (eds), *Formations of Belief: Historical Approaches to Religion and the Secular* (Princeton, NJ, 2019), 13–40.

[26] E. Cochrane, *Historians and Historiography in the Italian Renaissance* (Chicago, IL, 1981), discusses the genres of Renaissance historiography; see ch. 16 (pp. 445–78) for the relationship between humanist and 'sacred' history.

[27] O. Panvinio, *De vicecancellario* (1554), MS BAV, Chig. H II 24, fo. 39ᵛ: 'stilo plane tenui et iuxta rei exigentiam sermone scholastico et qui monachum potius quam litteratum redoleat'.

[28] Panvinio, *Reipublicae Romanae commentariorum libri tres* (Venice: Vincenzo Valgrisi, 1558), sig. Oo3ʳ: 'Antiquitatis enim et ceterarum disciplinarum cognitio non verborum splendore, sed rerum gestarum veritate continetur'.

false modesty). Many authors of historical works since Late Antiquity had affirmed that the art of oratory was unnecessary for the presentation of the Christian faith.[29] By adopting this *topos*, Panvinio placed himself in medieval tradition rather than adopting Renaissance attitudes to style. In contrast, Panvinio's predecessor as historian of the papacy, the humanist Platina, had prided himself on improving the Latin of medieval sources such as the *Liber pontificalis*. Panvinio quipped, somewhat sarcastically, that if anyone were able to combine their elegant presentation with painstaking historical research, they would deserve to be judged 'all but divine'.[30] In 1584, Panvinio's style was regarded by the renowned Latinist Silvio Antoniano as unrefined yet acceptable.[31]

Yet, Panvinio did adopt humanist techniques and tools. Examples of this are his philological attention and his awareness of the antiquity of sources deriving from the language in which they were written.[32] He knew that minute differences in the documents he quoted might prove decisive in constructing historical accounts such as the history of Roman noble families (although his attention to philology did not keep him from introducing small falsifications). In other respects, too, he went beyond Eusebius's method. Panvinio was a historian and antiquarian. As a typical antiquarian of the sixteenth century, he sought to include in his works not just sources written on paper but also, as has been said, epigraphic documentation—that is, for example, inscriptions from monuments. Lastly, Panvinio's critical attitude towards high prelates was also shaped by humanistic precursors. When he continued Platina's biographies, Panvinio inherited his frankness in criticizing the immoral behaviour of popes.

In summary, this is a study of history-writing at a key moment in early modern history as seen through the lens of an individual author and in the context of his time. It is also a re-examination of Rome during the Catholic Reformation. It shows that friction existed between the attempts at a top-down confessionalization of historiography, exerted by the Roman Curia,

---

[29] For what follows see S. Bauer, 'The *Liber pontificalis* in the Renaissance', *Journal of the Warburg and Courtauld Institutes* (forthcoming). On the tension between religion and rhetoric see also C. K. Pullapilly, *Caesar Baronius: Counter-Reformation Historian* (Notre Dame, IN, 1975), 147–52.

[30] Panvinio, *Reipublicae Romanae commentariorum libri tres*, sig. Oo3ʳ: 'prope divinus'.

[31] S. Antoniano to Giacomo Savelli, 3 September 1584, ed. Perini, *Panvinio*, 240: 'Lo stile non mi è parso né culto né ornato; è nondimeno tolerabile.'

[32] On humanist source criticism see, e.g., G. Ianziti, *Writing History in Renaissance Italy: Leonardo Bruni and the Uses of the Past* (Cambridge, MA, 2012); S. I. Camporeale, *Christianity, Latinity, and Culture: Two Studies on Lorenzo Valla*, ed. P. Baker and C. S. Celenza (Leiden, 2014).

and individual writers before Bellarmine and Baronio. These two authors, in the 1580s, saw themselves as consciously setting models for others to follow in controversial theology and history. Bellarmine, a theologian, was active also as a censor of historical works and, as such, typified the idea that historiography had to conform with the Church's ideals in the aftermath of the Council of Trent (1545–63). Baronio, as a historian, traced the origins of ecclesiastical institutions and traditions back to the time of the early Church and countered Protestant claims that these had ever been substantially modified—or corrupted—in the Middle Ages.[33] In the first volume of his *Annales ecclesiastici* (1588), Baronio stated his programme. He would restore the original image of the Church in its pristine beauty—a Church 'without spot or wrinkle' (Eph. 5:27) that was a shining reflection of the truth. His book would therefore first describe the foundations of Christian religion, pious services, sacred councils, and canons.[34] Having accomplished this description, Baronio would turn to *continuity* as his main theme:

> We shall demonstrate for every age that the visible monarchy of the Catholic Church was instituted by Christ our Lord, founded upon Peter and preserved inviolate by his legitimate and true successors, the Roman pontiffs, guarded religiously and never broken or suspended but continued forever.[35]

As a result, when Baronio judged the validity of historical sources, he often applied standards of assessment that were based on doctrinal foundations. For him, theological and historical truth could not diverge.[36] The Church's

---

[33] The main works of these two authors are: R. Bellarmine, *Disputationes de controversiis Christianae fidei adversus huius temporibus haereticos*, 3 vols (Ingolstadt, 1586–93); C. Baronio, *Annales ecclesiastici*, 12 vols (Rome, 1588–1607). A detailed comparison between Panvinio and Baronio is beyond the scope of this book; but see below, 178–180, 210–211 and *ad indicem* s.v. Baronio.

[34] Baronio, *Annales*, *Praefatio*, i. 1: 'pulcherrima ecclesiae facies "non habens maculam neque rugam" [Eph. 5:27]'; ibid., i. 4–5: 'Nos operae pretium facturos existimamus, si una cum nascentis ecclesiae primordiis, ipsa a Christianae religionis fundamenta primitus iacta, divinas leges, pias functiones, sacra concilia, editos canones, ut instituti ratio postulabit, sigillatim recensuerimus.' See also M. Mazza, 'La metodologia storica nella *Praefatio* degli *Annales ecclesiastici*', in Guazzelli et al., *Baronio*, 23–45.

[35] Baronio, *Annales*, *Praefatio*, i. 5. My translation is adapted from S. Ditchfield, *Liturgy, Sanctity and History in Tridentine Italy: Pietro Maria Campi and the Preservation of the Particular* (Cambridge, 1995), 283. On Baronio's 'projection of Tridentine practice back onto the apostolic age' see also G. A. Guazzelli, 'Cesare Baronio and the Roman Catholic Vision of the Early Church', in Van Liere et al., *Sacred History*, 52–71, at p. 61.

[36] A. Pincherle, 'Baronio, Cesare', in *DBI*, vi. 470–8; R. De Maio, 'Introduzione: Baronio storico', in R. De Maio, L. Gulia, and A. Mazzacane (eds), *Baronio storico e la Controriforma* (Sora, 1982), pp. XVII–XXIV; S. Tutino, ' "For the Sake of the Truth of History and of the Catholic Doctrines": History, Documents and Dogma in Cesare Baronio's *Annales Ecclesiastici*',

normative system after Trent included a confessionalized view of history; but these revised norms of historiography were not thoroughly internalized before the 1580s. In the final two decades of the sixteenth century, members of the church hierarchy discussed the extent to which writings from the 1550s and 1560s, such as Panvinio's works, were still acceptable. The Congregations of the Index and Inquisition removed numerous prohibited texts, Protestant and Catholic, from circulation. At the time of Panvinio's writing, however, theological concerns had not yet won an absolute precedence over historical considerations.

As has long been recognized, the Papal State was a peculiar case in the framework of early modern European political entities. State and Church not only co-operated but fell into one.[37] The staunchly religious ideological dimension of the Papal State made it different from other confessionalized states in the early modern era. In the Papal States, theology was an omni-present source of political legitimation. This book is a contribution to recent efforts to re-evaluate the role of theology in the theory of confessionalization, in which it was seen by its original propagators, Wolfgang Reinhard and Heinz Schilling, as an essentially negligible factor.[38]

Panvinio contributed to the aims of Catholic Reform; his *De varia creatione* showed that change and development—in a vital domain such as papal elections—had been possible in history. In this way, Panvinio provided a historical foundation for reforms of the conclave. In addition, several of his works on ecclesiastical history (*De primatu Petri* and *Historia ecclesiastica*) were explicitly aimed at countering the theories of Protestants. He was the only historian of a commission, instituted by the Roman Inquisition under Pius IV, to refute the *Magdeburg Centuries*.[39] One might justly wonder whether this

---

Journal of Early Modern History, 17 (2013), 125–59. See also the pithy statement by Pullapilly, *Baronius*, 151: 'Baronius removed the burden of proof from the ecclesiastical historian and placed a burden of belief on the reader.'

[37] P. Prodi, *Il sovrano pontefice. Un corpo e due anime: la monarchia papale nella prima età moderna*, new edn (Bologna, 2006); trans. S. Haskins, *The Papal Prince. One Body and Two Souls: The Papal Monarchy in Early Modern Europe* (Cambridge, 1987).

[38] See Lotz-Heumann, 'Confessionalization', 38; T. Brockmann and D. J. Weiß, 'Einleitung', in iid. (eds) *Das Konfessionalisierungsparadigma: Leistungen, Probleme, Grenzen* (Münster, 2013), 1–22; T. Kaufmann, 'Confessionalization', in F. Jaeger and G. Dunphy (eds), *Encyclopedia of Early Modern History* (Leiden, 2016–), iii. 362–74. Reinhard's articles on Rome have recently been made accessible in a collection: W. Reinhard, *Kleinere Schriften zur Rom-Forschung*, ed. B. Emich et al. (Rome, 2017), Web, http://dhi-roma.it/reinhard-kleinere-schriften.html.

[39] Panvinio, *De primatu Petri et Apostolicae Sedis potestate libri tres contra Centuriarum auctores* (Verona: Girolamo Discepolo, 1589); id., *Ecclesiastica historia pontificum Romanorum*, MS Madrid, Biblioteca del Monasterio de El Escorial, f-I-16. See below, 182.

type of historiographical response was an expression of the Counter Reformation rather than of the Catholic Reformation. As the example of Panvinio demonstrates, Catholic Reform and Counter Reformation are inherently difficult to distinguish.

I agree, up to a point, with Hubert Jedin's classic definition that 'the Catholic Reform was the Church's reorientation towards Catholic ideals of living through an internal process of renewal, while Counter Reformation was the self-assertion of the Church in the struggle against Protestantism'. Jedin made the case that 'it is impossible to speak of Catholic Reformation *or* Counter Reformation; rather one must speak of Catholic Reformation *and* Counter Reformation'.[40] In my book, I use the term Catholic Reformation in both a broader and a less apologetic sense than Jedin. Repressive mechanisms of church government in this period, such as Inquisition and censorship, should be considered part of the Catholic Reformation. For practical reasons, I also subsume under this term Catholic responses to Protestant historiography.

A thorough consideration of Panvinio's standing as a historian has long been overdue. More than any other author of his period, Panvinio stimulated historical research into post-classical Rome and medieval church history. I consider the wider implications of his writings and present an analysis from the inside of the cultural system that was early modern Rome. I aim to provide a better understanding of the changing priorities, mentalities, and cultural standards that flourished during the transition from the Renaissance to the Catholic Reformation at a time when philological precision began to undermine age-old religious traditions. These new findings are situated in the context of the uneasy relationship between history and theology, which is still strongly felt in debates today.

---

[40] H. Jedin, *Katholische Reformation oder Gegenreformation?* (Lucerne, 1946), 38; translation: 'Catholic Reformation or Counter-Reformation?', in D. M. Luebke (ed.), *The Counter-Reformation: The Essential Readings* (Oxford, 1999), 21–45, at pp. 44–5. For discussions of the terms Catholic Reformation and Counter Reformation see also J. W. O'Malley, *Trent and All That: Renaming Catholicism in the Early Modern Era* (Cambridge, MA, 2000); S. Ditchfield, 'Of Dancing Cardinals and Mestizo Madonnas: Reconfiguring the History of Roman Catholicism in the Early Modern Period', *Journal of Early Modern History*, 8 (2004), 386–408; G. Bedouelle, *The Reform of Catholicism, 1480–1620*, trans. J. K. Farge (Toronto, 2008), 4–13; M. Firpo, 'Rethinking "Catholic Reform" and "Counter-Reformation": What Happened in Early Modern Catholicism—a View from Italy', *Journal of Early Modern History*, 20 (2016), 293–312. The search for alternatives to the two terms is still ongoing, with 'Early Modern Catholicism' as a capacious frontrunner. As has recently been noted, 'today there is still no term that covers both the efforts at reform within the Church during the sixteenth century and the attempt to win back the Church's lost socio-political terrain' (R. Decot, G. Walther, and R. Kanz, 'Catholic Reformation', in *Encyclopedia of Early Modern History*, ii. 447–57, at p. 457).

In assessing Panvinio's works about ecclesiastical history, I have sometimes made reference to the state of knowledge as found in recent scholarship. It was not possible—and is, in my opinion, not appropriate—to draw such comparisons systematically. My aim was not so much to evaluate the validity of his research results as to explore the working methods of a sixteenth-century historian. The title of this book, *The Invention of Papal History*, is of course somewhat of a provocation. Scholars of Late Antiquity and medievalists will object that papal history was born much earlier, in texts such as the *Liber pontificalis*.[41] Although I make no attempt to trace the full story of papal historiography, I give examples throughout of how Panvinio used earlier sources. The reason why I believe it is legitimate to speak of the 'invention' of papal history is that Panvinio not only collected the largest quantity of material on papal history ever assembled by a scholar up to his time; he was also prepared to apply source criticism and ask hard questions about the reality of change in the Church's past. Panvinio's creative combination of both was daring and path-breaking.

---

[41] The *Liber pontificalis* was an anonymous series of biographies of popes from St Peter onwards; its first part was written in the sixth century. See Bauer, '*Liber pontificalis* in the Renaissance'. For an overview of the development of papal historiography see H. Fuhrmann, 'Papstgeschichtsschreibung: Grundlinien und Etappen', in A. Esch and J. Petersen (eds), *Geschichte und Geschichtswissenschaft in der Kultur Italiens und Deutschlands* (Tübingen, 1989), 141–83.

1

'The Clouds Roar'

Panvinio's Early Career

From Verona to Rome

Already during his lifetime, Onofrio Panvinio was immortalized in a contemporary biographical collection. The author was Girolamo Ruscelli, who in 1564 turned to Panvinio for information while he was preparing an entry on him in his *Imprese di uomini illustri* (Imprese of Famous Men). At the age of thirty-four, Panvinio therefore put together an account of his life and his deeds, which he sent to Ruscelli in a letter.[1] We shall see how Panvinio attempted to create a memorable image of himself, sometimes mixing fact and fiction. His early biography will be reconstructed by verifying what he sets out in the letter.

Panvinio was born in Verona as Giacomo Panvino; it was only later, upon entering the Augustinian Order, that he changed his name to Onofrio in memory of his father. By his own account, his date of birth was 24 February 1530, the day on which Charles V was crowned emperor by Pope Clement VII in Bologna.[2] Not only was this the day of the coronation, it was also the emperor's own birthday. The coincidence that Panvinio's birth fell on this day must surely be understood as a piece of literary fiction destined for publication in Ruscelli's *Imprese*. As we know from other sources, Panvinio was most likely born on 20 February.[3]

---

[1] For what follows see Panvinio's letter to G. Ruscelli, 4 November 1564, in G. Ruscelli, *Lettere*, ed. C. Gizzi and P. Procaccioli (Manziana, 2010), 186–93; G. Ruscelli, *Le imprese illustri* (Venice, 1566), 532–5 (section on Panvinio, also reprinted in Ruscelli, *Lettere*, pp. c–cvi).

[2] Panvinio to Ruscelli, 4 November 1564, in Ruscelli, *Lettere*, 188.

[3] Panvinio to Hans Jakob Fugger, 20 February 1563, Vat. lat. 6277, fo. 74^r: 'die natalis meo'. According to his brother Paolo, he was born on 'Sunday' (the feast day 'domenica parentevole'), 19 February 1530; but the 19th, in fact, fell on a Saturday that year. Panvinio's own indication of 20 February points to a Sunday and is compatible with Paolo's indication of the feast day. See Paolo Panvinio, *Vita del Reverendo Padre Onofrio Panvinio*, MS Milan, Biblioteca Ambrosiana (hereafter BAM), Q 115 sup., fos 68^r–73^v, ed. Perini, *Panvinio*, 214–24, at p. 214.

The Invention of Papal History: Onofrio Panvinio between Renaissance and Catholic Reform. Stefan Bauer, Oxford University Press (2020). © Stefan Bauer.
DOI: 10.1093/oso/9780198807001.001.0001

His family lived beyond the river Adige, near the walls of the medieval commune in the district of San Vitale, a populous and somewhat marginal district of Verona. Both his father, Onofrio Panvino, and his mother, Bartolomea Campagna, came from this district.[4] As has been said, their elder son was born Giacomo Panvino; by his own account, he amended his last name to Panvinio, 'according to the old manner and for better consonance' ('all'anticha et per maggior consonantia'). True to his attempt at scholarly self-fashioning in Ruscelli's *Imprese*, Panvinio provided a series of particulars about the history of his forebears. In the Middle Ages his family had belonged to the nobility in both Cremona and Verona. At some point, they experienced a steep decline but managed to remain citizens. In the early fifteenth century, they became craftsmen—in particular, furriers. By Panvinio's day they had given up this trade and lived on other income, although it is not clear of what sort.[5]

How much of this is true? Such information is not easy to verify, and some of the details may be dubious. Certainly, in the eighteenth century the history of this family was hardly known, even to the most erudite Veronese local historians. One of these historians, Giovanni Battista Biancolini, found evidence of the first Panvino in Verona only for the fifteenth century.[6] Another local historian, Bartolomeo Campagnola, was more persistent and established a genealogy of the 'de Panevino' family from c.1400 to 1600. Campagnola (1692–1781), who was judged by Lodovico Antonio Muratori to be 'a skilled hunter' of documents, dug deep into several Veronese archives.[7] Campagnola summed up his results in a preface which he composed for his planned re-publication of Panvinio's *Veronese Antiquities*: The Panvino were, at least since 1400, an honest, but not noble Veronese family. They subsisted modestly as craftsmen. The family was extinguished around 1600 upon the deaths of the last males who carried the name; females in the sixteenth century were successfully married to several scribes, notaries, and nobles.[8]

---

[4] See A. Tagliaferri, *L'economia veronese secondo gli estimi dal 1409 al 1635* (Milan, 1966), 45; Paolo Panvinio, *Vita*, 214.

[5] Panvinio to Ruscelli, 4 November 1564, 188: 'vivono d'entrata esercitando il palazzo'. See also Panvinio, *Antiquitatum Veronensium libri VIII*, ed. Marco Antonio Clodio et al. (first publ. Padua: Paolo Frambotto, 1647), 2nd edn (1648), 160.

[6] G. B. Biancolini, *Notizie storiche delle chiese di Verona*, 8 vols (Verona, 1749–71), ii. 517.

[7] B. Campagnola, 'Materiali per scrivere la vita e commentare le opere delle antichità veronesi di Onufrio Panvinio', MS Verona, Biblioteca civica, 2852, 57 fos. Muratori is quoted from M. Zorzato, 'Campagnola, Bartolomeo', in *DBI*, xvii. 311–12: 'un bravo cacciatore'.

[8] Campagnola, 'Ex notis quae per me, Bartholomaeum Campagnolam...parantur in libros *Antiquitatum Veronensium* Onuphrii Panvinii' (1739), in his 'Materiali', fos 42ʳ–43ʳ. On the *Antiquitates Veronenses* see below, 50–51.

More details can be gleaned from the various documents in Campagnola's collection. These specify that the 'Panevino' were a family of *sartores* (patchers, menders, or possibly tailors) from at least around 1400 onwards.[9] Among the documents is the will of our Panvinio's grandfather, Giacomo, after whom the boy was probably named.[10] Giacomo was the son of Paolo, a *sartor* from the district of San Vitale. Giacomo's uncle Matteo was a *varotarius*—that is, a furrier specializing in vair—though this seems to have been an exception in a family of otherwise more modest *sartores*. (Panvinio, in his letter to Ruscelli, turned this exception into the rule.)[11] Campagnola's conclusion that the Panvino were neither a noble nor an important family is also confirmed by the various lists of citizens which were drawn up according to nobility, civic functions, or income in the sixteenth and seventeenth centuries. The name does not appear in these lists.[12]

Panvinio's mother was a Campagna, which, according to Panvinio, was 'doubtless' a very noble family.[13] She was the daughter of Bernardo Maria and her grandfather was named Marino Campagna.[14] They were, like Panvinio's father, from the district of San Vitale. Her family had lost the largest part of its wealth through unlucky circumstances and wars. Panvinio counted among his ancestors the aristocrat Bernardo Campagna, a medical doctor under the della Scala in the thirteenth or fourteenth century, who was mentioned by Biondo Flavio in his *Italia illustrata*.[15]

We know that the Campagna were indeed part of the old Veronese nobility and had resided there already before the rule of the della Scala. Around 1600 they belonged to the aristocracy of medium rank and lived in well-to-do or, at any rate, respected districts in the centre, such as San Pietro Incarnario.[16] Biancolini, the local historian quoted above, however, questioned whether these were the same Campagna to which Panvinio belonged. Biancolini found that Panvinio's mother came not from this aristocratic

[9] Campagnola, 'Materiali', fo. 33ʳ (will of Dominicus de Panevino, 27 May 1440). See also the family tree on fo. 46ʳ.
[10] Ibid., fos 24ʳ, 31ʳ, 32ʳ⁻ᵛ (will of Iacobus de Panevino, 29 May 1521).
[11] Ibid., fos 24ʳ, 33ᵛ (will of Matthaeus de Panevinis, 24 August 1500) and 38ʳ. For the term *varotarius*, meaning 'pellicciao (di vaio)', see Tagliaferri, *Economia veronese*, 216.
[12] For such lists see F. Del Forno, *Case e palazzi di Verona* (Verona, 1973), 31–4; V. Chilese, *Una città nel Seicento veneto: Verona attraverso le fonti fiscali del 1653* (Verona, 2002).
[13] Panvinio to Ruscelli, 4 November 1564, 188: 'senza dubio in Verona è nobilissima'.
[14] Paolo Panvinio, *Vita*, 214: 'fu figliuola di Messer Bernardo Maria [figliuolo del] quondam Marino Campagna della detta contrà di San Vitale'.
[15] Biondo Flavio, *Italia illustrata*, in his *Opera* (Basel, 1531), 293–422, at p. 377.
[16] Del Forno, *Case e palazzi*, 25, 29, 32; Chilese, *Una città*, 74, 100.

house, but rather from the simpler Campagna Tagliapietra ('stone cutter'), who dwelt, as we have seen, in San Vitale.[17] Campagnola's collection also confirmed this. He labelled his set of notes from wills between 1471 and 1558 as pertaining to 'that Campagna family which is not referred to as noble'.[18] In a register for the district of San Vitale of 1519, Panvinio's maternal grandfather was mentioned as living there. In the same register, Campagnola found references to two Campagna who worked there as stone cutters (*lapicidae*).[19]

That Panvinio's brother Paolo was younger has been assumed based on the custom of giving the first son the name of the grandfather on the father's side, which in this case was Giacomo.[20] Panvinio also had at least one sister, by the name of Cassandra. She, too, was probably younger. Panvinio mentioned in 1564 that with his modest income he had to take care of the marriage of a sister, as his family was impoverished.[21] We know where the large dowry provided by Panvinio went: Cassandra married a rich wood merchant, with whom she had three children by the time he drew up his will in 1569.[22]

His brother and sister must have been born within six or seven years of Panvinio's birth, as, by Paolo's account, their father died in 1536. After this undoubtedly traumatic event, a relative from his father's side—who, as a cleric, possessed some benefices—persuaded Panvinio's mother to designate him for an ecclesiastical career. This Gieronimo Panvino promised that he would renounce his own benefices in favour of the boy. His mother's economic constraints must have played a big part in her agreeing to this plan. Gieronimo lived in the district of Santa Cecilia and was mentioned in

---

[17] Biancolini, *Notizie storiche*, ii. 517.

[18] Campagnola, 'Materiali', fo. 23[r–v]: 'familiae a Campanea quae nobilis non dicitur'. See also his 'Ex notis' (n. 8, above), fo. 42[r].

[19] Campagnola, 'Materiali', fos 45[r], 38[v]. Campagnola mistook one of them for the celebrated sculptor Girolamo Campagna, who was not born until 1549.

[20] K. A. Gersbach, 'Onofrio Panvinio's Brother, Paolo, and his Role in the Posthumous Edition of the *De primatu Petri et Apostolicae Sedis potestate* and the Purchase of Onofrio's Manuscripts for the Vatican Library', *Analecta Augustiniana* (hereafter *AAug*), 56 (1993), 241–64, at p. 244.

[21] Panvinio to Ruscelli, 4 November 1564, 189: 'ho maritata una sorella con buona dote'. In 1563 Panvinio mentioned 'sisters', in the plural, for whom he provided dowries; this was probably an exaggeration to underline his financial distress. See Panvinio's letter to an unnamed addressee, 20 November 1563, in K. A. Gersbach, 'Onofrio Panvinio's *De comitiis imperatoriis* and its Successive Revisions: Biographical Background and Manuscripts', *AAug*, 53 (1990), 409–52, at pp. 442–3; id., 'Brother', 255–6.

[22] Campagnola, 'Materiali', fos 27[r], 29[v], 31[v]–32[v] (will of Joannes Baptista de la Gobba, 24 July 1569). See also ibid., fos 28[r], 34[r].

documents of 1530 and 1551 as chaplain at the cathedral (*capellanus cathedralis*); he made a will in 1566.[23] It is likely that Gieronimo helped our Panvinio in his early childhood, during the three or four years (*c.*1537–40) in which the young boy attended the cathedral school ('scuola di domo').[24]

This school was the well-known *Scuola degli Accoliti*, the college of acolytes.[25] Despite its name, the school, since 1505, had also accepted secular pupils, so boys being prepared for their future in the ranks of the Church were educated side by side with others being trained for their roles in Verona's civic life. It is unclear whether Panvinio was an acolyte and what his funding arrangements were. At the school, Panvinio might have had his head shaved for the first time—the strict reformer Gian Matteo Giberti (bishop of Verona, 1524–43) arranged for a barber to visit the premises every week for this purpose. Giberti also took care to enforce school discipline and appointed a spiritual director to give simple introductions to Holy Scripture, teach the boys how to pray and hear their confession. The school's fame rested on its musical education; Vincenzo Ruffo, a renowned composer of masses and madrigals, was trained there in the 1520s. The grammar teachers were less famous, although in 1536–7 we find, for one year, the accomplished Greek scholar Bernardino Donato, who had also taught at the University of Padua. In any case, Panvinio would have received solid grammar teaching at a relatively ambitious school.

At the age of eleven, in 1541, Panvinio entered the Augustinian house of Sant'Eufemia and received the habit of the Augustinian hermits. The church, with a length of ninety metres, was one of the largest in Verona—a size which made it possible to host the general chapter of the Augustinian Order there in 1538. It is tempting to imagine Panvinio as a young boy, watching scores of Augustinians in their black habits, as they made their way through Verona for this gathering.[26] A small *studium* was active at Sant'Eufemia from at least 1294 and a 'very beautiful library' with numerous 'rare books' existed

---

[23] Ibid., fos 27ʳ, 29ʳ, 30ʳ, 37ʳ⁻ᵛ, 46ʳ.

[24] For his attending the school see Paolo Panvinio, *Vita*, 214.

[25] For what follows see A. Spagnolo, 'Le scuole accolitali di grammatica e di musica in Verona', *Atti e memorie dell'Accademia d'agricoltura, scienze, lettere, arti e commercio di Verona*, ser. iv, 5 (1904) no. 1, 97–330, esp. pp. 115–44, 311–27; A. Prosperi, *Tra evangelismo e controriforma: G. M. Giberti, 1495–1543* (Rome, 1969), 233–4.

[26] N. Zanolli Gemi, *Sant'Eufemia: storia di una chiesa e del suo convento a Verona* (Verona, 1991); E. Esteban, 'De capitulo generali Veronae celebrato anno 1538', *AAug*, 9 (1921–2), 263–71; L. Tacchella, *Il processo agli eretici veronesi nel 1550: Sant'Ignazio di Loyola e Luigi Lippomano (carteggio)* (Brescia, 1979), 58.

a hundred years later.[27] This *studium* was 'provincial'—that is, limited in the subject matter it taught—and concentrated mostly on logic. For advanced and theological studies, students were traditionally sent to a general *studium* in the Augustinian houses of Rome, Naples, Siena, Perugia, Bologna, Rimini, Padua, or Pavia; to these were added, between 1540 and 1544, Pisa, Venice, and Milan.[28]

Sant'Eufemia, with twenty-two professed brothers in 1537, was a larger-than-average Augustinian house. In 1540, the house suffered a major scandal when a leading member of the monastic community was convicted of heresy. Fra Niccolò da Verona had been the prior in 1537–8 and was on friendly terms with the Catholic reformer Girolamo Seripando (1492/93– 1563), who was elected general of the Augustinian Order in 1539.[29] Niccolò appears to have converted and began preaching Protestant doctrine as well as distributing Protestant books. Bishop Giberti was 'deeply disturbed' ('graviter commotus'), and Seripando, on a return visit to Verona in June 1540, had no choice but to expel Niccolò from the order. In evaluating this incident, it must be remembered, of course, that Martin Luther himself had defected from the ranks of the Augustinian hermits and had thrown the order into a crisis. In Germany, all the Augustinian provinces were seriously affected. Luther's influence also took root in several houses in France and Northern Italy. Until the Council of Trent and later, the Augustinians in general were suspected of Lutheran thinking, such that the order had every good reason to pursue heretics vigilantly within its own ranks. After the founding of the Roman Inquisition in 1542, Seripando acted as a commis- sary for the new institution to deal with cases inside the order. He empha- sized hierarchy and discipline and aimed to provide a better formation of young men to enable the order to survive this crisis.[30]

Sant'Eufemia must still have been reeling from the heresy incident when, in 1541, Panvinio stepped through its late-Gothic portal. Panvinio's age,

---

[27] On the 'bibliotheca pulcherrima' and its 'plurimi ac rari libri' see D. A. Gandolfo, *Dissertatio historica de ducentis celeberrimis Augustinianis scriptoribus* (Rome, 1704), 213. See also Zanolli Gemi, *Sant'Eufemia*, 24–5, 28.

[28] H. Jedin, *Girolamo Seripando: sein Leben und Denken im Geisteskampf des 16. Jahrhunderts*, 2 vols (Würzburg, 1937), i. 245–6.

[29] For what follows see ibid., i. 42–3, 140, 170–1, 185–6, 259–81, ii. 259; Tacchella, *Processo*, 56–60; *Hieronymi Seripando O.S.A. Registra generalatus, 1538–1551*, ed. D. Gutiérrez, 7 vols (Rome, 1982–96), vii (Index generalis), s.v. Nicolaus Veronensis.

[30] D. Gutiérrez, *The Augustinians from the Protestant Reformation to the Peace of Westphalia 1518–1648*, trans. J. J. Kelly (Villanova, PA, 1979), 30–2.

eleven, was the minimum for a novice.[31] As was customary, Panvinio changed his name to mark his entrance into the community. During his novitiate, the probation period of one year, Panvinio was, above all, expected to familiarize himself with the Rule of St Augustine and the severity of life in the community, as well as with singing and reciting the divine office at fixed hours. The master of novices trained them in the rites and rules of the common life: when and where not to speak, when to kneel down, when to prostrate themselves on the floor, how to be humble and love poverty. It seems that this master of novices in Verona also taught Latin.[32] The second master, Panvinio's principal teacher, was Giovanni Battista Marchesino, a close relative of the family, who served as prior from 1540 to 1542/43. It was on his initiative that the boy had entered the order. For two years Marchesino taught him in Sant'Eufemia.[33]

When the novitiate was over, in 1542, Panvinio proceeded to his profession. In this solemn ceremony, his habit was blessed by the prior; then Panvinio, on his knees, promised to be obedient to God, the Virgin Mary, and the authorities of the order, and to live without property and in chastity according to the Rule of St Augustine until the end of his life. Thus, from a novice he turned into a professed brother, who was assigned a new seat among the friars as an external sign of his new status.[34] His Augustinian habit was a black cowl, tied at the waist with a long belt; it had a short hood or capuche, which friars usually pulled over their head when they travelled. With worship, cloistered life, and penitential acts such as fasting, the Augustinians practised a fairly rigorous asceticism. While in the late Middle Ages the order witnessed a decline in observance and a rise of dispensations, in the sixteenth century it was well known for the reforms undertaken during the period prior to the Council of Trent. Priors general Giles of Viterbo (1506–18) and Girolamo Seripando (1539–51) persistently pursued a reform programme for the restoration of the common life.[35]

---

[31] Panvinio to Ruscelli, 4 November 1564, 188. Minimum age: Constitutions of 1290, ch. 16, in I. Arámburu Cendoya (ed.), *Las primitivas Constituciones de los Agustinos* (Valladolid, 1966), 59 (addition of 1348).

[32] Constitutions of 1290, ch. 17, in *Primitivas Constituciones*, 59–60, with other graphic details. See also Gutiérrez, *Augustinians 1518–1648*, 143. For Verona see *Hieronymi Seripando Registra*, v (1988), 109.

[33] Paolo Panvinio, *Vita*, 215. On Marchesino see also K. A. Gersbach, 'Giuseppe Panfilo, OSA, Papal Sacristan and Bishop of Segni: Biography, Literary Activity, and Relationship to Onofrio Panvinio, OSA', *AAug*, 58 (1995), 45–83, at p. 59.

[34] Constitutions of 1290, ch. 18, pp. 61–3.

[35] D. Gutiérrez, *The Augustinians in the Middle Ages 1357–1517*, with contributions by R. Arbesmann and A. Zumkeller, trans. T. Martin (Villanova, PA, 1983), 40–1, 109.

Marchesino, Panvinio's teacher, died about a year after Panvinio's profession. Marchesino's successor as prior, Ambrogio of Verona (prior 1543–6), then took care of the boy's education. According to Panvinio's brother Paolo, he taught him logic and some fundamentals of theology.[36] In 1544 Panvinio also attended the grammar school of a certain Daniele Aliense to improve his Latin, and he became passionate about ancient Roman chronology. Daniele's last name suggests that he may have been a foreigner (*alienus*).[37] In 1547 Ambrogio of Verona was sent to the Council of Trent.

In the same year, Panvinio, by his own account, came to Rome for the first time, in the services of Prior General Seripando, and then served Seripando for the next four years.[38] Seripando was Panvinio's protector and has sometimes been regarded as the discoverer of this young talent. The story of this discovery, as told by his brother, goes as follows: On the way to the Council of Trent, Seripando visited the Augustinian house at Verona. For this event, the fifteen- or sixteen-year-old Panvinio gave a Latin oration, composed by himself. Deeply impressed, the general probed the boy's talents by questioning him and decided to take an interest in him by sending him to the general houses in Naples and Rome for his studies.[39] A month-long visit by Seripando in Verona is, in fact, attested to have begun on 15 September 1545.[40]

In 1546 the Veronese Augustinian community was in great debt brought about by the dissipation of its goods by individual friars and the lavish entertainment of guests. Seripando therefore sent a special vicar to examine the situation, instructing him to cut spending and possibly reduce the number of members of the house.[41] It is probable that Panvinio departed from Verona in late summer 1546 to commence the academic year in Naples. Perhaps it was convenient for Sant'Eufemia at that moment to have one fewer mouth to feed.

---

[36] Paolo Panvinio, *Vita*, 215; on Ambrogio see K. A. Gersbach, 'A Letter of Ambrogio of Verona, O.S.A.', *Augustiniana*, 42 (1992), 207–12.

[37] Panvinio, *Fastorum libri V a Romulo rege usque ad Imperatorem Caesarem Carolum V Austrium Augustum; In Fastorum libros commentarii* (Venice: Vincenzo Valgrisi, 1558), sig. b5ʳ; Paolo Panvinio, *Vita*, 215. See also my section on the *Fasti*, below, 50–61.

[38] Panvinio to Ruscelli, 4 November 1564, 189. As we will see, it is more likely that he actually arrived in Rome in 1548 rather than in 1547.

[39] Paolo Panvinio, *Vita*, 215–16.

[40] In 1545, he stayed there from 15 to 18 May and from 15 September to 15 October. See D. Gutiérrez, 'Hieronymi Seripandi "Diarium de vita sua" (1513–1562)', *AAug*, 26 (1963), 5–193, at pp. 57–8, 61–2, 68; *Hieronymi Seripando Registra*, iv. 21–3, 159, 220–34, v. 108–9.

[41] *Hieronymi Seripando Registra*, v. 59–60, 74, 109.

Panvinio thus remained in Verona for about another year after his 'discovery' by Seripando. The first reference to Panvinio's presence in Naples is dated from 1547; in May 1547 and again in May 1548 he was listed among the students at the general study house (*studium generale*) of Sant'Agostino in Naples.[42] Naples may have been a particular choice of Seripando, for this was his home town, which he had left only upon becoming general in 1539. Although Panvinio was listed as a student in Naples in May 1547, this does not mean he arrived in May, as previous scholarship has assumed. The composition (*dispositio*) of each house of studies was sent to the prior general every year around May and showed the status quo at that moment. Because the academic year commenced in September, it is probably safe to assume that Panvinio began his studies in September 1546.[43] Here he met his new prior Aurelio della Rocca, a theologian who was very close to Seripando—an *intimus*—and had accompanied the prior general to Trent in 1545–6 to join in the theological discussions. Aurelio came to Naples shortly after Panvinio, in 1547, and remained there, like him, for about two years.[44]

More than philosophy and theology, Panvinio was fascinated by other topics, and pursued studies of pagan history and topography. By his own account, he had enthusiastically engaged in historical studies ever since he entered the Augustinian Order at age eleven.[45] Searching for the temple of the Cumaean Sibyl in 1548, for example, he travelled to Pozzuoli and Baia.[46]

Panvinio must have moved to Rome by September 1548, as in May 1549 he was listed among the members of the Roman *studium*.[47] The Augustinian house at Rome was attached to the church of Sant'Agostino near Piazza Navona. We are well informed about its architecture but not its internal

---

[42]   Ibid., v. 142 (29 May 1547) and vi. 14 (4 May 1548).

[43]   My thanks to Luis Marín de San Martín (Archivio Generale Agostiniano, Rome) for his help with this chronological question.

[44]   On Aurelio della Rocca see Jedin, *Seripando*, ii. 381, and *ad indicem*; Gutiérrez, 'Seripandi "Diarium"', *ad indicem* s.v. Aurelius de Roccacontracta; id., 'Patres ac theologi augustiniani qui concilio Tridentino interfuerunt', *AAug*, 21 (1947–50), 55–177, at pp. 121–3.

[45]   Panvinio, *De urbis Veronae viris doctrina et bellica virtute illustribus* (Verona: Angelo Tamo, 1621), 48; id., *Antiquitatum Veronensium libri VIII* (1648), 163: 'huic studio [historiae] adhuc puer neque aetatis duodecimum excedens annum impensissime vacare coeperim eo ipso tempore, quo Sancti Augustinianorum instituti vestes Veronae assumpsi'.

[46]   Panvinio, *De sibyllis et carminibus sibyllinis*, printed together with *De ludis saecularibus*, in his *Fastorum libri V* (1558), separate page numbering, 26–35, at p. 35. See K. A. Gersbach, 'The Books and Personal Effects of Young Onofrio Panvinio, O.S.A., in Vat. Lat. 7205', *AAug*, 52 (1989), 51–76, at p. 59.

[47]   *Hieronymi Seripando Registra*, vi. 151 (25 May 1549: under *studentes*).

life.[48] The prior from Naples, Aurelio della Rocca, was also transferred there and from spring 1549 was prior in Rome. If Seripando regarded himself as a protector of the young Panvinio, it may not be mere coincidence that he had him transferred at about the same time as his own *intimus* Aurelio. Moreover, from October 1548 until the summer of 1550 Seripando himself remained in Rome.[49] Panvinio's transferral may also have been connected to his task of compiling a chronicle of the Augustinian Order, as part of the new edition of the constitutions of the order, the production of which Seripando was supervising. Panvinio can be considered fortunate to have left Naples, as the Augustinian house there fell into disarray in 1551, when its prior was murdered under mysterious circumstances and several friars were arrested.[50]

We possess an inventory of Panvinio's books and personal belongings, which he drew up in 1549–50; it reveals information about the items at his disposal during his time as a student in Naples and Rome.[51] The inventory was followed by a list of his income and spending for the months of January and February 1550. The list of Panvinio's books certainly reflected the contents of his course of study. In the first five years of the *studium generale*, classes consisted of logic and philosophy, especially Aristotle. Among Panvinio's books we also find texts used for Latin teaching, which he may already have possessed in Verona, and many works of classical authors. Cicero's works are represented in large numbers. By virtue of this book list, Panvinio's study of ancient Greek is documented. Religious and devotional works are not predominant, but obvious texts such as the New Testament, the Breviary, and Offices were among his belongings.

Panvinio's passion for history and chronology becomes evident. Let us glance, then, at Panvinio's bookshelf at the age of nineteen. For reference works on the Roman emperors, we find Erasmus's edition of Suetonius's *Vitae Caesarum* and the *Scriptores Historiae Augustae*, issued in folio format in Basel or Cologne.[52] Panvinio also had *De Caesaribus*, a world history according to emperors compiled by Giovanni Battista Egnazio (1478–1553),

---

[48] *La chiesa, la Biblioteca Angelica, l'Avvocatura generale dello Stato: il complesso di Sant'Agostino in Campo Marzio* (Rome, 2009).

[49] Gutiérrez, 'Seripandi "Diarium"', 75–80; Jedin, *Seripando*, ii. 415.

[50] Jedin, *Seripando*, i. 466–7.

[51] 'Inventario de' libri e robbe di Frate Onofrio Panvino Veronese' (autograph), Vat. lat. 7205, fos 53ʳ–95ᵛ, partly published in Gersbach, 'Books', 60–74.

[52] C. Suetonius Tranquillus, Dion Cassius Nicaeus, Aelius Spartianus…, ed. Desiderius Erasmus (Basel, 1518), again published in Cologne (1527).

which was issued together with Egnazio's edition of the *Historia Augusta*.[53] Julius Caesar's *Commentaries* were available to him in the edition made by the Veronese scholar Giovanni Giocondo.

There was the edition of various chronicles, combined into one folio volume by Johannes Sichard and printed by Heinrich Petri in Basel (*Chronicon*, 1529/1536); it was typographically sophisticated for its tables and contained works by Eusebius, Jerome, Prosper of Aquitaine, Cassiodorus, Hermannus Contractus, Matteo and Mattia Palmieri.[54] Panvinio also had the *Chronographia* of the Pole Alexander Scultetus (Rome, 1546), which covered the entire period from antiquity to the present and was dedicated to Cardinal Alessandro Farnese. He owned a copy of the forged ancient sources published by Annius of Viterbo (Panvinio's copy: *Antiquitates variae*, Paris, 1512/1515).

On chronology, he had, furthermore, the lists of Roman office-holders, *Fasti Capitolini*, which had recently been discovered and published by Bartolomeo Marliani (*Consulum, dictatorum... series*, Rome, 1549). On Roman topography, we find Andrea Fulvio's *Antiquitates Urbis* in Italian translation (Venice, 1543), Marliani's *Topographia* (Rome, 1544/Basel, 1550), and an edition of the medieval description of the city, *Mirabilia Urbis*, also containing a catalogue of popes and other rulers. We encounter Machiavelli's analysis of republican forms of government (*Discorsi sopra la prima deca di Tito Livio*) and Polydore Vergil's cultural history (*De inventoribus rerum*). On a lighter note, Panvinio had a copy of Giovan Piero Valeriano's *Pro sacerdotum barbis apologia*; in fact, Panvinio wore a beard when he was portrayed in the 1550s (Figs 1.1 and 1.2).[55]

---

[53] G. B. Egnazio, *De Caesaribus libri III...*; Aelius Spartianus, Iulius Capitolinus..., ed. id. (Venice, 1516), again published in Florence (1519). Panvinio also possessed another copy of Suetonius with annotations by both Erasmus and Egnazio: Suetonius, *XII Caesares...*; G. B. Egnazio, *De Romanis principibus* (Lyon, 1532; and reprints).

[54] For a description with photographs see the catalogue by F. Hieronymus, *Griechischer Geist aus Basler Pressen*, http://www.ub.unibas.ch/cmsdata/spezialkataloge/gg, nos 417 and 418.

[55] The portrait (Fig. 1.1), which had previously been thought to be by Titian, was attributed to Tintoretto by E. A. Safarik in 1981; see P. Piergiovanni, *Galleria Colonna in Roma: catalogo dei dipinti* (Rome, 2015), 260–1. The painting's subject is believed to be Panvinio, although no conclusive evidence for this identification has come to light. For another portrait see the engraving (Fig. 1.2) in Cornelius Curtius, *Virorum illustrium ex Ordine Eremitarum Divi Augustini elogia cum singulorum expressis ad vivum iconibus* (Antwerp, 1636), 146. Curtius (ibid., sigs a4ᵛ–b1ʳ) implied that he had received the image that served as model for this engraving from Rome—that is, probably from Sant'Agostino. Compare also Panvinio's memorial bust, below, 78–80 (Figs 2.2–2.3).

Fig. 1.1 Onofrio Panvinio. Painting by Jacopo Tintoretto (attributed). Courtesy of the Galleria Colonna, Rome.

We can conclude that by this stage Panvinio was more interested in Aristotle than in theologians, more in antiquity than in the Middle Ages, and much more in emperors than in popes. Panvinio had a voracious intellect. His appetite for knowledge was immense but selective, concentrating on history and antiquities but leaving out other vast fields such as natural philosophy. Considering that reformers within his order regarded the practice of allowing quasi-private property (including books) to be an abuse,

ONVPHRIVS PANVINVS Veronenfis, Ord.
Ere. S. Aug; antiquitatum indagator folertiſsimus,
Panormi fato immaturo e vivis raptus eſt, Ætat
ſuæ A⁰ 39 incboato Dñi, 1568 dic 18 Kal April.
I.Fran.in.

Fig. 1.2 Onofrio Panvinio. Engraving by Jacob Franquart. From Cornelius Curtius, *Virorum illustrium ex Ordine Eremitarum Divi Augustini elogia* (Antwerp, 1636). Courtesy of the University Library, Ghent (Bib.Hist. 007503, 146).

Panvinio must have had a dispensation from his superiors. For the erudite Seripando, learning may have trumped poverty as an ideal. On the other hand, many of these books may have been part of the libraries of the Augustinian houses rather than being Panvinio's personal possessions.[56]

Meanwhile, Panvinio's former teacher Ambrogio of Verona lamented the absence of his pupil and their lack of contact. Ambrogio did not write to Panvinio directly, but through his prior Aurelio warned him not to be inflated with pride since he was making his career in Rome, and not to forget his former teacher. He quoted from the Old Testament an exhortation to be intellectually modest. One has the feeling, though, that Ambrogio was not speaking solely of intellectual modesty, but that Panvinio had also shown some personal ambition and, perhaps, arrogance:

My son is slipping away from me. Onofrio, what have I done to you? Where are you going? Do you see that there is written 'Seek not the things that are too high for thee'? You are in Rome, ascended above the stars of heaven. The clouds roar.[57]

Panvinio's Early Literary Production

Panvinio had connections to the higher echelons of the Augustinian hierarchy, and his first work seems to have been commissioned by Seripando himself. Tellingly, it dealt with Panvinio's passion, chronology; but here he was forced to set aside his beloved antiquity and deal with medieval history. His first work was a chronicle of the Augustinian Order. In his letter to Ruscelli, Panvinio stated that he had written the chronicle 'at the request' of Seripando in 1549, when he was nineteen years old.[58] The chronicle, entitled

[56] In fact, many of these books no longer appear in the inventory of his library drawn up in c.1564–7 ('Index librorum scriptorum bibliothecae Fratris Onophrii Veronensis', Vat. lat. 3451. ii, fos 1ʳ–29ʳ; cited as ILS). The reason for the disappearance of some of the books may also have been censorship; for example, Machiavelli's works had been placed on the Index of Prohibited Books in 1559.

[57] Ambrogio of Verona, Paola (Calabria), to Aurelio della Rocca, 24 July 1549, Vat. lat. 6412, fo. 380ʳ, ed. Gersbach, 'Ambrogio', 209: 'Mi si lontana il figlio. O Onoffrio, quid feci tibi? Quo tendis? Vedi che gli è scritto "Altiora ne te quesieris" [Sir 3:22]? A Roma sei: asceso supra astra celi. Nubila tonant'. Compare also the parable (Isa 14) about the king of Babylon's high aspirations ('ascendam super altitudinem nubium') and downfall.

[58] Panvinio to Ruscelli, 4 November 1564, 189: 'a instantia del Cardinal Seripando'. Panvinio received some money as a New Year's gift from the prior general on 1 January 1550; see the list of his income, Vat. lat. 7205, fo. 89ᵛ: 'Kalendis ianuariis ex strenna reverendissimi patris generalis argentei octo mihi supererant'. See also ibid., fo. 95ᵛ.

Commentarium rerum Ordinis Fratrum Eremitarum Sancti Augustini, was published in an edition of the constitutions of the Augustinian Order in May 1551, although the book had already been printed by July 1550. It was not written by Panvinio alone, but by a group of compilers.[59] Its preface was dated 1549, while the last events mentioned in it were the election of Pope Julius III and the appointment of Marcello Cervini as the new cardinal protector of the order (both in February 1550).

The chronicle began with the year AD 352, the first year of the pontificate of Pope Liberius. It then proceeded to the birth of St Augustine of Hippo, which was placed under the year 358. For the fourth and fifth centuries, the entries were always followed by indications of sources, such as Possidius's life of Augustine and Prosper of Aquitaine's *Chronicle*. As points of reference, popes were listed if their pontificates coincided with important events in the pre-history of the order or if they granted relevant privileges. Of course, the early history of the Augustinians is a complicated subject because the order was officially created only in the middle of the thirteenth century; before that date, its history was that of local congregations. Modern scholarship has shown that the order's claim to have been founded by St Augustine was a construction or 'myth';[60] but the chronicle, in keeping with late medieval practice, treated Augustine as the founder. For the period AD 500–723, the compilers simply stated, with disarming honesty, 'we have not found anything certain regarding our order'.[61] Accordingly, they did not cover this period. In AD 1244 several eremitical communities in Tuscany united themselves into a single religious order and called themselves the Order of Hermits of St Augustine; this was followed in 1256 by the inclusion of several other hermit groups. The Augustinians became a new mendicant order alongside the Dominicans and Franciscans. From this moment onwards, the chronicle became very detailed and provided, wherever possible, an

---

[59] [Panvinio et al.], *Commentarium rerum Ordinis Fratrum Eremitarum Sancti Augustini*, in *Constitutiones Ordinis Fratrum Eremitarum Sancti Augustini nuper recognitae* (Rome: Antonio Blado, 1551), separate numbering (but beginning with fo. 25ʳ), fos 25ʳ–58ʳ. The contents of the entire book are described by E. Esteban, 'De antiquarum constitutionum Ordinis praecipuis editionibus', *AAug*, 2 (1907–8), 35–41, 84–94, 109–14, at pp. 84–8. For a discussion of the chronicle's authorship see ibid. 86–7 n. 1; for the history of its publication, id., 'Excerpta e regestis Reverendissimi Seripandi circa Constitutiones Ordinis ab ipso in lucem editas', *AAug*, 2 (1907–8), 58–62, 79–84.

[60] A. Wesjohann, *Mendikantische Gründungserzählungen im 13. und 14. Jahrhundert* (Berlin, 2012), 499–671.

[61] *Commentarium rerum Ordinis*, fo. 28ᵛ: 'nihil de ordine nostro certi reperimus'. See also the preface to the chronicle, ibid., fo. 25r.

entry for every single year until 1550. Pieces of information and advice had been sent to the compilers from members of the order in different places.[62]

As an appendix, the compilers included a list of saints and blessed of the order, whose names they were reluctant to include since their dates were often not precisely known. Lastly, they added a page of corrections to the work, most likely in 1551, just before the book came out.[63] The corrections may foreshadow Panvinio's future working style, characterized by frequent modifications and rewriting. Although the text was anonymous, Panvinio later included it in the lists of his own publications. He must have been pleased with his first work, since the publisher Antonio Blado produced a typographically beautiful folio edition on fine paper, paid for by Seripando. The general of the Augustinians, worn-out and ill, abdicated his role by the time the chronicle had been successfully published in May 1551.[64]

Panvinio's further course of studies corresponded more or less to the programme that Seripando set out in the constitutions of 1551; this was a precise definition of the rights and duties of the students and teachers.[65] Panvinio's degrees were conferred by Seripando's successor, Christopher of Padua, who became prior general in May 1551. As has been mentioned, the *studium generale* consisted, first, of five years of philosophy—that is, two years of logic (the biennium which Panvinio spent in Naples) and three years of natural philosophy and metaphysics, based on Aristotle. After having passed the exams, the student could be named cursor and be admitted to the theological course of study. Panvinio was confirmed as a cursor at the general chapter in May 1551.[66] It is reasonable to assume that he had already passed his exams at the end of the previous academic year, between 15 August and 8 September when, as Seripando had ruled, examinations were to take place

---

[62] See Seripando's letter accompanying the constitutions, in *Constitutiones Ordinis*, 1551, sigs A3^r–A5^r.

[63] 'Elenchus sanctorum et beatorum', in *Commentarium rerum Ordinis*, fos 55^v–56^v; 'Errata in compendio', ibid., fos 57^v–58^r.

[64] Jedin, *Seripando*, i. 232, 282–7.

[65] For what follows see the constitutions of 1551, ch. 37, 'De forma circa studia et studentes ac lectores nostri ordinis servanda', repr. in D. Gutiérrez, 'Los estudios en la Orden agustiniana desde la edad media hasta la contemporánea', *AAug*, 33 (1970), 75–149, at pp. 140–8. Previous regulations are contained in the constitutions of 1290, ch. 36 (with additions of 1348), pp. 110–21. See also D. Gutiérrez, *The Augustinians in the Middle Ages 1256–1356*, trans. A. J. Ennis (Villanova, PA, 1984), 141–6; id., *Augustinians 1518–1648*, 143–7; E. L. Saak, *High Way to Heaven: The Augustinian Platform between Reform and Reformation 1292–1524* (Leiden, 2002), 370–82.

[66] *Christophori Patavini O.S.A. Registra generalatus, 1551–1567*, ed. A. Hartmann (Rome, 1985–), i. 47 (18 or 19 May 1551).

without exception.[67] Therefore, it seems that Panvinio studied only four years of philosophy (1546–50) instead of the five required by the new constitutions.

By May 1552 Panvinio had become a master of students (*magister studentium* or *studii*). This was a sort of assistant teacher who helped the regent organize the studies and oversee repetitions, lectures, and disputations.[68] In this function, Panvinio also had to ensure that students woke up early in the morning for church, and he taught them their first lessons in logic according to the Augustinian thinker Paul of Venice (d. 1429). After studying theology for three years, one could obtain the title of lector. As part of the exams, the candidate delivered one lesson in metaphysics and two in theology, in which he expounded the *Sentences* of Peter Lombard. Panvinio, having passed the exams no doubt in August or September, was appointed lector by the prior general on 25 December 1553.[69] He thus completed three full years of theology (1550–3).

The lectorate was not a university degree; it was a title and office within the Augustinian Order with specific functions which included teaching, examining, preaching, and participating in general chapters. Beyond the lectorate, the remaining higher degrees were bachelor and master of theology. These degrees required periods of successful teaching—usually at least three years for the bachelor—but no further examinations. For now, Panvinio was a lector and would have taught, as we have seen, Aristotle and Peter Lombard. In parallel to his university studies, Panvinio extended his scholarly networks. For example, in 1550 or 1551, Panvinio met the Benedictine monk Vincenzio Borghini, with whom he would later discuss ancient Roman *Fasti*. In 1553 Panvinio corresponded with the humanist scholar and printer Paolo Manuzio in Venice, who praised the young scholar's 'virtue'.[70]

Panvinio probably taught students in Rome until May 1554, when he was assigned to serve as lector in the *studium* at the Florentine house.[71] He

[67] Constitutions of 1551, ch. 37, in Gutiérrez, 'Los estudios', 145.

[68] *Christophori Patavini Registra*, i. 223 (21 May 1552: 'fit magister studentium'). See also P. F. Grendler, *The Universities of the Italian Renaissance* (Baltimore, MD, 2002), 358.

[69] *Christophori Patavini Registra*, ii. 150 (20 May 1553: listed as 'magister studii'), 314 (25 December 1553: 'lectorem…fecimus').

[70] V. Borghini to Panvinio, 17 October 1551, in id., *Il carteggio*, ed. D. Francalanci, F. Pellegrini, and E. Carrara (Florence, 2001–), i. 328–9; P. Manuzio to Panvinio, 13 September 1553, London, British Library, Add. MS 12107, fo. 7r–v. See also K. A. Gersbach, 'Onofrio Panvinio, OSA, and his Florentine Correspondents Vincenzio Borghini, OSB, Pietro Vettori, Francesco de' Medici', *AAug*, 60 (1997), 207–80.

[71] *Christophori Patavini Registra*, ii. 381, 385 (12 May 1554: 'locatur Florentiae'), 386 (17 May: 'Monuimus venerabilem priorem Florentinum ut…Fratrem Onufrium Veronensem venientem reciperet').

managed to delay and, eventually, avert this transfer when in August 1554 the prior general gave him permission to continue his studies outside the order (*extra ordinem*)—that is, permission to live in Rome outside the Augustinian house. The special dispensation was valid for two years.[72] Around the same time, Seripando complained about Panvinio's disobedience to him in an unspecified matter, so it is possible that Seripando was against this move.[73]

An academic degree already dispensed a friar from regular observance, allowing him to devote himself to studying while his brothers chanted mass in the choir, preached, or begged for alms and food. Permission to live apart from the community, however, was uncommon. Not many other cases of Augustinians with such dispensations are known; two of these, in the sixteenth century, are related to the Augustinian centre of theological studies, Salamanca (regarding Juan de Guevara and Luis de Léon).[74] Of course, those friars were granted this favour in their capacity as theologians. It was undoubtedly unique that Panvinio was dispensed to carry out research not in theology but in history. Accordingly, the prior general must have expected assiduous study and impressive results.

Panvinio's most important patron in the period between 1552 and 1555 was the cardinal protector of the Augustinians, Marcello Cervini. It is to Panvinio's relationship with Cervini that we now turn. Cervini, from Montepulciano in Tuscany, was born in 1501. He was a talented ecclesiastical administrator with a deep love for ancient books. Cervini was friendly with the Farnese family and was put in charge of the education of the young Alessandro Farnese. Because of this friendship with the Farnese, Cervini was given quick promotion through the ranks of the Church. Upon his appointment as cardinal in 1539, he showed his gratitude by including the Farnese fleur-de-lis in his coat of arms.[75]

---

[72] Ibid., iii. 91 (20 August 1554): 'Literis nostris apertis facultatem dedimus Fratri Honofrio Veronensi lectori manendi in Urbe extra ordinem per biennium'.

[73] Seripando to Francisco Torres, 15 November 1554, MS Naples, Biblioteca nazionale, XIII AA 60, fo. 125ʳ: 'F. Onofrio ben sape cioche li dissi quando passai per Roma. Non ha voluto udirme. Det illi Dominus intellectum [2 Tim. 2:7]'. See also Jedin, *Seripando*, ii. 278. The passage is strikingly similar to the complaint about Panvinio which, in 1549, Ambrogio of Verona had sent to the prior at the Roman house and *intimus* of Seripando, Aurelio della Rocca; see above, 29.

[74] Gutiérrez, *Augustinians 1518–1648*, 112, and *ad indicem* on the two men.

[75] For Cervini's education and early career see W. V. Hudon, *Marcello Cervini and Ecclesiastical Government in Tridentine Italy* (DeKalb, IL, 1992), 18–42; C. Quaranta, *Marcello II Cervini (1501–1555): riforma della Chiesa, concilio, Inquisizione* (Bologna, 2010), 39–184.

Among Cervini's learned friends were Angelo Colocci, Pietro Bembo, and Carlo Gualteruzzi. He also supported a circle of scholars (the 'Vitruvian Academy') founded at the beginning of the 1540s around Claudio Tolomei. His support for antiquarian studies extended to Stephanus Pighius, a scholar of ancient epigraphy, chronology, and mythology, who worked on a corpus of inscriptions. From about 1540 Cervini became involved with the Vatican Library, encouraging the publication of Greek works from the manuscript collection. Cervini collaborated with another eminent scholar of Greek, Guglielmo Sirleto, in search of manuscripts.[76]

During the 1540s Cervini's interests turned from classical authors, such as Cicero and Varro, more and more towards the Church Fathers and ecclesiastical writers.[77] Luigi Lippomano turned to Cervini for advice when preparing his monumental *Lives of the Saints* (*Sanctorum priscorum patrum vitae*, 1551–60). In 1548 Cervini became the first cardinal to direct the Vatican Library; in 1550 Pope Julius III appointed him cardinal-librarian. It was Cervini's conviction that nothing protected the faith better from heresy than the Vatican Library, with its access to original ancient sources.[78]

From 1550 Cervini strongly supported Seripando's reform efforts. He contributed his authorization to Seripando's new edition of the Augustinian Constitutions.[79] It thus seems likely that Panvinio was introduced to his new patron through Seripando. Panvinio probably impressed Cervini with his work on the chronicle of his order, and Cervini would have regarded Panvinio's further works as part of his own publication projects. Panvinio's research aligned with Cervini's agenda of elucidating late antique and early

---

[76] On Sirleto, who became a custodian of the Vatican Library in 1554 and a cardinal in 1565, see B. Clausi and S. Lucà (eds), *Il 'sapientissimo calabro' Guglielmo Sirleto nel V centenario della nascita (1514–2014)* (Rome, 2018). On Cervini's scholarly interests see P. Paschini, 'Un cardinale editore: Marcello Cervini', in id., *Cinquecento romano e riforma cattolica* (Rome, 1958), 183–217; P. Piacentini, 'Marcello Cervini (Marcello II): la Biblioteca Vaticana e la biblioteca personale', in *Storia della Biblioteca Apostolica Vaticana* (Vatican City, 2010–), ii, ed. M. Ceresa, 105–43; P. Sachet, 'Publishing for the Popes: The Cultural Policy of the Catholic Church towards Printing in Sixteenth-Century Rome' (doctoral thesis, Warburg Institute, University of London, 2015).

[77] S. Giombi, 'Lo studio umanistico dell'antichità cristiana nella riforma cattolica', *Rivista di storia e letteratura religiosa*, 28 (1992), 143–62, at p. 149; Hudon, *Cervini*, 40–1; Quaranta, *Marcello II*, 428–58.

[78] See Cervini's letter to A. Farnese, 16 September 1554, in L. Dorez, 'Le cardinal Marcello Cervini et l'imprimerie à Rome (1539–1550)', *Mélanges d'archéologie e d'histoire*, 12 (1892), 289–313, at p. 311: 'La libraria è il maggior thesoro ch'abbia la Sede apostolica perché in essa si conserva la fede dall'heresie'.

[79] *Constitutiones Ordinis*, 1551, sig. A2ʳ. On their relationship see Jedin, *Seripando*, ii. 298–9, and *ad indicem*; Hudon, *Cervini*, 108–9.

medieval sources to understand better the history of the early Church. An ultimate goal of Cervini was church reform according to an apostolic model, for which secure historical knowledge was a necessary foundation.

A letter from 1552 illustrates how Cervini advised Panvinio on the ancient Roman *Fasti*. The letter was dated 3 July 1552, when Panvinio was a master of students at the Roman house and still studying theology. Since the academic year ended on 28 June, in July Panvinio presumably had spare time to devote himself to historical studies. Cervini stated that Panvinio had not resolved a question regarding the *Fasti* (the date of the consulship of Ausonius, AD 379) to Cervini's satisfaction. We learn that Panvinio had turned to Cervini, in a previous letter of his own, to ask for specific advice about chronology, and that Cervini addressed him as 'dearest' ('carissimo'). In the second part of the letter Cervini pointed out that Panvinio, during the summer holidays, had time to continue the studies he had begun, which had evidently been interrupted by other duties at the *studium*. As regarded his future studies, Cervini promised to speak to the prior general.[80]

In 1553 Panvinio produced the first publication under his own name; but he later did not count it among his published works, probably because it consisted of only one printed sheet. Decorated with three woodcuts and printed by Antonio Blado, this sheet contained a list of Frankish tribal leaders and kings, starting with Priam and leading up to Henry II, the king of France from 1547 onwards.[81]

A project of a universal chronicle was mentioned in the draft dedication to Cervini of Panvinio's work *De primatu Petri* (On the Primacy of Peter), dated 1 November 1553. Panvinio apologized for not having been able to finish the work that Cervini commissioned—that is, the *Chronica ab orbe condito* (Chronicles from the Beginning of the World).[82] Panvinio's project

---

[80] M. Cervini (Gubbio) to Panvinio, 3 July 1552, Vat. lat. 6412, fo. 1a^r–v. See also Perini, *Panvinio*, 13; Ferrary, *Panvinio*, 10–11 n. 25. For the summer periods in Gubbio see Hudon, *Cervini*, 130–1.

[81] Panvinio, *Omnium Francorum ducum et regum quorum apud veteres auctores memoria est epilogus a Priamo duce usque ad Regem Heinricum II Valesium…Onophrius Panvinius Veronensis fecit Romae anno Christi MDLIII* (Rome: Antonio Blado, 1553). The sheet is preserved in Vatican City, Archivio Segreto Vaticano (hereafter ASV), Misc., Arm. I 20, fo. 12. See also A. Mercati, *Dall'Archivio Vaticano* (Vatican City, 1951), 84 n. 3.

[82] Panvinio, *De primatu Petri et sedis apostolicae urbis Romae dignitate*, Vat. lat. 6883, fos 1^r–52^v, dedication to Marcello Cervini, dated 1 November 1553, fos 1^r–4^r, at fo. 1^r (cited by Ferrary, *Panvinio*, 10 n. 24): 'Quum abs te, Reverendissime Praesul, delegatum michi munus *Chronicorum ab orbe condito* conficiendorum…adhuc absolvere non potuerim'. The medieval spelling of 'mihi' is owed to the scribe.

of a world chronicle led to his edition of ancient Roman *Fasti*, in 1557.[83] In the meantime, however, Panvinio proposed an intermediate remedy to appease Cervini until the world chronicle could be produced: *De primatu Petri*, a small treatise which he had extracted from the immense material of the larger book. *De primatu* was a digest of sources relating to the primacy of Peter. This was, as he said, the first fruit of his labours to go to press; he hoped that it would confirm and extend Cervini's hopes in him. In the preface to Book I of *De primatu*, Panvinio thanked for their help, in particular, the historian of canon law Antonio Agustín and the antiquarian Ottavio Pantagato. Augustinian friars had helped him, too.[84] Despite Panvinio's hopes, *De primatu* did not go to press; it was not printed during his lifetime and came out only in part in 1589.[85]

Another treatise dedicated to Cervini and mentioned in the preface was appended to *De primatu Petri*; it was entitled *De sacrorum cleri ordinum origine* (On the Origin of the Holy Orders of Clerics). Panvinio also mentioned his plans to write a treatise on the history of papal elections and the lives of the popes. (These later became separate, full-fledged works.)[86]

In his *Romani pontifices et cardinales* (Roman Pontiffs and Cardinals) of 1557 we find another, more elaborate statement about Cervini's influence on him. The statement appears in Panvinio's long preface, dated Parma, 1 May 1557, with which he dedicated the book to Cardinal Alessandro Farnese. He began, predictably, by extolling the value of history as a source of models for good and bad behaviour, 'witness of the times, light of the truth'.[87] Panvinio's preface then became autobiographical. He related that, when he was a young man (*adolescens*), a strong natural inclination had urged him to devote himself fully to researching the literary monuments of the ancients and putting into order what he found chaotically dispersed, so that it could be read conveniently. He then considered the notion that the world was ruled by two great forces: religion and the government of the State. While

---

[83] See below, 50–61.

[84] Panvinio, *De primatu Petri*, Preface to Book I, Vat. lat. 6883, fo. 7ʳ.

[85] See below, 84–87, 181–87.

[86] Panvinio, *De sacrorum cleri ordinum origine tractatus*, Vat. lat. 6883, fos 100ʳ–160ʳ (there are notes for a censorship of this text ibid., fo. 161ʳ⁻ᵛ); an extract of this work was published by A. Mai in *Spicilegium Romanum*, 10 vols (Rome, 1839–44) (hereafter *SR*), ix. 512–15. See also the dedication of *De primatu Petri* (cited in note 82), fo. 1ʳ, and an address to the reader in the same manuscript ('Candido lectori salutem', fo. 5ʳ⁻ᵛ), both cited by Ferrary, *Panvinio*, 11 n. 26.

[87] Panvinio, *Romani pontifices et cardinales Sanctae Romanae Ecclesiae ab eisdem a Leone IX ad Paulum Papam IV per quingentos posteriores a Christi natali annos creati* (Venice: Michele Tramezzino, 1557), 'Alexandro Farnesio . . . S.P.D.', sigs *3ʳ–**2ʳ, at sig. *3ʳ.

he thought that he should dedicate himself to the study of both, he had first laid hands on ancient Roman history, 'the most eminent and worthy of all'. After he had already engaged in serious studies of this subject, his work was interrupted when Marcello Cervini first advised, then ordered him to abandon, 'for some time' (*ad tempus*), his unfinished writings on Roman history and to shift entirely to 'church history—that is, the history of Christian religion'. The cardinal deemed Panvinio suitable to shoulder such a heavy responsibility.[88]

Panvinio explained Cervini's view of the state of historical studies in the first half of the 1550s. According to Panvinio, Cervini lamented that all the great scholars of his time worked on ancient Roman history or other profane disciplines while leaving behind and disdaining church history. The sacred historical texts of Christianity, especially those written in Latin, lay in darkness and obscurity. Eusebius and other well-respected church historians had written about the first four hundred years and had concentrated primarily on the Eastern Church. The history of churches, towns, and provinces, as well as the biographies of martyrs and of the famous and learned men of the Western Church, were still to be written. Numerous rites and ceremonies of the early Church had to be studied because modern heresies had arisen out of ignorance of them.[89]

To carry out Cervini's order, Panvinio started exploring source material under 'great physical strain' and even peril. In Rome, he searched all the churches, archives, and libraries, both public and private, for relevant material, which he then either copied himself or had copied. He also travelled to various parts of Italy for his investigations.[90] We can trust his statements about the difficulty of his task because he was working on a pioneering chronicle of popes and cardinals. His collection of information about the cardinals, in particular, was entirely new; Panvinio created the genre of an ecclesiastical chronicle which included the biographical dates of the princes of the Church. His work on cardinals was later continued by

---

[88] Ibid., sig. *3ᵛ: 'suasu primo, postea iussu beatissimae recordationis Marcelli II Pontificis Maximi, qui eo tempore cardinalis Sanctae Crucis erat, coactus fui ad tempus ea, quae in historia Romana conscripseram, imperfecta relinquere et totum ad historiam ecclesiasticam, religionis scilicet, me convertere'; ibid.: 'primoque hortatus est, postea praecepit ut ad historiam ecclesiasticam conscribendam, Romana vetere ad tempus relicta, animum, vires et calamum accommodarem'.

[89] Ibid., sig. *4ᵛ.   [90] On his archival visits see also below, 66–67.

Giovanni Antonio Petramellari in 1599 and served as a foundation for Alfonso Chacón's *Lives of the Popes and Cardinals* (1601).[91]

Panvinio's brother Paolo stated that Cervini, as cardinal-librarian, gave Panvinio permission to view and copy any material in the Vatican Library that was useful to him.[92] Having collected a wealth of documents, Panvinio began to write; but just when he had started to adapt his mind to writing, Cervini became pope as Marcellus II (9 April 1555) and died three weeks later (1 May 1555). Panvinio felt bereft of all protection but nevertheless decided to continue his work, though in a less happy frame of mind.[93]

The last work of this period to be mentioned is the *Collectio Avellana*, a collection of documents concerning popes and emperors from the fourth to sixth centuries. Panvinio would work on an edition of this collection again shortly before the end of his life, in the summer of 1567, when he had a title-page printed. From the draft of his dedication to Cardinal Otto Truchsess von Waldburg, we learn that Cervini had rediscovered an important medieval manuscript of the *Avellana* in his diocese of Gubbio. Cervini had handed a copy to Panvinio, urging him to produce an annotated edition.[94] Despite his best intentions, Panvinio was not able to fulfil his promise to do this before Cervini died. He took the occasion to reiterate how strong a blow Cervini's death had been to the course of his studies and plans.[95] Cervini's death was also a threat to Panvinio's way of life because his successor on the

---

[91] G. A. Petramellari, *Ad librum Onuphrii Panvinii De summis pontificibus et Sanctae Romanae Ecclesiae cardinalibus a Paulo IV ad Clementis VIII annum pontificatus octavum continuatio* (Bologna, 1599); A. Chacón, *Vitae et gesta summorum pontificum a Christo domino usque ad Clementem VIII necnon Sanctae Romanae Ecclesiae cardinalium cum eorundem insignibus*, 2 vols (Rome, 1601). In 1567 Girolamo Garimberti took a different line and published witty observations on selected cardinals, their virtues and vices (*La prima parte delle vite overo fatti memorabili d'alcuni papi et di tutti i cardinali passati*, Venice, 1567). For a list of biographical works on cardinals, beginning with Panvinio's book, see C. Weber, *Senatus Divinus: verborgene Strukturen im Kardinalskollegium der frühen Neuzeit (1500–1800)* (Frankfurt am Main, 1996), 534–8.

[92] Paolo Panvinio, *Vita*, 216.

[93] Panvinio, *Romani pontifices et cardinales* (1557), sig. *4ʳ: 'omni praesidio me destitutum esse crediderim'.

[94] Title page: *XV pontificum Romanorum, VI imperatorum, aliquot praeclari nominis sacerdotum, virorum et feminarum clarissimorum epistolae CCXL*, ed. Panvinio ('Dilingae excudebat N.N.N. anno salutis MDLXVII mense Iulii'), Vat. lat. 6206, fo. 219ʳ, cited in Ferrary, *Panvinio*, 17 n. 42; dedication of 1 May 1567, fos 221ʳ–223ʳ, cited ibid. 10 n. 24. An index of letters follows, but the edition itself is not contained in the manuscript. The edition was never published; the *Collectio* had to wait another 300 years for its first edition. See R. Gryson, *Répertoire général des auteurs ecclésiastiques latins de l'antiquité et du haut Moyen Âge* (Freiburg im Breisgau, 2007), 420–7, 484. See also below, 74–76, 165–66.

[95] *XV pontificum Romanorum … epistolae CCXL*, ed. Panvinio, dedication, cited in Ferrary, *Panvinio*, 10 n. 24: 'cursum studiorum cogitationumque mearum valde retardavit'.

papal throne, Paul IV Carafa (r. 1555–9), was a hard-line reformer who abolished privileges of friars. Panvinio, thus, faced the threat of returning to the cloister. Hope was on the horizon as Panvinio was creating contacts with Alessandro Farnese the Younger. Panvinio might well have been introduced to Farnese by Cervini, although his brother Paolo stated that Panvinio's connection with Farnese's *maggiordomo*, Curzio Frangipane (d. 1554), was also instrumental.[96]

The Histories of Noble Families

With Alessandro Farnese's patronage not yet fully secured, in 1555 Panvinio started composing the histories of several aristocratic families, in the clear hope of finding patrons. I will briefly mention his histories of the Frangipane, Savelli, Massimo, and Mattei families.[97] Panvinio's history of the Frangipane has been considered by a present-day medievalist to be 'a compilation of certain and uncertain materials'.[98] In Panvinio's view, the story of this family covered 2,000 years of history.[99] It began in antiquity, where Panvinio identified the Roman tribe of the Anicii as Frangipane ancestors—a connection which today is seen as a patent legend. Pope Gregory the Great (who died in 604) was claimed to be a family member; this was no doubt due to Panvinio's patrons' expectations. Especially for ancient times, Panvinio used not only literary sources, such as Livy and Plutarch, but also epigraphic material—that is, inscriptions. In Book III, Panvinio attempted to show that the Frangipane descended from the Anicii of the Late Empire.[100] He then dealt with the Michiel of Venice, citing sources

[96] Paolo Panvinio, *Vita*, 217.
[97] For a longer discussion see S. Bauer, 'History for Hire in Sixteenth-Century Italy: Onofrio Panvinio's Histories of Roman Families', *Erudition and the Republic of Letters*, 4 (2019), 397–438. There is good evidence that Panvinio also composed a history of the Cenci family. See his 'Le opere che ho composte le soglio dividere in quattro parti' (autograph list of his works, *c.*1564–5), in Vat. lat. 7762, fos 560ʳ–ᵛ, 563ʳ, at fo. 560ᵛ: 'dell'historia di casa di Cenci libri dua a M. Christoforo Cenci Chierico di Camera'. Cristoforo died in 1562.
[98] M. Thumser, 'Die Frangipane: Abriß der Geschichte einer Adelsfamilie im hochmittel-alterlichen Rom', *QFIAB*, 71 (1991), 106–63, at p. 107: 'ein wahres Panoptikum an gesicherten und ungesicherten Materialien'.
[99] Panvinio, *De gente Fregepania libri IV*, dedicated to Mario Frangipane (1 May 1556), MS BAV, Barb. lat. 2481, 139 fos (16th–17th c.). On the Frangipane family see also B. Arnold, 'Frangipani', in V. Reinhardt (ed.), *Die großen Familien Italiens* (Stuttgart, 1992), 277–86.
[100] For details see R. Bizzocchi, '*Familiae Romanae* antiche e moderne', *Rivista storica itali-ana*, 103 (1991), 355–97, at p. 384; É. Bouyé, 'Les armoiries imaginaires des papes: archéologie et apologétique romaines à la fin du XVIᵉ siècle', in F. Alazard and F. La Brasca (eds), *La papauté à la Renaissance* (Paris, 2007), 589–618, at pp. 600–1.

from Venetian archives, which shows that he must have been to Venice before May 1556.[101] When it came to the Middle Ages, he conducted archival research and cited documents, books, or monuments, to which he appended brief comments or conclusions. For example, he transcribed medieval documents from the monastery of St Andrew on the Coelian Hill.[102] He also used the archives of the church of Santa Maria Nova (Santa Francesca Romana), which are now recognized as the main source for the history of the Frangipane.[103]

The history of the Savelli family, written in 1556, discussed this family's ancestors over the preceding 400 years.[104] Here, Panvinio resisted the temptation to trace the family history back to earlier times. He said he would base himself on *monumenta* ('monuments');[105] by these he meant both inscriptions on stone and documentary sources on paper or parchment. The key figure in the family's history was Pope Honorius III (r. 1216–27). It is likely the family wished to give prominence to this pope rather than dwell on the antiquity of its origins. As we know now, Honorius III—who before becoming pope was referred to as Cencius Camerarius (Cencius, the pope's chamberlain)—was not actually a Savelli. Panvinio claimed that he was. To bolster that claim, he cited certain precedents: for example, the universal chronicle of St Antoninus of Florence (d. 1459) and the *De cardinalatu* (1510) of Paolo Cortesi, in which Cencius was called 'Sabellus'.[106] The thirteenth-century sources, however, provided no such information. To supply this missing link, Panvinio invented, or rather manipulated, an inscription. For prudence's sake, he made the manipulation in a document that could not be readily accessed: a bull of Pope Celestine III from the archives of the abbey

---

[101] The chapters on the Michiel are published in E. Celani, '"De gente Fregepania" di Onofrio Panvinio', *Nuovo archivio veneto*, 5 (1893), 479–86.

[102] A. Bartòla, 'Onofrio Panvinio e il Regesto del monastero dei Santi Andrea e Gregorio al Celio', *Nuovi annali della Scuola speciale per archivisti e bibliotecari*, 6 (1992), 101–12; id., 'Introduzione', in id. (ed.), *Il Regesto del monastero dei Santi Andrea e Gregorio ad Clivum Scauri*, 2 vols (Rome, 2003), i, pp. VII–LXIX, at pp. XVII–XXIV.

[103] A. Augenti, *Il Palatino nel Medioevo: archeologia e topografia (secoli VI–XIII)* (Rome, 1996), 186–7; Thumser, 'Frangipane', 109 n. 6.

[104] Panvinio, *Gentis Sabellae monumenta*, dedicated to Card. Giacomo Savelli (1 September [1555]), Rome, Archivio di Stato, Archivio Sforza Cesarini, I^a parte, 33 (AA XXI, 1), fos 1^r–40^v (copy dated 1587); *De gente Sabella liber*, dedicated to Flaminio Savelli (1 May 1556), Rome, Biblioteca Casanatense, 1347, 63 fos (16th c.) (extended version). Edition which made use of both MSS: E. Celani, '"De gente Sabella": manoscritto inedito di Onofrio Panvinio', *Studi e documenti di storia e diritto*, 12 (1891), 271–309; 13 (1892), 187–206. On the history of the Savelli family in general see I. Baumgärtner, 'Savelli', in Reinhardt, *Die großen Familien*, 480–4.

[105] Panvinio, *De gente Sabella*, ed. Celani, 280: 'ut ex certis constat monumentis'.

[106] P. Cortesi, *De cardinalatu* (San Gimignano, 1510), fo. 36^r (a book owned by Panvinio, see ILS, fo. 25^v); Antoninus of Florence, *Chronica*, 3 vols (Lyon, 1543), iii, fo. 30^v.

of San Benedetto in Polirone near Mantua. Where the bull said that it was issued by 'Cencius, cardinal deacon of Santa Lucia in Orthea, chamberlain of the pope', Panvinio turned the phrase into 'Cencius *de Sabello*, cardinal deacon' etc.[107] The small embellishment had significant consequences. Down to the 1970s, Honorius was universally reckoned a Savelli.[108] While Panvinio did not invent the idea that Honorius was a Savelli, he was certainly guilty of giving the semblance of historical proof to it.

In his history of the Massimo family (1556), Panvinio endeavoured to show that the Massimo descended from the Roman *gens* Fabia.[109] He again sought to give scholarly underpinning to traditions which already existed. A few years before, the family had commissioned frescoes depicting the life of Hannibal's great opponent, Quintus Fabius Maximus 'Cunctator' (d. 203 BC), who was considered the dynasty's founding father. Panvinio's text contained numerous correspondences to the events displayed in the fresco cycle, such as the mythical connection to Hercules, the selection of prominent figures of the *gens* Fabia, and the use of sources such as Livy, Plutarch, Valerius Maximus, Virgil, and Ovid.[110] In his final family history, that of the Mattei (1561), Panvinio faced the arduous task of proving that they derived from the medieval Guidoni-Papareschi and could trace their lineage back to Pope Innocent II (r. 1130–43).[111]

In yet another case, he encountered pressures beyond the usual expectations of patronage and the hope of rewards. Members of the Cibo family subjected Panvinio to threats of physical harm because he had written that the father of Pope Innocent VIII (Giovanni Battista Cibo, r. 1484–92) had been a medical doctor rather than, as the family expected, a knight.[112]

---

[107] Panvinio, *De gente Sabella*, ed. Celani, 280: 'per manum Cencii *de Sabello* Sanctae Luciae in Orphea diaconi cardinalis et domni papae camerarii' (my italics). Compare the edition of this bull in P. Torelli (ed.), *Regesto mantovano* (Rome, 1914), i. 344 (21 November 1194): 'per manum Centii Sancte Lucie in Orthea diaconi cardinalis domini pape camerarii'.

[108] Panvinio's manipulation was revealed by H. Tillmann, 'Ricerche sull'origine dei membri del Collegio Cardinalizio nel XII secolo (II.2)', *Rivista di storia della Chiesa in Italia*, 29 (1975), 363–402, at pp. 391–3. See also S. Carocci, *Baroni di Roma: dominazioni signorili e lignaggi aristocratici nel Duecento e nel primo Trecento* (Rome, 1993), 415–16.

[109] Panvinio, *De gente Maxima libri duo*, dedicated to Antonio Massimo (1 May 1556), MS Rome, Biblioteca Angelica, Ang. lat. 2581, fos 1ʳ–57ᵛ (partly autograph). For an edition based on Vat. lat. 6168, fos 165ʳ–224bᵇ (16th c.?), see *SR*, ix. 547–91 (dedication wrongly dated to 1558).

[110] R. Guerrini, 'Plutarco e l'iconografia umanistica a Roma nel Cinquecento', in M. Fagiolo (ed.), *Roma e l'antico nell'arte e nella cultura del Cinquecento* (Rome, 1985), 87–108, at p. 103.

[111] Panvinio, *De gente nobili Matthaeia liber*, dedicated to Giacomo Mattei (1 December 1561) and Muzio Mattei, MS Padua, Biblioteca universitaria, 263, fos 193ʳ–220ʳ (16th–17th c.).

[112] Panvinio, *Romani pontifices et cardinales* (1557), 327: 'ex mediocri genere, honorato tamen ortus patrem Aaron nomine medicum habuit'.

In 1558 Panvinio's friend Carlo Sigonio warned him that Alberico Cibo Malaspina, the marquis of Massa, was threatening Panvinio's life ('vi minaccia la vita'). This hot-headed nobleman, who was in his mid-twenties, fumed when he heard that Panvinio had laughed off his complaints ('vene siete riso').[113] Panvinio obliged. For his edition of Platina's *Historia de vitis pontificum* (Lives of the Popes, 1562), he rewrote the biography of Innocent VIII and inserted a bloated section filled with praise for the Cibo family and its ancestry.[114] After this act of submission, relations with the marquis improved. In 1568 Panvinio dedicated a series of engraved papal portraits (*XXVII pontificum maximorum elogia et imagines*) to him.[115]

Such 'politic' lapses aside, Panvinio's family histories had a sound methodological foundation grounded in his extensive research into archives and monuments. This suggests that genealogy, despite being commissioned by aristocratic families to glorify their ancestries, can be seen as a more serious field of historical investigation than is often assumed. Yet the position of this genre of history for hire in sixteenth-century Italian historiography is not straightforward. Panvinio struck a balance between fulfilling the expectations of the noble families who commissioned him and following his own scholarly instincts as a historian, but he nevertheless did not seek the publication of these texts.

The sheer size of his manuscript material on the Roman families is remarkable. It is the most abundant of all unpublished genealogical collections on Roman families compiled in the sixteenth century.[116] More manuscript copies of his genealogical works exist than was previously assumed.[117] Also, there was a lively interest in these manuscripts in the succeeding centuries. For example, they were used by Fioravante Martinelli, whose *Roma sacra* (1653) has been referred to as the best work on the Roman churches up to the twentieth century.[118] In the eighteenth century, the Marchese

---

[113]   C. Sigonio to Panvinio, 3 October 1558, in K. A. Gersbach, 'Onofrio Panvinio and Cybo Family Pride in his Treatment of Innocent VIII and in the *XXVII pontificum maximorum elogia et imagines*', *AAug*, 54 (1991), 115–41, at p. 132. Sigonio added: 'questo non è da ridere, cioè l'haver a far con giovani ricchi et sdegnati'.

[114]   B. Platina, *Historia de vitis pontificum Romanorum a Domino Nostro Iesu Christo usque ad Paulum Papam II*, ed. Panvinio (Venice: Michele Tramezzino, 1562), fos 264ᵛ–265ᵛ. On Platina see also below, 150–154, 162–163.

[115]   See below, 153–154.

[116]   See A. von Reumont, *Geschichte der Stadt Rom*, 3 vols in 4 pts (Berlin, 1867–70), iii.1, p. 476.

[117]   For details on the manuscripts see Bauer, 'History for Hire'.

[118]   F. Martinelli, *Roma ex ethnica sacra Sanctorum Petri et Pauli apostolica praedicatione profuso sanguine publicae venerationi exposita* (Rome, 1653), 117. On Martinelli see C. Hülsen, *Le chiese di Roma nel medio evo* (Florence, 1927), p. XLIII.

Pompeo Frangipane owned a set of copies, which he made available to scholars.[119] For the history of the Massimo family, in 1839 the genealogist Pompeo Litta cited Panvinio's manuscript work and stated that the friar was 'an authority of great weight'.[120] Regarding the history of the Savelli, Panvinio's manuscript was an important point of reference in Gaetano Moroni's influential historical dictionary (1853).[121]

Exile from Rome with Cardinal Farnese

It was not easy make contact with Cardinal Alessandro Farnese in the years leading up to 1555. Whereas Marcello Cervini in 1550–5 spent most of every year in Rome (and a smaller part in Gubbio), Farnese had fallen out with Pope Julius III for political reasons and was forced to flee Rome in 1551; he returned twice for brief periods but generally stayed away for most of the pope's pontificate.[122] This resulted in an overall disruption to Farnese's artistic patronage. It also explains why Cervini—and not Farnese—was surely Panvinio's key patron under Julius III.

Already in December 1554, Panvinio dedicated a piece of work to Farnese, *De vicecancellario* (On the Vice-Chancellor), where he traced the origins of this office, of which Farnese was the current holder.[123] He was lucky that the cardinal returned to Rome on the news of Cervini's election in April 1555 and that he stayed there for about a year, until June 1556. That year was long enough for Panvinio to win his patronage; he then followed

---

[119] See, e.g., F. M. Nerini, *De templo et coenobio Sanctorum Bonifacii et Alexii historica monumenta* (Rome, 1752), 192, 235, 329; A. Cassio, *Memorie istoriche della vita di Santa Silvia* (Rome, 1755), 28, 53, 67, 70–1; G. B. Mittarelli and A. Costadoni (eds), *Annales Camaldulenses Ordinis Sancti Benedicti*, 9 vols (Venice, 1755–73), iv. 354, Appendix, cols 600, 614.

[120] P. Litta, *Famiglie celebri di Italia*, 184 fascs (Milan, 1819–83), s.v. Massimo di Roma (1839), tav. i: 'autorità di molto peso'. See also R. Bizzocchi, *Genealogie incredibili: scritti di storia nell'Europa moderna*, 2nd edn (Bologna, 2009), 26. The private Biblioteca Massimo in Rome still today holds a set of Panvinio's histories of the Roman families.

[121] G. Moroni, 'Savelli, famiglia', in his *Dizionario di erudizione storico-ecclesiastica*, 109 vols (Venice, 1840–79), lxi. 294–304, at p. 296.

[122] C. Robertson, *'Il Gran Cardinale': Alessandro Farnese, Patron of the Arts* (New Haven, CT, 1992), 12; S. Andretta and C. Robertson, 'Farnese, Alessandro', in *DBI*, xlv. 52–70, at pp. 58–60.

[123] Panvinio, *De vicecancellario: excerpta ex libro de cardinalium origine*, MS BAV, Chig. H II 24, dedication, fo. 1r–v; ibid., fo. 39v, postscriptum dated 13 December 1554. Perini published this work without the date of the postscriptum (*Panvinio*, 262–99). On *De cardinalium origine* see below, 74, 97.

Farnese in leaving the city and moving to Parma.[124] Since Farnese was an avid collector of antiquities, Panvinio shifted his attention—no doubt with enthusiasm—back to profane history and to his *Fasti*. This also explains his earlier remark that Cervini had made him abandon profane history only 'for now' (*ad tempus*).

Alessandro Farnese had no equal as a private patron of artists in mid-sixteenth-century Rome.[125] He had been made a cardinal in 1534 and Vice-Chancellor of the Roman Church in 1535, then received many more lucrative benefices, so that his wealth was almost unlimited. In addition to his patronage of artists, Farnese enjoyed the company of scholars who joined him at his dinner table. In a famous account, Giorgio Vasari said that he received the idea for his writing of the *Lives of the Artists* from Paolo Giovio during a dinner party with humanists and poets, held by Farnese in 1546. Among the intellectuals connected to the cardinal's court were Annibale Caro, Romolo Amaseo, Antonio Agustín, Lorenzo Gambara, Latino Latini, Girolamo Mercuriale, Fulvio Orsini, and Ottavio Pantagato.[126]

The Farnese family was a relatively new arrival on the Roman scene, although it had long been established in the surrounding Lazio region. Alessandro Farnese senior (1468–1549) was elected pope as Paul III in 1534. He gave the cardinal's hat to his eldest grandson, Alessandro, and in 1545 also to Alessandro's younger brother, Ranuccio. For their father—that is, his son Pier Luigi—Paul III created first the Duchy of Castro, then that of Parma and Piacenza. Paul's election ushered in a continuation of the Golden Age of patronage, which had been sharply interrupted by the Sack of Rome in 1527. Commissions included a new phase in the reconstruction of St Peter's Basilica, Michelangelo's painting of the *Last Judgement* and his reorganization of the Campidoglio, as well as the construction of the family palace, Palazzo Farnese (to which Michelangelo contributed). An interesting development occurred in the patronage of Alessandro Farnese junior. Whereas in the 1530s and 1540s his religious commissions were very rare, in the 1560s he started a large-scale programme of building and renovating churches. Scholars disagree about the extent to which this ostentatious

---

[124] See below, 45–46. For the beginning of Farnese's patronage in 1554–5 see also Panvinio, *Fastorum libri V* (1558), dedicatory preface to A. Farnese, sig. a4ᵛ; Panvinio to Ruscelli, 4 November 1564, 189.

[125] On Farnese's artistic patronage see Robertson, *Farnese*; on his literary patronage, G. Guerrieri, 'Il mecenatismo dei Farnesi', *Archivio storico per le provincie parmensi*, ser. iii, 6 (1941), 95–130; 7–8 (1942–3), 127–67; ser. iv, 1 (1945–8), 59–119.

[126] P. de Nolhac, *La bibliothèque de Fulvio Orsini* (Paris, 1887), 13–15; Robertson, *Farnese*, 68.

show of piety was a result of the demands of the Catholic Reformation and part of his campaigns to become pope—and the extent to which it reflected a change in his religious beliefs.[127] What is certain is that, in Farnese, as in Cervini and Panvinio, a move from the secular to the spiritual could be traced.

Meanwhile, Panvinio's academic progress was steady. On 10 June 1556 the prior general, Christopher of Padua, extended his privilege to live outside the monastery for another two years and heaped praise on the young man for his contributions to history, through which he had brought much honour to the order. The general gave him three hundred *scutata* for his 'very poor sister' and conferred on him the degree of bachelor (*baccalaureus*) of theology.[128] On 20 August 1557 Panvinio received the license to obtain the degree of *magister et doctor* of theology. The general granted this license, not because of Panvinio's teaching experience (which was the normal requirement), but in recognition of his work on the popes and emperors and in praise of his virtues, 'which are certainly unique in our order'.[129] After this, Cardinal Farnese formally conferred the degree on Panvinio. This was not unusual, as theological degrees could be awarded by popes and other high members of the Curia.[130]

We are informed about Panvinio's moves in the years 1556–9 through an autobiographical account contained in the preface to his text *Creatio Pii IV Papae* (Election of Pope Pius IV).[131] He opened this preface with the observation that during the 'severe and difficult' pontificate of Paul IV (1555–9), the finest men of all classes left Rome temporarily and spread out to 'various

---

[127] Robertson, *Farnese*, 151, 158–62; C. Riebesell, *Die Sammlung des Kardinal Alessandro Farnese: ein 'studio' für Künstler und Gelehrte* (Weinheim, 1989), 3–5.

[128] *Christophori Patavini Registra*, iv. 155 (10 June 1556): 'Fratri Onufrio Veronensi baccalaureo literae patentes'.

[129] Ibid., v. 93 (20 August 1557). Panvinio's virtues, 'quae certe in ordine nostro singulares sunt', are mentioned in Christopher's corresponding letter to Panvinio of 21 August 1557, which is included in Farnese's 'open letter' (see below, n. 130).

[130] 'Open letter' by Farnese for Panvinio, undated, Vat. lat. 6412, fos 378ʳ–379ᵛ, ed. Perini, 233–6. After citing Christopher of Padua's letter (see previous note) and invoking the 'authoritas apostolica nobis per diversos summos pontifices concessa', Farnese continued: 'te Fratrem Onuphrium familiarem nostrum…sacrae theologiae magistrum et doctorem…constituimus et creamus'.

[131] Panvinio, *Creatio Pii IV Papae*, in id., *De varia Romani pontificis creatione*, Book X, MS Munich, Bayerische Staatsbibliothek, Clm 152, fos 409ʳ–439ᵛ, partial edn in S. Merkle, in *Concilium Tridentinum: diariorum, actorum, epistularum, tractatuum nova collectio*, 13 vols (Freiburg im Breisgau, 1901–2001), ii. 575–601; preface, 575–8. In his edition, Merkle left out the text of several letters.

parts of the world'.[132] Strongly anti-Spanish and anti-Habsburg, Paul allied with the French and provoked a war against the Spanish forces in Italy. The conflict lasted from September 1556 to September 1557 and threw Rome into confusion.[133] Cardinal Farnese foresaw this war and departed from the city around 5 June 1556. A week later, Panvinio left to follow his patron into exile; he went to Venice and then to Verona, where he visited his relatives for the first time in five years. In the meantime, Farnese began sitting out Paul IV's pontificate in Parma; and at the beginning of September 1556, Panvinio left Verona and joined Farnese. During a year in the 'very quiet town' of Parma from 1556 onwards, Panvinio was 'free from all concerns which usually vex men and not entangled in any business'. However, in truth, the beginning of Panvinio's period in Parma was not as peaceful as he made it appear. In October 1556 Panvinio left Parma temporarily for an unknown destination and he then fell ill in Bologna with a serious fever. He was cured in Verona by the physician and translator of Aristotle, Domenico Montesauro, and was back in Parma in January 1557.[134]

After this, Panvinio was able to put the finishing touches on his *Romani pontifices et cardinales* (Roman Pontiffs and Cardinals) (Fig. 1.3).[135] The antiquities dealer and editor Jacopo Strada published a first edition of this work under the title *Epitome pontificum Romanorum a Sancto Petro usque ad Paulum IV* in Venice in 1557, which did not satisfy the author.[136] Panvinio then issued a revised edition entitled *Romani pontifices et cardinales* with the printer Michele Tramezzino in Venice, 1557. When Panvinio dedicated

---

[132] Ibid. 575: 'Aspero et difficili Pauli IV pontificatu intractabilique et saevo eiusdem ingenio nobiliores quique omnium ordinum homines permoti Urbe relicta in diversas orbis terrarum partes concessere.'

[133] K. M. Setton, *The Papacy and the Levant (1204–1571)*, 4 vols (Philadelphia, PA, 1976–84), iv. 659–87.

[134] Panvinio, *De urbis Veronae viris... illustribus* (1621), 38; *Antiquitatum Veronensium libri VIII* (1648), 159. Panvinio to Farnese, 12 November 1556, in A. Ronchini, 'Onofrio Panvinio', *Atti e memorie delle RR. Deputazioni di storia patria per le provincie modenesi e parmensi*, ser. i, 6 (1872), 207–26, at p. 213; A. Agustín (Rome) to Panvinio, 16 January 1557, in id., *Epistolario*, ed. C. Flores Sellés (Salamanca, 1980), 243–4.

[135] Panvinio, *Creatio Pii IV*, ed. Merkle, 575–6: 'Quo anno ab omnibus quae homines angere solent curis liber et nullis negociis in civitate quietissima implicitus libro de cardinalibus extremam manum imposui, et eo qui secutus est anno MDLVII ipsum publicavi.'

[136] Panvinio, *Epitome pontificum Romanorum a Sancto Petro usque ad Paulum IV, gestorum videlicet electionisque singulorum et conclavium compendiaria narratio; cardinalium item nomina, dignitatum tituli, insignia legationes, patria et obitus* (Venice: Jacopo Strada, 1557). Autograph MS: Panvinio, *Epitome pontificum Romanorum*, BAV, Barb. lat. 2754. See also D. J. Jansen, *Jacopo Strada and Cultural Patronage at the Imperial Court: The Antique as Innovation*, 2 vols (Leiden, 2019), ii. 736–9 and *ad indicem* s.v. Panvinio.

ONVPHRII
PANVINII VERONENSIS
FRATRIS EREMITÆ AVGVSTINIANI,

ROMANI PONTIFICES

ET CARDINALES S. R. E.
ab eifdem à Leone I X. ad Paulum Papam I I I I.
per quingentos pofteriores a Chrifti
Natali annos creati.

**Cum Priuilegio fummi Pontificis, & Illuftrisfimi
Senatus Veneti ad annos decem.**

Fig. 1.3   Onofrio Panvinio, *Romani pontifices et cardinales* (Venice, 1557).
Courtesy of the Bayerische Staatsbibliothek, Munich (4 H.eccl. 587).

the *Romani pontifices* to Cardinal Farnese in 1557, he made it clear that Farnese had not commissioned this book and that the idea had come solely from Marcello Cervini. What Panvinio published under this title was not much more than a skeleton chronicle of popes and cardinals—a byproduct or off-shoot of his *Fasti*. Still, it proved to be influential because it was the only work of its kind and would later be used as an essential reference work by scholars such as Cesare Baronio. As Hubert Jedin noted, 'when the young Baronio started preparing his lectures on church history at the Oratory, he had only a single small, pertinent book at his disposal'—that is, Panvinio's brief history of popes.[137]

The *Romani pontifices* was meant to be the first volume of a work in three parts, containing a universal Latin and Greek church history from Christ to the present day. The contents of Volume 1—that is, the chronicle of popes and cardinals—were intended as a 'catalogue or foundation' ('index sive fundamentum') for the other parts. The second volume would deal with the history of the popes in a more detailed way and the third with universal church history.[138]

The *Romani pontifices* attracted some critical comments. Writing from Rome to Parma, Panvinio's friend Ottavio Pantagato related three points of criticism which he had heard about without yet having seen the book. The first point was that under each pope, Panvinio re-listed the cardinals created by his predecessor if these were still alive; this led to unnecessary repetitions. Secondly, he had changed the numbers of certain popes contrary to common usage. Thirdly, he had judged the actions of some popes negatively.[139] A few months later, having seen the book, Pantagato added critical observations about the dates of the first leaders of the Church, referring in particular to Peter, Linus, and Clement.[140]

Something must be said here about Panvinio's autobiographical account. To begin, Panvinio hid Alessandro Farnese's political activities; in the

---

[137] H. Jedin, *Kardinal Caesar Baronius: der Anfang der katholischen Kirchengeschichts-schreibung im 16. Jahrhundert* (Münster, 1978), 37. Jedin referred here to Panvinio's *Epitome* of 1557, probably not making a distinction between the *Epitome* and the *Romani pontifices*.

[138] Panvinio, *Romani pontifices et cardinales* (1557), sigs **1ᵛ–**2ʳ.

[139] O. Pantagato to Panvinio, 28 August 1557, in id., 'La correspondència', ed. A. Soler i Nicolau, 2 vols (doctoral thesis, Universitat Autònoma de Barcelona, 2000), i. 130: 'vi fate arbitro de le attioni di essi pontefici con poco vantaggio loro'.

[140] Pantagato to Panvinio, late 1557, ibid. 140. For an attempt to censor this work in the Congregation of the Index of Prohibited Books see below, 164–166. For printed copies with handwritten corrections and additions in view of a possible second edition (which never came out) see MSS Rome, Biblioteca Casanatense, 829; Venice, Biblioteca Marciana, Marc. lat. IX 83 (3724).

summer of 1556 Farnese was not the innocent bystander whom Panvinio tried to make him appear. The cardinal deftly changed his political affiliations; whereas he had previously been closely linked to the French, he now engaged in secret dealings with the Spaniards, with the aim of facilitating the restitution of Piacenza to his family. This became known to Paul IV, who subjected the cardinal to an angry outburst, allegedly shouting: 'You have always been a deceitful and wicked man, a heretic, but I will make you sorry for it!'[141] From then on, Alessandro was under suspicion and surveillance. He did not receive permission to go to France but was allowed to leave Rome. He went to Parma before an agreement was reached on 13 August 1556 between Alessandro's brother Ottavio and King Philip II of Spain, according to which Ottavio received Piacenza. Though Alessandro protested his innocence, maintaining that his brother alone was responsible for the coup, the episode was perceived as a defection of the Farnese family from the Holy See and its interests. The Farnese afterwards remained in the service of Philip II.[142] This helps explain why Panvinio dedicated several of his works to Philip II.

Panvinio failed to note that the last of his books mentioned in his account—that is, the combined volume containing *Romani principes* (Roman Emperors) and *De comitiis imperatoriis* (On the Imperial Elections)—came out in Basel. Given that Panvinio was including his autobiographical account in a history of a papal elections, it would hardly have been opportune for him to mention that the book had been published in a Protestant Swiss city.[143] In fact, in January 1559 Panvinio realized that this edition would be problematic because Protestant printers were included in Paul IV's Index of Prohibited Books, which had come into force on 30 December 1558. The publisher, Heinrich Petri, was on the list of 'printers from whose shops the works of various heretics had come forth' ('typographi e quorum officinis diversorum haereticorum opera prodiere'). This rendered all the works that he published highly suspicious. Though the prohibition seemed to refer

---

[141] G. Drei, *I Farnese*, ed. G. Allegri Tassoni (Rome, 1954), 103: 'Voi siete sempre stato un perfido, un malvagio, un eretico, ma io ve ne farò pentire!' For what follows see ibid. 94–119; H. Gamrath, *The Farnese: Pomp, Power and Politics in Renaissance Italy* (Rome, 2007), 70–1.

[142] Gamrath, *The Farnese*, 113: 'the family's absorption into the Spanish system'.

[143] Panvinio, *Romanorum principum et eorum quorum maxima in Italia imperia fuerunt libri IV; De comitiis imperatoriis liber* (Basel: Heinrich Petri, 1558). The printer Giordano Ziletti, son-in-law of Vincenzo Valgrisi, had given the manuscript to Petri (letter by Petri to Panvinio, 5 October 1558, Vat. lat. 6412, fo. 25ʳ, ed. Perini, *Panvinio*, 75 n. 1). On Ziletti see P. F. Grendler, *The Roman Inquisition and the Venetian Press, 1540–1605* (Princeton, NJ, 1977), 191. On *De comitiis* see also below, 138–141.

only to books published 'henceforth' ('posthac'), Panvinio's friends were sceptical that this mere specification would save his edition from a ban.[144] It was feared that, in practice, all the books that Petri had previously printed could be neither sold nor possessed without special permission from the Inquisition. Ottavio Pantagato suggested that Panvinio delete the printer's name and mark from all his copies, as this might solve the problem.[145] Antonio Agustín asked him—probably as a precautionary measure—to send the book directly to Naples, without letting it touch ground in Rome.[146]

Roman Antiquity and the Problem of Forgery

In these years, Panvinio also completed his *Fasti* and his *Commentaries on the Roman Republic*. To publish these works 'with more accuracy', as he said, Panvinio left Parma in October 1557 and moved to Venice. For the entire year of 1558 he was busy with their publication, for which the printer Vincenzo Valgrisi bore the costs.[147] Panvinio stayed in Venice for over a year and a half, until June 1559 (although the stay was interrupted by another few months in Parma in late 1558 and early 1559).[148] A return to Rome was

---

[144] J. M. de Bujanda (ed.), *Index des livres interdits*, 12 vols (Sherbrooke, Quebec; Geneva; Madrid, 1984–2016), viii. 38, 132, 332, 336; in particular, p. 786: 'opera...posthac excusa'.

[145] O. Pantagato to Panvinio, 28 January 1559, in id., 'La correspondència', i. 267: 'Dissi ad un amico vostro de lo libro *De imperio Romano* e de lo trattato *De comitiis imperatoriis*, che io dubitava del impressore interditto; ma risposse che era ben vostro, perché indubitatamente non piacerà a cui può molto sopra di voi; e così interditto non dispiacerà. Non giova che sia uscito prima che lo indice, ma gioverà bene quant'al impressore—se la materia non spiacerà loro—che si cancelli il nome, el segno et epistola del impressore, perché con questa moderatione se no posson leggere molti di materia non prohibita.' Pantagato perhaps took it for granted that there was a printer's epistle contained in this edition, but this was not in fact the case.

[146] Agustín to Panvinio, 6 February 1559, in id., *Epistolae Latinae et Italicae*, ed. J. Andrés (Parma, 1804), 363; also in J. Carbonell i Manils, 'Epigrafia i numismàtica a l'epistolari d'Antonio Agustín (1551–1563) (vol. 1)' (doctoral thesis, Universitat Autònoma de Barcelona, 1991), 318: 'Il libro *De comitiis imperator(iis)* vedete se potete mandarlo a Napoli senza che tochi in Roma.'

[147] Panvinio, *Creatio Pii IV*, preface, 576; Panvinio (Venice) to Farnese, 5 November 1557, in Ronchini, 'Panvinio', 213–14.

[148] For his departure from Venice see below, 63. For his time in Parma see the letter by Panvinio to Farnese, 18 June 1558, ed. Ronchini, 'Panvinio', 217–18; the letters by Pantagato in id., 'La correspondència', i. 245–77; and Carbonell, 'Epigrafia', 320 (Panvinio's second stay in Parma lasted from some time before November 1558 until early February 1559). In *c*.1559, Panvinio wrote his *Antiquitates Veronenses*; see K. A. Gersbach, 'A History of Biblioteca Angelica Latin Manuscript 64: Onofrio Panvinio's "Antiquitatum Veronensium libri VIII"', *AAug*, 55 (1992), 207–20.

still out of the question, as Paul IV became increasingly hostile not only to Panvinio's patron, but also to members of religious orders who lacked discipline. In July 1558, Paul published a bull against monks and friars who lived outside their religious houses; some of them were to be imprisoned if they did not immediately return to their institutions. In his letters, Agustín reported to Panvinio the effects of this bull (which he referred to as 'bolla contra apostatas').[149] In January 1559 Agustín advised Panvinio (in Parma) to sleep in a religious house but to eat at the table of the Farnese court without any worries.[150]

Panvinio's works on Roman antiquity from 1557–8 were the only texts dealing with pagan subject matter published by Panvinio during his lifetime. His edition of the *Fasti* was certainly the most weighty and important of these. Encouraged by the work of Heinrich Glarean, Panvinio allegedly started working on the *Fasti* already in 1544 at the age of fourteen. When fragments were discovered in the Roman Forum in 1546/47, he was excited and even more eager to do this work.[151] The *Fasti* were consular and triumphal lists which provided information about Roman kings, annual magistrates, and military victors who were granted triumphal processions. They had been compiled during the time of Emperor Augustus. After the discovery of the first fragments, Cardinal Alessandro Farnese sponsored

[149] Agustín to Panvinio, 6 August 1558, in his *Epistolario*, 314; his letters of 9 July 1558, ibid. 306, and 3 September 1558, ibid. 318.
[150] Agustín to Panvinio, 6 January 1559, ibid. 362; also published in Carbonell, 'Epigrafia', 297: 'Dormite pur in chiostro, et andate a tavola dell'Illustrissimo senza scrupulo.' In Venice (where he stayed from 1557), Panvinio lodged only initially in the Augustinian house of Santo Stefano; for most of 1558, he resided with the Spanish ambassador. Returning to Venice in February 1559, however, he began to lodge at Santo Stefano again. Back in Rome, he lived 'in casa di' or 'appresso' Cardinal Farnese, but it is not clear where exactly his rooms were. In 1567, a letter from Enea Vico was addressed to Panvinio at the Palazzo di San Giorgio—another name for the Palazzo della Cancelleria, Farnese's chief residence as Vice-Chancellor (Vat. lat. 6412, fo. 242ʳ⁻ᵛ). In 1568 Nicolaus Florentius searched for Panvinio and Fulvio Orsini in their respective rooms, possibly in Palazzo Farnese ('me n'andai dritto alla camera di Lei'; 'camera del…Messer Fulvio': letter to Panvinio, 21 March 1568, ibid., fo. 312ʳ⁻ᵛ). Alessandro Farnese had inherited Palazzo Farnese in 1565, but it was still partly unfinished in 1568.
[151] Panvinio, *Fastorum libri V* (1558), sigs b1ʳ–b5ʳ ('A quibus tabulae capitolinae primum editae…'), at sigs b4ᵛ–b5ʳ: 'Ego enim etsi ante ipsarum tabularum inventionem, Glareani et ipse [that is, just like Sigonio before him] exemplo adcensus, diu in hoc opere laborarim, quippe quod Veronae anno Domini MDXLIIII primo huic negocio vacare coeperim dum adhuc in scholis agerem doctissimi grammatici et de me benemeriti Danielis Aliensis, illud tamen fatebor me quoque earum tabularum inventione ad haec eadem peragenda promptiorem factum fuisse.' See also ibid., dedicatory preface to A. Farnese, sig. a3ᵛ: 'Quas [tabulas] divina prope voluntate erutas esse eo potissimum tempore existimo; quo paulo ante ipsum opus Veronae adhuc adulescentulus aggressus fueram'.

a further search in the area to excavate more pieces. The *Fasti* were then relocated to the Palazzo dei Conservatori on the Capitoline Hill and became known as *Fasti Capitolini*.[152] In 1549 Bartolomeo Marliani published their first edition. Panvinio immediately acquired a copy.[153] Carlo Sigonio produced an edition in 1550. Panvinio completed his own initial manuscript version in 1552, consisting of a copy of the inscriptions without commentary.[154]

Several problems arose with respect to producing a correct edition. First, the gaps between the fragments had to be filled. Second, the chronology of the *Fasti* had to be compared to the tradition of chronology derived from literary sources, most importantly Livy. They were consistently one year out of step with the Livian scheme. The *Fasti* placed the first year of the consulate in 244 AUC (*ab Urbe condita*: from the foundation of Rome), whereas the Roman antiquarian Varro had established 245 AUC, equivalent to 509 BC, as the standard date, which Livy followed. Sigonio recognized that two separate traditions existed and kept the chronologies of the historians and that of the *Fasti* separate. He stuck to this finding, so that in his editions, the numbering of years AUC is always one year behind. Panvinio realized that the numeration of the *Fasti* was unimportant: it was the sequence which mattered. Based on Sigonio's work, he therefore took the additional step of adapting the consular lists to the Varronian numeration of years. He presented the Capitoline numbers in the left column and the Varronian numbers in the right column. Panvinio also extended the *Fasti* beyond the end of the inscribed lists and continued the register of Roman rulers up to Emperor Charles V, in his own time.

Panvinio gave a manuscript to Jacopo Strada, around 1554. The edition which Strada published three years later failed to satisfy him. It is not clear why Panvinio was so enraged—whether it was really because of typographical errors and inaccuracies (he claimed it was 'not so much printed as mangled'), or whether he himself had changed his mind after he had given the manuscript to Strada and had wanted to delay publication because he was

---

[152] For what follows see Stenhouse, *Reading Inscriptions*, 103–12. For another recent discussion of the *Fasti Capitolini* and their discovery see M. Beard, *The Roman Triumph* (Cambridge, MA, 2007), 61–80.

[153] See above, 26.

[154] Panvinio, *Fasti*, Vat. lat. 3451.i, fo. 75ᵛ: 'Panvinius...fecit et scripsit Romae MDLII'. See also A. Degrassi, 'Fasti consulares et triumphales Capitolini', in id. (ed.), *Fasti consulares et triumphales* (Rome, 1947), 1–142, at p. 13. On other editions of the Fasti see W. McCuaig, 'The *Fasti Capitolini* and the Study of Roman Chronology in the Sixteenth Century', *Athenaeum*, 69 (1991), 141–59.

constantly making improvements and modifications.[155] It is often assumed that Strada had snatched the manuscript from Panvinio without his knowledge; but as we learn from letters from Agustín to Panvinio, the two actually had a contract. Agustín, a jurist, offered advice about the legal aspects of the question, saying he was ready to testify regarding the contract. He believed Panvinio could print a new edition of his own, but could not sell the same manuscript that he had sold to Strada to anyone else for three or four years.[156] It would have been risky for Panvinio to proceed with a new edition, as Strada had duly obtained his privileges: from Emperor Charles V for twelve years, from King Ferdinand for ten years (both issued in 1556), and from the Venetian Senate for ten years (issued on 27 April 1557).[157]

The *Fasti* raise some interesting questions regarding epigraphy and forgery. The first question is whether epigraphic sources were considered more accurate and, therefore, more authoritative than literary sources. Sigonio's edition demonstrates that he valued epigraphy more highly than the evidence of literary sources. Although he did not make a programmatic statement, it is clear from his edition that he assumed, firstly, that the *Fasti* were an official record and, secondly, that their text was particularly reliable because it was epigraphic. He therefore regarded Livy's differing chronology as that of a mere individual who followed his own norm.[158] Panvinio took a more pragmatic approach towards epigraphic sources. Though concerned with finding exact information, our friar did not revere inscriptions as absolutely reliable regardless of what other sources said. He generally gave preference to inscriptions but did not follow them slavishly. He was more interested in them as texts than in epigraphy as a discipline for its own sake.[159]

---

[155] Panvinio, *Fastorum libri V*, sig. b5ʳ: 'Maturavi quoque hoc opus edere, quod iam Venetiis meo nomine addito excusum sit inversum et male affectum. Nam triennio ante a me datum ut evulgaretur, ab imperitissimis typographis non excusum sed laceratum est, quod et me inscio et absente factum fuit'; J. Strada, preface to his edition of Panvinio's *Fasti et triumphi Romanorum a Romulo rege usque ad Carolum V* (Venice, 1557), dated 15 May (1557), sigs *2ʳ–*4ʳ, at sig. *3ᵛ: 'cum ante tres annos Romae in Illustrissimi Cardinalis Alexandri Farnesii Domini ac patroni mei aula, tanquam eius familiaris, versarer et eius libri copia mihi esset facta'. See also Jansen, *Strada*, ii. 736–9.

[156] Agustín to Panvinio, 27 November 1557, in id., *Epistolario*, 281. See also his letter of 11 December 1557, ibid. 283: 'la fede del contratto col Strada vi mandarò'; letter of 5 February 1558, 289: 'il testimonio per la stampa contra il Strada'.

[157] Panvinio, *Fasti et triumphi* (1557), at the end of the book (not paginated).

[158] McCuaig, '*Fasti Capitolini*', 146–7, 151.

[159] See Stenhouse, *Reading Inscriptions*, 8, 75. On the use by antiquarians of non-literary evidence (material objects) to supplement literary sources see I. Herklotz, 'Arnaldo Momigliano's "Ancient History and the Antiquarian": A Critical Review', in P. N. Miller (ed.), *Momigliano and Antiquarianism: Foundations of the Modern Cultural Sciences* (Toronto, 2007), 127–53.

Panvinio's attitude might have protected him from falling prey to just too many forgeries. The science of epigraphy had been widely practised and become intellectually reputable from only about 1500. Scholars had collected many thousands of ancient inscriptions and assembled them in manu-scripts. Fra Giovanni Giocondo (d. 1515) had applied rigorous philological standards to collections of inscriptions. Panvinio was part of a group of scholars who came together in Rome in the mid-sixteenth century and further developed principles for analysing inscriptions. Ironically, the very value that historical scholars placed on inscriptions increased the likelihood that forgers would invent them to support their own arguments or points of view. Annius of Viterbo, a notorious forger of historical works, also invented several inscriptions to prove that his hometown of Viterbo was a seat of an Etruscan civilization predating Greece and Rome. He had some of these carved; they survive today in the Museo Civico of Viterbo.[160] While forging inscriptions to provide evidence for one's own case was certainly the prime function of such forgeries, there were other possible motives as well.

Forged inscriptions have much in common with forged works of art from antiquity. Restorers and sculptors were tempted to create examples indistinguishable from the ancient originals, even to the expert eye. In a famous episode told by Giorgio Vasari in his life of Michelangelo, the artist created a sculpture of a Sleeping Cupid, which he covered with dirt so that it seemed as if it had been excavated. It passed for an ancient work of art with his patron, and Michelangelo was widely admired for this feat of deception. Vasari added his own judgement: He criticized the patron for spurning a perfect work of art when he discovered it was not ancient.[161]

It should come as no surprise that humanist culture was prone to forgeries. After all, humanists prided themselves on imitating classical Latin literature as perfectly as possible. When humanists wrote history, they did not typic-ally integrate original documents into the text as faithful citations; rather, they usually transformed and adapted original documents to the needs of a literary genre. Where evidence was missing, it was invented; writers

---

[160] A. Collins, 'Renaissance Epigraphy and Its Legitimating Potential: Annius of Viterbo, Etruscan Inscriptions, and the Origins of Civilization', in A. E. Cooley (ed.), *The Afterlife of Inscriptions* (London, 2000), 57–76; Stenhouse, *Reading Inscriptions*, 76.

[161] G. Vasari, *Le vite de' più eccellenti pittori, scultori ed architettori*, ed. G. Milanesi, 9 vols (Florence, 1878–85), vii. 147–9; M. Hirst, 'The Artist in Rome, 1496–1501', in *Making and Meaning: The Young Michelangelo* (London, 1994), 13–81, esp. pp. 13–28.

adhered, for example, to the classical technique of inventing speeches of generals. It was enough that a speech convincingly represented what the general could have said before a battle. This was a recreation of the past rather than a mere presentation of the fragmentary literary evidence which had come from antiquity. When scholars who had been trained as humanists or influenced by humanist culture devoted themselves to the study of epigraphy, a similar effect could be noted. By completing fragments of inscriptions, they could display their art.[162] An innocence is connected to this which, for us today, is difficult to understand. Anthony Grafton has cautioned us against assuming that these scholars had a different notion of historical truth from ours; still, it remains puzzling that even those scholars who otherwise practised rigorous historical research sometimes broke their own scientific rules.[163]

By inventing or altering inscriptions, scholars not only intended to show off their ability to emulate antiquity but also sometimes sought to make money. Although the market for inscribed tablets was smaller than that for sculpted antiques, they were regularly sold. The reason for forging might also be local or family pride. Another fascinating motive was to 'bewilder the ignorant and test the learned': a scholar's game. A well-known example in the field of poetry is Marc-Antoine Muret's deception of Joseph Scaliger by sending him two poems written in what seemed to be archaic Latin, simply to see if Muret could pull the wool over his learned colleague's eyes. The learned joke, which displayed Muret's mastery of Latin, was successful, and Scaliger printed the poems in an edition of Varro's *De re rustica* in 1573.[164] By demonstrating their ability to understand and emulate the past in this way, scholars enhanced their reputations. Suspicions are strong that Sigonio invented and then printed the complete version of a treatise by Cicero which had previously been known only in fragments. Sigonio never admitted to writing it and claimed that the manuscript had been given to him; the successful deception seems to have been entirely for his private pleasure.[165]

---

[162] On imaginary reconstructions of ancient monuments in the Renaissance and Baroque periods see V. P. Tschudi, *Baroque Antiquity: Archaeological Imagination in Early Modern Europe* (Cambridge, 2017).

[163] A. Grafton, *Forgers and Critics: Creativity and Duplicity in Western Scholarship* (Princeton, NJ, 1990), 49; id., Review of Stenhouse, *Reading Inscriptions, Sixteenth Century Journal*, 39 (2008), 911–13.

[164] Grafton, *Scaliger*, i. 161; Stenhouse, *Reading Inscriptions*, 96.

[165] W. McCuaig, *Carlo Sigonio: The Changing World of the Late Renaissance* (Princeton, NJ, 1989), 291–344.

The most notorious forger of inscriptions was the artist and antiquarian Pirro Ligorio (c.1518–83)—so notorious, indeed, that the nineteenth-century editors of the *Corpus inscriptionum Latinarum* (Corpus of Latin Inscriptions) rejected as false all the inscriptions known to us only through him. This amounted to almost 3,000 inscriptions concerning the city of Rome alone.[166] In the case of Pirro Ligorio one motive among others must have been to compensate for an inferiority complex. Originally trained as an artist, he felt that he was not always taken seriously, although as an artist and architect he was convinced that he could understand antiquity better than scholars trained in literature, law, and history.[167] Panvinio summarized Ligorio's achievements, especially praising his contribution to Roman topography and pointing out that he had corrected many errors committed by previous antiquarians.[168] Yet while Ligorio's research on antiquity was an important source for his friends and colleagues, he was never able to lose the stigma associated with being fundamentally an artist rather than a scholar.

In 1558, Panvinio promised to publish a collection of inscriptions. The material he put together, much later (1566–7), for such a collection is preserved in two manuscripts in the Vatican Library.[169] Nineteenth-century collectors of inscriptions argued that some of the examples in Panvinio's *Fasti* were sixteenth-century reconstructions or inventions; however, it is not clear whether he falsified them himself.[170] Fulvio Orsini accused

[166] S. Orlandi, M. L. Caldelli, and G. L. Gregori, 'Forgeries and Fakes', in C. Bruun and J. Edmondson (eds), *The Oxford Handbook of Roman Epigraphy* (Oxford, 2015), 42–65, esp. pp. 44–5; Stenhouse, *Reading Inscriptions*, 82.

[167] C. Occhipinti, *Pirro Ligorio e la storia cristiana di Roma da Costantino all'Umanesimo* (Pisa, 2007), pp. LXXII–LXXIV; F. Loffredo and G. Vagenheim (eds), *Pirro Ligorio's Worlds: Antiquarianism, Classical Erudition and the Visual Arts in the Renaissance* (Leiden, 2019); Ferrary, *Panvinio*, 38.

[168] Panvinio, *Reipublicae Romanae commentariorum libri tres*, Preface to Book I, sigs a6ᵛ–a8ᵛ, at sig. a8ʳ⁻ᵛ. For a critical edition of this preface (by Panvinio later given the title 'De his qui Romanas antiquitates scripto comprehenderunt') see Ferrary, *Panvinio*, 49–62. Ferrary also provided an exhaustive commentary, ibid. 68–132. For the relations between Panvinio and Ligorio see also A. Schreurs, *Antikenbild und Kunstanschauungen des neapolitanischen Malers, Architekten und Antiquars Pirro Ligorio (1513–1583)* (Cologne, 2000), 32, 48, 115–16, 366.

[169] G. B. De Rossi, 'Delle sillogi epigrafiche dello Smezio e del Panvinio', *Annali dell'Istituto di corrispondenza archeologica*, 34 (1862), 220–44; M. Buonocore, 'Onuphrius Panvinius et Antonius Augustinus: de codicibus Vaticanis Latinis 6035–6 adnotationes nonnullae', in M. H. Crawford (ed.), *Antonio Agustín between Renaissance and Counter-Reform* (London, 1993), 155–71.

[170] *Corpus inscriptionum Latinarum* (Berlin, 1862–), vi.5, pp. 214*–15* ('Falsae Panvinianae'). See also A. E. Cooley, *The Cambridge Manual of Latin Epigraphy* (Cambridge, 2012), 392–4; Orlandi et al., 'Forgeries and Fakes', 46–7.

Panvinio of being a 'planter of carrots'—that is, an inventor of lies; but we do not know exactly to what he was referring, whether to a specific work by Panvinio or his scholarship in general.[171]

Panvinio's *Reipublicae Romanae commentariorum libri tres* (Three Books of Commentaries on the Roman Republic) was a companion volume to the *Fasti*. The preface was dated 1 August 1558, so the book was completed shortly after the *Fasti*.[172] It was dedicated to Ferdinand I, who had become Holy Roman Emperor in the same year. Panvinio declared that by adding another work to the *Fasti*—that is, the description of the Roman Republic— he hoped to have produced two equally useful works. Although many others had treated the Republic, Panvinio thought that they had not explained it as carefully as he had done.[173] He gave a summary of the work's contents. In Book I, on topography, he treated the 'image of the old city—that is, the ancient buildings' ('priscae urbis imagino, id est, vetusta aedificia'). He included the origin, location, boundary, gates, streets, hills, and regions of the city. Book II dealt with institutions; it had a separate title-page and was called 'The Roman State' ('Civitas romana'). It was original in that it aimed to present not an organizational plan but a history—sacred and secular—of Roman institutions. Panvinio described them as connected to the historical periods in which they occurred, from Romulus to Constantine.[174] Book III was concerned with the Empire outside the city of Rome ('Imperium Romanum')—that is, the provinces. The dedicatory epistle to Ferdinand ended with references to Antonio Agustín and to Martín de Guzmán, a Spanish noble at Ferdinand's court, who was a diplomat and close advisor to the emperor. These two men had informed him about the emperor's interest in ancient history.[175]

In addition to the dedicatory epistle to Ferdinand, each book had a separate preface.[176] The preface to Book I contained a catalogue of previous

---

[171] Stenhouse, *Reading Inscriptions*, 4–5.

[172] Ibid. 7–11, 71–2, 101–3. See also G. Vagenheim, 'La critique épigraphique aus XVIᵉ siècle: Ottavio Pantagato, Paolo Manuzio, Onofrio Panvinio, Antonio Agustín et Pirro Ligorio: à propos des tribus romaines', *Aevum*, 86 (2012), 949–68.

[173] Panvinio, dedicatory epistle to Emperor Ferdinand I, dated 1 August 1558, in his *Reipublicae Romanae commentariorum libri tres*, sigs a2ʳ–a6ʳ, at sig. a3ᵛ.

[174] M. H. Crawford, 'Benedetto Egio and the Development of Greek Epigraphy', in id. (ed.), *Antonio Agustín*, 133–54, at p. 133.

[175] Panvinio, dedicatory epistle to Emperor Ferdinand I, in his *Reipublicae Romanae commentariorum libri tres*, sig. a5ᵛ.

[176] On these prefaces see M. Mayer i Olivé, 'El canon de los humanistas de su tiempo interesados en la epigrafía y las antigüedades clásicas según el criterio de Onofrio Panvinio', *Sylloge Epigraphica Barcinonensis*, 8 (2010), 29–65.

scholars who had studied Roman topography. Most of this preface was actually an expanded version of the first paragraph of the preface to Georg Fabricius's *Roma* (1551). Fabricius, in the second edition of his work in 1560, accordingly denounced Panvinio for copying him.[177] Like Fabricius, Panvinio first listed a number of ancient antiquarians: above all Varro, but also Frontinus, Aelius Aristides, Pseudo-Rufus, and Pseudo-Victor. He then lamented the ill fortunes of Rome during the Middle Ages, before arriving at Petrarch. Biondo Flavio came next, as the true founder of modern antiquarian studies. Then followed Giulio Pomponio Leto, Giovanni Tortelli, and Poggio Bracciolini; and after them Raffaele Maffei, Fabrizio Varano, and Francesco Albertini. More recent was Andrea Fulvio, while Bartolomeo Marliani was the latest writer to follow in the footsteps of these antiquarians. Panvinio then added two names which Fabricius did not mention: Benedetto Egio and Pirro Ligorio. He praised their excellence, though much of their work was unpublished.[178] After the end of Book III, Panvinio again turned to the works on which he had drawn, paying homage to two friends: Antonio Agustín and Carlo Sigonio.[179] Agustín was singled out for his help with the entire treatise, and especially with questions regarding Roman tribes, colonies, towns and their laws in the second and third books. Sigonio had shared with Panvinio his knowledge of ancient law when he was in Venice and when Sigonio was working on his *De antiquo iure Italiae* (published Venice 1560).

A second companion volume to the *Fasti*, also published in 1558, which has already been mentioned, was Panvinio's *Romani principes*.[180] Although Panvinio did not publish any other books on ancient Roman topics during his lifetime, his interest in pagan antiquity peaked again in the second half of the 1560s. In 1567 the *Reipublicae Romanae commentarii* were developed into an enormous project, inspired by Varro, of *Antiquitates Romanae* (Roman Antiquities) in one hundred books; the work was to be dedicated to Maximilian II.[181] From 1565 Panvinio also worked on Roman religion and hoped to write a book on *De antiqua Romanorum religione* (On the

---

[177] Ferrary, *Panvinio*, 66 n. 91, 119–20.

[178] Panvinio, *Reipublicae Romanae commentariorum libri tres*, Preface to Book I, sigs a6ᵛ–a8ᵛ. See above, n. 168.

[179] Ibid., afterword ('De iis quorum praecipue opera in his commentariis scribendis usus sum'), 948–53.

[180] Panvinio, *Romanorum principum...libri IV* (1558).

[181] J.-L. Ferrary, 'Panvinio (Onofrio)', in C. Nativel (ed.), *Centuriae Latinae* (Geneva, 1997), 595–9, at p. 597; id., *Panvinio*.

Ancient Religion of the Romans). At the time of his death, only part of it was ready for printing: *De ludis circensibus* (On the Circus Games). Panvinio intended for another extract, *De triumpho*, taken from his commentary on the triumphal lists in the *Fasti*, to appear in print at the same time. In 1565–6, he had plates engraved to help communicate the content of these works and enhance their appeal. Even so, the illustrated *De triumpho* was not published until 1571.[182] The illustrated *De ludis circensibus* (with the plates from 1565–6), which came out in 1600, was a particular scholarly success and remained the key work on Roman circus games for two centuries.[183] It gives us an idea of what Panvinio's other works on antiquity would have looked like, had he not died before their completion.

Panvinio's antiquarian works have received mixed judgements. His *Fasti* were considered a masterpiece in the sixteenth century. The eminent scholar of chronology Joseph Scaliger, for example, regarded Panvinio as the most authoritative commentator on the *Fasti*.[184] In terms of assembling other ancient sources, however, Panvinio's lack of critical acumen has tended to lower his reputation; he was more inclined to collect and compile than to select and scrutinize. Yet, this attitude was aligned with the widespread sixteenth-century practice of compiling. In many cases, historians were considered to have made scholarly progress precisely when they had assembled more sources on a given topic than their predecessors had.

Panvinio's review of the antiquarian research of other scholars in his preface to the *Reipublicae Romanae commentarii* is telling in many ways.[185] By sticking to Fabricius's scheme, he left aside many important works of the

---

[182] Panvinio, *De triumpho commentarius* (Venice: Michele Tramezzino, 1571). For the text of *De triumpho* see *Fastorum libri V, Commentarii*, 453–62; on the engravings, E. Lurin, 'Etienne Dupérac, graveur, peintre et architecte (vers 1535?–1604): un artiste-antiquaire entre l'Italie et la France' (doctoral thesis, Université Paris-Sorbonne, 2006), *passim* (with extensive sections on Panvinio). See also W. Stenhouse, 'Panvinio and *descriptio*: Renditions of History and Antiquity in the Late Renaissance', *Papers of the British School at Rome*, 80 (2012), 233–56, at p. 233: 'Panvinio's 1571 study of the Roman triumph embodies a central innovation of sixteenth-century classical scholarship, the use of visual reconstructions alongside textual accounts to communicate the details of ancient ceremonies'.

[183] Panvinio, *De ludis circensibus; De triumphis* (Venice: Giovanni Battista Ciotti, 1600). See S. Tomasi Velli, 'Gli antiquari intorno al circo romano: riscoperta di una tipologia monumentale antica', *Annali della Scuola Normale Superiore di Pisa, Classe di lettere e filosofia*, ser. iii, 20 (1990) no. 1, pp. 61–168, at pp. 127–60; I. Herklotz, *Cassiano Dal Pozzo und die Archäologie des 17. Jahrhunderts* (Munich, 1999), 220–2.

[184] Grafton, *Scaliger*, i. 119, ii. 66–7.

[185] See I. Herklotz, Review of Ferrary, *Panvinio*, *Wolfenbütteler Renaissance-Mitteilungen*, 22 (1998), 19–22; id., *Cassiano*, 204–26, 246–7.

sixteenth century, especially collections of antiquarian miscellanea and commentaries in the tradition of Angelo Poliziano. (Missing names include Alessandro D'Alessandri, Caelius Rhodiginus, Francesco Robortello, and Piero Vettori.) This may have been an expression of his own distance from philological research, since he saw himself primarily as an antiquarian and historian. Already in his day, philologists of Northern Europe were, in fact, beginning to outclass their Italian counterparts. Italians such as Panvinio, on the other hand, had daily access to archaeological monuments and made the most of this advantage.

In any case, Panvinio's classification of the various disciplines associated with research on antiquity shows that he was keenly aware of all the main sources of antiquarian knowledge. In the revised version of the preface to his *Commentaries on the Roman Republic*, dating from 1567/68, Panvinio divided the authors according to whether they studied topography, epigraphy, chronology, or customs and institutions.[186] He also showed a critical appreciation of the medieval topographical texts known as the *Mirabilia urbis Romae*; these were difficult to use because they were filled with legends, so his recognition of their historical value was a sign of his pragmatism.[187] Panvinio's approach to antiquity, as an organic whole, had two models: in antiquity, Varro, and in the fifteenth century, Biondo Flavio. Because Panvinio was more inclusive and systematic than Varro, his project could rightly be considered one of the first serious attempts at a Varronian treatment of antiquity in modern times.[188]

In several ways, therefore, Panvinio was innovative.[189] As we have seen, his gigantic project of *Antiquitates Romanae* attempted a synthesis of knowledge about the ancient Roman world. In his *Fasti*, he reconciled the Varronian numbering of years with that on the *Fasti* tablets. In his *Commentaries on the Roman Republic*, he attempted an integration of static antiquarian methods and historical-chronological narrative, using not only literary sources but also evidence derived from epigraphy, numismatics, and archaeology. Finally, his approach included a pioneering interest in

---

[186] On customs and institutions ('mores et instituta') see Herklotz, *Cassiano*, 187–239.

[187] Ferrary, *Panvinio*, 71–6.

[188] R. Fubini, 'Onofrio Panvinio: alle origini del mito di Varrone come fondatore della scienza antiquaria', in id., *Storiografia dell'umanesimo in Italia da Leonardo Bruni ad Annio da Viterbo* (Rome, 2003), 83–9.

[189] Ferrary, *Panvinio*, 167–9; id., 'Panvinio (Onofrio)', 597; E. Lurin, 'Les restitutions de scènes antiques: Onofrio Panvinio iconographe et inventeur d'images', in M. Hochmann et al. (eds), *Programme et invention dans l'art de la Renaissance* (Paris, 2008), 153–73.

'scholarly illustrations' as a means of enhancing the reader's knowledge of the ancient world; he himself employed artists to produce exact representations of ancient scenes. We will see further below how Panvinio used some of these creative approaches and techniques in his treatments of medieval history and church history.

2

Between Church and Empire

Panvinio's Final Decade

Journey to Germany and Return to Rome

Since 1558 Panvinio used his friend Antonio Agustín's contacts to prepare a trip to Germany. In fact, Agustín's own visit to Germany in the spring of 1558 may not only have paved the way for Panvinio in a practical respect but also inspired him to venture north. In April, Agustín reported on the state of the German libraries and suggested that Panvinio travel there: 'Do not miss the opportunity to go to Germany', he wrote.[1] He praised the richness of the cathedral libraries and especially commended the libraries in Worms, Passau, Mainz, and Speyer. Among collectors and patrons, he mentioned Cardinal Otto Truchsess von Waldburg (prince-bishop of Augsburg), who resided in Dillingen, and Hans Jakob Fugger in Augsburg. In May, Panvinio expressed his desire to visit Vienna with the Spanish diplomat Martín de Guzmán; in June, he wrote about his plans to visit Germany.[2] Between July 1558 and January 1559, Panvinio was even considering changing patrons, but Agustín advised against this and rebuked him for consulting Cardinal Michele Ghislieri (later Pope Pius V) about this plan.[3] In the preface to the *Fasti* of 1558, Panvinio stated that he had 'lived in Rome for a long time' in the past, which shows he was not at all sure when he would be able to return there.[4] According to his diary for 1556–9, he had sworn to himself that he would never again set foot there while Paul IV was alive. Because he could

---

[1] A. Agustín (Linz) to Panvinio (Venice), 11 April 1558, in his *Epistolario*, 290: 'non lasciate con ogni ocasione di venir in Germania'.
[2] Agustín to Panvinio, 11 June 1558 and 25 June 1558, ibid. 295–7.
[3] Agustín to Panvinio, 9 July 1558, ibid. 306; see also his letter of 6 January 1559 (above, 51).
[4] Panvinio, *Fastorum libri V, Commentariorum in Fastos consulares Appendix*, dedicatory preface to Francisco de Vargas dated 1 August 1558, sig. *2ʳ: 'Rome, ubi longo tempore vixi'.

The Invention of Papal History: Onofrio Panvinio between Renaissance and Catholic Reform. Stefan Bauer, Oxford University Press (2020). © Stefan Bauer.
DOI: 10.1093/oso/9780198807001.001.0001

no longer maintain himself in Venice, and he no longer liked Parma or Piacenza, he decided to proceed to the imperial court at Augsburg.[5]

Emperor Ferdinand had paid Panvinio a considerable sum of money as a reward for dedicating to him the *Commentaries on the Roman Republic*. In February 1559, Panvinio wrote to Ferdinand, seeking a permit to visit German libraries. In March, Ferdinand invited him to his court. Farnese gave his permission for the trip and wrote letters of introduction to the emperor, Cardinal Cristoforo Madruzzo (prince-bishop of Trent) and Otto Truchsess von Waldburg.[6] Panvinio remained in Venice in May 1559 to participate in the general chapter of the Augustinians held there.[7] He left Venice for Verona in late June, then went to see Cardinal Farnese in Piacenza around 7 July.

Because Paul IV was gravely ill, Panvinio was permitted to go to Germany only on the condition that he would return as soon as possible. Farnese promised to let Panvinio participate in the expected papal conclave either as his own assistant or for some other purpose. Travelling north, Panvinio went to Brixen and met Cardinal Madruzzo. He arrived in Augsburg on 26 July and visited Cardinal Otto Truchsess von Waldburg. Panvinio was received well in Augsburg, and Otto wrote to Farnese in complimentary terms about him.[8] With Otto's help, Panvinio managed twice to speak a few words to Ferdinand, who was in town holding the Imperial Diet. Panvinio remained in Augsburg for twenty days. 'I admirably achieved everything I had come to do', he recorded.[9] This last remark requires some comment. He did not, in fact, complete everything he wanted to do, as he did not travel around the country and carry out research in other German cities. We know at least that he copied several ancient Roman inscriptions in Augsburg.[10]

---

[5] Panvinio, *Creatio Pii IV*, preface, 576. For what follows see ibid. and Panvinio, DVC-X, Clm 152, fos 409ᵛ–411ʳ.

[6] Undated and unsigned letter (but no doubt by Farnese) to Emperor Ferdinand, Vat. lat. 6412, fo. 336ʳ; Farnese to Otto Truchsess von Waldburg, 8 July 1559, Vat. lat. 6412, fo. 360ʳ⁻ᵛ. Both these letters are cited in Perini, *Panvinio*, 22. The third letter, to Madruzzo, is mentioned, together with the others, by Panvinio in his *Creatio Pii IV*, 577.

[7] O. Pantagato to Panvinio, 20 April 1559, in id., 'La correspondència', 293.

[8] O. von Waldburg (Augsburg) to A. Farnese (Piacenza), 16 August 1559, in Perini, *Panvinio*, 23; Panvinio, *Creatio Pii IV*, 577. On Otto see T. Groll (ed.), *Kardinal Otto Truchseß von Waldburg (1514–1573)* (Augsburg, 2015).

[9] Panvinio, *Creatio Pii IV*, 577: 'cuncta pro quibus veneram egregie confeci'. See also Ferdinand's letter of recommendation for Panvinio (facilitating his visits to libraries and archives), 8 August 1559, ed. C. L. Grotefend, 'Zur Literaturgeschichte', *Anzeiger für Kunde der deutschen Vorzeit*, n. s. 19 (1872), cols 4–9, 38–43, at col. 43.

[10] O. Hartig, 'Des Onuphrius Panvinius Sammlung von Papstbildnissen in der Bibliothek Johann Jakob Fuggers (Codd. lat. monac. 155–160)', *Historisches Jahrbuch*, 38 (1917), 284–314,

The true purpose of his journey may have been to establish contacts with new patrons. In addition to Otto von Waldburg, Panvinio also tried to meet Hans Jakob Fugger, who was not in Augsburg at the time. In a letter written a few months later, Fugger expressed regrets over not having been able to make Panvinio's acquaintance in Augsburg but thanked him for having left some books for him.[11] As we shall see, in the 1560s both Otto von Waldburg and Fugger became important new sponsors in addition to Farnese.

Panvinio was on his way back to Italy, and had just crossed the Alps, when he received news of the pope's death. He hurried to Rome, where Alessandro Farnese was expecting him for the conclave. On 12 September 1559 Panvinio arrived in the Eternal City, where he would spend the rest of his life.[12] Pius IV was elected after one of the longest conclaves in history, lasting from 5 September to 26 December 1559. After the Spanish and French factions had blocked each other for months, they finally settled on a compromise candidate. Unlike his predecessor, the new pope Giovanni Angelo Medici of Milan (unrelated to the Florentine Medici family) was not a fanatic. He steered the Holy See back into friendly relations with Emperor Ferdinand and Philip II of Spain. He also reversed some of the more excessive 'reform' measures of Paul IV, freeing apostate monks and friars from persecution, limiting the powers of the Inquisition and beginning to revise the impossibly strict Index of Prohibited Books. In a move which was controversial with the cardinals but popular among the faithful, he had two rich and depraved nephews of Paul IV tried and executed (although Pius IV himself also indulged in large-scale nepotism). The great diplomat Cardinal Giovanni Morone, who had been imprisoned on suspicion of heresy, was rehabilitated. Pius IV not only reopened the Council of Trent but also brought it to a successful conclusion. Crucially, he revived the papal tradition of giving support to scholars and artists. Pius listened to advisers such as the reformers Carlo Borromeo and Filippo Neri, as well as the theologians Seripando, Alfonso Salmerón, and Diego Laínez.

While it is an exaggeration to claim that Pius IV found 'his ideological and cultural points of references in the pro-Habsburg works of Onofrio

---

at pp. 288–9; M. Ott, *Die Entdeckung des Altertums: der Umgang mit der römischen Vergangenheit Süddeutschlands im 16. Jahrhundert* (Kallmünz, 2002), 213–19.

---

[11] H. J. Fugger (Augsburg) to Panvinio, 15 October 1559, MS BAM, D 501 inf., fo. 290ʳ. Fugger wrote that he had returned home and found a letter by Panvinio from 18 August.

[12] Panvinio, *Creatio Pii IV*, 577. Panvinio noted his arrival in Rome on 12 September also in Clm 152, fo. 318ᵛ.

Panvinio',[13] it is striking that from the conclave onwards, the Medici pope was well disposed towards him. Panvinio's brother Paolo related that a few days after his election, the new pope sent a small bag with a considerable sum of money to Panvinio. As Panvinio himself told Girolamo Ruscelli, Pius IV repeated such donations several times.[14] One of the reasons for this generosity may have been that Panvinio had been present at the conclave.[15]

Pius IV may have expected future favours from Panvinio, such as the composition of well-meaning descriptions of the conclave, his life, and his pontificate. Panvinio's account of the conclave was part of his ongoing work on the history of papal elections. Farnese had pressured him to write such a work since at least the spring of 1559, when Panvinio was still in Venice. Likely, the cardinal wanted this work in expectation of, or preparation for, the death of Paul IV. Panvinio's study of papal conclaves was also a natural transition from his work on imperial elections. As we have seen, the treatise *De comitiis imperatoriis* had been published along with his *Romani principes* in 1558, both with dedications to Philip II of Spain. In 1563 Panvinio would dedicate an expanded manuscript version of *De comitiis* to Maximilian II; he enlarged this manuscript again for the copy that he produced for Hans Jakob Fugger in 1565.[16] Panvinio's history of papal elections, *De varia creatione Romani pontificis*, was also constantly revised and enlarged; it became perhaps the most widely diffused and popular of Panvinio's unpublished works.[17]

According to Panvinio's brother, Pius IV considered making Panvinio a bishop; but Panvinio declined because he wanted to retain his freedom to study while he was still young. This account is highly improbable, for we know that Panvinio was always in search of money and a benefice which would permanently maintain him. To be sure, in 1561 Cardinal Marcantonio da Mula, bishop of Verona, urged Alessandro Farnese to give a vacant bishopric—which seemed to have been at his disposal—to Panvinio.[18] In August 1563, with the help of Cardinal Vitellozzo Vitelli, Panvinio attempted to obtain Spanish benefices from the pope, explaining that he did not expect to

---

[13] F. Rurale, 'Pio IV', in *Enciclopedia dei papi*, 3 vols (Rome, 2000), iii. 142–60, at p. 150: 'trovando i suoi referenti ideologici e culturali nell'opera filoasburgica di Onofrio Panvinio'.

[14] Paolo Panvinio, *Vita*, 219: 'Creato che fu Papa Pio IV, da lì a pochi giorni li mandò a donare in un sachetto dosento scudi d'oro'; Panvinio to Ruscelli, 4 November 1564, 189.

[15] For the conclave see below, 129–132.

[16] On *De comitiis* see above, 49–50; below, 138–141.   [17] See below, Chapter 3.

[18] M. da Mula (Rome) to A. Farnese (Caprarola), 2 August 1561, in R. Fulin, 'Onofrio Panvinio', *Archivio veneto*, 4 (1872), 158.

receive any other secure source of income. Panvinio was even trying to buy the Spanish citizenship which would have been required for this purpose.[19]

In September 1563 Panvinio obtained from Pius IV an open letter of recommendation ('breve apertum') addressed to the Christian hierarchy of Italy and Europe, ranging from patriarchs to cathedral chapters, asking that all libraries and archives be made accessible to him. Pius apparently placed great trust in him; he referred to him as a member of his household ('familiaris noster').[20] In the same September, Panvinio visited the libraries of the Benedictine monasteries of Montecassino and Cava.[21] Fugger wrote to him in November 1563 saying he was glad to hear that Panvinio had returned from Naples in October, because he was urgently waiting for some texts from him.[22] In 1564 Panvinio, with Francesco Davanzati, was supposed to travel to Sicily and 'some other provinces' by papal order. They were to obtain Greek, Arabic, and Latin manuscripts of works of Church Fathers which could be used to confute Protestant errors; Marcantonio da Mula was to oversee their publication.[23] The cardinal had been charged with helping Paolo Manuzio found a printing press for the critical edition of works of the Fathers. The project proved to be premature and abortive due to a lack of personnel and philological experience in Rome at the time.[24] From a letter of Fugger, we learn that Panvinio intended to be away from Rome, leaving after Easter and remaining away for the entire month of May 1564.[25] The extent of Panvinio's travels to archives during his lifetime can be seen in the list he published in 1568 at the beginning of his *Chronicon ecclesiasticum* (a long table in whose parallel columns he synchronized the histories of Church and Empire). Panvinio's list of research visits was impressive; by his own account, he had consulted over fifty archives. These included cathedral

---

[19]   Panvinio to V. Vitelli, 20 August 1563, ed. Gersbach, '*De comitiis*', 441: 'non ci vedo altro modo di haver da questo papa alcuna cosa ferma'. See also ibid. 415.

[20]   Pius IV, 'Breve apertum pro Honofrio Panvinio', 13 September 1563, ASV, Arm. XLIV, 11, fos 355ᵛ–356ᵛ. See also Baumgarten, *Hispanica IV*, 32–3, 44–5.

[21]   Perini, *Panvinio*, 26–7.

[22]   Fugger to Panvinio, 18 November 1563, Vat. lat. 6412, fo. 100ʳ.

[23]   C. Baronio, O. Rinaldi, G. Laderchi, and A. Theiner, *Annales ecclesiastici*, 37 vols (Bar-le-Duc, 1864–83), continuation by O. Rinaldi, ad AD 1564, xxxiv. 495, no. 53.

[24]   See G. Gullino, 'Da Mula, Marcantonio', in *DBI*, xxxii. 383–7; L. von Pastor, *Geschichte der Päpste seit dem Ausgang des Mittelalters*, 16 vols (Freiburg im Breisgau, 1886–1933), vii. 313, 581, 655; F. Barberi, *Paolo Manuzio e la Stamperia del popolo romano (1561–1570)* (Rome, 1942), 109; Sachet, 'Publishing for the Popes'.

[25]   H. J. Fugger (Augsburg) to Panvinio, 11 March 1564, in W. Maasen, *Hans Jakob Fugger (1516–1575)*, ed. P. Ruf (Munich, 1922), 109.

archives as well as archives of monasteries, religious orders, and other churches all over Italy.[26]

As mentioned, in 1564 Panvinio provided information for the biographical entry about him that was to appear in Ruscelli's *Imprese di uomini illustri*.[27] Though he had been in Alessandro Farnese's service for eighteen years, 'with honest conditions and treatment', Panvinio had not found a benefice or regular income which sustained him financially.[28] He listed the sums of money which various rulers had given to him: from Pope Pius IV he had received 200 scudi; from Emperor Maximilian II he had received 200 scudi (and, in addition, had been promised 70 scudi annually); from King Philip II of Spain he had received 500 scudi in total; and smaller amounts had come from various other powerful men, including Cardinal Farnese. Panvinio had spent much of this money helping his poor relatives—maintaining his poor widowed mother, supplying the dowry for the marriage of his sister, and paying for the release of his brother Paolo, who had been captured by the Ottomans in the Battle of Djerba in 1560. The rest of the money was spent on having manuscripts copied for his studies, as well as distributing his works.[29]

In the final year of his pontificate, on 24 January 1565, Pius IV gave Panvinio a position in the Vatican Library as a *corrector* and *revisor* of manuscripts.[30] This included a good regular income of 10 cameral ducats a month, which was twice the salary of his predecessors in the same post, Gabriele Faerno (d. 1561) and Giovan Francesco Manfredi. Paolo Panvinio stated that his brother replaced someone who had fallen into disgrace and was imprisoned in Castel Sant'Angelo.[31] This unlucky employee can be

[26] Panvinio, 'Auctores quibus tum in hoc Chronico sive Fasteis, tum in Historia ecclesiastica conscribenda usi sumus', in his *Chronicon ecclesiasticum a C. Iulii Caesaris dictatoris imperio usque ad Imperatorem Caesarem Maximilianum II* (Cologne: Maternus Cholinus, 1568), sigs *3ʳ–A2ᵛ, at sigs *4ᵛ–A1ʳ ('Variarum ecclesiarum archivia a nobis visa').

[27] See above, 16.

[28] Panvinio to Ruscelli, 4 November 1564, 189; ibid. 193: 'in XVIII anni che sono in Roma con tanti favori, amicitie et introduttioni non ho ancora un quattrin d'entrata'.

[29] Ibid. 189. On Paolo Panvinio's captivity see Gersbach, 'Brother', 245–6.

[30] Pius IV, *motu proprio* of 24 January 1565, ASV, Arm. LII, 3, fos 60ʳ–61ʳ, partial edn. in G. Marini, *Degli archiatri pontifici*, 2 vols (Rome, 1784), ii. 307–10. The tasks of a *corrector* and *revisor* are laid out in Pius IV's brief of 8 January 1562 (ASV, Arm. LII, 1, fos 257ᵛ–258ᵛ, partial edn. in Marini, *Degli archiatri*, ii. 305–6 n. 3). For what follows see Paolo Panvinio, *Vita*, 219; R. De Maio, 'La Biblioteca Vaticana sotto Paolo IV e Pio IV (1555–1565)', in *Collectanea Vaticana in honorem Anselmi M. Cardinalis Albareda*, 2 vols (Vatican City, 1962), i. 265–313, at pp. 288–93; C. Grafinger, 'Servizi al pubblico e personale', in *Storia della Biblioteca Apostolica Vaticana*, ii. 217–36, at p. 228.

[31] Paolo Panvinio, *Vita*, 219.

identified as Manfredi. It seems, in addition, that Matteo Devaris, the corrector of Greek manuscripts, was also dismissed to make Panvinio's double salary possible. In this job we find Panvinio again involved with Cardinal Marcantonio da Mula (who was appointed Vatican librarian in September 1565). Despite his new role, Panvinio maintained his hopes of travelling to Vienna and meeting Emperor Maximilian II, as he informed Fugger in a letter of 4 March 1565.[32] Panvinio's job in the Vatican Library lasted for less than a year because the austere reformer Pius V, who was elected in January 1566, did not confirm this provision—a decision in line with his general policy of reducing papal spending.

Nevertheless, Panvinio continued to receive payments until his death in 1568; there was probably some ambiguity about Panvinio's position.[33] Just after Panvinio's death, Pietro Galesini hoped to apply for Panvinio's post as corrector, which, he stated, Panvinio had held 'in absentia' while he was in the service of Farnese.[34] Galesini was the chief collaborator and scholarly consultant to Carlo Borromeo in Milan and hoped to obtain the post at the Vatican 'in absentia', too. Another example of an absent officeholder, according to Galesini, was Gaspare Viviani, bishop of Sitia. At any rate, Panvinio, from first-hand experience, wrote a short history of the Vatican Library.[35] Paolo Panvinio maintained that Pius V promised his brother 'something bigger' than the small but regular income from the library, but it was not forthcoming.[36]

From 1559 Panvinio spent much of his time on research into ecclesiastical matters. The first fruit of these endeavours was a short treatise on the rites involved in the blessing of the Agnus Dei (*De baptismate paschali*),

---

[32] H. J. Fugger (Taufkirchen) to Panvinio, 18 April 1565, ed. Maasen, *Fugger*, 118. Fugger recommended that Panvinio should go in September when the emperor would have returned from Bohemia.

[33] J. Bignami Odier, *La Bibliothèque Vaticane de Sixte IV à Pie XI: recherches sur l'histoire des collections de manuscrits* (Vatican City, 1973), 62 n. 63.

[34] Pietro Galesini to Carlo Borromeo, 25 May 1568, MS BAM, F 40 inf., fos 158ʳ–160ᵛ, ed. M. Lezowski, *L'Abrégé du monde: une histoire sociale de la bibliothèque Ambrosienne (v. 1590–v. 1660)* (Paris, 2015), 381–5, at p. 384: 'questo offitio... altri... l'hanno in absentia avuto'; ibid.: 'Onofrio era absente a servitio del suo Cardinal Farnese'.

[35] Panvinio, *De Bibliotheca Vaticana*, published posthumously in Juan Bautista Cardona, *De regia Sancti Laurentii Bibliotheca, De Pontificia Vaticana, De expungendis haereticorum propriis nominibus, De dyptichis* (Tarragona: Felipe Mey, 1587), 37–49. On this work see P. Nelles, 'The Renaissance Ancient Library Tradition and Christian Antiquity', in R. De Smet (ed.), *Les humanistes et leur bibliothèque/Humanists and their Libraries* (Leuven, 2002), 159–73. The text about the Vatican Library was part of Panvinio's larger description of the St Peter's Basilica, for which see below, n. 39.

[36] Paolo Panvinio, *Vita*, 219: 'con dirli il papa [Pius V] che gli voleva dar maggior cosa che il pane, ma non li dette né questo né altro'.

published on the occasion of Pius IV's consecration of the Lamb of God on 20 April 1560.[37] It has been shown, however, that, apart from an added dedicatory preface to Cardinal Farnese and some minor modifications, Panvinio had only translated a text, published in 1556 by another scholar, from Italian into Latin—though he claimed that the treatise was his own. The other author was a fellow Augustinian from Verona, Giuseppe Panfilo. Since Panfilo never complained about this, Karl Gersbach has argued that the two men may have collaborated on the original version.[38] Panvinio also wrote descriptions of churches, such as St Peter's Basilica and the Basilica of St John Lateran (with its Baptistery and the Lateran Palace); he produced a guidebook to the seven principal churches of Rome, which contained historical and archaeological considerations.[39] Research into Christian antiquity led him to explore and write about catacombs.[40]

While working on his history of the conclaves and elections and his new edition of Platina's *Lives of the Popes* (1562),[41] Panvinio remained in the service of Cardinal Farnese, who was now based predominantly in Rome and had resumed his regular patronage of artists and scholars. Some summers were spent with the cardinal and his circle at the Palazzo Farnese at Caprarola, situated some 50 km from Rome, in Latium. Because the palace

[37] Panvinio, *De baptismate paschali, origine et ritu consecrandi Agnus Dei liber ex commentariis Onuphrii Panvinii…in historiam ecclesiasticam excerptus* (Rome: Antonio Blado, 1560).

[38] Gersbach, 'Giuseppe Panfilo'.

[39] Panvinio, *De rebus antiquis memorabilibus et praestantia basilicae Sancti Petri apostolorum principis libri VII* (long extract), in *SR*, ix. 192–382; id., *De sacrosancta basilica, baptisterio et patriarchio Lateranensi libri IV*, ed. P. Lauer, *Le Palais de Latran* (Paris, 1911), 410–90; id., *De praecipuis urbis Romae sanctioribusque basilicis, quas septem ecclesias vulgo vocant, liber* (Rome: heirs of Antonio Blado, 1570); id., *De ecclesiis Christianorum*, in *SR*, ix. 141–80; Vat. lat. 6780–1 (material on Roman churches, including important notes on St Paul's Outside the Walls). See also C. Jobst, 'La basilica di San Pietro e il dibattito sui tipi edili: Onofrio Panvinio e Tiberio Alfarano', in G. Spagnesi (ed.), *L'architettura della Basilica di San Pietro* (Rome, 1997), 243–6; I. Herklotz, 'Basilica e edificio a pianta centrale: continuità ed esclusione nella storiografia architettonica all'epoca del Baronio', in L. Gulia (ed.), *Baronio e le sue fonti* (Sora, 2009), 549–78, at pp. 551–3; P. C. Claussen, *Die Kirchen der Stadt Rom im Mittelalter 1050–1300*, 3 vols (Stuttgart, 2002–10), *ad indices*; Occhipinti, *Ligorio*, *passim*.

[40] Panvinio, *De ritu sepeliendi mortuos apud veteres Christianos et eorundem coemeteriis liber* (Cologne: Maternus Cholinus, 1568). See G. Ferretto, *Note storico-bibliografiche di archeologia cristiana* (Vatican City, 1942), 93–8; V. Fiocchi Nicolai, 'San Filippo Neri, le catacombe di San Sebastiano e le origini dell'archeologia cristiana', in M. T. Bonadonna Russo and N. Del Re (eds), *San Filippo Neri nella realtà romana del XVI secolo* (Rome, 2000), 105–30, at pp. 108–13 ('il primo studio in qualche modo moderno e critico suo cimiteri paleocristiani della città', 108; for Panvinio's signature in the Catacomb of the Giordani see fig. 4 in this article); I. Herklotz, 'Christliche und klassische Archäologie im sechzehnten Jahrhundert', in D. Kuhn and H. Stahl (eds), *Die Gegenwart des Altertums* (Heidelberg, 2002), 291–307, at pp. 301–2; id., 'Chi era Priscilla?', 432–4.

[41] On the Platina editions see below, 150–154, 162–163.

was in the process of being decorated, Panvinio was asked to participate in a fitting manner and lend his talents to the enterprise. Annibale Caro, Fulvio Orsini, and Panvinio were assigned the task of collaborating on the invention of iconographical programmes. Panvinio may have helped devise the selection and arrangement of the history scenes in the Room of Farnese Deeds.[42] Some of these scenes may have been taken from Panvinio's life of Paul III, which he wrote for his new edition of Platina. In September 1562 each day Cardinal Farnese would listen to a section of this biography, which was read to him.[43] Panvinio's role as an artistic advisor is far from clear; he was probably an intermediary. In some cases, we know that he entrusted to his friend Paolo Manuzio, an excellent Latin stylist, the composition of the inscriptions which Panvinio was asked to write. Panvinio helped decorate the cardinal's *studiolo*, whose theme—the solitude of the spiritual life—was particularly fitting work for a learned friar such as Panvinio. It was Annibale Caro, not Panvinio, who dealt with the problems of practical execution.[44]

At the end of his fragmentary biography of Panvinio, his brother Paolo included two episodes from the scholar's life which are not entirely credible.[45] One day, when Panvinio joined a banquet that Cardinal Farnese had organized, Cardinal Madruzzo caused a stir by mocking the lowly friar loudly for joining the feast table. Farnese came to Panvinio's defence. Madruzzo soon changed his mind when he heard that Panvinio was working on a volume which contained the lives of all the cardinals. The story may, in fact, show us two things: (a) that Panvinio had high self-esteem and did not mind consorting with cardinals and (b) that his pen as a historian was powerful and, perhaps, sometimes even feared. The second story concerned Panvinio's planned trip to Vienna in 1565. According to his brother Paolo, Prospero d'Arco, the imperial ambassador in Rome, tried to convince Panvinio to go there, as the emperor was eager to meet him. Farnese was at first reluctant to sanction the trip because he was afraid that Panvinio might

[42] For what follows see L. W. Partridge, 'Divinity and Dynasty at Caprarola: Perfect History in the Room of the Farnese Deeds', *Art Bulletin*, 60 (1978), 494–530; Lurin, 'Les restitutions', 154–7; E. Leuschner, 'Otium und Virtus: Kontemplation als Tugendübung in der Stanza della Solitudine von Caprarola', in T. Weigel and J. Poeschke (eds), *Leitbild Tugend: die Virtus-Darstellungen in italienischen Kommunalpalästen und Fürstenresidenzen des 14. bis 16. Jahrhunderts* (Münster, 2013), 229–53; Robertson, *Farnese*, 220–3.

[43] Tommaso Gigli (Ronciglione) to Panvinio (Rome), 21 September 1562, ed. Perini, *Panvinio*, 253. See also Panvinio, 'Paulus III', in Platina, *Historia de vitis pontificum*, ed. Panvinio (1562), fos 289ʳ–301ʳ.

[44] A. Caro to Panvinio, 15 May 1565, in id., *Lettere familiari*, ed. A. Greco, 3 vols (Florence, 1957–61), iii. 237–40.

[45] For what follows see Paolo Panvinio, *Vita*, 221–4.

abandon him and remain at the Viennese court. The journey was cancelled when news arrived that the Turkish army was about to leave from Constantinople, which might have made travelling too dangerous.[46] This second story, too, seems to be an attempt to boast about Panvinio's importance. In truth, of course, it was Panvinio who courted Emperor Ferdinand and King Maximilian (emperor from 1564). In March 1562 Panvinio planned to visit either of them, and for this purpose he obtained a letter of recommendation from Ottavio Farnese; yet he never travelled there.[47]

German Patrons

Panvinio's relations with Germany were intense from 1562, when he found an additional, and very keen, patron in Hans Jakob Fugger (1516–75), one of the most important book collectors of the sixteenth century.[48] As a young man, Fugger had travelled to several countries, including Italy, for his studies. He studied in Bologna for a couple of years in the 1530s. Remaining a Catholic during the Reformation, he was involved in the politics of his hometown, Augsburg, and often acted as an intermediary between the confessions. He maintained good personal relations with Ferdinand and his son Maximilian. Although he had neither the talent nor the inclination for business, Fugger was asked to co-direct the merchant business of the Fugger family from 1560. In addition, Fugger spent lavishly on his library and on artistic and scientific sponsorship. In 1563 Fugger declared personal bankruptcy and, the year after, stepped down from the direction of the family business. Because of his strong connections to the Wittelsbachs, Fugger soon received new roles in the administration of the Duchy of Bavaria. He travelled with Albrecht V, Duke of Bavaria, in 1563. In 1565 he resigned from his political offices in Augsburg and moved to Taufkirchen castle, situated between Munich and Landshut. He advised the duke on his acquisitions of art and antiques from Italy. In 1571 Fugger's personal library passed into the duke's court library. With 12,000 volumes, including 900

---

[46] See also the letters exchanged between Panvinio and Fugger, in Maasen, *Fugger*, 119–22.

[47] Ottavio Farnese (Rome) to 'Sacra Cesarea Maestà' (that is, Emperor Ferdinand I or his son Maximilian), 12 March 1562, Vat. lat. 6412, fos 323ʳ, 331ʳ, ed. Perini, *Panvinio*, 251. Ferdinand was in Prague in March 1562: see S. Steinherz (ed.), *Nuntiaturberichte aus Deutschland*, 2. Abtheilung, iii (Vienna, 1903), 26–33.

[48] On Fugger see Maasen, *Fugger*; H. Kellenbenz, 'Hans Jakob Fugger', in *Lebensbilder aus dem Bayerischen Schwaben* (Munich etc., 1952–), xii, ed. A. Layer, 48–104; M. Häberlein, *Die Fugger: Geschichte einer Augsburger Familie (1367–1650)* (Stuttgart, 2006).

manuscripts, his collection abruptly made the Munich library a major European centre of learning.[49]

Fugger had built up his collection using the network of agents of the family business across Europe; in this way, he had access to almost any book he wanted, especially since he was ready to pay almost any price for it.[50] Venice was a centre for his acquisitions. Fugger employed the eminent scholar of Greek, Hieronymus Wolf, as a librarian in the years 1551-7. In 1552 he acquired the library of Hartmann Schedel from Nuremberg. In addition to classical authors, Fugger was interested in ecclesiastical writers and documents such as acts of church councils, which could be used in the religious discussions of his time. In accordance with humanist taste, he furnished his library with a mixed arrangement of sculptures and books.[51] From the 1540s the Mantuan antiquarian Jacopo Strada worked for him and assembled a monumental work with illustrations of coins as well as an array of coats of arms of popes, cardinals, and nobles of Italy.[52]

Panvinio had not managed to meet Fugger on his trip to Augsburg in 1559. On 3 October 1562 he sent Fugger a list of some of his works. In the following years, the German patron commissioned numerous manuscripts. Panvinio's and Fugger's extensive exchange of letters allows us to trace in detail the progress of the composition of Panvinio's larger and smaller works from October 1562 to 1567.[53] These included a history of papal elections and the history of the imperial elections, *De comitiis* (dedicated to Maximilian II in 1563). *De comitiis* was sent to Fugger in 1564-5.[54] In addition, Panvinio sent to Fugger the portraits of the popes from Christ to Pius V, with their coats of arms and those of the cardinals (*Pontificum Romanorum imagines*, 1566).[55]

---

[49] In 1919 the Munich court library took the name Bayerische Staatsbibliothek.

[50] On Fugger's library see O. Hartig, *Die Gründung der Münchener Hofbibliothek durch Albrecht V. und Johann Jakob Fugger* (Munich, 1917).

[51] R. von Busch, 'Studien zu deutschen Antikensammlungen des 16. Jahrhunderts' (doctoral thesis, Universität Tübingen, 1973), 194–8.

[52] See also below, 153–154.

[53] Most of Fugger's letters to Panvinio (from Vat. lat. 6412) are published in Maasen, *Fugger*, 96–126; others are listed with short summaries ibid. pp. VI–VIII. The volume does not include Panvinio's letters to Fugger, which remain unpublished in Vat. lat. 6277.

[54] MS Clm 153: Panvinio, *De iure, potestate, officio et comitiis imperatoris* [*sic*] *libri V ad Caesarem Maximilianum Iuniorem*, dedicated to Maximilian II, 1 November 1563 (fo. 2[r-v]). See *Catalogus codicum manu scriptorum Bibliothecae Regiae Monacensis*, iii.1, 2nd edn (Munich, 1892), 36 (this catalogue also provides information on the other MSS in Munich mentioned below); Maasen, *Fugger*, pp. VI–VII; Gersbach, '*De comitiis*', 418–19; and below, 138–141.

[55] MSS Clm 155–60. See below, 153–154.

Among the works offered to the German merchant were also the ceremonial books of the Roman Curia and diaries of the masters of ceremonies (1565).[56] It was a special privilege for Fugger to receive these manuscripts, as the diaries were kept under lock and key in the Vatican. Even important Roman families or religious orders were not allowed to make copies during Panvinio's lifetime.[57] The Master of Ceremonies Paride Grassi had protested a few decades earlier when, against his will, Cristoforo Marcello had published the papal ceremonial. Grassi had a point because Protestants were eager to pounce on details about the papacy contained in these works. Luther's friend Wenzeslaus Linck had used the printed version to make a selection of extracts and translate them into German; his compilation of papal forms of pomp (1539) aimed to deride and scorn the papacy. With the same aim, Pier Paolo Vergerio, in 1556, had used extracts from the ceremonial to ridicule papal elections.[58] Panvinio's collection included various liturgical texts, diaries by Jacopo Gherardi and Pier Paolo Gualtieri, and diaries by masters of ceremonies from Johannes Burckard (from 1484) to Biagio Martinelli (1518–38). Burckard's diaries, in particular, contained scandalous material; when Gottfried Wilhelm Leibniz published extracts concerning Alexander VI from a manuscript in Wolfenbüttel (*Specimen historiae arcanae*, 1696), the publication was placed on the Index of Prohibited Books. A complete edition of Burckard's diaries came out only in 1883–5.[59]

---

[56] MSS Clm 132–45: Panvinio, *Vetusti aliquot rituales libri* (Clm 132–3); *Diaria caeremoniarum magistrorum et aliorum* (Clm 134–45). See M. Andrieu, *Les 'Ordines Romani' du Haut Moyen Age*, 5 vols (Leuven, 1931–61), i. 213–14.

[57] According to Jörg Bölling, Panvinio's copies might have been the first copies of the ceremonial diaries ever made; see his 'Römisches Zeremoniell in Bayern: Herzog Albrecht V., Kardinal Otto Truchseß von Waldburg und die Fugger', in R. Becker and D. J. Weiß (eds), *Bayerische Römer, römische Bayern: Lebensgeschichten aus Vor- und Frühmoderne* (Sankt Ottilien, 2016), 167–98, at pp. 174, 194 ('die weltweit ersten Abschriften außerhalb der päpstlichen Kapelle'); id., 'Bereinigte Geschichte? Umstrittene Päpste in der Historiografie des 15. Jahrhunderts', in H. Müller (ed.), *Der Verlust der Eindeutigkeit: zur Krise päpstlicher Autorität im Kampf um die Cathedra Petri* (Berlin; Boston, 2017), 187–213. On Panvinio's difficulties to get hold of Paride Grassi's diaries see also his letter to Farnese, 17 July 1564, in Ronchini, 'Panvinio', 220.

[58] W. Linck, *Bapsts gepreng, ausz dem Cerimonien Buch* (Strasbourg, 1539); P. P. Vergerio, *Ordo eligendi pontificis et ratio* (Tübingen, 1556). See N. Staubach, '"Honor Dei" oder "Bapsts Gespreng"? Die Reorganisation des Papstzeremoniells in der Renaissance', in id. (ed.), *Rom und das Reich vor der Reformation* (Frankfurt am Main, 2004), 91–136, at pp. 125–30; Bölling, 'Römisches Zeremoniell', 191.

[59] J. Burckard, *Diarium*, ed. L. Thuasne, 3 vols (Paris, 1883–5). See also A. Badea, 'Geschichte schreiben über die Renaissancepäpste: römische Zensur und Historiographie in der ersten Hälfte des 18. Jahrhunderts', in H. Wolf (ed.), *Inquisition und Buchzensur im Zeitalter der Aufklärung* (Paderborn, 2011), 278–303.

In his long dedication to Fugger of the first volume of his collection, entitled *Vetusti aliquot rituales libri*, Panvinio explained his reasons for including the various liturgical texts.[60] It has been found, however, that Panvinio copied most of the texts in his first volume from two editions of liturgical texts that had been published by Georg Cassander in Cologne in 1558 and 1561.[61] To hide his plagiarism, Panvinio modified the titles of the liturgical pieces.[62] To the liturgies copied from Cassander, Panvinio added the *Ordo Romanus* of Cencius Camerarius, for which he wrote a separate preface.[63] *Vetusti aliquot rituales libri* also contained two works written by Panvinio: a brief dictionary of ecclesiastical terms and a historical explanation of the *stationes* (station days and station churches) in Rome, both of which were then published in Panvinio's revised edition of Platina in 1568.[64]

Further works which Fugger and Panvinio discussed included his book on colours (*Liber de coloribus*);[65] a world chronicle (*Indici delli anni del mondo*); a work on the ancient history writers; a collection of instructions to the papal nunci; a collection of donations and concessions to the Church; engravings of ancient sacrifices; the treatise on the origins of the college of cardinals (*De cardinalium origine*); and the collection of papal and imperial letters (*Collectio Avellana*). Moreover, Fugger asked for printed books from

[60] Panvinio, Clm 132, *Vetusti aliquot rituales libri*, dedication to Fugger, 1 January 1565, fos 3ʳ–8ʳ. This dedication was published by J. C. von Aretin, *Beyträge zur Geschichte und Literatur*, 9 vols (Munich, 1803–7), i.6, pp. 63–72, and by Thuasne in his edition of Burckard, *Diarium*, iii, pp. LXII–LXVI n. 1.

[61] Before it was dedicated to Fugger, this first volume had already been dedicated to Alessandro Farnese on 1 June 1564. Panvinio's original MS of *Vetusti aliquot rituales libri*, with corrections, is Vat. lat. 6112; the draft dedication to Farnese is on fos 40ʳ–44ʳ. Other MSS include: Vat. lat. 4973; Barb. lat. 724; BAM, H 142 inf.; Naples, Biblioteca nazionale, I D 2, fos 6ʳ–189ʳ; Paris, Bibliothèque nationale de France (hereafter BNF), Lat. 939, fos 1ʳ–216ᵛ; Rome, Biblioteca Vallicelliana, G 87; Vatican City, Archivio dell'Ufficio delle celebrazioni liturgiche del Sommo Pontefice, vol. 137. On the BAV manuscripts see P. Salmon, *Les manuscrits liturgiques latins de la Bibliothèque Vaticane*, 5 vols (Vatican City, 1968–72), iii. 7–9, 102–3, 113; Andrieu, *Ordines Romani*, i. 301–10.

[62] G. Cassander, *Liturgica de ritu et ordine dominicae coenae celebrandae* (Cologne, 1558); id., *Ordo Romanus de officio missae* (Cologne, 1561). See also M. Andrieu, 'Note sur quelques manuscrits et sur une édition de l'"Ordo romanus primus"', *Revue des sciences religieuses*, 2 (1922), 319–30, at pp. 328–30; Ferrary, *Panvinio*, 19–23.

[63] Panvinio's preface was published in J. Mabillon, *Museum italicum*, 2 vols (Paris, 1687–9), ii. 165.

[64] Panvinio, *Interpraetatio multarum vocum ecclesiacarum quae obscurae vel barbarae videntur; item De stationibus urbis Romae libellus*, dedication to Laurentius Celsus, 1 September 1567, in Platina, *Historia de vitis pontificum*, ed. Panvinio (Cologne: Maternus Cholinus, 1568), separate pagination. On the *Interpraetatio* see also Herklotz, 'Christliche und klassische Archäologie', 302.

[65] This book may have been connected with sections of Clm 133 (vol. ii of the liturgical texts). See the *rubricae* of this MS in Aretin, *Beyträge*, i.6, pp. 54–60, at p. 56: 'De coloribus quibus Sancta Romana Ecclesia in sacris vestibus solet uti'.

the Italian book market—for example, the decrees of the Council of Trent; printed bulls by Pius IV; the Index of Prohibited Books of the Council of Trent (1564); and the new editions of the Catechism, Missal, and Breviary. Panvinio, for his part, received from Fugger volumes of the *Magdeburg Centuries* from Volume 7 onwards, and enquired about (unnamed) books cited by the authors of these *Centuries*. From late 1562 Panvinio also wrote regular political news reports (*avvisi*) for Fugger.[66] Fugger lost interest in these reports as early as 1563, evidently not satisfied with Panvinio's abilities as a diplomatic correspondent and court journalist.

In general, Fugger generously offered to pay for the scribes who worked on the production of Panvinio's works and to give him regular financial subsidies. In the 1560s, Panvinio seems to have been caught in a sort of vortex; his frenetic activity as a writer (by which he aimed to satisfy his patrons) obliged him to spend ever more money on scribes and writing materials and, therefore, to search for new funding. In 1565, for example, Panvinio maintained three scribes, an illustrator, and even a cook.[67]

From September 1566 to 1567, as the frequency of his correspondence with Fugger decreased, Panvinio was being helped by another patron in Germany: Cardinal Otto Truchsess von Waldburg, prince-bishop of Augsburg. As we have seen, Panvinio had visited the cardinal in Augsburg in 1559. Panvinio wrote to Otto in November 1566, saying that he had encountered problems publishing some of his works in Rome as the ecclesiastical authorities had held them up.[68] Otto, who noted that German Catholics held Panvinio's works in high esteem, suggested having his unpublished texts revised by Jesuits in Germany (especially Peter Canisius) and then printed.[69] Other letters showed that Otto considered having the works published either in the Jesuit university town of Dillingen or in Cologne. These works included *De primatu Petri*, the collection of ceremonial books, the *Collectio Avellana*, and the letters of Gregory VII. Otto received the *Collectio* in July 1567 and handed it to Canisius.[70] Panvinio also seems to have sent Otto the

---

[66] Panvinio's *avvisi* are contained in Vat. lat. 6277. They have not yet been scrutinized for their value as a source illustrating events at the Curia; for some preliminary observations see C. Zwierlein, 'Fuggerzeitungen als Ergebnis von italienisch-deutschem Kulturtransfer 1552–1570', *QFIAB*, 90 (2010), 169–224, at pp. 190–5.

[67] See below, 168–169.

[68] Otto von Waldburg to Panvinio, 5 December 1566, Vat. lat. 6412, fo. 224ʳ⁻ᵛ: 'dice...che dalli superiori costà li vien fatta tanta difficultà et prolongatione in rivederle [le opere], onde non può darle alla stampa come sarebbe suo desiderio'. See also Ferrary, *Panvinio*, 16–18.

[69] Otto von Waldburg to Panvinio, 28 September 1566, Vat. lat. 6412, fo. 220ʳ⁻ᵛ.

[70] Otto to Panvinio, 24 July 1567, ibid., fos 294ʳ–295ᵛ. See also P. Canisius, *Epistulae et acta*, ed. O. Braunsberger, 8 vols (Freiburg im Breisgau, 1896–1923), vi. 70–3, 656. On Otto's efforts to publish *De primatu* see also below, 183.

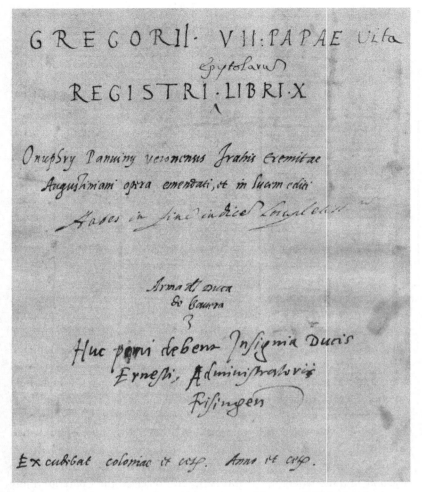

GREGORII· VII:PAPAE *vita*
epistolarum
REGISTRI·LIBRI·X

Onuphry Panuiny veronensis fratris Eremitae Augustiniani opera emendati, et in lucam editi·

fates in fine indice longioris

Arma et duca & bauera
?

Huc poni debent Insignia Ducis Ernesti, Administratoris Frisingen

Excudebat coloniae et ccip. Anno et ccip.

Fig. 2.1 Onofrio Panvinio, *Vita* and *Registrum* of Gregory VII, draft title page. Partly autograph. Courtesy of the Biblioteca Ambrosiana, Milan (G 31 inf., fo. 1ʳ).

manuscript of the letters of Gregory VII (*Registrum*), which were given to the printer Gerwin Calenius in Cologne. For the *Registrum*, Panvinio drafted both a title page and a dedicatory preface to Ernst of Bavaria, bishop of Freising (Fig. 2.1).[71]

---

[71] Gregory VII, *Registrum*, ed. Panvinio, MS BAM, G 31 inf. (partly autograph); BAV, Ottob. lat. 764 (16th–17th c.). In 1570 Peter Canisius wrote that the letters of Gregory VII had been

Overall, however, Otto's and Canisius's attempts proved mostly abortive. The printer Calenius was interested in printing some works (*De primatu Petri*, ceremonial books, and a universal chronicle), but he was wary of others. He feared that the *Collectio Avellana* was so 'great and sumptuous' that it would take many years to sell out the first print run. Canisius, on the other hand, liked this project and suggested adding scholia to confirm Catholic truths and turn the collection into a weapon against the Protestants. As regards Gregory VII's *Registrum*, Canisius thought that this book should rather be printed in Venice, so that it could be more easily distributed and sold in countries such as Italy, France, and Spain.[72]

The humanist Jean Matal unsuccessfully attempted to help Panvinio publish works on Roman antiquity in Cologne. Cardinal Antoine Perrenot de Granvelle's initiatives to help Panvinio publish his works with Christophe Plantin in Antwerp were also abortive.[73] Only a new edition of Platina's *Lives of the Popes* and the *Chronicon ecclesiasticum* were printed in Cologne in 1568 by the printer Maternus Cholinus (who had already published an edition of the *Lives* in 1562). Seeking to strengthen his ties with Spain, Panvinio dedicated the Platina edition to Pedro Afán de Ribera, viceroy of Naples.

Panvinio's Death and the Fate of His Manuscripts

Panvinio died during a trip to Monreale near Palermo in Sicily.[74] He had travelled there with Cardinal Farnese, who was archbishop of the city. Panvinio may have been asked to help in some way with the organization of

'given to Calenius, if I am not mistaken' ('Calenio, ni fallar, traditis'); see his *Epistulae et acta*, vi. 384. The planned edition included a life of Gregory: *Gregorii VII Papae vita* (G 31 inf., fos 5ʳ–22ᵛ; Ottob. lat. 764, fos 6ʳ–23ʳ). For Panvinio's dedication to Ernst of Bavaria, dated 1 November 1567 (G 31 inf., fos 2ʳ–3ᵛ), see 'Catalogus codicum hagiographicorum Latinorum Bibliothecae Ambrosianae Mediolanensis', *Analecta Bollandiana*, 11 (1892), 205–368, at pp. 324–6. Both the preface and Panvinio's life of Gregory VII were published from Ottob. lat. 764 in *Appendix ad opera edita ab Angelo Maio*, ed. G. Cozza-Luzi (Rome, 1871), 78–94 (edition and notes by A. Mai).

[72] Canisius (Dillingen) to Panvinio, 29 September 1567, in his *Epistulae et acta*, vi. 69–74. See also below, 84.
[73] Ferrary, *Panvinio*, 15–26.
[74] On Panvinio's death see G. Lagomarsini, commentary to his edition of G. Poggiani, *Epistolae et orationes*, 4 vols (Rome, 1756–62), iv. 91–7 n. a; L. A. Biscardi, 'Lettera intorno al giorno della morte di Frate Onofrio Panvinio all'Illustrissimo Signore…Girolamo Tiraboschi', *Nuovo giornale de' letterati d'Italia*, 39 (1788), 107–30.

a synod over which Farnese would preside; but no doubt he was also planning to visit monuments and conduct archival research. His last surviving letter, from Naples, is dated Wednesday, 18 February 1568.[75] After a long and extremely strenuous journey, during which Farnese's party travelled mostly by land (except for the ferryboat passage across the Strait of Messina), they arrived in Palermo on 28 March. The cardinal entered Monreale on 2 April.[76] At some point between 28 March and 20 April, Onofrio Panvinio died unexpectedly of a fever.

A few years later, unnamed 'friends' installed a memorial bust and plate in the church of Sant'Agostino in Rome. It is the only public memorial devoted to Panvinio in Rome. The monument was first mentioned in 1581 by Giuseppe Panfilo, Panvinio's Veronese compatriot, fellow Augustinian, and friend, in his chronicle of the order.[77] Panfilo wrongly stated that this was a tomb (*sepulchrum*), which later caused confusion among writers. The bronze bust was accompanied by a black marble plate with an inscription.[78] We do not know who commissioned this monument, nor who the artist was. During a restoration of the church by the architect Luigi Vanvitelli in the eighteenth century, the original monument was destroyed; it was then refashioned. The new version of the Panvinio monument, sculpted by Gaspare Sibilla in 1758 and still visible today to the right of the sacristy door, is composed of a white marble bust and a yellow marble plate (Figs 2.2–2.3).[79]

The inscription was copied from the old monument and inserted into the new one in 1758. It specifies the place and date of Panvinio's death: 'Panormi obiit XVIII Kal. Apr.' ('he died in Palermo on the 18th day before the Kalends

---

[75] Panvinio (Naples) to Cardinal Sirleto, 18 February 1568, Vat. lat. 6189.iii, fo. 541ʳ, ed. Lagomarsini, in Poggiani, *Epistolae*, iv. 93–4 l. n. a. On the practicalities of this journey see also Farnese's letters in ASV, Fondo Borghese, ser. ii, 461, fos 7ʳ⁻ᵛ, 16ʳ⁻ᵛ, 27ᵛ–28ʳ, 29ᵛ–30ʳ; P. M. Baumgarten, *Von den Kardinälen des sechzehnten Jahrhunderts* (Krumbach, 1926), 67.

[76] N. Giordano, 'Alessandro Farnese (con documenti inediti)', *Archivio storico siciliano*, ser. iii, 16 (1965–6), 191–227, at pp. 203–5.

[77] G. Panfilo, *Chronica Ordinis Fratrum Eremitarum Sancti Augustini* (Rome, 1581), fo. 126ʳ⁻ᵛ: 'Romae postea in templo Sancti Augustini marmoreo sepulchro cum eius imagine ahenea condecoratus fuit, quod amici honoris causa posuere.'

[78] Angelo Rocca, *Bibliotheca Apostolica Vaticana* (Rome, 1591), sig. d3ʳ: 'huius effigies ad vivum ex aere expressa in ecclesia Sancti Augustini Romae visitur; infra vero epitaphium...in marmore nigro incisum legitur'. Rocca, the founder of the Biblioteca Angelica, was an Augustinian.

[79] For a payment to Sibilla dated 1 October 1758 see Rome, Archivio di Stato, Agostiniani in Sant'Agostino, busta 99, receipt no. 458; ibid., busta 303, p. 97. See also U. Donati, 'Gli architetti del convento di Sant'Agostino a Roma', *L'Urbe: rivista romana*, 5 (1940) no. 8, pp. 20–6, at p. 26 n. 31. Fig. 1.2 (on which see above, 26) might contain some clues about the appearance of the original monument.

Fig. 2.2 Onofrio Panvinio. Bust by Gaspare Sibilla (1758). Sant'Agostino, Rome. Photo courtesy of the Bibliotheca Hertziana – Max-Planck-Institut für Kunstgeschichte, Rome.

Fig. 2.3 Onofrio Panvinio. Bust by Gaspare Sibilla (detail).

of April').[80] The Kalends were the first day of every month. This date, however, would be an incorrect and very unlikely way of referring to the Ides of March (15 March). It is best to assume it was simply a mistaken representation of 'XVIII Kal. Mai.' ('the 18th day before the Kalends of May')— that is, 14 April. (This emendation avoids the problem regarding the Ides, which in April fall on the 13th.) The date of 14 April is, furthermore, confirmed by a note in manuscripts of Panvinio's work on St Peter's Basilica.[81]

---

[80] The inscription (Fig. 2.2) reads: 'D(eo) O(ptimo) M(aximo). / F(ratri) Onuphrio Panvinio Veronensi / Eremitae Augustiniano / viro ad omnes et Romanas / et ecclesiasticas antiquitates / e tenebris eruendas nato / qui Alexandr(um) Farn(esium) Card(inalem) Vicecan(cellarium) / in Siciliam prosequutus alienissimo / et sibi et historiae tempore / Panormi obiit (ante diem) XVIII Kal(endas) Apr(iles) MDLXVIII / praeclaris multis et perfectis / et inchoatis industriae suae / monumentis relictis vix(it) an(nos) XXXIX / amici honoris caussa posuerunt.' There are some similarities between this inscription and the dedication by Orazio Blado to Alessandro Farnese, in Panvinio, *De praecipuis urbis Romae...basilicis* (1570).

[81] Note, by an unknown author, in Panvinio, *De rebus antiquis memoratu dignis basilicae Sancti Petri in Vaticano*, Vat. lat. 6115, fo. 92ʳ: 'obiit Panormi die XIIII mensis Aprilis 1568'. The same note is found at the end of other manuscript copies of the same work.

The most likely date of Panvinio's death, 14 April 1568, was the Wednesday of Holy Week. On the 20th (that is, on the Tuesday after the festivities of Easter) a letter by Antonio Elio went out, reporting the news of Panvinio's death. Elio, the titular patriarch of Jerusalem and a member of Farnese's entourage, wrote to Cardinal Sirleto and mentioned Panvinio's death. From this letter, we learn that Girolamo Mercuriale, the cardinal's learned medical doctor, had remained at Panvinio's side until the end. For Farnese, it was as if he had lost a son; the entire household bemoaned Panvinio's death.[82] Elio spoke of the arrangements that had been made to carry out Panvinio's will.[83] Panvinio was buried in the church of the Augustinian house in Palermo, as Rocco Pirri attested in his description of Sicilian churches (1630).[84] It may be true that Panvinio's remains lay 'in the burial place which is common to the friars' (as was believed in the eighteenth century),[85] but then again it cannot be excluded that he had an individual tomb which was later covered up or destroyed during a restoration of the church.

On his deathbed, Panvinio decided that Antonio Elio should take care of his worldly belongings. He asked Elio to act as his procurator; Elio was to ensure that his poor mother received as much money as possible and that some (unspecified) items went to the Augustinian house in Verona.[86] According to Panvinio's brother Paolo, Panvinio's manuscripts were deposited with Elio; furthermore, Panvinio had named four trusted friends to revise his works and see them through the press: Giuseppe Panfilo (the fellow Augustinian from Verona), Fulvio Orsini (librarian of Alessandro Farnese), Latino Latini (a scholar of the Church Fathers), and Girolamo Mercuriale.[87] According to Cardinal Granvelle, Panvinio's will stated something slightly different—namely, that only Orsini and Mercuriale were to be literary

[82] Antonio Elio (Monreale) to Sirleto, 20 April 1568, in Poggiani, *Epistolae*, iv. 95–6 n. a: 'Monsignor Illustrissimo patrone...certo ha sentito la perdita di tanto huomo con quella tenerezza che si conviene da padre a figlio, et noi di casa lo piangemo tuttavia'.

[83] Ibid.: 'così ho fatto notar ne lo instrumento de la accettatione et de la procura che mando in persona di Messer Titio et di Messer Giovan Battista Argenti'. Tizio Chermadio was Farnese's *maggiordomo* in Rome, Argenti a secretary.

[84] R. Pirri, *Notitiae Siciliensium ecclesiarum* (Palermo, 1630), 219: 'in eo coenobio iacet Onuphrius Panvinus'.

[85] Biscardi, 'Lettera', 109: 'in quella sepoltura ch'è a' frati comune'. The historiographer of the king of Naples, Francesco Daniele (1740–1812), was given this information on a visit to Palermo. Daniele does not appear to have seen a death register or memorial book.

[86] Elio to Sirleto, 20 April 1568; G. Mercuriale to Sirleto, 21 April 1568, in Poggiani, *Epistolae*, iv. 96–7 n. a.

[87] Paolo Panvinio, 'Lectori' (draft preface to Panvinio's *De primatu Petri*, c.1584–5), MS BAM, Q 115 sup., fo. 67[r–v], ed. S. Maffei, *Verona illustrata*, 4 vols (Verona, 1731–2), ii. 349–52.

executors and that they were allowed to do as they pleased with the manuscripts.[88] In 1569, Carlo Sigonio hoped that Antonio Elio could give him access to a Chronicle of Parma from Panvinio's collection.[89] Be that as it may, we do not know much about how Elio and the four friends carried out their tasks.

Sant'Eufemia charged Giuseppe Panfilo (the papal sacristan) with attempting to recover all Panvinio's belongings, of which the Augustinian house was the rightful owner.[90] It appears that Panfilo may have gained possession of the manuscript of Panvinio's *Antiquitates Veronenses* (Veronese Antiquities) by July.[91] He also obtained some of Panvinio's material on consistories and conclaves, which in 1569 he passed on to Silvio Antoniano, secretary to the college of cardinals.[92]

Other members of the group of four friends took other texts into their possession. Fulvio Orsini laid his hands on several manuscripts: *De ludis* (Vat. lat. 3393), the *Fasti* (Vat. lat. 3451.i), and other material concerning Roman antiquity (Vat. lat. 3439).[93] Orsini (d. 1600) then left his collection to the Vatican Library in his will. Some volumes of Panvinio-related material are now in the Biblioteca Ambrosiana in Milan. These include a collection of letters received by Panvinio from Orazio Orsini, Pantagato, Agustín, Sigonio, and others (BAM, D 501 inf.); Panvinio's *Vita* of Gregory VII and his edition of this pope's *Registrum* (G 31 inf., partly autograph); and material connected to publication projects in Germany (P 244 sup., fasc. 6, partly

---

[88] Granvelle (Rome) to Christophe Plantin (Antwerp), 15 May 1568, in M. Van Durme (ed.), *Supplément à la Correspondance de Christophe Plantin* (Antwerp, 1955), 83: 'Panvino…ha enchargé en son testament audict Fulvio et un medecin dudict Seigneur Cardinal Farneze de reveoir ses papiers et oeuvres et d'en faire ce quil leur semblera'. See also J. Matal's letter from Cologne to Orsini, 25 May 1578, Vat. lat. 4103, fos 112ʳ–113ʳ, mentioning 'Onufrii scripta quorum, ut audio, es heres'. On Orsini see R. Mouren, 'La bibliothèque du palais Farnèse avant Fulvio Orsini', *Mélanges de l'Ecole française de Rome: Italie et Méditerranée*, 107 (1995), 7–14.

[89] C. Bastia, 'Per una ricostruzione della genesi e delle vicende censorie dell'*Historia Bononiensis* di Carlo Sigonio', *Schede umanistiche*, n. s. 3 (1993) no. 2, pp. 99–113, at p. 113.

[90] Paolo Panvinio, worried about losing his inheritance, wrote to A. Farnese, 11 May 1568 (ed. Ronchini, 'Panvinio', 223–4). Panfilo was named papal sacristan and master of the papal chapel in Rome on 10 May 1568; see Gersbach, 'Panfilo', 52, 74–5.

[91] A. Farnese to Elio, 4 July 1568, ed. Gersbach, 'Angelica Latin Manuscript 64', 214 n. 19. According to Campagnola ('Ex notis', fo. 42ᵛ), Paolo Panvinio then obtained this manuscript by 1574.

[92] See Antoniano's notes in ASV, Arch. Concist., Acta Misc., 54, fo. 1ʳ, and 70, fo. 1ʳ, where he also referred to Panvinio with unqualified appreciation as 'vir ecclesiasticae historiae peritissimus et in conquirenda antiquitate diligentissimus'. See also Mercati, *Dall'Archivio Vaticano*, 83–4.

[93] Orsini wrote to Gian Vincenzo Pinelli on 29 November 1573, mentioning that he had taken two or three volumes; see De Nolhac, *Bibliothèque de Fulvio Orsini*, 262 n. 4. For these manuscripts see ibid. 398–9; Ferrary, *Panvinio*, 27 n. 67, 32–3, 156, 217; Lurin, 'Les restitutions'.

autograph). One wonders whether the letters in MS D 501 inf. might have been removed by the executors and passed on to Gian Vincenzo Pinelli, much of whose collection later entered the Ambrosiana. Pinelli possessed copies of Panvinio's library catalogue, probably made from a manuscript kept by Fulvio Orsini.[94]

In May 1568, Pope Pius V seems to have instructed Cardinal Sirleto to review Panvinio's manuscripts and publish 'for the common benefit' those of his works which seemed 'worthy of being approved'.[95] In January 1569, however, the pope—known as a strict reformer—changed his mind about Panvinio. He took the drastic step of banning all Panvinio's works from printing. This all-out prohibition concerned both reprints and hitherto-unpublished manuscripts.[96] Word had spread in Rome that someone was planning to publish Panvinio's works in Venice, so the papal nuncio there was asked to intervene. The reason was that Pius V wanted to 'have the works accurately revised, since there are many things that need consideration and correction'.[97] We do not know precisely why this decision was made, but it certainly stopped any plans for publication which Panvinio's four friends may have had. Pius V's step also likely reflected either a lack of protection of Panvinio's memory by superiors in the Augustinian Order or a lack of influence of the order at the papal court. Lastly, rumours claimed

---

[94] Vat. lat. 3451.ii; copies: BAM, P 189 sup., I 129 inf. The letters from Orsini to Pinelli (BAM, D 422–3 inf.) might yet yield additional clues.

[95] Report from Rome dated 8 May 1568, in Naples, Archivio di Stato, Archivio Farnesiano, busta 283.I, fasc. 1, fo. 10ʳ: 'Dicono che Sua Beatitudine ha ordinato al Cardinale Sirleti che veda le compositioni et scritture de la bona memoria di Frate Honofrio…et tutte quelle che li parranno degne d'essere approvate le faci mettere in luce et in stampa a comune utilitade'. See also A. Aubert, *Paolo IV: politica, Inquisizione e storiografia* (Florence, 1999), 184. However, it is not very likely that Sirleto, who went on to become Cardinal-Librarian in 1572, actually received these manuscripts; in 1576 Orazio Muti, a Lateran canon and collector of antiquities, still offered to obtain them for the cardinal (as mentioned in a letter by Filippo Gambardelli from Naples to Sirleto, 2 March 1576, Vat. lat. 6185, fo. 175ʳ⁻ᵛ: 'far havere a Vostra Signoria Illustrissima…tutte le scritture che lasciò Frate Honofrio Panvinio'). It is unclear how Muti planned to procure the manuscripts.

[96] Cardinal Michele Bonelli (Rome) to Nuncio Giovanni Antonio Facchinetti, 12 January 1569, in F. Gaeta et al. (eds), *Nunziature di Venezia* (Rome, 1958–), viii. 481: 'Si è inteso che si cerca di stampar furtivamente l'opre di Fra Onofrio bonae memoriae costà; il che darebbe fastidio a Nostro Signore quando seguisse. Però faccia ogni diligenza per impedir questa stampa, avisandomi quel che se ne sarà presentito et particolarmente quel che se ne fosse comminciato a stampare'. See also Facchinetti's replies, ibid. 484 (19 January), 487 (26 January) and 491 (2 February).

[97] Bonelli to Facchinetti, 26 January 1569, ibid. 488–9: 'Nostro Signore vuole ch'ella prohibisca in ogni modo ai stampatori che non debbiano stampare l'opere di Fra Honofrio, così quelle che non sono più state stampate come quelle che si havessero a ristampare di nuovo, perché Sua Santità vuol farle rivedere accuratamente prima, essendovi molte cose c'hanno bisogno di consideratione et correttione insieme'.

that there had been strong tensions between Pius V and Panvinio because of the latter's inadequate religious discipline.[98]

In 1570, Canisius wrote to his Jesuit brethren in Cologne to inform them about demands from Rome that the letters of Gregory VII should not be printed; Panvinio's edition allegedly swarmed with errors. Canisius was to return the manuscript to Rome.[99] Had Panvinio's work been published, it would have been the first printed edition of this main historical source on Gregory VII. Instead, the *princeps* was published in 1591 by Cardinal-Librarian Antonio Carafa (who owned a copy of Panvinio's *De varia creatione*) and Antonio d'Aquino.[100]

Despite Pius V's ban, in 1570 the heirs of the papal printer Antonio Blado managed to publish Panvinio's guidebook to the seven main churches of Rome (*De praecipuis urbis Romae... basilicis*) in both Latin and Italian. Orazio Blado dedicated the Latin edition to Cardinal Farnese.[101] In the preface to the Italian version (dedicated to Beatrice Ferella Orsini, duchess of Gravina), Marco Antonio Lanfranchi from Verona stated that Panvinio had urged him to make the translation.[102] Blado's heirs had received privileges for both editions. A passage in this book, in which Panvinio discussed the legend about the Holy Stairs at the Lateran, was denounced to the Congregation of the Index in 1587 by Alfonso Chacón.[103] Panvinio's *De triumpho*, as a work of antiquarian scholarship on pagan Rome, was not at risk of running into trouble with the authorities; it was published in 1571 with Pius V's permission.

By 1578 Panvinio's manuscripts had been given to Cardinal Giacomo Savelli (a member of the Congregation of the Inquisition since 1557 and its dean from 1577), in whose residence they were kept locked up.[104] The owner

---

[98] See Francesco Sansovino's continuation of Giacomo Filippo Foresti, *Sopplimento delle croniche universali del mondo* (Venice, 1575), 709: 'Si morì [Panvinio] assai fresco huomo per dolor d'animo, percioché havendolo Pio V con agre parole ripreso perché non stesse nel suo monistero, accorandosi, dubitando di qualche travaglio, mancò con dolore universale de' letterati.'

[99] Canisius (Augsburg) to Petrus Busaeus (Cologne), 8 January 1570, in id., *Epistulae et acta*, 384–7, at p. 384: 'Postulant enim ex Urbe uarios, quod uariis scatet erroribus, primum Augustam ad me ac deinde Romam remittatur neque typis modo excudatur.'

[100] In A. Carafa and A. d'Aquino (eds), *Epistolae decretales summorum pontificum*, 3 vols (Rome, 1591), iii. 549–885.

[101] Panvinio, *De praecipuis urbis Romae... basilicis*, dedication by Orazio Blado to A. Farnese (not paginated).

[102] Panvinio, *Le sette chiese romane* (Rome, 1570), dedication to B. Ferella Orsini (not paginated): 'essendo stato astretto... di tradurre'.

[103] See below, 143–144.

[104] Latino Latini to J. Matal (Cologne), 21 March 1579, in id., *Epistolae*, 2 vols (Rome; Viterbo, 1659–67), ii. 176–8: De Nolhac, *Bibliothèque de Fulvio Orsini*, 62 n. 3, 226 n. 1. On

of the rights to Panvinio's works, however, was now his brother. He had received these rights as a donation from Sant'Eufemia.[105] In his draft preface to Panvinio's *De primatu Petri*, Paolo recounted how, in 1583, he had gone to Rome, where he had spent a year trying to ensure that his brother's works were published.[106] He lamented that Antonio Elio had deposited all the manuscripts with Savelli. Only *De primatu* had remained with Cardinal Marcantonio Colonna, to whom Panvinio had given this work before he had set off on his ill-fated journey to Sicily.[107] According to Paolo, many other works, including a 'Chronicon Augustinianorum' had been snatched away by Giuseppe Panfilo (d. 1581) under the false pretence that he wanted to see them through the press; Paolo claimed that Panfilo had actually wanted to publish them under his own name.[108] Cardinal Savelli allegedly promised Paolo Panvinio that his brother's finished works ('quelle che saranno in perfettione') would be printed.[109]

During these years a number of Panvinio's works were kept privately by popes. At his death, Gregory XIII (r. 1572–85) had both an unbound manuscript of *De primatu Petri* and a large manuscript volume of *De varia creatione Romani pontificis* in his private study; they were then taken into possession by Sixtus V (r. 1585–90).[110] The fact that these manuscripts were held separately by the popes themselves might indicate both a special

---

Savelli see H. H. Schwedt, *Die Anfänge der römischen Inquisition: Kardinäle und Konsultoren 1542-1600* (Freiburg im Breisgau, 2013), 231–2; J. Hasecker and J. Schepers, *Römische Inquisition und Indexkongregation, Grundlagenforschung 1542-1700: Personen und Profile* (Paderborn, forthcoming).

[105] Will of Paolo Panvinio, 9 October 1586, in Campagnola, 'Materiali', fos 25^r–25b^r.

[106] Paolo Panvinio, 'Lectori' (draft preface to Panvinio's *De primatu*). See also his letter to A. Farnese, 30 June 1584, ed. Ronchini, 'Panvinio', 225–6.

[107] Book I of *De primatu* was eventually published in 1589. See also below, 181–187.

[108] This was a misunderstanding: Panfilo did publish a *Chronica Ordinis Fratrum Eremitarum Sancti Augustini* (1581), but it was different from the Chronicle of the Augustinian Order published by Panvinio in 1551 (*Commentarium rerum Ordinis Fratrum Eremitarum Sancti Augustini*). See Gersbach, 'Panfilo', 66–73. On Panfilo see also above, 68–69.

[109] Paolo Panvinio, 'Lectori' (draft preface to *De primatu*), fo. 67^r, ed. Maffei, *Verona illustrata*, ii. 350: 'il quale Signor Cardinal mi ha promesso di farmi gratia d'ogni cosa, acciò faccia stampare quelle [opere] che saranno in perfettione'.

[110] 'Inventarium sive nota quorundam librorum et scripturarum quae tempore obitus felicis recordationis Gregorii Papae XIII, ut asseritur, repertae sunt in eius studio', MS Rome, Biblioteca dell'Accademia dei Lincei e Corsiniana, Corsin. 671, fos 172^r, 197^r, 202^r, 210^r, 233^r. This MS of *De varia creatione* ('volumen magnum', fos 197^r, 233^r) might have been Vat. lat. 6107 (on which see below, 197–198). As far as *De primatu* is concerned, the entry says 'M.S. in foliis magnis solutis' (fo. 210^r). See also G. L. Masetti Zannini, 'Biblioteche bolognesi a Roma', *L'archiginnasio*, 63–5 (1968–70), 489–511, at pp. 494, 501.

interest on their part and a specific caution, which could have led them to keep these texts unavailable for consultation.

The presence of Cesare Baronio's concurrent labours on ecclesiastical history certainly did not help Panvinio's cause.[111] Nonetheless, there were several important initiatives in the 1580s and 1590s to produce editions of Panvinio's works. In December 1587 Sixtus intended to have Panvinio's works on ecclesiastical matters ('di sacra scrittura') printed so that others would not publish his works under their own name.[112] Sixtus knew Panvinio's works, as he not only kept the manuscripts of De primatu and De varia creatione with him but he also owned some of Panvinio's printed books (such as the Fasti with commentaries of 1558 and the papal biographies), which he deposited in his private library.[113]

After Cardinal Savelli's death, all Panvinio's manuscripts went to Cardinal Girolamo Rusticucci's residence.[114] From there they went to Cardinal Giulio Antonio Santoro, head of the Inquisition, in 1592.[115] This included the manuscript of De primatu Petri (now together with related censorship notes), which was still stored in the 'wardrobe' (guardaroba) of Clement VIII in the Apostolic Palace in 1592. Together with a ceremonial (put together by Panvinio) also held there, it was given on loan to Santoro.[116] In that year a commission headed by Santoro and created by Clement VIII considered

---

[111] Baronio's Ecclesiastical Annals were published from 1588 onwards. See below, 178–180.

[112] Avvisi di Roma, 16 December 1587, MS BAV, Urb. lat. 1055, fo. 542ᵛ, ed. J. A. F. Orbaan, 'La Roma di Sisto V negli Avvisi', Archivio della Società romana di storia patria, 33 (1910), 277–312, at p. 302: 'S'intende che Nostro Signore voglia si stampino le belle opre et fatiche di Frate Honofrio Veronese dell'ordine di Sant'Agostino, altre volte famigliare del Cardinal Farnese et poco fa di Savello, di sacra scrittura, acciò altri non si orni delle lunghe vigilie et laboriosi studii di questo valente padre, con scommunica a chi occultarà sue opre, fatti et scritture.' See also P. M. Baumgarten, Neue Kunde von alten Bibeln, 2 vols (Rome; Krumbach, 1922–7), i. 340.

[113] G. Cugnoni, 'Documenti chigiani concernenti Felice Peretti, Sisto V, come privato e come pontefice', Archivio della Società romana di storia patria, 5 (1882), 1–32, 210–304, 542–89, at pp. 247 ('Onofrii...Fasti', 'Commentarii in Fastis', 'de vitis pontificum Romanorum') and 281 ('Onofrio de vitis pontificum'). An entry for 'Baptistae Platinae opera omnia' is found on p. 217. Sixtus also owned Panvinio's 'liber de primatu Sancti Petri'; see ibid. 248.

[114] 'Lista de' libbri di Frat'Onofrio Panvini che già furono in deposito appresso il Cardinal Savello di buona memoria et hora sono appresso l'Illustrissimo et Reverendissimo Signor Cardinale Rusticucci, havuta da Sua Signoria Illustrissima a dì V di Aprile 1588', MS Corsin. 671, fos 80ʳ–82ᵛ, ed. L.-G. Pelissier, 'Catalogue des manuscrits de Panvini', Revue des bibliothèques, 1 (1891), 192–4 (for a copy see Vat. lat. 7762, fos 559ʳ⁻ᵛ, 564ʳ⁻ᵛ).

[115] List of manuscripts received from Cardinal Rusticucci, compiled by Geronimo Fosco, secretary to Cardinal Santoro, 18 September 1592, Vat. lat. 7762, fos 558ʳ⁻ᵛ, 561ʳ–562ᵛ.

[116] 'Onuphrii Panvini De primatu in foliis solutis numero 54', 'Cerimoniale...manuscriptum, folia 196 ex papyro in pergamena'; see A. Bertolotti, 'Varietà archivistiche e bibliografiche', Il bibliofilo, 3 (1882), 33–5; Baumgarten, Neue Kunde, i. 341; MS Vat. lat. 7030, fo. 3ᵛ. On the censorship of De primatu see below, 183–187.

whether to publish Panvinio's works. Panvinio's manuscripts were sorted by subject matter and what was perceived as their usefulness. *De varia creatione* and the *Historia ecclesiastica* were subjected to special scrutiny.[117] Afterwards, Panvinio's manuscripts were incorporated into the Vatican Library.

Later efforts to publish Panvinio's collected works were unsuccessful. Lukas Holste, Cardinal Francesco Barberini's librarian and, from 1653, first custodian of the Vatican Library, aimed to publish several of Panvinio's works in the 1640s and 1650s. He found, however, that the Congregation of the Index still knew about and respected Pius V's ban on the publication of Panvinio's works.[118] In this context, it was noted that Panvinio's works on St Peter's and the Lateran Basilica could not be published because silence had been imposed on the question of the prerogatives between the two basilicas; Panvinio had spoken out in favour of St Peter's.[119] Pope Alexander VII staged a search for Panvinio's manuscripts in 1659; Holste bequeathed three of them (i.e., the descriptions of St Peter's and the Lateran Basilica as well a manuscript of lives of popes) to Alexander two years later at his death.[120] At any rate, in 1647 Veronese scholars managed to publish Panvinio's *Antiquitates Veronenses* (Veronese Antiquities), while in 1656, his short *De baptismate paschali* was reprinted in Rome with a dedication to Alexander VII.[121]

In the eighteenth century Filippo Argelati (d. 1755) took an interest in Panvinio's works. The Milanese editor and publisher sought to put together Panvinio's collected works ('tutte l'opere del Panvinio') for his press.[122]

---

[117] See below, 189–200.

[118] See the letters by L. Holste to Cardinal Barberini, 2 July 1646, MS Rome, Biblioteca Vallicelliana, Allacci 96, fo. 318ʳ; 5 October 1546 and 29 July 1547, BAV, Barb. lat. 6490, fo. 5ʳ⁻ᵛ, 50ᵛ–51ʳ. See also Barberini's letters to Holste, 11 October and 28 November 1646, Barb. lat. 6492, fos 41ʳ–44ᵛ, 52ʳ–53ᵛ. On Holste see P. Rietbergen, *Power and Religion in Baroque Rome: Barberini Cultural Politics* (Leiden, 2006), 256–95. My thanks to Paul Nelles for references.

[119] MS BAV, Chig. S V 15, fasc. 10, fo. 3ʳ. See also Gersbach, 'Angelica Latin Manuscript 64', 218; Gersbach, '*De comitiis*', 420 n. 35.

[120] MS BAV, Chig. S V 15, fasc. 10: section of a letter by Filippo Visconti, prior general of the Augustinian Order, 24 January 1659, fo. 1ʳ⁻ᵛ. For the three manuscripts inherited by Alexander VII see H. Rabe, 'Aus Lucas Holstenius' Nachlass', *Centralblatt für Bibliothekswesen*, 12 (1895), 441–8, at p. 445. For Holste's collection of printed books by Panvinio see A. Serrai, *La biblioteca di Lucas Holstenius* (Udine, 2000), *ad indicem*.

[121] Panvinio, *Antiquitatum Veronensium libri VIII* (1647), 2nd edn (1648); id., *De baptismate paschali* (Rome: Angelo Bernabò, 1656).

[122] See C. Vianello, 'Introduzione', in *Edizione nazionale del carteggio di L. A. Muratori* (Florence, 1975–), iii, ed. ead., 1–12, at p. 12; F. Argelati's letters, ibid., *ad indicem*; L. A. Muratori, *Epistolario*, ed. M. Càmpori, 14 vols (Modena, 1901–22), viii. 3666, 3685, 3715, ix. 3775, 3783, 3801 (letters from 1737–8); id., letter to Campagnola, 12 March 1739, in Campagnola, 'Materiali', fos 18ᵛ–19ʳ; Argelati's letter to Pope Benedict XIV, c.1740–7, in C. M. Grafinger, *Die Ausleihe vatikanischer Handschriften und Druckwerke im 18. Jahrhundert*, 2 pts (Vatican City, 2002), i. 137–8.

Argelati, who had edited Carlo Sigonio's works in six volumes, proposed this idea to Lodovico Antonio Muratori in 1737 and the two collaborated on the project. They soon found out that a publisher in Verona, Jacopo Vallarsi, was working on a similar project. It seems that Argelati's project prevailed and Vallarsi withdrew; but the project stalled a few years later because the Viennese court stopped paying Argelati's pension.

It was left to nineteenth-century scholars to rediscover Panvinio's works. Chief among them was Cardinal Angelo Mai, a custodian of the Vatican Library (1819–33), who presented a selection of unpublished works in the ninth volume of his *Spicilegium Romanum* in 1843.[123] The last major edition of a previously unpublished work was Philippe Lauer's publication of Panvinio's description of the Lateran Church in 1911.[124]

In the next chapter, I will explore one of Panvinio's works, his history of papal elections, in detail.

---

[123] *SR*, ix includes, among shorter extracts: *De ecclesiis Christianorum liber*, 141–80; *De rebus antiquis...basilicae Sancti Petri*, 192–382; *De cardinalium origine liber*, 469–511; *De Fabiorum familia, De Maximorum familia*, 549–91. See also Panvinio, *Gregorii Papae VII vita*, in *Appendix ad opera edita ab Angelo Maio*, 78–94.

[124] Panvinio, *De sacrosancta basilica, baptisterio et patriarchio Lateranensi*, ed. Lauer.

3

Panvinio's History of Papal Elections

Introduction

Writing the history of the papacy through the history of the papal elections gave Panvinio the opportunity to trace changes in the distribution of power inside the Church over the course of the centuries. Whoever elected a new pope after the death of the previous one had, momentarily, the greatest power of the Church in their hands. The rules for this election were modified throughout the centuries to adapt to varying historical necessities. In the middle of the sixteenth century a history of this subject had not yet been written; Onofrio Panvinio was the first to write it.

The work *De varia creatione Romani pontificis* (On the Various Ways of Electing the Roman Pope) had its place among Panvinio's studies of the history of the Church. Panvinio began composing a history of the papal elections from late 1558 onwards, which suggests a connection with the preparations for the conclave after the death of Paul IV. As we saw in Chapter 1, Panvinio and his patron, Cardinal Farnese, had left Rome three years earlier. Panvinio was at the cardinal's residence in Parma in December 1558 when he asked his friend Ottavio Pantagato in Rome, with the help of other friends such as Gabriele Faerno, to collect materials on conclaves for him.[1] Panvinio also approached Antonio Agustín about this matter, who advised him where to look. In particular, Angelo Massarelli, bishop of Telese, was said to have the most material.[2] On 11 April 1559 Farnese reminded Panvinio, who was back in Venice, that he had promised to send him

---

[1] Letters by O. Pantagato to Panvinio, 22 December 1558, in id., 'La correspondència', 258; 31 December 1558, ibid. 259; 7 January 1559, ibid. 262; 17 June (below, n. 4). See also the letter by G. Faerno to Panvinio, 24 December 1558, in L. Ceretti, 'Gabriele Faerno filologo in otto lettere inedite al Panvinio', *Aevum*, 27 (1953), 307–31, at p. 328.

[2] A. Agustín (Piedimonte d'Alife) to Panvinio, 6 January 1559, ed. Carbonell i Manils, 'Epigrafia', 297, where Agustín also suggested contacting Tommaso Gigli, Carlo Gualteruzzi, and Gabriele Salvago. See also Gigli's letter to Panvinio, 7 January 1559, MS BAM, D 501 inf., fo. 289^r, and Gualteruzzi's three letters written between 7 April and 19 June 1559, ibid., fos 227^r–229^r.

The Invention of Papal History: Onofrio Panvinio between Renaissance and Catholic Reform. Stefan Bauer, Oxford University Press (2020). © Stefan Bauer.
DOI: 10.1093/oso/9780198807001.001.0001

material on conclaves.[3] On 17 June 1559 Pantagato wrote to Panvinio, commenting that *De varia creatione* was an 'interesting work'.[4] He promised to try to obtain more material for him.

It may be that Panvinio initially intended to write a version in one book; this seems to be indicated by a title found in a list of his works from 1559 ('De varia creatione Romani pontificis liber I').[5] If so, the idea lasted for only a short time, as he then aimed for a five-book version; but, as we will see, he finished only the first three books of this version, which he dedicated to Cardinal Farnese. A few years later, Panvinio created a new version in ten books for Hans Jakob Fugger.

On 24 June 1559 Panvinio wrote to Farnese, sending him the first two books of *De varia creatione* and explaining his plan for the rest of the work.[6] In this letter, Panvinio specified that after the first two books, three more were to come, so the work would consist of five, leading up to the election of Paul IV, if he managed to get hold of all the conclave reports. Panvinio explained the method he had observed in the first two books. First, he had described the mode of each papal election. Then he had provided an account of all popes elected in this way. Finally, with 'examples from history' (that is, the presentation of historical source material) he had illustrated and proved his points. He would follow the same order for the third and fourth books up to Urban VI (r. 1378–89)—that is, up to the beginning of the Great Western Schism. From the fifth book onwards (beginning with Urban VI), Panvinio would include all the individual conclave reports he could find. Panvinio believed the work would please Cardinal Farnese because it was 'full of a variety of information on many things and diverse events' ('piena di varia cognitione di molte cose et diversi accidenti'). Lastly, he urged Farnese to have skilled writers create a clean copy so that the manuscript would be easier to read, as he himself did not have the time to write 'neat letters' ('belli charatteri'). Another reason why Panvinio suggested a clean manuscript was that he had no intention of having the work printed within the next few years. Panvinio also pointed out that Farnese could keep a copy with him when he moved between his various residences. This was an indication that the cardinal was particularly interested in this matter at the

---

[3] A. Farnese (Parma) to Panvinio (Venice), 11 April 1559, ed. Gersbach, '*De comitiis*', 430.

[4] O. Pantagato (Rome) to Panvinio (Venice), 17 June 1559, in id., 'La correspondència', 305: 'È curiosa opera *De varia creatione summi* [*sic*]'.

[5] Panvinio, *Antiquitatum Veronensium libri VIII* (1648), 164.

[6] For what follows see Panvinio (Venice) to A. Farnese, 24 June 1559, ed. Ronchini, 'Panvinio', 218–19.

time—perhaps, as has been said, in preparation for the next conclave. There were projects to reform the rules of papal election, which will be discussed further below.

A few days after this letter of 24 June, Panvinio left for Germany.[7] As we have seen, in August 1559 he was in Augsburg when news arrived that Paul IV was about to die. Panvinio hurried back to Rome where he arrived in September. Cardinal Farnese was one of the protagonists at the conclave which followed. For Panvinio, a particularly emotional experience ensued, as he witnessed the election of the new pope on Christmas Day.[8]

In what way did Panvinio present the history of papal elections? To answer this question, we shall first consider briefly what we know today about the subject.[9] Roughly, we can divide this history into two millennia: the period from St Peter up to the year 1000 and the second millennium until today. In the early times, except for the particular case in which Peter appointed his own successor, the election of a pope was carried out like the election of a bishop. The clergy and the laity of the city, likely together with bishops from near Rome, designated the bishop of Rome. We do not know the practical details of how this form of election took place.[10] After Emperor Constantine's Edict of Milan of 313 (legalizing Christianity) and when Christianity had become the official religion of the Empire (380), Roman emperors interfered with the papal elections. They decreed laws to influence it and even directly installed popes on the Roman See. Emperor Constantius II famously supported Antipope Felix (II) against Liberius, whom he sent into exile in AD 357. Roman emperors reserved the right to intervene when the result of an election was unclear. For example, Emperor Honorius sided with Boniface I in AD 419 against Boniface's competitor,

---

[7] See above, 63–64.

[8] For these episodes see Panvinio's autobiographical account in his text *Creatio Pii IV*, 575–86. For the conclave see also below, 129–132.

[9] The key stages of the history of papal elections are described in H. Fuhrmann, 'Die Wahl des Papstes: ein historischer Überblick', *Geschichte in Wissenschaft und Unterricht*, 9 (1958), 762–80. For a longer treatment based directly on the sources see P. Hinschius, *Das Kirchenrecht der Katholiken und Protestanten in Deutschland*, 6 vols (Berlin, 1869–97), i. 217–94. For studies focusing on specific epochs see A. Paravicini Bagliani, *Morte e elezione del papa: norme, riti e conflitti; il Medioevo* (Rome, 2013); M. A. Visceglia, *Morte e elezione del papa: norme, riti e conflitti; l'età moderna* (Rome, 2013); G. Wassilowsky, *Die Konklavereform Gregors XV. (1621/22): Wertekonflikte, symbolische Inszenierung und Verfahrenswandel im posttridentinischen Papsttum* (Stuttgart, 2010); M. Pattenden, *Electing the Pope in Early Modern Italy, 1450–1700* (Oxford, 2017). For a selection of sources see G. J. Ebers (ed.), *Der Papst und die römische Kurie*, i (no more publ.) (Paderborn, 1916).

[10] A. Thier, *Hierarchie und Autonomie: Regelungstraditionen der Bischofsbestellung in der Geschichte des kirchlichen Wahlrechts bis 1140* (Frankfurt am Main, 2011), 15–62.

Eulalius. The western Roman Empire collapsed but the Ostrogothic kings continued the Roman emperors' tradition of interference, as did the Byzantine emperors. The Byzantine emperors devised an elaborate procedure by which a newly elected pope had to prove his orthodoxy through a confession of faith before the emperor would confirm him. If doubts existed about his faith, he could be invited to Constantinople for a personal interview to verify his orthodoxy. For the most part, the Carolingians required only that the newly elected popes notify the emperors of their elections. From 824 onwards, new popes had to swear an oath of loyalty to the imperial legate before they could be consecrated. When Carolingian power in Italy had faded, papal elections during the tenth century came under the influence of competing Roman nobles, which led to the most chaotic period in the history of the papacy. Interventions by Emperor Otto I had only short-lasting effects. Finally, in 1046 Henry III deposed three simoniac popes and successively installed several German popes.

At that moment, the reform party inside the Church reacted. The reformers wanted to eliminate lay influence on the choice of popes. The decree on papal elections issued by Pope Nicholas II (1059) limited the group of electors to the cardinals. With this event began the millenarian break in the history of the elections, which we have already mentioned; although this decree was not initially fully respected, the new norm had been established. An addition in 1179 brought the decree to its complete affirmation, with the idea of a majority of two-thirds, which stabilized the result of the election. Finally, in 1274 Gregory X introduced the conclave: the election under the total exclusion of the outside world. This electoral principle has been followed, in principle, until today.

How did Panvinio, the first analytic historian of the papal elections, treat this subject? He approached it by distinguishing the various ways in which the elections had occurred.[11] As mentioned, in his letter to Farnese of 24 June 1559, Panvinio had briefly presented this method. The general preface of *De varia creatione* (dated Venice, 1 June 1559) provided more information. Panvinio said here that he sought to recount a story of divine providence; according to him, it was only through the intervention of God that the Church had survived and emerged unscathed from the many challenges it encountered. By way of examples, he mentioned wars, threats from heretics

---

[11] For short summaries of the contents of *De varia creatione* see Mabillon, *Museum italicum*, ii, pp. cix–cxv; *SR*, ix. 530–1; Perini, *Panvinio*, 149–51 (all based on Panvinio's epitome, on which see below, 135–138).

and persecutions, tyrants, schisms, and internal quarrels. That the forms of papal election were manifold and inconstant was also an expression of divine will. It would be useful, necessary, and delightful for those interested in church history to learn about these elections.[12]

He recounted that he had worked on similar subject matter 'quite extensively' by order of Marcello Cervini 'five years earlier' (that is, c.1554). By this earlier work, he may have meant the beginning of his *De primatu Petri* (dedicated to Cervini in 1553).[13] Cardinal Farnese often asked Panvinio to proceed with a more diligent examination of the topic—a request that Panvinio obeyed. Therefore, in this preface, he explained that it was Farnese who made him finally turn from 'profane things' to 'sacred history' (although he claimed elsewhere that Cervini had done the same thing for him).[14]

In the preface to Book I which follows, Panvinio said that he wanted to demonstrate two things: first, that several different forms of election had existed from St Peter's time to his own time and, second, that no variation in the elective process had taken place without the authority and consent of the popes themselves.[15] These changes were made at assemblies or councils and by 'solemn rite'. Historical sources revealed that the election of popes varied immensely, and Panvinio aimed to show the reasons for such diversity. As far as he knew, nobody else had treated this subject before him.

---

[12] Panvinio, *De varia creatione Romani pontificis libri tres*, dedicated to Alessandro Farnese (1 June 1559) (hereafter DVC-III), general preface, inc. 'Orbem terrarum', MS Rome, Biblioteca Angelica, Ang. lat. 83, fo. 3^{r-v} (16th–17th c.). For similar ideas see Panvinio's dedicatory preface to Platina, *Historia de vitis pontificum* (1568), sigs †3^r–†4^r. Other MSS of DVC-III: Bologna, Biblioteca universitaria, 1173 (16th c.); Copenhagen, Det Kongelige Bibliotek, GKS 539 2° (16th–17th c.) (from the library of Gaspar de Guzmán, d. 1645); Rome, Biblioteca Angelica, Ang. lat. 293 (17th c.); Florence, Biblioteca nazionale, II V 38 (17th c.?); Bologna, Biblioteca arcivescovile, 4915 (Book I only); BAV, Boncompagni-Ludovisi, C.8 (Books II–III); Vat. lat. 6779 (16th c.) (incomplete; contains material for Book III, partly written in Panvinio's hand).

[13] As he wrote in DVC-III, Preface to Book I (MS Ang. lat. 83, fo. 5^v): 'in libro quem *de dignitate sedis apostolicae* scripsi'. This phrase was later excluded from the preface to Book I in the ten-book version (hereafter DVC-X), which is otherwise mostly identical. See also below, nn. 15, 37, 44.

[14] DVC-III, general preface, fo. 4^{r-v}: 'Te enim auctore nunc a rebus prophanis ad sacras historias tractandas me converti'. See the preface to *Romani pontifices et cardinales* (1557), where he made a similar statement about Cervini (above, 36–37).

[15] This preface to Book I, inc. 'Variam admodum', was published from the ten-book version (DVC-X) by Merkle, 'Prolegomena', in *Concilium Tridentinum*, ii, pp. XIII–CLXXVII, at pp. CXXX–CXXXI. See especially p. CXXX: 'nullam in comitiis ipsis varietatem praeter eiusdem Romani pontificis auctoritatem et consensum factum fuisse'; ibid.: 'eiusmodi comitia non nisi ex eorundem decretis et voluntate facta fuisse intelligendum est, qui non casu vel fortuito, sed ita varia temporum conditione exigente (qua nihil magis mutationibus obnoxium est) ipsam creandis summum religionis christianae antistitem rationem saepius conciliis congregatis et solenni ritu immutavere'. On DVC-X see below, n. 37.

Panvinio's claim that the popes themselves had always authorized changes to the rules was relevant in connection to the concurrent discussions about church reform at the Council of Trent (1545–63). The pontiffs from Paul III to Pius IV did everything to keep a 'reform of the Church's head' (*reformatio in capite*)—which would have included a revision of the rules of papal elections—out of the council's hands. In the aftermath of Trent, the papacy claimed the exclusive right to interpret and implement the conciliar decrees.[16] At first sight, Panvinio's *De varia creatione* provided a simple justification for the papacy's claim to its right to self-reform. However, the text's legitimizing functions were more complex. By showing that change in the Church had always occurred, Panvinio opened a Pandora's box—which could potentially play into the hands of both Protestant and Catholic reformers who denied the papacy its privilege to self-reform. Panvinio's approach towards the description of historical change contrasted, in particular, with that of Catholic controversial theologians who argued that dogma, liturgy, piety, and institutions had been founded in the early Church: the older these were, the truer they could be considered. When Cesare Baronio composed his *Ecclesiastical Annals* (from the 1570s), he made it a point to stress continuity over change.[17]

Furthermore, Panvinio showed that in the late antique and early medieval periods, the emperors had played a role in designating the popes. From Pope Gregory VII (r. 1073–85) onwards, the Church sought to eliminate this influence and began to strive for greater secular power. Panvinio implied that this was not a beneficial development for the Church. In doing so, he placed himself in the vicinity of Catholic reformers such as Girolamo Seripando who, while maintaining obedience to the popes, saw the papacy's exercise of temporal power as a root of corruption.[18] In private notes from the second half the 1550s, the former general of the Augustinians Seripando distinguished four ages of the Church: first, a golden, apostolic age; second, a silver, patristic age; third, a bronze age, in which the clergy began to exercise secular power (which the apostles had rejected); and fourth, the present, a leaden age, in which churchmen—suffering, as it were, under the weight of

---

[16] G. Wassilowsky, 'Posttridentische Reform und päpstliche Zentralisierung: zur Rolle der Konzilskongregation', in A. Merkt, G. Wassilowsky and G. Wurst (eds), *Reformen in der Kirche: historische Perspektiven* (Freiburg im Breisgau, 2014), 138–57.

[17] See above, 24–25; below, 210–211.

[18] For what follows see Jedin, *Seripando*, ii. 284–5. On Seripando's association with reformers see also C. Russell, 'Dangerous Friendships: Girolamo Seripando, Giulia Gonzaga and the *Spirituali* in Tridentine Italy', in W. François and V. Soen (eds), *The Council of Trent: Reform and Controversy in Europe and Beyond (1545–1700)*, 3 vols (Göttingen, 2018), i. 249–76.

this base metal—were deprived of virtue and discipline. A comparable theory of decadence, involving the Church's development from apostolic purity to greed and selfishness, had previously been held by another general of Panvinio's order, the humanist Giles of Viterbo (d. 1532).[19] A more cautious Catholic reformer, Marcello Cervini, like Seripando upheld the notion of supreme papal power within the Church. Both Cervini and Seripando—as legates—represented papal interests at the Council of Trent. Although Cervini believed that some popes had slipped from their position of moral authority in the early Church, he argued that curial reforms were to be carried out through papal, rather than conciliar, action. Cervini discussed these ideas with Cardinal Farnese.[20]

Massarelli's *Modes*

Panvinio's claim that nobody had worked on the topic of papal elections before him should be taken with a grain of salt. In fact, in April 1554 his friend Angelo Massarelli (1510–66) had put together a list of forms of papal elections entitled *Modi seu formae observatae diversis temporibus in elec-tione summorum pontificum a Petro usque ad Iulium III* (Modes or Forms Observed at Various Times in the Elections of Popes from Peter to Julius III).[21] This work might have been inspired by Cervini and Julius III. As we shall see below, Julius III prepared a reform of the rules of the conclave in 1554.[22] Massarelli had worked for Cervini from 1542 as a secretary, before becoming secretary of the Council of Trent (from 1546 until 1563) and a papal secretary (from 1550).[23] In 1557 he became bishop of Telese. Massarelli

---

[19] J. W. O'Malley, *Giles of Viterbo on Church and Reform: A Study in Renaissance Thought* (Leiden, 1968), 100–38.

[20] Hudon, *Cervini*, 72–81. See also H. Jedin, *Papal Legate at the Council of Trent: Cardinal Seripando* (St Louis, MO; London, 1947).

[21] The short treatise was published by A. Mai in 1843 under the title *De modis seu formis per diversa tempora observatis in electione pontificum maximorum a Divo Petro usque ad Iulium III*, in *SR*, ix. 518–30. A MS copy, entitled *Modi seu formae observatae diversis temporibus in elec-tione summorum pontificum a Petro usque ad Iulium III* (Vat. lat. 12125, fos 42^r–47^v), ends with the following autograph colophon (not included in the version published by Mai): 'Collect(ae) per me Angelum Massarellum Septempedanum Picentem ipsius Iulii III Pontificis Maximi secretarium anno Domini 1554 mense Aprilis'.

[22] See below, 128–129.

[23] For his career see S. Giordano, 'Massarelli, Angelo', in *DBI*, lxxi. 706–9. For Cervini's possible commissioning of the *Modi* see A. Tallon, 'Les conclaves dans l'historiographie de la Contre-Réforme', in M. Firpo (ed.), *'Nunc alia tempora, alii mores': storici e storia in età postri-dentina* (Florence, 2005), 25–46, at p. 30. The title of this volume ('*Nunc alia...*') was drawn

not only wrote the acts and diaries of the Council of Trent, but also conducted historical research. He put together much material on the history of popes and cardinals, collecting biographies, coats of arms, bulls, and epitaphs.[24] The scholar of diplomatics Paul Fridolin Kehr (1860–1944) used the following words to judge Massarelli's work, together with that of Panvinio:

> Any history of papal diplomatics should begin with Massarelli and Panvinio. This is because these men engaged in the serious effort of bringing together copies and facsimiles of papal bulls; they put together the rotas, collected the monograms, copied thousands of datings, and transcribed the signatures of the popes in the most exact ways, representing all diplomatic peculiarities. I was shocked to encounter a method which shows that these men had a perfect understanding of the peculiar nature of such works…They collected material which has remained undigested and unknown until today, and which does not need to shun comparison even with the collections of the Maurists.[25]

Massarelli concentrated on the history of cardinals; his specialty knowledge of this topic was exalted by Panvinio. In his *Romani pontifices et cardinales* of 1557, Panvinio profusely thanked Massarelli for his assistance. Massarelli not only helped with the entire work in general but provided, in particular, the material on the Avignon popes from Urban V (r. 1362–70) to Benedict (XIII) (antipope 1394–1417) and on the cardinals they created.[26] Massarelli revised Panvinio's book after its publication, pointing out numerous errors. As a result, he urged Panvinio to not hurry in the subject matter of cardinals.[27] Massarelli said that, in making his many corrections, he had worked extremely

---

from a letter by Sigonio to Panvinio, 26 November 1558: Sigonio, *Opera omnia edita et inedita*, ed. F. Argelati, 6 vols (Milan, 1732–7), vi, col. 1002.

[24] The material is listed by S. Merkle, 'Prolegomena', in *Concilium Tridentinum*, i, pp. XI–CXXIX, at pp. XCVIII–CI, CXV–CXV. See especially Vat. lat. 12125–7. For the coats of arms see Bouyé, 'Les armoiries imaginaires'.

[25] P. F. Kehr, 'Diplomatische Miszellen, iv: Die Scheden des Panvinius' (first publ. 1901), in id., *Papsturkunden in Italien: Reiseberichte zur Italia Pontificia*, 6 vols (Vatican City, 1977), iii. 1–26, at p. 2 (my trans.).

[26] Panvinio, *Romani pontifices et cardinales* (1557), preface to the section from AD 1305 onwards, p. 184. For more praise of Massarelli see Panvinio, *Fastorum libri V* (1558), 403.

[27] Agustín to Panvinio, 3 July 1557, ed. Carbonell, 'Epigrafia', 158: '"Andate adaggio et non correte in freta", dice un certo madrigale, che vi canta Messer Angelo Massarello nella materia di cardinali'; Massarelli to Panvinio, 13 November 1557, Vat. lat. 6412, fo. 12ʳ: 'ho trovato assai o vogliam dire scorrettioni o errori'.

diligently and had endured intolerable toils to do Panvinio a favour should he wish to issue a second edition of his work.[28]

Panvinio's *Romani pontifices et cardinales* included, as an appendix, the treatise *De episcopatibus, titulis et diaconiis cardinalium* (On the Bishoprics, *tituli*, and *diaconiae* of the Cardinals).[29] It has some passages in common with Panvinio's longer treatise *De cardinalium origine* (On the Origin of Cardinals) from 1555.[30] The manuscript copies of this last work were included among both Panvinio's and Massarelli's materials and do not carry a title with an author's name; only further research could determine whether Massarelli had a hand in its composition.[31]

Regarding the subject matter of papal elections, Massarelli had written a detailed diary of the conclave which led to the election of Julius III in 1549–50.[32] As we have seen, in 1559, when Panvinio was looking for sources, Agustín told him that Massarelli had extensive material on conclaves. Therefore, the concept of distinguishing ways of election in a historical sequence should be attributed to Massarelli so long as no other evidence comes to light. His work is a relatively brief commented list in which, for each mode, he provided a few sentences of explanation and added a reference or two to his sources. Perhaps Massarelli's work on this topic from April 1554 was already known to Panvinio at the time when he himself worked on *De primatu Petri* (dedicated to Cervini in November 1553), which he considered a first phase of his work on *De varia creatione*. Massarelli ultimately distinguished twenty-two modes up to the decree *Licet de vitanda* of Alexander III (1179), then went on to add another four modes up to his own time, for a total of twenty-six. As we shall see, Panvinio stopped counting with *Licet de vitanda*, which for him was the eighteenth

---

[28] Massarelli to Panvinio, 30 April 1558, Vat. lat. 6412, fo. 18ʳ, cited by Merkle, 'Prolegomena', in *Concilium Tridentinum*, i, p. IC: 'una diligentia esatissima et fatiga intollerabile per farvi piacere et honore'. The revised edition of *Romani pontifices* never came out. See also above, 48.

[29] Panvinio, *De episcopatibus, titulis et diaconiis cardinalium*, in his *Romani pontifices et cardinales* (1557), Appendix, 51–75. See pp. 51 and 75 for references to *De cardinalium origine* (on which see the following note).

[30] Panvinio, *De cardinalium origine*, in *SR*, ix. 469–511. The *terminus post quem* for the redaction of this work is the election of Paul IV on 23 May 1555; see ibid. 508. On p. 481 there is a reference to Panvinio's earlier treatise *De sacrorum cleri ordinum origine* (dedicated to Cardinal Cervini, i.e. written before his election as pope on 9 April 1555).

[31] MSS of *De cardinalium origine*: BAV, Vat. lat. 6111, fos 174ʳ–210ʳ (16th–17th c.); Vat. lat. 12125, fos 9ʳ–39ʳ (16th c.); Ottob. lat. 2961, fos 121ʳ–159ᵛ (16th c.); BAM, G 41 inf., fos 4ʳ–56ᵛ, 139ʳ–158ᵛ (16th c.). Perini (*Panvinio*, 262) voiced doubts about Panvinio's authorship.

[32] See below, 127.

and final mode. Massarelli, like Panvinio, began with the 'institution' of
Peter by Christ. However, from then on, the distinction of modes differed
slightly from that of Panvinio. It is not necessary to discuss the details of the
differences here. Massarelli's text was a sort of outline from which Panvinio's
work departed. Massarelli also indicated some of the major sources such
as Gratian's *Decretum* and writers of papal biographies (such as the *Liber
pontificalis*, Martin of Troppau, Ptolemy of Lucca, and Platina). As a different slant from Panvinio, Massarelli tended to minimize the emperors' roles
whenever possible and clearly thought their influence was negative.[33] Hubert
Jedin regarded Massarelli as an extremely industrious and diligent secretary
and collector of materials, although his skills as a historian had some well-
defined limits. His Latin was imperfect, he had never studied theology, and
he possessed only such sporadic knowledge of canon law and older theological literature as he may have gleaned from copying texts as a secretary.[34]
Though Panvinio clearly took inspiration from Massarelli's *Modi*, his *De
varia creatione*, as will become obvious, is a much more extensive treatise
based on a far greater number of sources and on Panvinio's own brand of
critical spirit.

The Shorter and Full Versions of *De varia creatione*

It is useful at this point to look at the various versions of Panvinio's work to
understand the content. Though Panvinio sent the first two books to
Farnese on 24 June 1559, with plans to write five books, what he eventually
presented to Farnese was a three-book version. There is preparatory material for the five-book version, but he never finished the work in this form.[35]
Some confusion may have arisen because Panvinio included the five-book

---

[33] See, e.g., Massarelli, *De modis*, ed. Mai, 526, on Emperor Otto I's choice of popes: 'cum is
modus contra libertatem ecclesiasticam indecens atque incongruus videretur ...'
[34] H. Jedin, *Das Konzil von Trient: ein Überblick über die Erforschung seiner Geschichte*
(Rome, 1948), 15–16; id., *A History of the Council of Trent*, trans. E. Graf, 2 vols (no more publ.)
(London, 1957–61), ii. 505–9.
[35] A draft preface to Book V, designed to be the last book of the work (inc. 'Tandem
aliquando ad quintum et ultimum instituti mei librum perveni') and leading up to the
sixteenth century, is in Vat. lat. 6778, fo. 491^{r-v}. At another moment, there might have been
a plan to write fifteen books, though this is an indication which might have been wrongly
introduced by a scribe; see the titles in Vat. lat. 6777, fos 1a^r ('XV', corr. ex 'X') and 80^r
(scribal hand).

version in the list of his works published by Ruscelli in 1566, most likely before he had written it.[36]

The three-book version carried a preface dated Venice, 1 June 1559. The contents of this version are rather more limited than what Panvinio announced to Farnese in his letter. The third book ended with the schism between Alexander III (r. 1159–81) and Antipope Victor IV (1159–64). The work therefore ended with the last way of election *before* the promulgation of the decree on papal elections of 1179, which made a two-thirds majority of all voting cardinals mandatory for a valid election (the basic rule followed until today). In this version, Panvinio distinguished seventeen modes of election up to Alexander III and before the decree of 1179. Book I covered the first four modes of election up to Silverius (r. 536–7). Book II started with Vigilius (r. 537–55), elected in the fifth mode, which was marked by the consent of the Byzantine emperor. It ended with the tenth mode and Gregory VI (r. 1045–6). Book III began with Clement II (r. 1046–7), elected in the eleventh mode, inaugurating a series of popes installed by the Emperor Henry III. It ended with the seventeenth mode. It is possible that at this point, for two reasons, Panvinio stopped working on *De varia creatione* and did not carry on to finish the fourth and fifth books he had promised to Farnese: first, because he left for Germany and second, because he had difficulty finding copies of the conclave reports up to the present, about which he had asked his friends and contacts.

Only in 1563 was a full version accomplished, not in five but in ten books. The full version was commissioned by Hans Jakob Fugger and its preface was dated 1 May 1563. Only one complete presentation version was produced and survives in Munich.[37] In the Vatican Library, most parts of the ten-book version are available but must be pieced together from various drafts and fragments.[38] For this version, in the general preface Panvinio made a change to the text and added a new final section. He changed the story of how he had been motivated to produce the work, recounting that

---

[36] See Ruscelli, *Le imprese* (1566), 534. See also Panvinio, 'Le opere che ho composte', Vat. lat. 7762, fo. 560ᵛ: 'Cinque libri della varia creatione del papa'. He also specified here that the length of this work was 'come dua volte Livio'—that is, twice as long as Livy. This version, however, has not been found; there are only fragmentary epitomes of it, for which see below, 137.

[37] Panvinio, *De varia Romani pontificis creatione libri X*, dedicated to Hans Jakob Fugger (DVC-X), Clm 147–52, 6 vols (containing notes and corrections in Panvinio's hand). Fugger confirmed the receipt of the work on 20 November 1563; see his letter to Panvinio, Vat. lat. 6412, fo. 105ʳ.

[38] Vat. lat. 6107.i–iii, 6775.i–ii, 6777, 6778, 12121, 12181 (all partly autograph).

he had already worked on a similar subject matter 'quite extensively' by order of Marcello Cervini ten years earlier (that is, around 1553), but that he was often asked by certain serious and important friends to pursue a more diligent examination of the topic.[39] Thus, Alessandro Farnese was not mentioned specifically. Lastly, in a new final section of the preface, Panvinio stated that in the ten books he would first deal with the institution of the Church and its vicar by Christ, then with everything which had to do with the elections of successive popes. He would include matters which were 'very serious and obscure' and which had not received treatment from anyone before him. To describe them, he would explain the greater part of church history of all the different periods, which, of course, meant including material which was already known. All this he would do for 'the public benefit' ('communis utilitas').[40] Here—only in the preface of the version dedicated to Fugger—Panvinio also mentioned that he desisted from publishing this work 'for very serious reasons', though he refrained from explicating these reasons.[41] As Panvinio wrote to Fugger in a letter dated 31 October 1562, he intended to have printed only the first book, which contained everything he could say 'catholically' ('catholicamente') on the authority and power of the pope. Not only were the other nine books not to be printed, Panvinio hoped nobody would see them as long as he lived. Fugger would recognize the reasons for this when he read the work. The German was asked to show the work to few people and to not let it leave his house. Even if the first book was published, it would be worthwhile for Fugger to have the manuscript version because it would be more correct and longer.[42]

In the ten-book version the modes of creation themselves (up to the seventeenth mode) were identical to the three-book version; however, the distribution of the modes over the books were different, as Table 3.1 shows:

The First Centuries and the Carolingians (Books I–III)

What had previously been Book I, was now spread out over two books (Books I and II). Book I contained modes 1–2 and dealt with Peter and

[39] Panvinio, DVC-X, general preface, inc. 'Orbem terrarum', Clm 147, fos 2ʳ–3ᵛ, ed. Merkle, 'Prolegomena', in *Concilium Tridentinum*, ii, pp. CXXIX–CXXX.
[40] Ibid., p. CXXX.
[41] Ibid.: 'gravissimas ob causas ab eo publicando desistam'. See H. Grauert, 'Das Dekret Nikolaus II. von 1059', *Historisches Jahrbuch*, 1 (1880), 502–602, at p. 592.
[42] Panvinio to Fugger, 31 October 1562, Vat. lat. 6277, fos 3ᵛ–4ʳ, cited by Perini, *Panvinio*, 152; Wassilowsky, *Konklavereform*, 38 n. 12.

Table 3.1 Contents of Panvinio, *De varia creatione Romani pontificis* (DVC)

DVC in III Books		DVC in X Books	
Book	Contents	Book	Contents (years of election according to *Oxford Dictionary of Popes*)
I	*Modes described:* 1–4	I	*Contents:* Christ–Evaristus (*c*.100). *Modes described:* 1: Peter (uncertain year) 2: Clement (*c*.91)
		II	*Contents:* Fabian (236)–Vigilius (537). *Modes:* 3: Clement's successors–Liberius (352) 4: Felix II (355)–Vigilius
II	*Modes:* 5–10	III	*Contents:* Pelagius I (556)–Gregory VI (1045). *Modes:* 5: Pelagius I–Benedict II (684) 6: John V (685)–Hadrian I (772) 7: Leo III (795)–Hadrian III (884) 8: Stephen V (VI) (885)–Benedict V (964) 9: John XIII (965)–Silvester II (999) 10: John XVII (1003)–Gregory VI
III	*Modes:* 11–17	IV	*Contents:* Clement II (1046)–Calixtus II (1119–24). *Modes:* 11: Clement II–Victor II (1055) 12: Stephen IX (X) (1057) only 13: Nicholas II (1058) only 14: Alexander II (1061), Gregory VII (1073) 15: Victor III (1086)–Paschal II (1099) 16: Gelasius II (1118)–Innocent II (1130)
		V	*Contents:* Honorius II (1124)–Alexander III (1159). *Modes:* 17: Celestine II (1143)–Alexander III 18: Decree *Licet de vitanda* (1179)
	Not in DVC-III	VI	Lucius III (1181)–Benedict XI (1303)
		VII	Clement V (1305)–Clement (VIII) (1423)
		VIII	Urban VI (1378)–Nicholas V (1447)
		IX	Calixtus III (1455)–Paul III (1534)
		X	Julius III (1550)–Pius IV (1559)

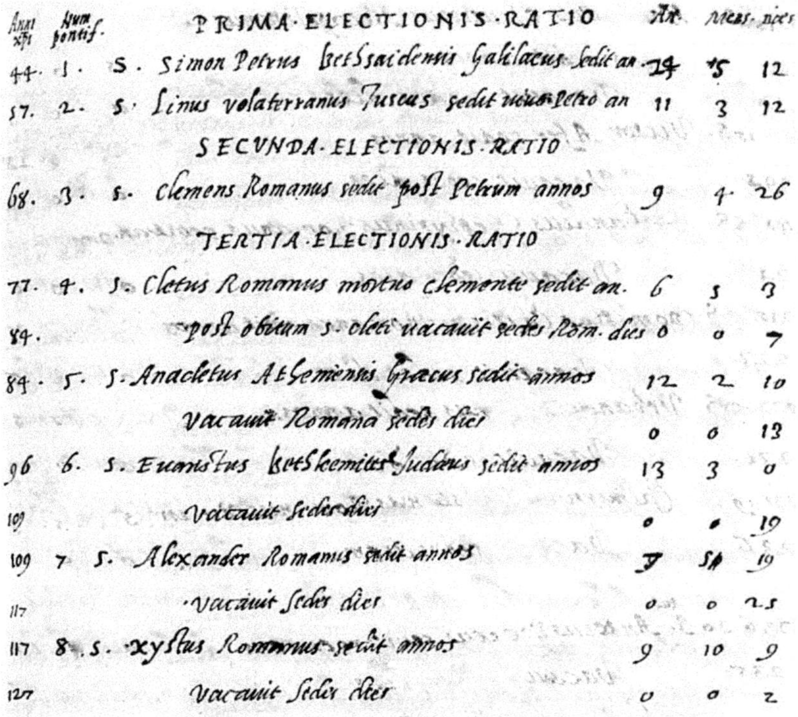

Fig. 3.1 The first three modes of papal election (detail). From Panvinio, DVC-X, Book II. Autograph. Courtesy of the Bayerische Staatsbibliothek, Munich (Clm 147, fo. 249ʳ).

Clement (Fig. 3.1). Rather than being an account of the ways of papal election, this first book presented primarily material on the primacy of Peter, much of which was taken from Panvinio's *De primatu Petri*. According to Panvinio, Christ had appointed St Peter as the first pope. Panvinio used the term *institutio* to refer to this first form of election—or, rather, designation of this spokesman among the apostles and leader of the youthful Church. The second form of election was the *substitutio* or *subrogatio*: St Peter nominated Clement as his successor—a form that Panvinio described using sources which today are considered apocryphal (Pseudo-Clement). In Fugger's version of *De varia creatione*, at the end of Book I Panvinio added a long treatise by Cardinal Reginald Pole (*De officio pontificis Romani*); this was a text written during the conclave after the death of Paul III.[43] It is interesting here, too, that Panvinio referred to his own previous work as *De Romani pontificis institutione et potestate liber* (Book on the Establishment and Power of the Roman Pope), which showed again that he saw *De varia creatione* as closely connected to *De primatu Petri*.[44]

Book II contained modes 3–4. The third mode of election was that which, as has been said, has been shown by modern scholars to have existed during the first three centuries (though we do not know many details about the practical process): the election by the clergy and laity of Rome. For this third elective mode, Panvinio collected proofs from the letters of Cyprian, which are today still considered the most important source on the elections. Panvinio's third mode began soon after the death of Clement (Panvinio did not give a precise beginning for it).[45] The last pope elected in the third way was Liberius (r. 352–66). Mode 4 arrived after Constantine had given peace to the Church and the emperors reserved for themselves a right of intervention or oversight. This form was observed from the election of Antipope Felix II (355) to that of Vigilius (537).

Book III (formerly Book II) contained modes 5–10, from the election of Pelagius I (556) to Gregory VI's deposition (1046). In this chapter Panvinio discussed, among other questions, the territorial donations that the Frankish kings had made to the Church. One striking example of Panvinio's criticism of sources was his discussion of a document of Louis the Pious, Charlemagne's son and successor—the so-called *Pactum Hludowicianum* (817). It was the first document in which the agreements between the Carolingian emperors and the popes, which had taken place from 754 onwards, were manifested in writing; over fifty years of Franco-papal history were thus condensed here. This pact between Louis and Pope Stephen IV represented a renewal

---

[43] R. Pole, *De summo pontifice Christi in terris vicario eiusque officio et potestate* (Leuven, 1569). On this text see T. F. Mayer, 'Il fallimento di una candidatura: il partito della riforma, Reginald Pole e il conclave di Giulio III', *Annali dell'Istituto storico italo-germanico in Trento/ Jahrbuch des italienisch-deutschen historischen Instituts in Trient*, 21 (1995), 41–67.

[44] DVC-X, Book I, Clm 147, fos 149ʳ–241ʳ (R. Pole, *De officio pontificis Romani*), preface to Pole's treatise by Panvinio, fo. 148ᵛ: 'Huic a me edito *de Romani pontificis institutione et potestate libro* commodissimum visum est Reginaldi Poli cardinalis Britanni viri doctissimi dialogum adiungere'. (My italics.)

[45] DVC-X, Book II, Clm 147, fo. 242ᵛ: 'Tertia Romani pontificis deligendi ratio. Mortuo igitur Clemente episcopo Romano, quem Petrus Apostolus adhuc vivens sibi successorem designaverat, sive aliquo ex suis successoribus, puta Cleto, Anacleto vel Evaristo, mos invaluit, ut nemo in posterum episcoporum Romanae sedis se vivente futurum pontificem renuntiaret'. In Panvinio's chronology the order of succession was Clement (r. 68–77), Cletus (77–84), Anacletus (84–96), and Evaristus (96–109), whereas in today's reckoning, the order is believed to have been Anacletus (*c*.79–*c*.91), Clement (*c*.91–*c*.101), Evaristus (*c*.100–*c*.109), with Cletus considered non-existent. See in Fig. 3.1 the chronological lists regarding modes 1–3.

of the Franco-papal alliance and listed the territories of the Papal State which had previously been granted to the Church by the Frankish rulers. It also assured free papal elections, in which the newly elected popes had only to notify the emperors of their election and did not have to ask for their confirmation. Panvinio included this document, in a somewhat abbreviated version, then commented that he doubted its authenticity. He found it 'strongly suspicious' because historical practice showed that newly elected popes had to be confirmed by the emperor before they could be consecrated. A document of this kind had to be spurious, as this was not how the emperors actually behaved.[46]

It is worth looking at how and in which context Panvinio reached such a conclusion. He was not the first to doubt the authenticity of this document. It had become 'guilty by association'—suspicious simply because the Donation of Constantine (to which this document seemed to bear several similarities) had been proved a forgery. In 1440 Lorenzo Valla had already cast doubts on Louis's donation but had not closely analysed the text.[47] No contemporary copies existed and the tradition of the document began only from the eleventh century onwards—this also made it a source of suspicion among careful scholars during the middle of the sixteenth century. The first to cast it into doubt extensively and systematically seems to have been the French Calvinist legal scholar Charles Du Moulin (1500–66).[48] Du Moulin, a passionate enemy of the papacy, claimed that no territories were donated in this document, just as they had not been donated in the false Donation of Constantine. The document, according to him, was fabricated by a papal

---

[46] After citing the document (DVC-X, Book III, Clm 148, fos 43^r–44^r) Panvinio commented (fo. 44^{r-v}): 'Hanc donationem (si modo vera est) ego exscripsi ex antiquissimo codice Bibliothecae Vaticanae. Nam eam forte suspectam facere id potissimum posset quid, quamquam aperte intelligatur neque Carolum Magnum neque eius filios absolutam creandi papam potestatem sibi oblatam accepisse, id tamen longo atque diuturno annorum intervallo septima hac comitiorum ratione manifeste observavi ipseque mox suggeram, Romanos pontifices a clero, senatu populoque Romano liberis suffragiis creatos non ante consecrari mos fuisse quam eorum comitia a legatis imperatoriis examinata et probata essent, ipsos quoque coram legatis imperatoris inaugurari solitos. Quae consuetudo usque ad Hadrianum Papam III [r. 884–5] perduravit.' For an edition of the *Hludowicianum* see T. Kölzer et al. (eds), *Die Urkunden Ludwigs des Frommen*, 3 pts (Wiesbaden, 2016), i. 312–20, esp. p. 319. See also See W. H. Fritze, *Papst und Frankenkönig: Studien zu den päpstlich-fränkischen Rechtsbeziehungen zwischen 754 und 824* (Sigmaringen, 1973), 15–19.

[47] L. Valla, *On the Donation of Constantine*, ed. and trans. G. W. Bowersock (Cambridge, MA, 2007), 132–6. See also W. Setz, *Lorenzo Vallas Schrift gegen die Konstantinische Schenkung: De falsa credita et ementita Constantini donatione* (Tübingen, 1975), 61–2; Camporeale, *Christianity, Latinity, and Culture*, 69, 101–9.

[48] C. Du Moulin, *Commentarius ad edictum Henrici II Regis Galliarum contra parvas datas et abusus curiae Romanae* (Basel, 1552), 229–34; he summarized his view in his notes to his edition of the *Decretum Divi Gratiani* (Lyon, 1554; reprint 1559), D. 63 c. 30, p. 221 n. †.

librarian. Among other arguments in his analysis, he observed that Paschal I (elected 817) sent a letter of apology to the emperor when he had been consecrated without having received the emperor's confirmation; and that even after Louis's presumed decree, and while Louis was still alive, Gregory IV (elected 827) asked the emperor for his confirmation before he could be consecrated. The entire argument of Du Moulin, several pages long, was included by another arch-enemy of the papacy, Matthias Flacius Illyricus, in his *Catalogus testium veritatis* (Catalogue of Witnesses to the Truth) of 1556.[49]

It is not clear whether Panvinio knew Du Moulin's works or Flacius's *Catalogus*. In any case, Panvinio was surely aware that it was perilous to question the Donation of Constantine—and subsequent donations—in Rome at this time.[50] It is noteworthy that Panvinio had the courage to challenge the authenticity of the *Pactum Hludowicianum* even though it had been included in venerable collections of sources from the eleventh and twelfth centuries, such as Cardinal Deusdedit's collection of canons, Ivo of Chartres's and Gratian's *Decretum*, and the *Liber censuum* of the Roman Church. A *guerre des savants* over the authenticity of the *Hludowicianum* was waged until well into the twentieth century. Influential deniers of its veracity included Antoine Pagi, a key editor of Baronio's *Annales ecclesiastici* (1743); Georg Heinrich Pertz, co-director of the *Monumenta Germaniae Historica* (1837); and Ferdinand Gregorovius, author of *The History of the City of Rome in the Middle Ages*.[51] The authenticity of the document was established in definitive fashion by Theodor Sickel in 1883.[52]

The underlying question was fundamentally whether the Carolingian rulers allowed free papal elections or whether they reserved their right of confirmation. The latter was suggested by the fact that Paschal I sent the letter of 817 mentioned by Du Moulin—which was considered a letter of apology by some circles on the Frankish side, but it may have been merely the act of notification stipulated in the pact.[53] With all these uncertainties, Panvinio understandably questioned the validity of the passage. Perhaps he

---

[49] M. Flacius, *Catalogus testium veritatis qui ante nostram aetatem reclamarunt papae* (Basel, 1556), 211–16.

[50] Bauer, *Censorship*, 149–66.

[51] C. Baronio, *Annales ecclesiastici*, ed. A. Pagi, 19 vols (Lucca, 1738–46), xiii, ad AD 817, cols 591–2; G. H. Pertz's edition of the *Hludowicianum*, in *Monumenta Germaniae Historica*, Leges, ii (Hannover, 1837), pt 2, pp. 9–11; F. Gregorovius, *Geschichte der Stadt Rom im Mittelalter*, 8 vols (Stuttgart, 1859–72), iii. 39–40.

[52] T. Sickel, *Das Privilegium Otto I. für die römische Kirche vom Jahre 962* (Innsbruck, 1883). The history of scholarship on the *Hludowicianum* is discussed by T. F. X. Noble, *The Republic of St. Peter: The Birth of the Papal State, 680–825* (Philadelphia, PA, 1984), 148–53.

[53] For Paschal's letter see A. Hahn, 'Das Hludowicianum: die Urkunde Ludwig des Frommen für die römische Kirche von 817', *Archiv für Diplomatik*, 21 (1975), 15–135, at pp. 109–12.

placed too much weight on the precise meaning of 'confirmation' by the emperor and expected that this right was exercised in a formal sense rather than informally, as was often the case with political influence on elections. Panvinio's doubts reflect a fundamental problem still present today: We do not know with any certainty the Carolingian rulers' attitude towards the question of the confirmation of papal elections. Some sources suggest a reluctance on their part to interfere, while others suggest a more active influence on the elections.[54] If Louis the Pious had guaranteed the freedom of election and consecration in 817, then his son Lothair in 824 (while Louis was still emperor) went against this same rule by decreeing that no consecration was permitted before the newly elected pope swore his allegiance to the imperial legate. Lothair's 'Roman constitution' was created in agreement with Pope Eugenius II (r. 824–7). Today, scholars believe that, on the whole, actual practice in the ninth century conformed with the practice described in Lothair's decree. This practice was disregarded after the end of the Carolingian rule over Italy but was reinstated by Otto I in 962. Panvinio believed that Pope Leo VIII renewed a privilege for Otto, which had been first given by Hadrian I to Charlemagne in 785, according to which the power to elect the popes was conceded to the emperors. Although both privileges were high medieval forgeries, at least Otto's control over papal elections was a historical fact, as will be discussed below in the section on Gregory VII.[55]

The Investiture Controversy (Book IV)

Book IV (formerly the first part of Book III) began with Clement II (r. 1046–7) and ended with Calixtus II (1119–24). It contained modes 11–16.[56] Panvinio split the former Book III into Books IV and V. In the preface to this crucial book, Panvinio wrote that this period saw devastating changes in the history of the Church. In his previous chapters, Panvinio said,

---

[54] For what follows see Hahn, 'Hludowicianum', 101–15; Noble, *Republic*, 202–3, 313; E. Boshof, *Ludwig der Fromme* (Darmstadt, 1996), 135–40; S. Scholz, *Politik, Selbstverständnis, Selbstdarstellung: die Päpste in karolingischer und ottonischer Zeit* (Stuttgart, 2006).

[55] DVC-X, Book III, Clm 148, fos 41ᵛ (Hadrian I), 54ʳ, 73ʳ⁻ᵛ (Leo VIII). See also below, 112–114.

[56] Passages from Panvinio's descriptions of the elections of Benedict X (1058), Nicholas II (1058), Alexander II (1061), Gregory VII (1073), and Victor III (1086) are cited in M. Stroll, *The Medieval Abbey of Farfa: Target of Papal and Imperial Ambitions* (Leiden, 1997), 157–8, 179–99.

we have seen a humble, dejected, poor Church of God, which was tossed about by the command of profane rulers and (as I will explain) plunged into disgraceful servitude. We will see that the same Church, shortly after, not without manifest divine help, became the ruler of the whole world and master of those who had ruled it before.[57]

In previous chapters, 'we have read that the emperors in the manner of the ancient Roman rulers gave the Church laws, that they installed and removed popes, that all ecclesiastical matters were handled according to their judgement and that all sacred things were oppressed because of a very grave servitude to the laymen'.[58] Now the Church 'gradually grew to such a height that it laboured under its immense size and appeared to break under its own weight'.[59] The Church now, in turn, commanded the emperors and 'treated them like the lowest slaves'.[60]

Panvinio then copied, without acknowledging this fact, a passage from Otto of Freising (d. 1158), the most significant historical thinker of the German High Middle Ages. In his *Chronicle or History of the Two Cities* Otto had expounded an Old Testament prophecy of Daniel (2:31–45), which he believed had been fulfilled.[61] In Daniel's account of a dream of the Babylonian king Nebuchadnezzar, the king saw a large statue made of several different materials arranged in descending order of value and durability: 'The head of the statue was of pure gold, its chest and arms were of silver, its belly and hips of bronze, its legs of iron, and its feet partly of iron and partly of terra cotta'.[62] The peculiar mixture of material at the feet, its weak spot, allowed the statue to be struck and destroyed at this point. Its feet were crushed by a stone that had been cut 'without a hand being put to

---

[57] DVC-X, Preface to Book IV, Clm 148, fo. 84^r: 'Vidimus hactenus Dei ecclesiam humilem, abiectam, vilem, solo profanorum principum nutu iactari et (ut ego nunc exponam) teterrima servitute demersam, quam eandem paulo post non sine manifesto divinitatis auxilio orbis terrarum principem et omnium qui ei aliquando dominati sunt dominam aspiciemus.'

[58] Ibid.

[59] Ibid.: 'atque in eam postremo gradatim amplitudinem crescere, ut magnitudine iam immensa laborans mole sua nunc ruere videatur.'

[60] Ibid., fo. 84^v: 'eosque tanquam vilia mancipia tractaret'.

[61] Ibid., fos 84^v–85^r ('qui Romanum imperium…tenebris haec etas comparatur'); Otto of Freising, *Chronica sive Historia de duabus civitatibus*, 2nd edn, ed. A. Hofmeister (Hannover; Leipzig, 1912), VI.36, pp. 305–6. Edition owned by Panvinio: Otto of Freising, *Rerum ab origine mundi ad ipsius usque tempora gestarum libri octo*; Otto and Rahewin of Freising, *De gestis Friderici*, ed. Johannes Cuspinianus (Strasbourg, 1515), fos 73^v–74^r; see ILS, fos 25^r, 26^v. See also H.-W. Goetz, *Das Geschichtsbild Ottos von Freising* (Cologne; Vienna, 1984), 258–64.

[62] For this and the following citations see *The Book of Daniel*, trans. L. F. Hartmann (Garden City, NY, 1978), 136–7.

it'. The statue collapsed and fell into pieces, which became 'fine as the chaff on the threshing floor in the summer'. The destructive stone then grew into an enormous mountain which 'filled all the earth'. Daniel explained that the four materials in the statue represented four kingdoms. The last would be replaced by a kingdom of God. As the fourth kingdom Daniel probably intended Hellenistic Greece; in the Christian tradition, it was usually thought to represent the Roman Empire. The stone was seen, by Hippolytus of Rome and other Christian thinkers, as representing Christ.[63] The interpretation of the statue's destruction presented interpretative difficulties for the Christian exegetes. If the Roman Empire had been destroyed, had the divine kingdom already arrived? Some extended, therefore, the duration of the Roman Empire into their present, pointing out that the Empire had been renewed and continued by the German emperors. The central idea of Otto of Freising's *Chronicle* was that the Holy Roman Empire was a continuation of the Roman Empire.[64] In his interpretation of the Book of Daniel, Otto claimed that the Roman Empire had been destroyed at a precise historical moment: when the Church had struck the emperor with the sword of excommunication. Otto had in mind Gregory VII's ban of Henry IV in 1076, which he thought was unprecedented in history.[65] The Church then grew into the huge 'mountain' before everyone's eyes. For Otto, this did not mean that a blissful divine kingdom had arrived; rather, the reign of the Church led to a gloomy and chaotic period. Otto lamented the devastating consequences of the Church's growth. Among these were numerous calamities and wars; Rome was often besieged, captured, and laid waste; in schisms, popes stood against popes, emperors against emperors. Otto showed himself displeased with having to describe all this. Where Otto wrote 'tedet memorare' ('it is a weariness to record'), Panvinio made an intervention and changed this expression to 'horret animus referre' ('the mind shudders at having to describe it')—thus making it more dramatic.[66]

---

[63] J. C. Collins, *Daniel: A Commentary on the Book of Daniel* (Minneapolis, MN, 1993), 112–13.

[64] W. Goez, *Translatio imperii: ein Beitrag zur Geschichte des Geschichtsdenkens und der politischen Ideen im Mittelalter und in der frühen Neuzeit* (Tübingen, 1958), 111–30.

[65] Otto of Freising, *Chronica*, VI.35, p. 304.

[66] DVC-X, Preface to Book IV, Clm 148, fo. 84^v; Otto of Freising, *Chronica*, VI.36, p. 306. While Panvinio mostly attained to Otto's view, there were, of course, other modes of interpreting Daniel's prophecy in the sixteenth century; see E. Cameron, 'The Bible and the Early Modern Sense of History', in id. (ed.), *The New Cambridge History of the Bible*, iii (Cambridge, 2016), 657–85.

Having stealthily assimilated this entire train of thought from Otto, Panvinio also added some of his own thoughts. For him, the origin of, and reason for, such great misery was the eleventh mode of election of the popes. Emperor Henry III (1017–56) had assumed too many powers for himself, which gave the Church occasion to set itself free—causing the succeeding mayhem of disturbances and wars.[67] Where Otto spoke of Henry IV's unprecedented excommunication, Panvinio inserted a remark of his own, stating that the pope 'despoiled the emperor of his greatest and most important powers of jurisdiction, which he often abused'.[68] Thus, Panvinio did concede that the Church, to some degree, had good reasons to rebel against imperial domination. To explicate these events, Panvinio, from Book IV onwards, had to change his way of writing. He now had to explain not only the modes of election but also, in a detailed way, the biographies and deeds of the popes. Only in this way, he wrote, could the changes in the modes be understood.[69]

As in the case of the *Pactum Hludowicinianum*, Panvinio was again misled when discussing Pope Nicholas II's decree on papal elections of 1059. This decree provided precise instructions for the order of a canonical election of the pope; in addition, it restricted the right of election to cardinals— a fundamental feature that is still in existence today. There were two versions of this decree in circulation, which differed in how they described the emperor's role in the election. Panvinio was the first scholar to recognize the differences between the 'papal' and the 'imperial' versions of this decree and to discuss them critically. He concluded that the 'imperial' version, which gave a leading role to the emperor, must have been authentic (though in the nineteenth century it was proved to be a forgery). Panvinio's main reason for this conclusion was that he thought that the 'imperial' version aligned with historical practice at the time. (For a longer discussion of the election decree see my Appendix.)[70]

In Book IV, Panvinio also included a life of Pope Gregory VII (r. 1073–85) which was critical of Gregory's actions towards the Empire—another strong reason for him to not publish his work. Gregory VII's importance was clear: Gregory, who had been chief policy advisor to Nicholas II and Alexander II

---

[67] DVC-X, Preface to Book IV, Clm 148, fo. 85ʳ. This preface had previously been the preface to Book III in DVC-III.

[68] Otto of Freising, *Chronica*, VI.36, p. 305; Panvinio, DVC-X, Preface to Book IV, Clm 148, fo. 84ᵛ: 'gladio anathematis potentissime feriit *et maximis insignibusque iurisdictionibus, quibus plerumque abutebatur, spoliavit.*' (Panvinio's addition is set in italics.)

[69] DVC-X, Preface to Book IV, fo. 85ʳ⁻ᵛ.   [70] See below, 213–220.

before becoming pope, set out on a programme to exalt the power of the papacy over temporal rulers. This began after his own election, when he broke with tradition by not asking for the approval of King Henry IV. Along with a programme to eradicate moral abuses within the Church, Gregory aimed to abolish royal control of bishops. This led to the well-known dramatic conflict with the Empire, in the course of which Henry IV was twice excommunicated and an antipope, Clement III, was created.

Panvinio's extensive life of Gregory began conventionally enough. This pope was a 'most memorable man' and 'very necessary' to the Roman Church; for the liberty of the Church, he had done many things against the emperor which were worthy of memory.[71] Treating the early life of Gregory, however, Panvinio showed himself a sceptic. He recounted two omens which foretold of the young boy's future greatness. As some purported that he was the son of carpenter, an omen was connected to his family background. The little child had played with shavings of wood on the ground and formed with them the words 'dominabor a mari usque ad mare' ('I will have dominion from sea to sea', Psalm 72:8), projecting his future rule over the universal Church. A learned man who saw this convinced his father to let him have an education. Panvinio commented that he did not know which 'story-teller' (*fabulator*) had invented this clumsy tale.[72] In the course of his education, the young man Hildebrand arrived at the imperial chancery, where—this is the second omen—the emperor Henry III received a warning in a dream. He saw Hildebrand with horns with which he crushed his son, Henry IV. He therefore had Hildebrand thrown into jail, from which the empress Agnes freed him and let him move on to a Cluniac monastery. Panvinio concluded that the inventor of these stories was 'a very fickle man who should be laughed at'.[73]

One can suspect that Panvinio rejected these stories not simply because they patently belonged to the realm of legends; had they served his purpose,

---

[71] DVC-X, Book IV, *Gregorii Papae VII electio*, Clm 148, fos 111ʳ–134ʳ, at fo. 111ʳ, published in J. Gretser, *Apologia pro Gregorio VII*, in his *Controversiarum Roberti Bellarmini Sanctae Romanae Ecclesiae Cardinalis amplissimi defensio*, 2 vols (Ingolstadt, 1607–9), ii, separate numbering, cols [235]–273, at col. [235]: 'vir maxime memorabilis et Romanae ecclesiae pernecessarius'; 'tot tantaque memoratu digna contra Imperatorem Henricum IV pro libertate ecclesiae gesserit'.

[72] DVC-X, Book IV, *Gregorii Papae VII electio*, Clm 148, fo. 111ᵛ, ed. Gretser, cols [235]–[236]: 'comminiscitur nescio quis fabulator inconcinnas fabellas'.

[73] Ibid., fo. 111ᵛ/col. 234: 'somnio admonitus imperator de eodem tum scriniario suo quod cornua videretur habere quibus filium eius contereret, hominem in vincula coniecisse; sed ab imperatrice Hagnete vinculis liberatum, Cluniacense monasterium petiisse…Sed ego levissimum hominem ridendum duco.'

he might well have endorsed them. In fact, in other cases he cited stories of such type without qualms—for example, when he recounted the story of the dove which settled on Giovanni Angelo Medici's cell in the Sistine Chapel to foretell his election many days before it occurred. This recalled the election of Fabian (r. 236–50), who was chosen following the same divine sign when a dove settled on his head.[74] Another reason came into play here with regard to Gregory VII. By ridiculing certain stories about Gregory, Panvinio elegantly and ironically cast a shadow of doubt over his career and his claim to temporal dominion. This attitude became more explicit as the *Vita* continued. Regarding Hildebrand's election as pope, Panvinio insistently made it clear that the election took place without the emperor's consent. Not only did Panvinio state this once, he repeated it half a dozen times over the course of a few pages. It is worth citing these passages because they make clear how heavy-handedly Panvinio drove home this point. Gregory VII was elected 'without the consent of the emperor'; 'without consulting the emperor'; 'against the customary practice of those times, without consulting the emperor and awaiting his authority and that of the German bishops and princes'; 'without the consent of the emperor and the German princes, against customary practice'; 'against customary practice and the privileges of his ancestors granted to the emperors by the Apostolic See'; 'contrary to the customary practices of the ancestors, the king not even having been consulted'.[75]

In addition, Panvinio maintained, using a passage from the *Annals* of Lampert of Hersfeld (d. after 1081), that after his election Gregory was eager to receive the Henry IV's consent and refused to be consecrated before he obtained it. Gregory feared the king's wrath and justified himself by explaining that he had not been able to withstand the raving Romans who had chosen him against his own will.[76] Henry IV granted his approval, although many of the German prelates, bishops, and abbots had expressed their

---

[74] Panvinio, *Creatio Pii IV*, 585. Panvinio's description of the election of Fabian in DVC-X, Book II, Clm 147, fo. 251ʳ, was taken from Eusebius, *Ecclesiastical History*, VI.29. See also Tallon, 'Les conclaves', 42.

[75] DVC-X, Book IV, *Gregorii Papae VII electio*, ed. Gretser, cols 241, [242] (twice), 244, 245, 247.

[76] Ibid., cols 246–7: 'quia populi furentis voluntati resistere non potuisset'; 'se, Deo teste, honoris huius apicem nunquam per ambitionem affectasse, sed electum se a Romanis et violenter sibi impositam fuisse ecclesiastici regiminis necessitatem'. The second passage was taken from Lampert of Hersfeld, *Annales*, in his *Opera*, ed. O. Holder-Egger (Hannover; Leipzig, 1894), 3–304, at p. 145; trans. I. S. Robinson, *The Annals of Lampert of Hersfeld* (Manchester, 2015), 170. For the traditional *topos* of popes being elected against their own will see A. T. Hack, 'Papst wider Willen: zur Geschichte eines Motivs', *QFIAB*, 96 (2016), 3–34, esp. pp. 25–9 (on Gregory VII).

grave doubts to him, as, from Hildebrand's previous diplomatic missions to the imperial court, they were only too familiar with his 'character, accomplishments, unfailing constancy, most fervent zeal for the honour of God, and tenacious sense of purpose'.[77] When the emperor's consent arrived, Gregory VII finally felt legitimate. He then started showing his real face. Not long after his consecration, Gregory (Fig. 3.2) began to execute what he had been planning for a long time. Not only did he aim to exclude the emperor from papal elections, he also tried to deprive him of any authority in choosing prelates, bishops, and abbots.[78] Therefore, in 1074 Gregory began laying the foundations for 'recovering the liberty of the Church' ('principia recuperandae ecclesiasticae libertatis iecit') and issued the principles for this programme in his *Dictatus papae*.

What followed was a description of the Investiture Controversy with an historical *excursus* on certain privileges which the emperor, in Panvinio's view, had received from the popes, and which enabled them to play an important role in papal elections. At this point, Panvinio reached back into history and summarized the development of imperial intervention into papal election from the Carolingians onwards, repeating many details from Book III, where he had dealt with this period. He did this to show why Gregory VII's actions were so unusual in comparison with what Panvinio thought were long-established privileges of the emperors. Panvinio assumed that Hadrian I, at a synod in the Lateran in 785, had given over to Charlemagne the rights to both elect the popes and invest bishops. The reports about this synod were actually false; they were an invention from the late eleventh century. Panvinio took this information from Gratian's *Decretum*.[79] Gratian had also included a false decree by Leo VIII, assigned by Panvinio to the year 962, in which the pope, at a Lateran synod, renewed and confirmed Hadrian's decree.[80] Although this decree, too, is now

---

[77] DVC-X, Book IV, *Gregorii Papae VII electio*, col. 246: 'mores, res gestas, inflexibilem constantiam, ferventissimum divini honoris zelum, et tenacem propositi sui voluntatem'. For the 'zelus ferventissimus' see Lampert of Hersfeld, *Annales*, ed. Holger-Egger, 288.

[78] DVC-X, Book IV, *Gregorii Papae VII electio*, col. 248.

[79] Ibid., col. 254. Panvinio copied the description of the synod, with some variation, from Gratian, *Decretum*, D. 63 c. 22, ed. E. Friedberg, in *Corpus iuris canonici*, 2nd edn, 2 vols (Leipzig, 1879), i, col. 241. It was also contained in Sigebert of Gembloux, *Chronica cum continuationibus*, ed. L. C. Bethmann, in *Monumenta Germaniae Historica*, Scriptores, vi (Hannover, 1844), 300–474, at p. 393 (in the addition 'Auctarium Aquicinense'), where it was dated to AD 773. Panvinio owned the first edition of Sigebert's *Chronicon*; see below, 203.

[80] Panvinio, *Gregorii Papae VII electio*, col. 255; Gratian, *Decretum*, D. 63 c. 22 (ed. Friedberg, col. 241). On the false privileges by Hadrian I and Leo VIII see also C. Märtl (ed.), *Die falschen Investiturprivilegien* (Hannover, 1986).

Fig. 3.2 Gregory VII. From Panvinio, *Pontificum Romanorum imagines*, vol. ii. Courtesy of the Bayerische Staatsbibliothek, Munich (Clm 156, fo. 66^r).

considered false, it reflected the historical fact that Emperor Otto I had gained near total control over papal elections. In fact, in Book III, Panvinio included an authentic source by a contemporary (Liutprand of Cremona, d. c.972) documenting that the Romans gave an oath to Otto in 963, promising they would never again elect a pope without the emperors' consent.[81] Such control was achieved again under Henry III and was one of the reasons why Gregory VII reacted against imperial power.[82]

Gregory VII became most explicitly hostile in the Lateran synod of 1080, during which 'openly spewed out what he had long designed and what he had gradually indicated in other decrees'. On this occasion, he promulgated a decree by which he sought to strip the emperor not only of his right to elect the popes, which had been granted to his predecessors 300 years earlier, but also of the right to invest any other prelates—a reference to what Panvinio thought was an authentic privilege that Hadrian I had given to Charlemagne.[83]

These examples may make it seem as though Panvinio plainly stood on the emperor's side in his treatment of the Church-State conflict. Many of his arguments certainly offended Roman censors, as we will see below in Chapter 4. Panvinio's course can best be described as idiosyncratic. He praised Gregory for many of his qualities at both the beginning and the end of his treatment of him. At the beginning, Panvinio labelled him as a 'most memorable man who was very necessary to the Roman Church', as we have seen above.[84] At the end of the treatment, Panvinio praised him twice. He was 'venerable, very prudent, Catholic, worthy of being loved by God, a steady hammer of the heretics, a very clever rescuer and defender of the

[81] DVC-X, Book III, Clm 148, fo. 62ʳ; Liutprand of Cremona, *Historia Ottonis*, in id., *Opera*, 3rd edn, ed. J. Becker (Hannover, 1915), 159–75, at p. 164. Panvinio owned a printed edition (see ILS, fo. 29ʳ): Liutprand of Cremona, *Rerum ab Europae imperatoribus ac regibus gestarum libri VI*, in Widukind of Corvey, *Rerum ab Henrico et Ottone I imperatoribus gestarum libri III…*, ed. Martin Frecht (Basel, 1532), 219–314; see here p. 308. On the oath see also H. Zimmermann, 'Parteiungen und Papstwahlen in Rom zur Zeit Kaisers Ottos des Großen', in id. (ed.), *Otto der Große* (Darmstadt, 1976), 325–414, at pp. 334–8. For other sources regarding Otto I and papal elections see Ebers, *Der Papst*, i. 32–6.

[82] See above, 109.

[83] *Gregorii Papae VII electio*, cols 260–1: 'quod diu ante agitaverat aliquotque decretis ante sensim praenotaverat, tunc primum aperte evomuit. Constitutionem illam enim tunc primum edidit, qua imperatorem non solum auctoritate instituendi Romanum pontificem, quam trecentis prope annis ante praedecessores sui habuerant, sed et omnibus etiam caeterorum sacerdotiorum investituris privare conatus est, omnemque episcoporum et abbatum instituendorum rationem ad electionis capitulorum et monachorum formam reduxit'. On the Lent synod of 1080 see H. E. J. Cowdrey, *Pope Gregory VII, 1073–1085* (Oxford, 1998), 194–9, 548–9.

[84] See above, 110.

rights of the Church, and worthy of perpetual memory'.[85] He also had 'particular zeal and authority' and was

> a very constant man, tenacious in his right pursuits, one who never— neither because of threats nor because of requests—strayed a finger's breadth, as they say, from the right path. He was a man of the ancient stamp and should be compared to those early popes who endured various forms of torture for Christ; he was bold, prudent, cautious, and the greatest restorer of the liberty of the Church.[86]

Of course, such praise could hide some criticism. For example, when Francesco Guicciardini (1483–1540) summed up Pope Alexander VI's character, he stated that Alexander's virtues included 'singular cleverness and sagacity, excellent judgement, a marvellous efficacy in persuading, and an incredible dexterity and attentiveness in dealing with weighty matters'.[87] Although both Guicciardini and Panvinio underlined a heightened cleverness (*solertia*), Panvinio took a different approach, focusing more on obstinacy. He may have praised Gregory's tenaciousness to make it clear that he was, in fact, a hard-headed fanatic. While he had shown that Gregory was 'tenacious', 'bold', and incorruptible, he had much less convincingly illustrated that Gregory was 'prudent' and 'cautious'. Since there is no conclusive proof of Panvinio's intentions, we should take the praise at face-value and conclude that Panvinio aimed to furnish a comprehensive picture of this pope. He did not include Gregory's defects when he described his character; but they were included in the account of his actions, where Panvinio revealed that he disapproved of Gregory's over-ambitious attempts to secure temporal authority and power for the Church.

---

[85] *Gregorii Papae VII electio*, col. 270: 'vir vita venerabilis, prudentissimus, catholicus, Deo amabilis, haereticorum malleus indefessus, ecclesiastici iuris redemptor ac conservator solertissimus perpetuaque memoria dignus'.

[86] Ibid., col. 271: 'Fuit enim hic pontifex vir constantissimus, recti proposti tenax, et qui a recta via nec minis, nec precibus unquam ne latum quidem, ut dicitur, unguem discessit. Homo antiqui exempli, et priscis illis Romanis pontificibus, qui diversa pro Christo cruciatuum genera pertulere, comparandus, audax, prudens, cautus et maximus ecclesiasticae libertatis assertor'. For the citation 'precipui zeli ac auctoritatis erat' see ibid. and Otto of Freising, *Chronica*, VI.36, p. 306.

[87] F. Guicciardini, *La historia di Italia* (Florence, 1561), 3; translation adapted from id., *The History of Italy*, trans. S. Alexander (New York, 1969), 10. For Alexander's vices see below, 126; for a summary of his pontificate: V. Reinhardt, *Pontifex: die Geschichte der Päpste von Petrus bis Franziskus* (Munich, 2017), 492–502.

Panvinio's account of Gregory VII's papacy ended with a discussion of the historical sources. The pamphlets of Cardinal Beno (d. 1100) against Gregory contained accusations which Panvinio branded 'partly false, partly ridiculous, and of no importance'.[88] He then listed the sources that he considered more useful. Among German authors, these were Paul of Bernried (d. c.1146), Gerhoch of Reichersberg (d. 1169), Lampert of Hersfeld (d. after 1081), and 'Konrad of Lichtenau, Abbot of Ursberg'.[89] Among the Italians, Panvinio cited Leo Marsicanus with his Montecassino Chronicle (d. 1115/17).[90] Panvinio ended his review of sources with St Anselm of Lucca (d. 1086), whom he recommended highly both as a writer and as a person. He included praise for Gregory VII from Anselm's Liber contra Wibertum (Against Wibert), in which Anselm compared Gregory to Pope Cornelius (r. 251–3) by quoting Cyprian's description of this early pope. As it turns out, Panvinio had not looked up Anselm's Liber; without saying so, he had instead taken the passage—including the praise for Anselm and Anselm's praise for Gregory—from the Chronicle of the 'Abbot of Ursberg'.[91]

Of the six source authors whom Panvinio named and presented as useful, both German and Italian, five clearly supported Gregory VII's reform ideas. The Chronicle of the 'Abbot of Ursberg' was a more difficult case because it had been composed by several authors. In the sixteenth century, it was believed to be a work of Konrad of Lichtenau. Later it was regarded as wholly a work of Burchard, provost of Ursberg (d. after 1230), until nineteenth-century scholars recognized that Burchard had included the previous chronicles of Frutolf of Michelsberg (d. 1103) and Ekkehard of Aura (d. after 1125). For the period concerning Gregory VII, this source was

---

[88] Gregorii Papae VII electio, col. 272. Panvinio owned Beno's pamphlets (Vita et gesta Hildebrandi) as published in Ortwin Gratius (ed.), Fasciculus rerum expetendarum et fugiendarum (Cologne, 1535), fos 39ᵛ–43ᵛ (see ILS, fo. 21ᵛ). Sources critical of Gregory were also reviewed, for example, by Robert Bellarmine; see his Disputationes de controversiis Christianae fidei, i, 3rd gen. controversy, IV.13, cols 1026–33.

[89] Gregorii Papae VII electio, col. 272. Paul of Bernried's Vita Gregorii VII and parts of Gerhoch's works were published for the first time by Jakob Gretser in 1610–11. Panvinio possessed a printed copy of Lampert's Annales—that is, Germanorum res praeclare olim gestae, ed. Ludwig Schradin, with a foreword by Philipp Melanchthon (Tübingen, 1533). See ILS, fo. 23ᵛ. On the 'Abbot of Ursberg' see below, n. 91.

[90] For Panvinio's own printed edition see below, 215–216.

[91] Gregorii Papae VII electio, cols 272–3; Chronicle of the 'Abbot of Ursberg', i.e., Frutolf of Michelsberg, in Frutolfi et Ekkehardi Chronica, ed. F.-J. Schmale and I. Schmale-Otte (Darmstadt, 1972), ad AD 1080, p. 92. Panvinio's printed copy of this chronicle was the Chronicum abbatis Urspergensis, with a continuation by an unnamed author (i.e., Kaspar Hedio) for the years 1230–1537/38 and a preface by Philipp Melanchthon (Strasbourg, 1537 or 1540) (see ILS, fo. 20ʳ).

not openly pro-imperial. Frutolf did not polemicize against the papacy's power as such, but he thought that Gregory's methods of implementing church reform were unorthodox. Dealing with the early twelfth century, Ekkehard supported unity with the Apostolic See and hated Henry IV.[92] Burchard denied papal authority over imperial office and made some explicit remarks that denied Gregory VII's power to depose Henry IV; but his part of the Chronicle mainly dealt with later periods up to 1230 (throughout which he showed an antipapal stance).[93] Thus, Panvinio, despite his criticism of Gregory VII, clearly wanted to demonstrate that he had based his work on this pope on pro-papal sources. By not citing sources critical of Gregory, Panvinio implicitly signalled to the reader that the criticism in his text consisted of his own ideas. However, this was not the full truth; Panvinio did incorporate other works critical of Gregory. One example is the German humanist Johannes Aventinus (1477–1534). In his section on Gregory VII, Aventinus heavily criticized Gregory for having occupied St Peter's throne against the emperor's wish and for laying the foundations of the papal empire. Panvinio paraphrased Aventinus without naming him as a source. He did so, poignantly, just before he embarked on his list of pro-papal sources.[94]

Licet de vitanda (Books V–VII)

Book V (still formerly Book III) began with Honorius II (r. 1124–30). It included mode 17 and Alexander III's schism. Then, in describing the decree *Licet de vitanda* of 1179 and the ensuing 18th mode, the book moved into new territory. This 18th mode was the last one for Panvinio. In the preface, Panvinio said that after describing so many schisms and so much turmoil in

---

[92] Schmale and Schmale-Ott, 'Einleitung', in *Frutolfi et Ekkehardi Chronica*, ed. iid., 1–45, esp. pp. 14, 30; T. J. H. McCarthy, 'Introduction', in id. (ed.), *Chronicles of the Investiture Contest: Frutolf of Michelsberg and his Continuators* (Manchester, 2014), 1–83, at pp. 38–41, 69–74.

[93] *Chronicum abbatis Urspergensis* (1537), 286–7; Burchard of Ursberg, *Chronicon*, 2nd edn, ed. O. Holder-Egger and B. von Simson (Hannover; Leipzig, 1916), 6–7. See also C. L. Neel, 'The Historical Work of Burchard of Ursberg, V: The Historian, the Emperor and the Pope', *Analecta Praemonstratensia*, 60 (1984), 224–55, at pp. 224–7. 'Abbas Urspergensis' was also included among Flacius's 'witnesses to the truth' in his *Catalogus testium veritatis* (1556), 858–62.

[94] *Gregorii Papae VII electio*, cols 271–2. 'Primus omnium…ausus est' was paraphrased from J. Aventinus; see his *Annales ducum Boiariae*, ed. S. Riezler, 2 vols (Munich, 1882–4), ii. 111–12. See also E. Schirmer, *Die Persönlichkeit Kaiser Heinrichs IV. im Urteil der deutschen Geschichtschreibung* (Jena, 1931), 26–30.

Book IV, he had hoped to deal with a quieter and more peaceful period which should have followed the Concordat of Worms. But this was not possible because the Church, although freed from external fear, was now riven by internal fighting and sedition occasioned by papal elections.[95] When the emperor's intervention was excluded from papal elections, the principal role in the elections fell to the clergy and the people of Rome—that is, to a crude, frantic, and mad crowd ('incondita, furiosa et insana multitudo').[96] No laws reined in and prevented electoral quarrels. The immoderate ambition of certain men ('immodica hominum ambitio') could proliferate, and two or three times within a few years, two popes were proclaimed in schism. This continued until Alexander III (r. 1159–81) created the excellent law ('optime providit') that elections were limited to the cardinals and were valid only when two-thirds of the cardinals had agreed that a candidate should become pope. Therefore, in Book V Panvinio described how the elections were first limited to people and clergy, then to the clergy, and eventually to the cardinals.

In this book, for the first section on Honorius II, Panvinio availed himself (as he himself noted) of sources such as Pandulphus Pisanus, Ptolemy of Lucca, and Martin of Troppau.[97] The 17th mode began for Panvinio with the election of Celestine II (1143); according to Panvinio, this mode was characterized by the exclusion of the Roman people from voting.[98] This was also explained in Panvinio's annotation to Platina's life of Innocent II (1562), where he named his sources: an anonymous book in the Vatican Library and Otto of Freising (both his Chronicle and his *Deeds of Frederick Barbarossa*).[99] It is thought today that such neat distinctions cannot actually be made for the development of papal elections in the twelfth century. After the influence of the Roman nobility had been averted in the election of Celestine II, in the following elections the Roman nobles—notably, the Frangipane—exerted a great influence again. This led to schisms. Panvinio described these schisms and, again, he noted his sources. For the description

---

[95] DVC-X, Clm 148, Preface to Book V, fo. 197[r–v].

[96] The folly ('insania') and rage ('furor') of the Romans were also mentioned by Otto of Freising (*Chronica*, VII.31, pp. 358–60), who described the revolt of the Romans against the pope in AD 1143–5 during the creation of the Commune.

[97] See Panvinio's remark in DVC-X, Book V, Clm 148, fo. 203[r]. Panvinio owned the first edition of Martin of Troppau's *Chronicle*—that is: Marianus Scotus, *Chronica*; Martinus Polonus, *Historia* (Basel, 1559). See ILS, fo. 24[r].

[98] DVC-X, Book V, Clm 148, fo. 220[v].

[99] Platina, *Historia de vitis pontificum* (1562), fo. 148[v]; (1568), 195. See also Otto of Freising, *Chronica*, VII.27, pp. 352–3; Otto and Rahewin of Freising, *Gesta Friderici I imperatoris*, 3rd edn, ed. G. Waitz and B. von Simson (Hannover; Leipzig, 1912), II.28, p. 134.

of the schism between Alexander III and Victor IV, he relied principally
on the contemporary author Rahewin and his continuation of Otto of
Freising's *Deeds of Frederick Barbarossa*, from which Panvinio copied a
large portion.[100]

During that century, it gradually became usual practice for the cardinals
to play the decisive role in the papal elections. Panvinio recognized the fundamental significance of Alexander III's decree *Licet de vitanda*, which fixed
this practice into normative writing. Mode 18 was the electoral principle
introduced by Alexander and the Third Lateran Council (1179).[101] The
decree had two key points. First, it required an election by cardinals only.
Second, a majority of two-thirds was necessary to elect a pope. Mode 18
remained in use until Panvinio's own time. He acknowledged some variations:
if the two-thirds majority could not be achieved by the formal casting of
votes, it could be reached by the procedures of compromise, *accessus*, or
adoration. Panvinio did not regard these procedures as separate electoral
modes.[102]

The remaining books (VI–X) dealt with particular elections and included
copies of particular bulls concerning elections. What was new in the
ten-book version, therefore, began in Book VI, which ran from Lucius III
(r. 1181–5) to Benedict XI (1303–4), after whose death the papacy was transferred to France. In the preface to this book, Panvinio explained that while
in the previous two books (that is, Books IV–V) he had described discord
and sedition, he had now landed on a more peaceful shore.[103] Panvinio
apologized to his 'pious and Christian readers' for having caused them
annoyance ('molestia'). He felt as if a great burden, which had caused him

[100] DVC-X, Book V, Clm 148, fos 239ʳ, 249ᵛ–277ʳ; Otto and Rahewin, *Gesta Friderici*, IV.60–84, pp. 297–341, regarding the years 1159–60.
[101] DVC-X, Book V, Clm 148, fos 291ᵛ–292ʳ. For *Licet de vitanda* see also *Conciliorum oecumenicorum generaliumque decreta: editio critica* (Turnhout, 2006–), ii.1, pp. 127–8. On Panvinio's copy of this decree see J. B. Sägmüller, *Die Thätigkeit und Stellung der Cardinäle bis Papst Bonifaz VIII.* (Freiburg im Breisgau, 1896), 140.
[102] Panvinio, 'Ratio creandi Romani pontificis' (annotation to Clement V), in Platina, *Historia de vitis pontificum* (1562), fos 191ᵛ–192ʳ (*accessus*, adoration); DVC-X, Book V, Clm 148, fo. 295ᵛ (compromise). For these procedures see Wassilowsky, *Konklavereform*, 41–133; for the medieval procedures of *scrutinium* and inspiration: P. Herde, 'Die Entwicklung der Papstwahl im dreizehnten Jahrhundert: Praxis und kanonistische Grundlagen', *Österreichisches Archiv für Kirchenrecht*, 32 (1981), 11–41.
[103] DVC-X, Preface to Book VI, Clm 149, fo. 1ʳ⁻ᵛ, at fo. 1ʳ: 'Tandem aliquando ex civilium et parricidialium armorum procellis exitiabiliumque dissentionum fluctibus emersum longe placidissimum deinceps aequoris tranquilli littus me excipiet.' See also Vat. lat. 6107.ii (this MS contains a full version of Book VI), fo. 258ʳ⁻ᵛ; and, for the new material, Table 3.1.

pain and troubles, had now been lifted from him.[104] The Apostolic See had freed itself from potent enemies such as Henry IV, Henry V, and Frederick Barbarossa and had become a ruler (*domina*) itself. By and large, this allowed it to look peacefully after its own affairs (although it was still harassed by certain emperors through wars and sedition). Therefore, from this point onwards, Panvinio changed his way of writing. Because the way of election always remained uniformly the 18th mode, he could concentrate on what had happened during the elections. He gave the biographical details no wider space, as these did not elucidate events which occurred at the elections. As the source material on many of these elections was scarce and they were, to his knowledge, not described by contemporary writers, Panvinio intended to make them clearer by inserting letters which popes had sent out to explain their elections. He was to both write his own prose and to include long passages extracted from other writers. Panvinio now also included sources in the Italian vernacular; an example of this is the section on the abdication of Celestine V and a section on Boniface VIII taken from the *Florentine Chronicle* of Giovanni Villani (d. 1348).[105] For Boniface VIII, Panvinio also included a fragmentary Chronicle of Orvieto (which he copied from a continuation of Martin of Troppau's Chronicle).[106] Likely, he received this manuscript from Monaldo Monaldeschi (d. 1589), a member of Alessandro Farnese's entourage, canon of St Peter's, and chronicler of Viterbo, with whom Panvinio was in close contact. (Panvinio dedicated his work *De ritu sepeliendi mortuos* to Monaldeschi in 1568.)[107]

This book thematically fit with Panvinio's summary of the reasons for the creation of the conclave, which he had published in a note to the life of Gregory X (r. 1271–6) in his edition of Platina. Panvinio dealt here with Gregory's bull *Ubi periculum* (1274), which established how conclaves

---

[104] DVC-X, Preface to Bk VI, Clm 149, fo. 1ʳ: 'Ita ut si pio et Christiano lectori superioribus enarrandis molestiae aliquid, imo plurimum attuli in tantorum compensationem malorum, sequentia laetiora accipiat. Nam etiam me ipsum grandi hercle onere levatum sentio, quum his exarandis multum doloris et molestiae subierim.' For what follows see ibid., fo. 1ʳ⁻ᵛ.

[105] Abdication of Celestine V: DVC-X, Book VI, Clm 149, fos 131ʳ–132ᵛ. See Panvinio's printed copy (ILS, fo. 23ʳ) of Giovanni Villani's chronicle, *La prima [– seconda] parte delle historie universali de' suoi tempi*, 2 vols (Venice, 1559), i. 259–60. For the death of Boniface VIII see ibid. 298–302; Clm 149, fos 145ᵛ–150ʳ.

[106] *Ex chronicis Urbevetanis ab eo, qui hoc tempore vixit, scriptis*, DVC-X, Book VI, Clm 149, fos 150ᵛ–155ᵛ; L. Fumi and A. Cerlini, 'Una continuazione orvietana della Cronaca di Martino Polono', *Archivio Muratoriano*, 14 (1914), 97–139. Fumi and Cerlini published the text from the MS in Perugia (Biblioteca comunale Augusta, 2895) which was probably used by Panvinio. They included variants from Panvinio's copy in their apparatus.

[107] Fumi and Cerlini, 'Una continuazione orvietana', 105; Panvinio, *De ritu sepeliendi mortuos* (1568), 3.

should be efficiently organized and carried out. Its key point was the isolation of cardinals (*conclave* in Latin means 'a room that can be locked with a key'). Their confinement, it was hoped, would ensure speedy elections for the future. With this bull, Gregory reacted in particular to his own election at Viterbo, which had been completed after almost three painful years of wrangling, with many cardinals habitually absent.[108]

Book VII reached from Clement V (r. 1305–14) to the election of Clement (VIII) (r. 1423–9), a late antipope in the Avignon line. The prodigious election of Clement V gave rise to numerous novelties and mutations in the Roman Church whose repercussions were felt throughout Christianity. Panvinio said that it was by divine providence that the Apostolic See was nearly destroyed, crushed by its old and perpetual enemy ('antiqui perpetuique hostis machinis quassata'). It was restored and reformed with divine help only when all hope had nearly vanished.[109] Important sources for this book were Giovanni Villani and, for the time from the beginning of the Great Western Schism in 1378 onwards, Dietrich of Niem's *De scismate* (On the Schism).[110]

The Great Schism (Book VIII)

Book VIII went a step backwards and began with the situation after the death of Gregory XI (1378), the pope who had returned to Rome from Avignon. This book included the election of his successor, Urban VI (r. 1378–89), as well as those of the other popes chosen after the return of the papacy to Rome until Nicholas V (r. 1447–55). Therefore, this book comprised two schisms: the beginning of the Great Schism and the schism of the Council of Basel, which ended under Nicholas V, when Antipope Felix V abdicated (1449). A new element from Book VIII onwards was that

---

[108] Panvinio, 'Ratio cur conclavis usus in creatione Romani pontificis inventus fuerit', in Platina, *Historia de vitis pontificum* (1562), fos 176ʳ–177ᵛ; DVC-X, Book VI, Clm 149, fos 68ᵛ–69ᵛ (Gregory X's election), 82ᵛ–85ʳ (conclave bull). Panvinio could have copied *Ubi periculum* from the *Liber sextus decretalium*, of which he owned a quarto edition (with *Clementinae* and *Extravagantes*; ILS, fo. 27ʳ). For a critical edition of the bull see *Conciliorum oecumenicorum generaliumque decreta*, ii.1, pp. 326–34. See also Herde, 'Entwicklung', 18–22; Paravicini Bagliani, *Morte*, 34–9.

[109] DVC-X, Preface to Book VII, Clm 149, fo. 159ʳ. See also Vat. lat. 6107.iii (containing a full version of Book VII), fo. 391ʳ.

[110] Dietrich of Niem (d. 1418), *De schismate...libri III* (Nuremberg, 1536); id., *De scismate libri III*, ed. G. Erler (Leipzig, 1890). For Panvinio's ownership of a folio edition of Dietrich of Niem see ILS, fo. 27ᵛ.

Panvinio claimed to have included conclave reports only from authors who had been eyewitnesses (whereas, for the previous sections, he himself had assimilated the material from 'old authors'). Panvinio himself would therefore write even less, letting the other authors speak directly, and wherever possible he included material from two or more authors who had simultaneously described the same election.[111]

A case in point is the election of Urban VI (1378), which was, in fact, the best-documented election of any pope in the Middle Ages.[112] His election in April 1378 was not at first controversial, but became so when Antipope Clement VII was elected in September 1378 and the Great Western Schism broke out. Panvinio presented an important array of diverse sources concerning the election of Urban. They included the treatise on the Great Schism by Dietrich of Niem, an employee at Urban's Roman Curia (d. 1418);[113] the chronicle of emperors and popes by Petrus de Herenthals (d. 1391), a prior at the Premonstratensian abbey of Floreffe who was convinced of the validity of Urban's election;[114] and a deposition of Italian cardinals which was later used against Urban VI.[115] Two points are interesting to note here. The first is the order in which Panvinio presented his material. He began with an orthodox source and ended with a source which cast some doubt on the canonical validity of Urban's election. The order demonstrates that he may have intended to give more weight to the orthodox views. The second point is that Panvinio offered a range of historical documentation, both

---

[111] DVC-X, Preface to Book VIII, Clm 150, fo. 1ʳ.

[112] The sources used by Panvinio regarding Urban's election—mentioned below—are noted in Panvinio's library catalogue (ILS, fo. 8ᵛ) and in M. Souchon, *Die Papstwahlen in der Zeit des großen Schismas*, 2 vols (Braunschweig, 1898–9), i. 21 n. 2. Contents of the rest of Book VIII are listed in ILS, fo. 13ʳ (this leaf is currently misbound and belongs after 8ᵛ). On other eyewitness reports of Urban's election see A. Rehberg, 'Ein "Gegenpapst" wird kreiert: Fakten und Fiktionen in den Zeugenaussagen zur umstrittenen Wahl Urbans VI. (1378)', in H. Müller and B. Hotz (eds), *Gegenpäpste: ein unerwünschtes mittelalterliches Phänomen* (Vienna, 2012), 231–59.

[113] *Urbani Papae VI creatio* (added in the margin in Panvinio's hand: 'ex Theoderico a Niem libro I de schismate pro Urbano VI'), DVC-X, Book VIII, Clm 150, fos 15ᵛ–19ʳ. See Dietrich of Niem, *De scismate*, ed. Erler, I.1–3, pp. 7–16.

[114] *Schismatis descriptio inter Urbanum Papam VI et Clementem VII Antipapam* (added in the margin in Panvinio's hand: 'ex vetusto libro vitarum pontificum Petri Leodiensis, qui hoc tempore vixit, pro Urbano VI'), DVC-X, Book VIII, Clm 150, fos 19ᵛ–36ʳ. See Petrus de Herenthals, *Secunda Vita Clementis VII*, in É. Baluze and G. Mollat (eds), *Vitae paparum Avenionensium*, 4 vols (Paris, 1914–22), i. 519–35.

[115] *Urbani VI Papae creatio* (added in the margin in Panvinio's hand: 'ex informatione habita a iuris consultis Gallis et Hispanis pro Clemente VII contra Urbanum VI'), DVC-X, Book VIII, Clm 150, fos 39ʳ–43ʳ, published in J. J. I. von Döllinger, *Beiträge zur politischen, kirchlichen und Culturgeschichte der sechs letzten Jahrhunderte*, 3 vols (Regensburg; Vienna, 1862–82), iii. 354–9.

favourable and less favourable to Roman orthodoxy, which other historians of his time would have avoided—or included only if such documentation were accompanied by an extensive commentary or narration that disproved the arguments of the polemical document.

This especially regarded the declaration of the cardinals. The version of this declaration that Panvinio presented had been drawn up by Italian cardinals in Tivoli in July 1378. Though relatively neutral, it began casting some doubt on Urban's election.[116] This document contained a question posed to the jurists by the cardinals, namely 'whether his election was canonical' ('utrum istius electio fuerit canonica').[117] In August, French cardinals used this document to draw up a radical new manifesto in which they declared Urban's VI election invalid.[118] Panvinio presented the first version of the document as an interesting historical testimonial, without worrying much about rectifying the doubts regarding Urban's election. Other editors had made sure to state the correct answers. When the jurist Baldo degli Ubaldi (d. 1400) included the same document at the beginning of his legal opinion on the case, he used it as a basis from which to disprove the cardinals' arguments. Bartolomeo Saliceto followed an analogous method in 1378–9.[119] In his continuation of Baronio's *Annales*, Odorico Rinaldi (1595–1671) steered an even clearer course. When he published much of the manifesto of the French cardinals, he first remarked that it was written by 'pseudo-cardinals'. He then frequently interrupted the text to remind the reader that he was being confronted with a text by 'schismatics' ('inquiunt schismatici' etc.).[120] By presenting the document as it was, Panvinio seems to have employed a more 'neutral' technique than other historians.

Panvinio then continued with the next pope of the Roman line, Boniface IX (r. 1389–1404), as he had already treated the popes of the Avignon line in

---

[116] A. M. Voci, 'Giovanni I d'Angiò e l'inizio del grande scisma d'Occidente', *QFIAB*, 75 (1995), 178–255, at pp. 193–9.

[117] *Urbani VI Papae creatio*, DVC-X, Book VIII, Clm 150, fo. 43ʳ; ed. Döllinger, 359.

[118] The redaction of the French cardinals, made in Anagni on 2 August 1378, was published side by side with that of the Italians in M. Dykmans, 'La troisième élection du pape Urbain VI', *Archivum historiae pontificiae*, 15 (1977), 217–64, at pp. 226–39.

[119] Baldo degli Ubaldi, *Quaestio de scismate*, in id., *In sextum Codicis librum Commentaria*, ed. Alessandro Tartagni, Andrea Barbazza, and Filippo Decio (Venice, 1577), fos 117ʳ–121ʳ, at fo. 117ʳ⁻ᵛ; N. Del Re, 'Il "Consilium pro Urbano VI" di Bartolomeo da Saliceto', in *Collectanea Vaticana in honorem... Cardinalis Albareda*, i. 213–63, at pp. 234–40.

[120] Baronio, Rinaldi, Laderchi and Theiner, *Annales*, xxvi, continuation by Rinaldi, ad AD 1378, nos 63–71, pp. 326–30.

Book VII. He again included a contemporary source on the election.[121] Panvinio commended such material to his readers because it contained material about the deeds of many famous men.[122] He especially praised the beauty and dignity of Pius II's descriptions of both Nicholas V's election and his own election, as well as Jacopo Ammannati Piccolomini's account of the election of Paul II.[123] The descriptions of the elections of Hadrian VI and Clement VII by learned contemporaries were also very delightful ('lectu iucundissimae').[124]

In this book, Panvinio incorporated material on the councils of Constance and Basel. The election of Martin V at Constance in 1417 was momentous because it ended the Great Schism. Martin's election violated the electoral decree of 1059, because not only cardinals, but also the five nations present at the council voted in the conclave. It was stipulated that two-thirds of the cardinals and two-thirds of the representatives of each nation had to agree on a new pope. Panvinio did not dwell on the fact that this exception also violated his own statement at the beginning of his *De varia creatione*, in which he assured his readers that, throughout history, the popes themselves had authorized all changes to the modes of papal election. It is worth bearing in mind that the council decreed that it did not wish to change the electoral rules permanently; only 'for this time' should an election be carried out according to the new procedure.[125] Panvinio provided the council's decrees on the electoral procedure as well as a narrative source from a participant.[126]

[121] *Conclave quo Bonifacius IX creatus est*, DVC-X, Book VIII, Clm 150, fo. 46^r–v; published from Panvinio's manuscript by Döllinger, *Beiträge*, iii. 361–2. On this source see also Souchon, *Papstwahlen in der Zeit des großen Schismas*, i. 45.

[122] DVC-X, Preface to Book VIII, Clm 150, fo. 1^v.

[123] On Pius II as historian see S. Bauer, 'Enea Silvio Piccolomini', in G. Galasso et al. (eds), *Il contributo italiano alla storia del pensiero: storia e politica* (Rome, 2013), 137–43; German trans. with illustrations: 'Enea Silvio Piccolomini als Geschichtsschreiber', in M. Dall'Asta (ed.), *Anwälte der Freiheit! Humanisten und Reformatoren im Dialog* (Heidelberg, 2015), 91–103.

[124] DVC-X, Preface to Book VIII, Clm 150, fo. 1^v.

[125] Council of Constance, Session 40 (30 October 1417), 'De modo et forma eligendi papam', in *Conciliorum oecumenicorum generaliumque decreta*, ii.1, p. 621: 'hanc autem formam et hunc modum electionis approbat…pro hac vice'.

[126] DVC-X, Book VIII, Clm 150, fos 129^r–141^v. See also *Concilia omnia tam generalia quam particularia*, ed. Petrus Crabbe, 2 vols (Cologne, 1538), ii, fos 557^v–560^v (Council of Constance, Sessons 40–41). The author of the 'Narracio de forma et modo eleccionis facte de domino nostro papa Martino V' (Clm 150, fos 138^r–141^r) has been identified as the Dominican Jean de Puydenoix (d. 1431); see D. Girgensohn, 'Berichte über Konklave und Papstwahl auf dem Konstanzer Konzil', *Annuarium historiae conciliorum*, 19 (1987), 351–91. The 'Narracio' is also contained in Vat. lat. 12121, fos 354^r–356^v (material for DVC-X) and Vat. lat. 12123, fos 338^r–341^r (a collection of material put together partly by Panvinio); see Girgensohn, 'Berichte', 367. On the election of Martin V see also A. Frenken, *Das Konstanzer Konzil* (Stuttgart, 2015), 142–53.

As in his *Romani pontifices et cardinales*, Panvinio also listed the electors from the nations who had voted for Martin.[127]

Panvinio included in this book, furthermore, Enea Silvio Piccolomini's description of the election of Felix V from his history of the Council of Basel, and the same author's oration on the election of Nicholas V (*De morte Eugenii IV creationeque et coronatione Nicolai V*). Among other material in this book there was a document which discussed the origin of the electoral capitulations in the conclaves, the first of which originated in the election of Boniface VIII (1294).[128]

Renaissance and Contemporary Conclaves (Books IX–X)

Book IX left behind the troubles of the schisms and turned to the elections from Calixtus III (r. 1455–8) to Paul III (r. 1534–49)—that is, up to the last election before Panvinio's first arrival in Rome.[129] Panvinio now included conclaves either about which he heard reports from persons who had personally been present or which he excerpted from the writings of those who had lived 'at the time of our fathers or grandfathers'. Panvinio added that he himself had been in Rome since the last years of Paul III's pontificate and that he had seen with his own eyes ('oculis ipsis') what had happened following Paul's death in 1549.[130] Important sources for this book included: Stefano Infessura's *Diario della città di Roma*, Platina's life of Pius II, Pius II's *Commentarii* (for the election of Calixtus III and Pius's own election), Jacopo Ammannati's *Commentarii*,[131] Jacopo Gherardi's *Diarium Romanum*, Paolo Giovio's *Historiae*[132] and the same author's biographies of

---

[127] Panvinio, *Romani pontifices et cardinales*, 279–80; DVC-X, Book VIII, Clm 150, fos 135ᵛ–136ᵛ.

[128] *La causa et la historia come sono stati fatti et continuati li capitoli del conclave*, in Panvinio, DVC-X, Book VIII, Clm 150, fos 207ʳ–209ᵛ, published in Döllinger, *Beiträge*, iii. 343–6. This document was discussed by M. Souchon, *Die Papstwahlen von Bonifaz VIII. bis Urban VI. und die Entstehung des Schismas 1378* (Braunschweig, 1888), 16–23.

[129] For a table of contents of Book IX made by Panvinio see ILS, fo. 13ʳ⁻ᵛ.

[130] DVC-X, Preface to Book IX, Clm 151, fo. 1ʳ: 'Cuius [*i.e.*, Pauli III] pontificatus extremis annis in Urbem quum me adhuc adulescens contulissem, quae post eius mortem acciderunt oculis ipsis vidi et his omnibus interfui'.

[131] J. Ammannati Piccolomini, *Epistolae et commentarii* (Milan, 1506). Panvinio owned this work; see ILS, fo. 23ʳ.

[132] P. Giovio, *Historiae sui temporis*, 2 vols (Florence, 1550–2). Panvinio had a folio edition of this work; see ILS, fo. 25ᵛ.

Leo X, Hadrian VI, and Cardinal Pompeo Colonna.[133] They also included Panvinio's own life of Leo X (from his edition of Platina), Paride Grassi's *Diaria* as well as Romolo Amaseo's funeral oration on Paul III.[134]

It would have been particularly unacceptable to any readers in the Curia that Panvinio included the account by Francesco Guicciardini, found in his *Historia di Italia* (1561), describing the election of Alexander VI. Guicciardini accused Alexander VI of buying the votes of numerous cardinals at the conclave which led to his designation as pope. The venal cardinals were oblivious to the teaching of the Gospels, and Alexander was characterized here as faithless, dishonest, shameless, obscene, and barbaric.[135] In the life of Alexander in his continuation of Platina, Panvinio also denounced the role which simony played in his election.[136]

Book X dealt with those conclaves which Panvinio either witnessed or during which time he was present in Rome ('quae vel ipse vidi vel his inter-fui')—that is, those leading to the elections of Julius III (1550), Marcellus II (1555), Paul IV (1555), and Pius IV (1559).[137] Panvinio was intentionally vague here. He was surely not present at the conclaves of Julius III and Marcellus II, although he witnessed Marcellus II's coronation on 10 April 1555 in St Peter's Basilica.[138] It is doubtful whether he was present at Paul IV's conclave; his descriptions were accurate and he did not name another source but his personal attendance cannot be proved.[139] His presence in the conclave on the election day of Pius IV was already noted above. Regarding descriptions from other testimonies, he had either received them in writing or written down what the informants had told him.[140]

---

[133] Id., *Vita Leonis X Pontificis Maximi; Hadriani VI Pontificis Maximi et Pompeii Columnae Cardinalis vitae* (Florence, 1548). Panvinio possessed a printed copy in folio; see ILS, fo. 25ᵛ.

[134] R. Amaseo, *Oratio habita in funere Pauli III Pontificis Maximi* (Bologna, 1563).

[135] Guicciardini, *La historia di Italia* (1561), 3–4; DVC-X, Book IV, Clm 151, fos 156ᵛ–157ᵛ. On the conclave of 1492 see also V. Reinhardt, *Der unheimliche Papst: Alexander VI. Borgia, 1431–1503* (Munich, 2005), 60–71.

[136] Panvinio, 'Alexander VI', in Platina, *Historia de vitis pontificum* (1562), fo. 268ᵛ; (1568), 357. See also J. N. Hillgarth, 'The Image of Alexander VI and Cesare Borgia in the Sixteenth and Seventeenth Centuries', *Journal of the Warburg and Courtauld Institutes*, 59 (1996), 119–29, at p. 125.

[137] DVC-X, Preface to Book X, Clm 152, fo. 1ʳ (ed. Merkle, 'Prolegomena', in *Concilium Tridentinum*, ii, p. CXXXI). For a table of contents of Book X see ILS, fo. 13ᵛ.

[138] DVC-X, Book X, Clm 152, fo. 282ᵛ (ed. Merkle, *Concilium Tridentinum*, ii. 253 n. 2): 'quum omnes cardinales denuo (me praesente) ad obedientiam sibi praestandam pedumque, manus et oris oscula suscepisset'; ibid., fo. 285ᵛ (Merkle, 255 n. 3): 'in Vaticanam basilicam delatus coronationis insignia me praesente, ut supra dixi, suscepit'.

[139] Merkle, 'Prolegomena', in *Concilium Tridentinum*, ii, pp. CXXV, CXXXIII.

[140] DVC-X, Preface to Book X: 'descriptiones vel ab his qui interfuerunt factas habui, vel iisdem referentibus ego digessi'.

Julius III's conclave—which, at two and a half months, was the second-longest conclave of the sixteenth century (after that of Pius IV)— received significant coverage by Panvinio. He presented Angelo Massarelli's extremely detailed diary, followed by texts from Sebastiano and Pier Paolo Gualtieri and Cardinal Bernardino Maffei. Massarelli's diary was published in 1911 by Sebastian Merkle, who found that Panvinio's copy was the only extant manuscript containing the second half of this diary.[141] Merkle noted that Panvinio offered a nearly complete version of Massarelli's diary, with few of his own interventions, corrections, or additions: 'Panvinio's recension gives the best compensation [for the loss of half of Massarelli's autograph] that we can desire.' He concluded that Massarelli must have given Panvinio a copy.[142]

Bernardino Maffei (1514–53) was born in Rome but came from a Veronese family. After having been a secretary to Alessandro Farnese, he was named a cardinal by Pope Paul III in 1549. In the dedicatory preface to Achille Maffei of his work *De ludis saecularibus* (1558), Panvinio noted that Achille's brother Bernardino had been one of the main figures through whose support and encouragement he had started dealing with ancient Roman history and monuments.[143] Panvinio, like other scholars, used the great manuscript and numismatic collections of Achille Maffei (the *Museum*) and, we can suppose, Bernardino's manuscripts as well.[144] It seems that Bernardino Maffei's stimulating diary of the election of Julius III was transmitted only in Panvinio's copy.[145]

Panvinio searched as many reports about Julius III's election as possible. In addition to Massarelli's and Maffei's diaries, he added texts from Sebastiano Gualtieri (1513–66) and Pier Paolo Gualtieri (1501–72).

---

[141] A. Massarelli, *Diarium V: de conclavi post obitum Pauli III (1549–50)*, ed. S. Merkle, in *Concilium Tridentinum*, ii. 1–145. Merkle published much of Maffei's and Gualtieri's texts in the footnotes to Massarelli's fifth diary.

[142] Merkle, 'Prolegomena', pp. XVI–XVII: 'Panvinii enim recensio compensationem praebet, qua meliorem desiderare non possemus.' For other MSS see ibid., pp. XVII–XXIII. See also S. Merkle, 'Das Concilium Tridentinum der Görresgesellschaft', *Zeitschrift der Savigny-Stiftung für Rechtsgeschichte*, 33, Kanonistische Abteilung, 2 (1912), 345–60, at p. 352: 'in der (schonenden) Bearbeitung O. Panvinios'.

[143] Panvinio, *De ludis saecularibus*, in id., *Fastorum libri V* (1558), dedication to Achille Maffei, 3–4.

[144] Panvinio thanked Achille in his *Fastorum libri V* (1558), *Commentarii*, 403. On these libraries see J. Ruysschaert, 'Recherche des deux bibliothèques romaines Maffei des XVe et XVIe siècles', *La bibliofilía*, 60 (1958), 306–55.

[145] B. Maffei, *Iulii III Papae conclave*, in DVC-X, Book X, Clm 152, fos 251ʳ–264ᵛ. See also Merkle, 'Prolegomena', in *Concilium Tridentinum*, ii, p. XXVI; and id., 'Das Concilium Tridentinum', 351: 'geistvoller Essay des Kardinals Bernardino Maffei'.

Sebastiano Gualtieri was an assistant (*conclavista*) of Cardinal Farnese in Julius III's conclave and later became bishop of Viterbo and apostolic nuncio in France; Pier Paolo was one of the literary figures surrounding Marcello Cervini (and was therefore also probably close to Massarelli). Gualtieri's reports are somewhat less remarkable than the others; however, by including him in a wide selection of accounts, Panvinio presented two things: first, different angles on the assembly reproducing, as it were, its physiognomy; and second, several sources which validated one another in terms of the events they described.[146] Although different in character, all these are first-rate sources in one respect: Each of the writers was personally present at the election for at least part of the conclave. These were the same eye-witness reports that Ludwig von Pastor later used in his *History of the Popes*.[147]

To this material Panvinio added Julius III's bull on the reform of the conclave, the first draft of which (1550), as it appears, was again transmitted only by Panvinio. Julius thought that a reform was necessary after seeing the abuses in the extremely long conclave in which he himself had been elected. In this first draft, *Ad universalis ecclesiae regimen*, Julius and the cardinals who drew up the bull (Bernardino Maffei and Giovanni Angelo Medici) proposed an especially tough version of the proposals for reform. Important points in both the stricter and more moderate versions (1554) regarded the urgency with which the conclave should begin after a pope's death (without waiting for cardinals who arrived late), and limits to the distribution of food after a certain time.[148] The second version, *In eligendis ecclesiarum praelatis*, though milder in some details, included three new points: a prohibition against waiting for cardinals who arrived late to the conclave (cap. 2), a prohibition against letting delegates of princes enter the conclave as assistants to cardinals (cap. 10), and a prohibition against agreements among the

---

[146]   B. Defrenne, 'Les "Diaria" et les "Acta" du Concile de Trente', *Revue bénédictine*, 30 (1913), 346–53, at p. 347. See also Merkle, 'Prolegomena', in *Concilium Tridentinum*, ii, p. XXXIX.

[147]   Pastor, *Geschichte der Päpste*, vi. 4 n. 1.

[148]   Panvinio, DVC-X, Book X, Clm 152, fo. 267^r: 'Iulius III Papa duas bullas pro reformatione conclavis fecit, primam strictissimam, quae locum non habuit, alteram mitiorem, quae aedita quidem fuit et cardinalium subscriptionibus confirmata. Sed quia eam pontifex non publicavit, paulo enim post excessit, locum et ipsa non habuit, prioris exemplum sequens est.' For more details see the two versions of the bull published from this MS by J. B. Sägmüller, *Die Papstwahlbullen und das staatliche Recht der Exklusive* (Tübingen, 1892), 285–98. See also ibid. 17–35; Wassilowsky, *Konklavereform*, 69.

cardinals to exclude certain candidates (cap. 19).[149] In any event, the bull was not published, probably because Julius III died.

Regarding the elections of Marcellus II and Paul IV, Panvinio's sections were much shorter and he relied more heavily on information that he assembled himself.[150] He focused more attention on the election of Pius IV. Panvinio presented his own long autobiographical report, *Creatio Pii IV*, as well as a diary by the Mantuan Antonio Guidi.[151] Ludwig von Pastor considered Panvinio's material, Guidi's text, and the diary of the Master of Ceremonies Lodovico Firmano (not provided by Panvinio) to be the most important sources on the conclave.[152] With a duration of more than three and a half months, this was the longest conclave of the sixteenth century. In his own report Panvinio gave a particularly vivid account of it, including all the votes from the first to the 68th scrutiny and a description of Pius IV's election, which Panvinio witnessed in the conclave.[153]

The conclave began on 5 September 1559. Panvinio, who returned to Rome on 12 September, begged Farnese to be admitted to the assembly; however, he was allowed to enter only on 24 December, among other religious, to hear the confessions of the cardinals and their assistants. The pope was unexpectedly elected on Christmas Day.[154] Panvinio described how, on joining the assembly, he went to see several of the cardinals with whom he was acquainted. These included Madruzzo and Otto Truchsess von Waldburg, whom he had met on his travels to Brixen and Augsburg in July, as well as some cardinals he possibly had not seen since his departure from

---

[149] Julius III, *In eligendis ecclesiarum praelatis*, 12 November 1554, in *Concilium Tridentinum*, xiii.1, ed. V. Schweitzer and H. Jedin, 228–32.

[150] Panvinio, DVC-X, Book X, Clm 152, fos 278ʳ–290ʳ (*Marcelli II Papae conclave*). Much of this material was published by Merkle in his notes to A. Massarelli, *Diarium VII: a Marcello II usque ad Pium IV (1555–61)*, in *Concilium Tridentinum*, ii. 245–362, at pp. 248–57. For Paul IV see fos 291ʳ–310ʳ/pp. 258–73 (*Pauli IV Papae conclave*). For accounts of the elections of Marcellus II and Paul IV largely based on Panvinio's narrative see Setton, *The Papacy and the Levant*, iv. 611–13, 617–21. See also Sägmüller, *Papstwahlbullen*, 35–6.

[151] Panvinio's other material on the election, *Pii IV Papae conclave* (fos 311ʳ–385ᵛ), was published in part (regarding fos 311ʳ–319ᵛ) by Merkle in his notes to Massarelli's *Diarium VII*, 332–40, and by Pastor, *Geschichte der Päpste*, vii, Appendix, pp. 621–7 (on the scrutinies). See also A. Guidi, *Acta interregni…a Pauli IV Papae obitu usque ad Pii IV…creationem* (Clm 152, fos 386ʳ–408ᵛ).

[152] Pastor, *Geschichte der Päpste*, vii. 11. L. Firmano's description of the election of Pius IV was published by Merkle (Firmanus, *Diaria caerimonialia*, in *Concilium Tridentinum*, ii. 491–571, at pp. 518–31). On the sources see also Wassilowsky, *Konklavereform*, 74–83.

[153] Panvinio's account of the election was summarized by Setton, *The Papacy and the Levant*, iv. 721–3, 734–8, and by Pastor, *Geschichte der Päpste*, vii. 49–56.

[154] See Panvinio, *Creatio Pii IV*, 577–8.

Rome in June 1556 (such as Rodolfo Pio da Carpi and the future pope, Giovanni Angelo Medici).

Panvinio described the many schemes and machinations (*machinae*) between the rival factions.[155] He tended to exaggerate his own role. First, several cardinals inquired his opinion. Otto asked him what he thought of Medici as a candidate for the papacy. Panvinio then met Galesio Regard, the chamberlain (*cubicularius*) of Giovanni Angelo Medici, whom he referred to as an old friend. Panvinio kissed Medici's hand and Medici himself exclaimed that he had known Panvinio well for a long time. Panvinio's reporting that Medici offered to do him any favour he wished was also surely a strategic point in the text, intended to help him obtain actual support after the text's publication.[156] Cardinal Madruzzo asked Panvinio not only what he thought of Medici as a candidate, but also wondered, 'What name shall we give him?' and jokingly suggested the name 'Aesculapius', with the god of medicine alluding to Medici's family name. When Panvinio received the hint from Farnese that the pope was soon to be elected, he remained in Medici's cell the entire time to observe what would happen and to gather first-hand information (Fig. 3.3).[157]

When a majority had been all but established, Carlo Carafa allegedly addressed Panvinio, who was standing in the back of the crowd in front of Medici's cell, and asked him for his opinion about this choice. Of course he was delighted, answered Panvinio, because Medici would make for a modest, pious, and temperate pope. Carafa agreed. Ranuccio Farnese again wanted to know from Panvinio what name the pope would give himself.[158] Panvinio labelled those petty conversations 'trifles' (*ineptia*) and a waste of time, but it seems certain that he was pleased to be involved in them, considering he gave them so much prominence in his account.[159]

Panvinio also claimed that he personally spurred Cardinal Giovanni Morone into action when it seemed that Medici's election, although nearly secure, could still slip away. Panvinio had asked Carlo Carafa when the election would take place. Morone had overheard Carafa's answer ('tomorrow

[155] Ibid. 582: 'tantis machinis'.
[156] Ibid. 578: 'Te meum antiquum familiarem optime novi, mi Onuphri. Salvus sis. Si quid tibi deest, pete, et me paratissimum habebis.'
[157] Ibid. 579.
[158] Ibid. 584: 'Tunc Sancti Angeli [i.e., Ranuccio Farnese] me compellans: "Quod nomen pontifici (inquit) dabimus, Onuphri?"', Panvinio suggested: 'Eum Stephanum X vocari debere censerem ob diei quae instat celebritatem divo Stephano dicatam, Stephani IX memor, qui id nomen obtinuit, quod die Sancti Stephani papa ante quingentos annos creatus fuisset.'
[159] Ibid.

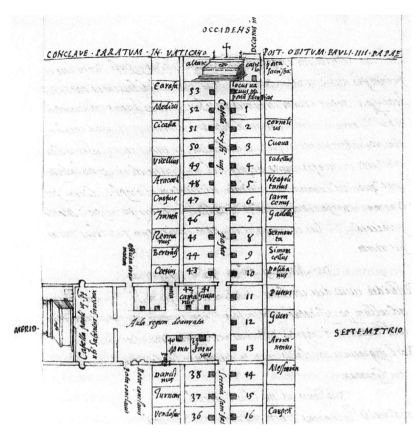

Fig. 3.3 Plan of the conclave leading to the election of Pius IV, 1559 (detail).
From Panvinio, DVC-X, Book X. Autograph. Courtesy of the Bayerische
Staatsbibliothek, Munich (Clm 152, fo. 319ʳ). Cardinal Medici's cell was in the
Sistine Chapel (no. 52) while Alessandro Farnese's cell was in the Sala Regia (no.
39). The Pauline Chapel, where the scrutinies were held, can be seen on the left.

morning') and showed himself surprised that the election should be
deferred. At this point, Panvinio came up with a maxim; he remarked that
'many things may come between the mouth and the morsel' ('multa possunt
inter os et offam cadere').[160] This was a classical aphorism, deriving from

[160] Ibid.: 'Moro...dixit: "Usque ad mane differenda est electio?" Ego inquam: "Ita enim
rettulit Cardinalis Carafa; sed quia multa possunt inter os et offam cadere, cur non potius nunc
omnibus patribus convocatis ea transigitur?" Tum Moro: "Recte dicis."' As a prominent nephew
of Paul IV, Carafa was condemned to death by Pius IV in 1561.

Cato the Elder and better known in English in the variant 'twixt cup and lip there's many a slip'. Morone agreed and 'asked all the fathers who were present, in a loud voice, what they were waiting for. Should they not take Medici immediately into the Pauline Chapel, place him on St Peter's chair, and thus do quickly what they had long desired for?'[161] Morone, according to Panvinio, then added a few more classical quotations to his exhortations, citing what he thought was from Virgil ('Delay has always been harmful to those who are prepared')—but was actually from Lucan—and also citing Sallust ('Before you begin, consider; but having considered, use dispatch').[162]

Events accelerated after the combined efforts of wisdom exhibited by Panvinio and Morone. Panvinio ran to Alessandro Farnese's cell to wake him up, and it was he who announced to his incredulous patron the news of the general consensus.[163] The cardinals flocked to the Pauline Chapel to elect Pius IV *viva voce* by adoration. Carlo Carafa wanted to expel the conclavists and assistants, but the protests of Panvinio and others were allegedly decisive in enabling them to stay. Panvinio gave a lively description of the ceremony to which even the sick cardinals insisted on being carried.[164] After the ceremony Panvinio, too, went to adore the new pope and kiss his feet. On this occasion, the new pope was asked by Cardinal Vitellozzo Vitelli if he knew Panvinio. Pius IV pronounced that he knew the friar 'very well, for he makes himself known everywhere in his books'.[165] The next morning, a ballot was cast to confirm the election which had already taken place the night before through the sudden act of adoration.[166]

---

[161] Ibid.: 'et omnes qui aderant patres intuitus alta voce "Et quid (inquit) moramini, patres? Cur lucem expectare vultis? Nonne melius est ut tantam rem nunc transigamus et optimum senem in Paulinam aedem deductum in Petri sede, quod diu desideravimus, collocemus?"'

[162] Lucan, Phars., I.281; Sallust, Catil. I.6.   [163] Panvinio, *Creatio Pii IV*, 584.

[164] For a description of this election see also Panvinio's letter to Seripando, 30 December 1559, Naples, Biblioteca nazionale, XIII AA 53, fo. 158^{r-v}, ed. Jedin, *Seripando*, ii. 627–8: 'tutti insieme corrivano come pazzi, chi alla capella, chi alla stantiola del papa a suffragare... viva voce fu eletto'.

[165] Panvinio, *Creatio Pii IV*, 585: 'Optime nosco; libris enim suis se ubique cognosci facit'.

[166] It has recently been underlined by Wassilowsky (*Konklavereform*) that in the sixteenth century this was usual practice, of which Panvinio's report gives another confirmation. Panvinio also described this custom in his note to Platina's life of Clement V (r. 1305–14), 'Ratio creandi Romani pontificis', fo. 192^r: 'Alius est quoque creandi pontificis mos, qui per adorationem dicitur. Hoc autem est cum duae partes cardinalium non expectato, ut vocant, scrutinio, sed voce tenus omnium consensu et voluntate quempiam ex cardinalibus in Romanum pontificem salutant atque venerantur. Qua ratione Iulius III, Marcellus II et Paulus etiam IV renuntiati fuerunt'. In the 1568 edition of the *Vitae* see pp. 252–3. This note was reprinted together with the note on Gregory X (see above, n. 108) in a booklet of eight leaves entitled Panvinio, *Sommario di capitoli et leggi che si osservano nell'elettione del sommo pontefice*, trans. Cornelio Massimini (Venice: Domenico Imberti, 1590).

Pius IV's Conclave Bull, 1561–3

As with Julius III, Panvinio included the bulls for a reform of the conclave prepared by Pius IV—that is, both the draft version of 1561/62 and the published version (9 October 1562).[167] It was decreed in November 1561 that work on the bull should begin. Pius IV, as a cardinal, had been a collaborator on the draft of Julius III's bull, and it was therefore not surprising that his own bull, *In eligendis ecclesiarum praelatis*, was based mostly on Julius's second version. Major differences concerned only the place of the conclave (Castel Sant'Angelo) and the procedure of voting. Pius devised an elaborate system to ensure more secrecy in the voting process—a system modelled on elections in Venice. Pius met with resistance in the college of cardinals, but on 18 March 1562 he declared his intentions to publish the bull. Modifications were negotiated to placate the cardinals. The location of Castel Sant'Angelo was removed and the dispositions concerning the voting system were deleted. The cardinals were to remain free to vote as they wished. (Secret balloting would be introduced only in 1621/22 by Gregory XV.)

The published version (which can be seen as the fourth version of Julius III's original draft) was approved and promulgated, after numerous negotiations, on 9 October 1562.[168] Although the bull was affixed in Rome in the usual public places on 21 November, Pius IV on 31 October instructed his legates at the Council of Trent to not make it public for the time being.[169] On 3 March 1563 Emperor Ferdinand wrote to Pius, urging him to submit the bull to the judgement of the Council of Trent and to include sharper provisions against simony at conclaves. This meant that the emperor wanted to modify the published version of *In eligendis*, which his ambassador at the Holy See had sent to him in October 1562.[170] Pius IV prepared a draft reply to Ferdinand, which he never actually sent; it enables us to understand more closely some of his thoughts. Pius expressed the notion that so many laws

---

[167] Pius IV, *In eligendis ecclesiarum praelatis*. For the draft see Clm 152, fos 440^r–447^v (ed. Sägmüller, *Papstwahlbullen*, 298–307). For the version published by Pius see *Bullarum, diplomatum et privilegiorum sanctorum Romanorum pontificum Taurinensis editio*, 25 vols (Turin; Naples, 1857–85), vii. 230–6. See also Sägmüller, *Papstwahlbullen*, 110–85; Wassilowsky, *Konklavereform*, 144–54; Visceglia, *Morte e elezione*, 158–61.

[168] See Baronio, Rinaldi, Laderchi, and Theiner, *Annales*, xxxiv, continuation by Rinaldi, ad AD 1562, no. 188, p. 311.

[169] Letter by Carlo Borromeo (Rome) to the legates in Trent, 31 October 1562, ed. J. Šusta, *Die römische Kurie und das Konzil von Trient*, 4 vols (Vienna, 1904–14), iii. 55–6.

[170] Letter of Prospero d'Arco (Rome) to the emperor, 10 October 1562, ed. T. Sickel, *Zur Geschichte des Concils von Trient* (Vienna, 1872), 389–90.

had been passed on this subject by previous councils and popes that it may have seemed as though nothing could be added to further improve conclaves. His intention, nonetheless, was to prevent abuses in the election of his successor, which was why he had published the bull. The pope also admitted to thinking that the bull's submission to the council would make its approval nearly impossible.[171] Pius expressed more ideas in a consistory of 12 April 1563; he maintained that while others wanted new and inappropriate changes in the conclave, he himself desired both a strict reform and the preservation of the statutes of the ancient councils.

News of Pius's reform intentions, brought to Innsbruck ten days later by the legate to the council, Cardinal Morone, seem to have calmed Ferdinand somewhat, although the emperor kept pressing for a discussion of the conclave at the council. In truth, however, Pius never had an intention to involve the council with the conclave bull. By referring to 'new and inappropriate changes', Pius surely meant the idea that the pope, at the time of a general council, could be elected by the council itself—an idea that had been present since the reform councils of the early fifteenth century and from which his bull provided solid protection by confirming the election through the cardinals in a conclave.

Although the emperor and the legates continued to discuss a further reform of the conclave during the final period of the Council of Trent, the bull *In eligendis* remained as it was. A contentious point was the interference of worldly powers in the decision process during the conclave—which, ironically, many cardinals welcomed because it gave them the possibility of obtaining 'worldly' (that is, financial) favours in return for their votes. Ironically, again, it was the emperor who aimed to exclude such lay interference. *In eligendis* in this respect presented a compromise. Though in principle it prohibited cardinals from heeding lay interference, it left the observation of this prohibition rather open, as the cardinals were never threatened with effective and precise sanctions—such as excommunication—if they disobeyed.[172] The cardinals, in fact, obtained the concession that the threat of excommunication would be removed before the bull's publication in 1562. In exchange for this removal, as it were, the pope added the prohibition against lay interference, which had not been present in the first draft.[173]

---

[171] Pius IV to Ferdinand, 18 March 1563 (draft replies), in *Concilium Tridentinum*, xiii.2, ed. K. Ganzer, 346–51, esp. pp. 349–50.

[172] Pius IV, *In eligendis* (in *Bullarum, diplomatum...*), cap. 26, p. 235.

[173] See the first draft of the bull in Clm 152, cap. 16, ed. Sägmüller, 306. This threat of excommunication had been taken over from Julius III's version of *In eligendis* (ibid. 297).

To sum up, Panvinio was at pains to highlight the importance of this bull. Much time had been spent on its preparation, and it put the forms of papal election into more precise terms than the decrees of previous popes had done.

The Epitomes

As *De varia creatione* was very detailed—and the version in ten books was made available only to Fugger—Panvinio prepared an abridgement. The epitome's intended purpose was to be useful for Pius IV's conclave reform. It was probably never meant for publication in print. Manuscripts are preserved with separate dedications to Fugger, Pius IV, and Cardinal Carlo Borromeo. The epitome for Fugger carried the same general preface as the ten-book version produced for him and it was dated 1 May 1563.[174] In the versions for Borromeo and Pius IV, new dedicatory prefaces were added before the general preface. Whereas the version for Pius carried no date, Borromeo's version was dated 14 May without any indication of a year.[175] The last document contained in the epitome was Pius IV's bull *In eligendis* of 9 October 1562. While the dedication for Pius might therefore have been drawn up some time after late 1562, the dedication for Borromeo should no doubt be dated 14 May 1563.

The dedicatory prefaces to Pius IV and his nephew Carlo Borromeo were identical except for a few words. Panvinio commented on Pius IV's attempts to reform the procedure of papal election.[176] The pope, according to Panvinio,

---

[174] Panvinio, *Librorum X de pontificis Romani creatione epitoma* (cited henceforth as DVC-X-Epitome), general preface, Clm 154, fos 2ʳ–3ʳ. The preface lacked only the last section, which addressed the German patron personally.

[175] *Librorum X de pontificis Romani varia creatione epitoma*, dedicated to Pius IV (*c.*1562–3), MSS Vat. lat. 6107.iii, fos 490ʳ–604ᵛ (16th c.) (with corrections in Panvinio's hand); Vat. lat. 6111, fos 1ʳ–131ᵛ (16th–17th c.); BNF, Lat. 4244B, fos 8ʳ–108ᵛ (17th c.); *Librorum X de varia creatione pontificis Romani epitome*, dedicated to Carlo Borromeo (14 May [1563]), MSS Rome, Biblioteca Angelica, Ang. lat. 1112 (16th c.); BAM, A 68 inf., fos IIIʳ–IVᵛ, 1ʳ–86ʳ (16th–17th c.); Naples, Biblioteca nazionale, I D 2, fos 195ʳ–290ʳ (17th c.); Florence, Biblioteca nazionale, II III 391 (17th c.); BNF, Lat. 939, fos 218ʳ–316ʳ (17th c.); Paris, Bibliothèque Sainte-Geneviève, 149, fos 82ʳ–197ʳ (17th c.).

[176] DVC-X-Epitome, dedication to Pius IV, adapted for C. Borromeo, Vat. lat. 6107.iii, fo. 492ʳ⁻ᵛ, at fo. 492ʳ: 'Inter multas Romano pontifice vere dignas curas, quas libenter ac studiose pro universa republica christiana Sanctissimus avunculus tuus Pius IV [*corr. ex:* Sanctitas Vestra] quotidie suscipit, ea vel praecipua est quod pontificalium comitiorum rationem vel temporum iniuria vel hominum licentia iamdiu labefactatam ad pristinam integritatem ac maiestatem totis viribus revocare contendit: quippe qui probe cognoscit, totam rerum ecclesiasticarum summam in ea versari.' The greater part of this preface was published in *SR*, ix. 516. See also Tallon, 'Les conclaves', 31.

wanted to bring the rules of elections, which had been loosened and undermined by the 'injustices of the times' and the 'unruly behaviour of men', back to their original integrity. When Panvinio heard that Pius had set his mind on this reform, he decided to revise and expand what he had already worked on ten years earlier at the suggestion of Marcello Cervini. He included everything that was worth knowing in this field, from Christ to the election of Pius IV, together with the electoral decrees. He hoped the events and documents contained in this book would create a helpful foundation for the conclave reform. Pius could read the relevant information either personally (in one version of the dedication), or else Borromeo (in the other version), after reading the book, could make relevant suggestions to his uncle. We may conclude that, for this reason, despite the brevity of the epitome, several electoral decrees were included in full, as they may have seemed useful for Pius.

It may be surprising how critical Panvinio was of the chaos caused by papal elections and that he had the courage to present his work to Cardinal Borromeo and the pope. In the general preface, Panvinio included a remark about the 'many dissensions, schisms, and disagreements of the elections, amid which most of the Roman pontiffs were appointed'.[177] This criticism may, in fact, have been welcome to Pius IV, precisely because he argued for a solid basis for legitimate elections; therefore, examples of past misbehaviour may have served to underline his points. Nevertheless, it is unlikely that the version for Pius IV was ever presented to the pope. Sebastian Merkle made an interesting suggestion as to why it may not have been appropriate for Panvinio to dedicate the epitome to Pius IV: It was not proper for a pope to receive a smaller version of a text which, in a longer version, had already been dedicated to someone of lower rank (Cardinal Farnese).[178] In addition, the work's criticism of the Church made the pope—its highest

---

[177] DVC-X, general preface, Clm 147, fo. 2ʳ, ed. Merkle, p. CXXIX: 'Ut enim miranda illa omittam, quibus historiae omnes iam inde a Christi passione refertae sunt, ex quibus certissimis clarissimisque argumentis intelligere facile possumus ex horrendis tempestatibus, inruentibus procellis saevissimisque ventorum turbinibus solo divinitatis gubernaculo Petri navem saepissime receptam et conservatam, illud certe divinitus accidisse nemo est sacrae antiquitatis quamquam leviter peritus qui non intelligat, quod quum in tot tyrannorum et haereticorum persequutionibus, tum *in tantis comitiorum dissensionibus, schismatibus et dissidiis, quibus Romanorum pontificum pars maxima creata est*, apostolica sedes integra perpetuo et absque labe ulla incorrupta permanserit.' (My italics.) The phrase 'tum in tantis comitiorum dissensionibus, schismatibus et dissidiis' was added above the line in the general preface to the DVC-X-Epitome, Vat. lat. 6107.iii, fo. 496ʳ. See also BNF, Lat. 4244B, fo. 10ʳ.

[178] Merkle, 'Prolegomena', p. CXXXV. Some copies of the DVC-X-Epitome also circulated without any dedication; see MSS Vat. lat. 3554, fos 1ʳ–125ʳ (first owned by Cardinal-Librarian Antonio Carafa, d. 1591); Rome, Deutsches Historisches Institut, Minucciani, 17, fos 1ʳ–333ʳ (16th–17th c.); BAV, Barb. lat. 2604, fos 24ʳ–169ʳ (16th–17th c.); BAV, Barb. lat. 2487 (17th c.).

representative—an unlikely dedicatee. Thus, Panvinio changed the dedication and put Borromeo in his place.

Panvinio's epitome included the complete prefaces of the ten books, with the criticisms of the Church contained in them. The abridgement inevitably included far fewer documents than the full version and Panvinio selected such pieces as could shed light most efficiently on the electoral forms and reforms. This also meant that much controversial material regarding papal biographies and anecdotal evidence of the behaviour of popes and cardinals was left out. To be sure, the epitome included the title headings of most of the eliminated material, so that the reader could get an overview of the contents of the full version. These headings were not complete, however. In Book IX, for example, the epitome excised the title headings for Alexander VI, making it appear as if Panvinio had never treated this pope's election in the full version.[179] Documentary material included for Book IX was limited strictly to the bulls concerning papal elections by Julius II, Clement VII, and Paul III. For Book X, the material consisted of Julius III's, Paul IV's, and Pius IV's bulls on papal elections.

While we can be sure that Panvinio himself prepared this type of epitome, there were two other kinds of abridgements whose compilers are uncertain. The first was the fragmentary epitome of the five-book version (corresponding to Panvinio's original plan from 1559). Although this abridgement carried the title *Epitome librorum V de varia creatione Romani pontificis*, it bore neither the author's name nor a dedication or general preface; nor was the text itself divided into books. It began with the preface to Book I and broke off after the tenth mode of elections (corresponding to the first two books in the three-book version or the first three in the ten-book version).[180]

The other type, *Modus eligendi pontifices ab electione Beati Petri usque ad haec tempora* (The Manner of Choosing the Popes from the Election of St Peter until the Present), was a compendium of Panvinio's epitome of the ten-book version, covering all books. This proved to be the most popular of all versions and was transmitted in numerous manuscripts, often in collections of conclave reports. It omitted the prefaces and started directly with an extract from Book I. Since it usually also lacked the author's name, it was only rarely encountered in manuscripts together with other works by

---

[179] See DVC-X-Epitome, BNF, Lat. 4244B, fo. 83ʳ, where the headings jump from Pius II to Julius II.

[180] *Epitome librorum V de varia creatione Romani pontificis*, MSS Rome, Deutsches Historisches Institut, Minucciani, 16, fos 1ʳ–23ᵛ (16th–17th c.); Biblioteca Casanatense, 401, fos 7ʳ–17ᵛ (16th–17th c.).

Panvinio.[181] What is striking is the similarity of the title to Massarelli's *Modi seu formae observatae diversis temporibus in electione summorum pontificum a Petro usque ad Iulium III*—which is not to say that Massarelli was the compiler, but that perhaps this compendium was an attempt to imitate Massarelli's short text.

Lastly, in the seventeenth century an epitome of the three-book version was made by Ilarione Rancati (1594–1663), the Cistercian abbot of Santa Croce in Gerusalemme in Rome. Rancati, who was a consultant to the Inquisition and Index and enjoyed high esteem as a scholar, included occasional remarks about Panvinio's sources. It has yet to be established if Rancati had a motive for making this abridgement above and beyond his personal interest in papal history.[182]

Panvinio's History of Imperial Elections

Around the same time as he worked on *De varia creatione*, Panvinio also wrote a history of imperial elections, *De comitiis imperatoriis liber*. The printed text was dedicated to Philip II in 1558.[183] Panvinio hoped to receive financial rewards in return; but these efforts, carried out between 1558 and 1563 (in 1562–3 by Panvinio's uncle Girolamo Campagna in person), were largely ignored by the Spanish court. As Gersbach has surmised, a book about imperial elections under the patronage of Philip II may have seemed inappropriate because the succession to the imperial throne was disputed between the two branches of the Habsburg family.[184] Panvinio kept pressing with the help of the king's secretary, Gonzalo Pérez, and members of the

---

[181] I identified about forty copies of *Modus eligendi*, including, e.g., Vat. lat. 12120, fos 1ʳ–46ᵛ (16th c.); BAM, D 357 inf., fos 1ʳ–21ᵛ (16th c.); Bologna, Biblioteca universitaria, 1117, vol. vi, fos 185r–238r (16th c.); London, British Library, Add. MS 48073, fos 2ʳ–55ʳ (16th–17th c.).

[182] I. Rancati, *Onuphrii Panvini De varia Romani pontificis creatione...epitome*, MSS BAM, B 238 suss., fos 1ʳ–34ʳ (17th c.); Rome, Biblioteca nazionale, Sess. 268, fos 3ʳ–49ᵛ (17th–19th c.). This epitome may have been made from DVC-III, MS Rome, Biblioteca nazionale, Sess. 236 (17th c.). On Rancati see H. H. Schwedt, *Die römische Inquisition: Kardinäle und Konsultoren 1601 bis 1700* (Freiburg im Breisgau, 2017), 497–9.

[183] The full title was: Panvinio, *De comitiis imperatoriis liber, in quo praeter caetera septem imperii electorum origo demonstrata est atque communis quae adhuc obtinuit fama refutata*, in id., *Romanorum principum...libri IV* (1558), 333–450.

[184] See also the slightly oblique comment by the king's secretary, Gonzalo Pérez, in his letter to Panvinio, 5 May 1563, ed. Gersbach, 'De comitiis', 433: 'Y es de mucha curiosidad solo en lo que toca al derecho y uso de la elección que agora hazen los electores; me paresce que lo que Vuestra Señoría sobrello dize no será bien recibido de los Alemanes, que tanto se fundan en su Bula Aurea.'

Farnese family. In April 1563 Philip finally granted him 300 ducats for the release of his brother (who had been captured by the Ottomans three years earlier) and promised help with another of Panvinio's works, the *Historia ecclesiastica*. In November 1563, Panvinio turned also to Maximilian II and hoped to impress him with *De comitiis*. The expanded manuscript versions of the work (1563–5) carried dedications to Maximilian.[185] Panvinio sent his brother to Vienna to present the three-book version to Maximilian. In May 1564, the response was positive and Paolo Panvinio received 300 florins.

Panvinio was the first historian to study in detail the election of emperors from ancient Rome up to Ferdinand and Maximilian.[186] His research into the origins of the electoral college, in particular, became influential. Panvinio rejected the traditional idea that the college was an institution created at the time of Pope Gregory V (r. 996–9) and Emperor Otto III (r. 996–1002), instead putting forward the hypothesis that the college was created either during the Interregnum which followed the death of Frederick II (1250–73) or shortly afterwards. He admitted that he had not found any precise evidence for this dating but conjectured that the college could have been formed at the time of Pope Gregory X (r. 1271–6), since he also reorganized papal elections.[187] (Panvinio surmised that previous historians had mistaken Gregory X for Gregory V.) Panvinio was not the first historian to challenge the early dating; he cited Johannes Aventinus, who had already pointed to a foundation of the college after the death of Frederick II and a confirmation by Gregory X. Although Aventinus had touched on the issue only in passing, Panvinio was overjoyed that he did not have to fight a scholarly battle completely on his own.[188]

---

[185] The dedicatory preface to Maximilian II, dated 1 November 1563, was published in J. Chmel, *Die Handschriften der k.k. Hofbibliothek in Wien*, 2 vols (Vienna, 1840–1), i. 517–18. For the manuscripts see Gersbach, '*De comitiis*', and above, 72; for Paolo's captivity, above, 67.

[186] On Panvinio's achievement see M. Buchner, 'Die Entstehung und Ausbildung der Kurfürstenfabel: eine historiographische Studie', *Historisches Jahrbuch*, 33 (1912), 54–100, 255–322, at pp. 309–12 (not only was he thorough, skilful, and astute but also ingenious and independent); E. Menke-Glückert, *Die Geschichtsschreibung der Reformation und Gegenreformation* (Leipzig, 1912), 96–9 (he had more critical acumen than Baronio).

[187] Panvinio, *De comitiis*, 401–2. Recent research still posits that the electoral college was formed in the thirteenth century and became a political reality during the Interregnum; see A. Begert, *Die Entstehung und Entwicklung des Kurkollegs* (Berlin, 2010). The question of its precise development, however, remains a 'fundamental mystery of German constitutional history' (ibid. 11).

[188] J. Aventinus, *Annales Boiorum* (Ingolstadt, 1554), 510: 'ego illos demum post fata Friderici II institutos et a Gregorio X Pontifice Maximo confirmatos esse compertum habeo'; Panvinio, *De comitiis*, 404: 'incredibili quodam gaudio affectus fui quod unum saltem hominem invenerim…cuius testimonio hanc rem conferma possem, ne solus contra tot doctissimorum scriptorum aciem in campum descenderem'.

De comitiis seemed to suggest that Panvinio had pro-imperial leanings, which is why, in 1592, the censor of *De varia creatione* denounced it as well.[189] The censor's judgement needs to be qualified, however. Panvinio's late dating of the creation of the electoral college proved to be highly unpopular in Germany. He also cast doubt on the crucial idea that the electoral college was instituted by an emperor. Furthermore, he supported Rome's interpretation of the papal *translatio imperii* ('translation of empire') to Charlemagne in 800 by stating that a newly elected emperor still needed to be confirmed by the pope. Panvinio demonstrated that this had been the usual practice in the Middle Ages. He chided recent German historians who thought otherwise for their lack of objectivity: 'It is the duty of a historian to describe what actually happened, and not what he thinks should have happened.'[190]

Lastly, Panvinio declared that Ferdinand's election as successor to the reigning emperor, Charles V, had been 'not so much free' as 'practically forced' by Charles.[191] This was an especially sensitive issue in 1558 because Ferdinand's succession to the imperial throne was contested by Paul IV.[192] It is, in fact, astonishing that Ferdinand, in his letter of recommendation for Panvinio (1559), stated that he had published works which 'were bound together with the dignity and greatness of the Holy Roman Empire'.[193] One wonders whether Ferdinand and his advisors had read the printed edition of *De comitiis*.

It is surprising, too, that Panvinio's book was published in Protestant Basel and, moreover, that he dedicated the enlarged manuscript version of *De comitiis* (in three books) to Maximilian II in 1563.[194] When Panvinio

[189] See below, 195.

[190] Panvinio, *De comitiis*, 369: 'historici munus est res gestas eadem ratione narrare qua factae sunt, et non ut fieri debuisse sibi videatur'. See also Aristotle's distinction between history and poetry: 'one tells what happened and the other what might happen' (Poet. 1451b); and Francesco Robortello, *In librum Aristotelis De arte poetica explicationes* (Florence, 1548), 89: 'poetae non est proprium narrare res gestas, sed ut fieri debuerint'.

[191] Panvinio, *De comitiis*, 371: 'electio vero non adeo libera, sed quasi coacta'.

[192] Ibid. 370: 'Prima enim Germaniae principum electio est, quae imperatorem re ipsa facit. Pontificis vero inauguratio est, quae eum imperatorem rite renuntiatum fuisse imperioque dignum declarat atque ei speciosa imperatoris et Augusti nomina indidit'. For the dispute between Paul IV and Ferdinand see Pastor, *Geschichte der Päpste*, vi. 571–9. On the curial theory of translation see Goez, *Translatio*; A. Seifert, *Der Rückzug der biblischen Prophetie von der neueren Geschichte* (Cologne, 1990), 38–48.

[193] Ferdinand's letter, 8 August 1559 (above, 63–64 n. 9): 'plura etiam volumina in lucem ediderit, quae cum sacri Romani imperii dignitate et amplitudine sunt coniuncta'.

[194] On the publication in Basel see A. Burckhardt, *Johannes Basilius Herold: Kaiser und Reich im protestantischen Schrifttum des Basler Buchdrucks um die Mitte des 16. Jahrhunderts* (Basel, 1967), 56–7; and above, 49–50.

sent the five-book version to Fugger in 1564–5, he expressly asked him to keep it secret. Possible motives for this were his wish to safeguard his unpublished intellectual property but also his expectation of criticism, not only from Catholics, but also from German Protestants.[195] Indeed, in 1566 the theologian Matthias Flacius and the jurist Simon Schard published sharply polemical treatises to rebut Panvinio's 1558 *De comitiis*, attacking his late dating of the electoral college and the curial theory of translation.[196] Schard warned his readers that Panvinio's theses shook the constitutional foundations of the Empire.[197] The two treatises came out in Basel, where Panvinio had published his work, and both authors offered their treatises to Maximilian II, to whom Panvinio had dedicated his enlarged manuscript.[198] Perhaps Flacius and Schard sprang into action in about 1565 (and not earlier) because by then word had spread in Germany that Panvinio had not only written *De comitiis* but was also working on a grand-scale *Church History* to counter the *Magdeburg Centuries*. After Panvinio's death in 1568, more criticism ensued in the Protestant fold but also came from the Catholic camp. In the 1580s the theologian Robert Bellarmine (a nephew of Panvinio's former patron Cervini) dealt harshly with the opinions of Flacius, Aventinus, and Panvinio. He branded Flacius a liar for denying that both the 'translation of empire' and the institution of the electoral college had been made by the authority of the papacy. Aventinus and Panvinio were reprimanded for their 'arbitrary' late dating of the electors.[199]

Panvinio and Chacón on the Roles of Change and Variation

This chapter has shown how Panvinio's history of papal elections evolved from 1559 to its conclusion in 1563. As far as Panvinio's method is

---

[195] Gersbach, 'De comitiis', 419. See also above, 72.

[196] M. Flacius, *De translatione Imperii Romani ad Germanos* (Basel, 1566); S. Schard, *De principum, quibus electio imperatoris in Germania commendata est, origine seu institutione*, in id. (ed.), *De iurisdictione, autoritate et praeeminentia imperiali ac potestate ecclesiastica...* (Basel, 1566), 861–914. (Schard dedicated the volume to Maximilian but his tract against *De comitiis* to the electors.) Flacius's work was also translated into German a year later.

[197] Schard, *De principum...origine*, 865.

[198] On these and later polemics in Germany, which lasted well into the seventeenth century, see A. Dürrwächter, *Christoph Gewold* (Freiburg im Breisgau, 1904), 39–47; Burckhardt, *Herold*, 56–76 (who argues that Panvinio's erudition was greatly superior to that of Flacius and Schard).

[199] R. Bellarmine, *De translatione Imperii Romani a Graecis ad Francos, adversus Matthiam Flaccium Illyricum* (Antwerp, 1589), 276–95 (on Panvinio); for 'Onuphrii temeritas' see p. 277.

concerned, his distinction of eighteen modes of election up to the sixteenth century certainly went beyond what was necessary—that is, he saw more modes of election than had actually existed. Of the eighteen modes, he placed the first thirteen in the period up to AD 1059. In doing so, he put excessive weight on a period about which we have little certainty. An adequate description would have limited itself more prudently to a shorter list. Panvinio, however, gave proof of his sensibility regarding the evolution of the papacy throughout its history, and he managed to include the main stages (the election by clergy and laity, the decree of 1059, etc.). The interesting point here is not the inflated refinement in the distinctions, but the quantity of documentary material which Panvinio collected and which allowed him to recognize the major stages of development. Panvinio's *De varia creatione* remains the only comprehensive source-based history of papal elections to have been written until today.

Panvinio showed that the history of these elections was characterized by great diversity and sharp discontinuities. This observation contained an explosive force. In sixteenth-century historical discourse, Catholics usually aimed to justify their legitimacy and superiority through demonstrations of historical continuity. Panvinio's arguments are therefore difficult to integrate into this line of theological and historical debate.[200] Perhaps to prevent criticism of his book, in his preface to Book III, Panvinio made efforts to create a distinction between eternal, divine rules (*immutabilia*) and areas of human experience which could be changed (*mutabilia*). These last areas included the laws governing papal elections. Panvinio thus displayed an unusually dynamic perception of church traditions.[201] In the course of the history of papal elections, the participation of secular powers changed over time, while their participation itself was a constant force. Panvinio not only argued that the intervention of secular powers was a long-standing tradition, he also seemed to imply that it was a beneficial custom. This was hardly acceptable to reforming forces in the sixteenth century; they aimed to eliminate this worldly interference. Despite his work's length, Panvinio left out several areas that would have found much interest in the sixteenth century. In particular, he did not go into detail about the actual process of elections—that is, he did not illustrate how elections by compromise, *accessus*, or adoration actually functioned.[202]

---

[200] Wassilowsky, *Konklavereform*, 35–6.
[201] DVC-X, Preface to Book III, Clm 148, fos 1ʳ–2ʳ.
[202] Wassilowsky, *Konklavereform*, 40.

In evaluating Panvinio's method, it will be useful to draw a brief comparison with another historical author: the Spanish Dominican friar Alfonso Chacón, who lived in Rome from 1567 until his death in 1599. Chacón's *Vitae et gesta summorum pontificum* (Lives and Deeds of the Popes) was published posthumously in 1601.[203] He used both Platina's and Panvinio's works to compile his text, and he was involved, to small degrees, in the censorship of both. In 1587 Chacón denounced to the Congregation of the Index a passage by Platina about Pope John XXI.[204] In the same year, he also denounced a passage in Panvinio's guidebook to the Roman churches, in which Panvinio had put forward a hypothesis about the history of the Holy Stairs (*scala sancta*) at the Lateran Palace. Chacón was not pleased that Panvinio had cast doubt on one of Rome's holiest relics. Panvinio had chosen to implicitly ignore the legend that these were the stairs which Christ had ascended on his way to trial in Jerusalem and which St Helena had then brought to Rome in the fourth century. Panvinio simply explained that these stairs belonged to the old Lateran Palace.[205] He knew the twelfth-century sources regarding the Lateran Palace (such as the description of the Lateran by Johannes Diaconus and the ceremonial texts by Benedictus Canonicus and Cencius Camerarius) and was thus keenly aware that those earlier sources had not referred to the stairs as 'holy'.[206] In fact, the legend about the holiness of the stairs gained wide circulation only around the time of the jubilee of 1450. Pious devotion intensified in the sixteenth century

---

[203] Chacón, *Vitae et gesta summorum pontificum*. His manuscript was incomplete at the time of his death; it was completed, for the period from Alexander VI (elected 1492) onwards, by Francisco Morales Cabrera. On Chacón see I. Herklotz, 'Historia sacra und mittelalterliche Kunst während der zweiten Hälfte des 16. Jahrhunderts in Rom', in R. De Maio et al. (eds), *Baronio e l'arte* (Sora, 1985), 21–74; id., 'Alfonso Chacón e le gallerie dei ritratti nell'età della Controriforma', in P. Tosini (ed.), *Arte e committenza nel Lazio nell'età di Cesare Baronio* (Rome, 2009), 111–42; A. Recio Veganzones, 'Alfonso Chacón, O.P., hacia una primera Roma subterránea (1578–1599)', in M. D. Rincón González (ed.), *Doce calas en el Renacimiento y un epílogo* (Jaén, 2007), 349–95.

[204] Bauer, *Censorship*, 114, 120. For Chacón's dependence on Platina, Panvinio, and Baronio as his models see Tallon, 'Les conclaves', 33.

[205] A. Chacón, 'Sententia de expurgandis denuo aliquot libris catholicorum qui cum multa utilitate expurgati legi possent, vel quorum authores suspecti sunt', Vatican City, Archivio della Congregazione per la dottrina della fede (hereafter ACDF), Index, Diari, 1, fo. 29ʳ; Index, Prot., B, fos 64ʳ, 243ᵛ (26 November 1587): 'Panvinius in libro *De septem ecclesiis* offendit dum dicit scalas sanctas non esse eas per quas Christus ascendit, sed ad usum solum palatii apostolici factas'. See Panvinio, *De praecipuis urbis Romae . . . basilicis*, 181: 'porta, quae respicit gradus scalae (quam nunc sanctam vocant) antiquitus vero patriarchii erat'. See also ibid. 171–2; id., *De sacrosancta basilica, baptisterio et patriarchio Lateranensi*, 487. On Panvinio's point of view see C. D'Onofrio, *Scalinate di Roma* (Rome, 1974), 110; N. Horsch, *Ad astra gradus: Scala Santa und Sancta Sanctorum in Rom unter Sixtus V. (1585–1590)* (Munich, 2014), 127.

[206] Horsch, *Ad astra gradus*, 123.

after Leo X publicly venerated the stairs as a holy relic.[207] By not mentioning the legend, Panvinio's guidebook stood in stark contrast to previous pilgrims' guides, as well as later ones such as Gregory Martin's *Roma sancta* (1581).[208] Sixtus V demolished and rebuilt the Lateran Palace from 1585 onwards and, because of their importance, the Holy Stairs had to be moved. They were transported to their present location at the Sancta Sanctorum chapel in 1588.

At some point between 1588 and 1590, Chacón wrote to Pope Sixtus V and explained that he wanted to produce a new *History of Popes and Cardinals*, updating and expanding Panvinio's short book on the same subject from 1557. Many details had to be added to Panvinio's work and many errors—regarding dates, names, and coats of arms—had to be corrected (though Chacón did not provide examples of errors). Chacón's mentioning of coats of arms indicates that he referred to the Strada edition rather than the 'authorized' Tramezzino edition of Panvinio's work (*Romani pontifices et cardinales*), which did not contain coats of arms.[209] He asked the pope if he could have the manuscripts of Panvinio's *Church History* (*Historia ecclesiastica*), as a loan from Cardinal Rusticucci, for two to three weeks.[210] It is unclear whether he received them; but we know that he was given the first three volumes for inspection in 1592.[211]

Chacón's historiography was characterized by a type of apologetics that avoided too much polemic. Direct attacks against Protestant historians were not characteristic of his style; much like Baronio, he preferred a strict chronological structure that portrayed a positive image of papal history.[212] Chacón hardly mentioned the modes of papal election. The reason for this was surely that the post-Reformation papacy was embarrassed that there had been, first, so many historical variations and, second, so many disputed and troubled elections. Chacón did mention some of the troubles connected

---

[207] Ibid. 75–93; D'Onofrio, *Scalinate*, 103–10.

[208] G. Martin, *Roma sancta*, ed. G. B. Parks (Rome, 1969), 35, 93. See also Horsch, *Ad astra gradus*, 322–3.

[209] Giovanni Antonio Petramellari, on the other hand, was at pains to point out that he continued the Tramezzini edition rather than the Strada edition: see Petramellari, *Ad librum Onuphrii Panvinii De summis pontificibus... continuatio* (1599), sig. †3ʳ.

[210] See the outline for the new work sent by Chacón to Sixtus V ('De libro pontificum maximorum et cardinalium a se edendo'), MS Fano, Biblioteca comunale Federiciana, Amiani 80, fos 91ʳ, 92ʳ⁻ᵛ; as well as the summary of this plan which he made for Silvio Antoniano, ibid., fo. 94ʳ⁻ᵛ. For a simpler continuation of Panvinio's *Romani pontifices et cardinales* from 1587, with lists of cardinals from 1557 to 1586 (by an unknown author), see Vat. lat. 5559 (*Appendix libri Fratris Onuphrii Panvinii de pontificibus et cardinalibus*).

[211] See also below, 180–181.

[212] Tallon, 'Les conclaves', 33–4. For what follows see ibid. 31–40.

to elections, but used these troubles to recount cautionary tales. Temporal influence in the elections was shown to have caused confusion in medieval elections; simony, when it occurred, was punished. This stance was highly relevant in the 1590s, when Pope Clement VIII attempted to push back Spanish influence in his conclave reform.

No pope has ever managed to officially designate his own successor.[213] The institution of the conclave, according to Chacón, ensured free elections of the popes and was the best remedy against confusion, so long as its rules were strictly observed. While Chacón was glad to cite elections from the Middle Ages as examples, his continuator, Francisco Morales Cabrera, was much more hesitant about mentioning the disorder which pervaded more recent conclaves. Julius III's long conclave was treated in only one phrase—a fact which Alain Tallon has judged as self-censorship, aimed at presenting an official history of the papacy.[214]

Chacón found an elegant way to explain why conclaves were places of intrigue. When he mentioned these machinations at all, he argued that they were the result of divine intervention, as the Holy Spirit caused many sudden turns in such negotiations which could not be foreseen by the participants. Chacón could not completely avoid the subject because it triggered much curiosity among readers and also because numerous sources circulated which documented recent conclaves. In general, however, Chacón recognized that papal elections were not a subject that added to the glory of the papacy; he preferred to dwell much more on ceremonies such as the papal coronations.[215] Set against this background, Panvinio's *De varia creatione* stood out even more strongly as a work of risky historical criticism. In my next chapter, I will situate Panvinio's views on the dynamics of church history within the contexts of the confessionalization and censorship.

---

[213] This option was the subject of some discussion in the sixteenth century. Paul IV threatened to make the papacy hereditary, and Pius IV considered publishing a decree prohibiting this option once and for all. Panvinio's *De varia creatione* supported Pius's stance, as Panvinio argued that this idea went against church tradition. See J. B. Sägmüller, 'Ein angebliches Dekret Pius' IV. über die Designation des Nachfolgers durch den Papst', *Archiv für katholisches Kirchenrecht*, 75 (1896), 413–29, at pp. 423–4; Baumgarten, *Von den Kardinälen*, 43–51; Visceglia, *Morte e elezione*, 157–8.

[214] Tallon, 'Les conclaves', 41.   [215] Ibid. 32, 42–6.

4

Church History, Censorship, and Confessionalization

The Interrelationship of History and Theology

From the time of the Reformation, church history presented a challenge to each confession in its own right.[1] Protestants felt compelled to devise particularly creative answers because, as Euan Cameron noted, 'the core message of the Reformation called for a shift in perceptions of the Christian past'.[2] This was because Protestants, who sought to revert to the Church's pristine early state, confronted the key issue of explaining why error had entered the Church after apostolic times. The prevailing models of church history did not suit their view of the degeneration of the medieval Church. Thus, Protestant historians had to re-invent the discipline. Protestant reformers were imbued with humanism to varying degrees; again according to Cameron, a transition from humanist-inspired to 'doctrinal-apocalyptic' Protestant church history occurred in the sixteenth century. Early Swiss reformers such as Johannes Oecolampadius, Joachim Vadian, Huldrych Zwingli, and Heinrich Bullinger showed a strong interest in the humanist historical method. They emphasized human fallibility and the deterioration of what had, initially, been good intentions in religious life. On the other hand, the doctrinal-apocalyptic variants employed a stricter view: for example, the *Magdeburg Centuries* (published 1559–74), maintained that incorrect teachings and the dilution of the ideas of the Gospel had led to inevitable degradation. Similarly, Johann Sleidan, in his *Four Empires* (*De quatuor summis imperiis*, 1556), viewed history as an unfolding of constant

---

[1] For further discussions of this subject see W.-F. Schäufele, 'Theologie und Historie: zur Interferenz zweier Wissensgebiete in Reformationszeit und konfessionellem Zeitalter', in W.-F. Schäufele and I. Dingel (eds), *Kommunikation und Transfer im Christentum der Frühen Neuzeit* (Mainz, 2007), 129–56, as well as my forthcoming article 'Theology and History', in K. G. Appold and N. H. Minnich (eds), *The Cambridge History of Reformation Era Theology, c.1500–1675*.

[2] For what follows see E. Cameron, 'Primitivism, Patristics, and Polemic in Protestant Visions of Early Christianity', in Van Liere et al., *Sacred History*, 27–51 (quotation p. 29).

The Invention of Papal History: Onofrio Panvinio between Renaissance and Catholic Reform. Stefan Bauer, Oxford University Press (2020). © Stefan Bauer.
DOI: 10.1093/oso/9780198807001.001.0001

decline, leading to an apocalyptic end.[3] The second line of thought—the apocalyptic streak—prevailed in the most influential Protestant views of history.

For Martin Luther, a crucial insight gained from the study of historical evidence was that the papal primacy had not been established by divine right but instead created by mere human actions. His short-lived but intense research on this topic at the time of the Leipzig Disputation (1519) was instrumental in paving the way for his later rejection of the papacy as an institution.[4] Philipp Melanchthon's *Loci communes* (Theological Commonplaces, 1521) were the first systematic treatment of Luther's theology; he sought to show that Lutheran ideas were consonant with the doctrines of the first centuries of Christianity.[5] Melanchthon had a keen interest in universal history and developed the influential idea that a long historical continuity had existed in the proclamation of the truth of the Gospels. This continuity was expressed by small groups of believers who throughout history had stuck to the true faith despite the worsening corruption in the Church. Matthias Flacius Illyricus's *Catalogus testium veritatis* (Catalogue of Witnesses to the Truth, 1556) was the most striking example of this line of argumentation. Just as the Catholics maintained the existence of an uninterrupted succession of bishops of Rome, Flacius argued that there had never been a time during which no protest was made against the popes' domination of the Church.[6]

By around 1560 the battle lines of interconfessional polemics had become more clearly drawn. On the Protestant side, this was reflected by the *Magdeburg Centuries*, composed by Flacius, Johannes Wigand, and their

---

[3] A. Kess, *Johann Sleidan and the Protestant Vision of History* (Aldershot, 2008), 84. For a discussion of providential views of history see Cameron, 'The Bible and the Early Modern Sense of History'.

[4] See B. Lohse, *Martin Luther's Theology*, trans. R. A. Harrisville (Edinburgh, 1999), 118–26; S. E. Schreiner, *Are you Alone Wise? The Search for Certainty in the Early Modern Era* (Oxford, 2011), 148–65; M. Thompson, 'Luther on God and History', in R. Kolb, I. Dingel, and L. Batka (eds), *The Oxford Handbook of Martin Luther's Theology* (Oxford, 2014), 127–42.

[5] H. Bollbuck, 'Testimony of True Faith and the Ruler's Mission: The Middle Ages in the *Magdeburg Centuries* and the Melanchthon School', *Archiv für Reformationsgeschichte/Archive for Reformation History*, 101 (2010), 238–62.

[6] H. Scheible, 'Der Catalogus testium veritatis: Flacius als Schüler Melanchthons', in id., *Aufsätze zu Melanchthon* (Tübingen, 2010), 415–30; H. Bollbuck, *Wahrheitszeugnis, Gottes Auftrag und Zeitkritik: die Kirchengeschichte der Magdeburger Zenturien und ihre Arbeitstechniken* (Wiesbaden, 2014), 80–103; I. Dingel, J. Hund, and L. Ilić (eds), *Matthias Flacius Illyricus: biographische Kontexte, theologische Wirkungen, historische Rezeption* (Göttingen, 2019). On Flacius's use of medieval sources see M. Hartmann, *Humanismus und Kirchenkritik: Matthias Flacius Illyricus als Erforscher des Mittelalters* (Stuttgart, 2001).

collaborators. In the *Centuries*, doctrine took centre stage. In their preface, the Centuriators argued that they had employed a new method: While their predecessors as historians of the Church (from Eusebius onwards) had concentrated on persons and events, they instead dealt with religious ideas. They saw doctrine as an action of God's Church.[7] This work divided each century into sixteen chapters, of which the one on doctrine was the most important. Those on liturgy, church government, and synods were also concerned with doctrine. All shared a markedly polemical character, no doubt supplying proof texts for sermons and controversialist tracts.

Many of the historical questions the Centuriators covered had been chosen for controversial reasons. For instance, they decided to uphold the authenticity of the legend of Pope Joan. According to this well-known story, a female pope occupied the chair of St Peter during the ninth century; she pretended to be a man and then died in childbirth during a procession. The Centuriators argued against Panvinio's refutation of the legend, dating from 1562. He had put forth compelling reasons as to why the story had to be false, drawing on historical, philological, and theological reasoning. Most convincing was Panvinio's proof of the silence of contemporary sources, including the *Liber pontificalis*.[8] The Centuriators were interested in upholding the authenticity of the story not only because it ridiculed the papacy but also because Pope Joan interrupted the continuity of apostolic succession. Therefore, they compiled a list of references to sources which, though they were not contemporary, mentioned the story. According to the Centuriators, the story's relatively long circulation inside the Catholic Church proved its authenticity. They countered Panvinio's key argument of the silence of contemporaries by throwing overboard a fundamental rule of source criticism: that the highest value should generally be assigned to contemporary sources. Instead they claimed that the authors of the ninth-century sections in the *Liber pontificalis* had 'deliberately omitted her name and

---

[7] Flacius et al., *Ecclesiastica historia* [i.e., *Magdeburg Centuries*], Centuria I, sigs α4ᵛ, α6ʳ.

[8] Panvinio's annotation to Johannes VIII, in Platina, *Historia de vitis pontificum* (1562), fos 102ʳ–104ᵛ; (1568), 134–7. See A. Boureau, *The Myth of Pope Joan*, trans. L. G. Cochrane (Chicago, IL, 2001), 245–7; Bauer, *Censorship*, 95–6. Panvinio's dismissive comments about one of the sources of the legend, Martin of Troppau (Martinus Polonus), stirred up polemics among Polish students at Padua: see W. McCuaig, 'Andreas Patricius, Carlo Sigonio, Onofrio Panvinio, and the Polish Nation of the University of Padua', *History of Universities*, 3 (1983), 87–100. On Baronio and Pope Joan see S. Zen, *Baronio storico: Controriforma e crisi del metodo umanistico* (Naples, 1994), 211–22.

dates because of the disgrace and because she was a woman'.[9] Here emerged a fundamental aspect of history's role in early modern polemical writing: Source criticism was appreciated, but overarching theological and political needs often had a higher priority.

A similar pattern could be observed among the Catholics. While numerous works on doctrine and specific questions of church history were published at the beginning of our period, during the second half of the sixteenth century large works of synthesis appeared. In general, the viewpoints of Catholic authors were less personal and more homogeneous than those of Protestant authors. Johann Eck, Luther's most famous opponent, published his *Enchiridion locorum communium* (Manual of Commonplaces) for the first time in 1525; there, he laid out Catholic doctrine, explained the primacy of the papacy, and defended the institutional Church, councils, tradition, good works, the sacraments, and the cult of images. This made his book the blueprint for polemical handbooks of the sixteenth century.

Catholics prominently deployed historical arguments to demonstrate the development of papal power as a means of bolstering the pope's primacy against the challenge mounted by Protestants. Furthermore, papal lists and papal histories proved that this succession had been uninterrupted until the present day.[10] Excursions into church history, however, remained personal and isolated initiatives. Among such initiatives can be mentioned, for example, the editions of ancient church historians (*Autores historiae ecclesiasticae*, 1523) by Erasmus's friend Beatus Rhenanus as well as the editions of conciliar decrees by Jacques Merlin (*Quatuor concilia generalia*, 1524) and Petrus Crabbe (*Concilia omnia*, 1538). Melchior Cano (*De locis theologicis*, 1563) was an exception among Catholics in this period, as he expressed more detailed opinions about the role of human history in ecclesiastical studies and advocated the execution of critical studies within the limits of authorization by the Church.[11]

---

[9] Flacius et al., *Ecclesiastica historia*, Centuria IX (1565), cols 332–3, 500–2; quotation, col. 502: 'nomen autem et tempus eius pontificios scriptores consulto omisisse propter foeditatem rei et sexum foemineum'. See also Boureau, *Myth*, 247–8; Bollbuck, *Wahrheitszeugnis*, 346–9.

[10] For a papal list see J. Eck, *De primatu Petri adversus Ludderum* (Paris, 1521), Book II, fos 33ʳ–39ʳ.

[11] A. Biondi, 'La storiografia apologetica e controversistica', in N. Tranfaglia and M. Firpo (eds), *La storia: i grandi problemi dal Medioevo all'età contemporanea*, 10 vols (Turin, 1986–8), iv. 315–33, esp. pp. 316–17, 331 n. 2.

Papal Biography

The history of papal biography in the sixteenth and seventeenth centuries awaits a basic stocktaking. Therefore, in this section I offer some preliminary thoughts.[12] In doing so, I assume that three main factors influenced the practice of writing papal biographies. First was the social condition of their creation in the ever-changing balances of power in the various pontificates. The weight of the papal relatives and favourites was determined and balanced anew each time, and it was by no means taken for granted that a biography made sense under the successor of the pope it described. The decision as to whether a predecessor's biography should be published was sometimes delicate. Second was the overarching interest of the Curia in its self-representation as a perfect model for the outside world. Interests connected to points of importance for theology and politics had to be defended and maintained vis-à-vis both Catholics and Protestants. Third was the increasing importance of empirical methods and attempts at making papal historiography more 'scientific', which constantly wrestled with the other two factors.

Biography as a classical literary genre was concerned with the particular nature and traits, as well as the public actions, of its subject. It revealed not only positive but also negative features and activities, with the goal of providing a comprehensive picture of a lifetime's achievements.[13] In what follows, I shall leave aside sources such as diaries of the papal masters of ceremonies and encomia delivered at papal funerals. Although they contain relevant material, they are not, properly speaking, biographies. It is also necessary to distinguish between serial and individual biographies. The serial biographies are best known; by continuing Bartolomeo Platina's *Lives of the Popes*, which itself was a transformation of the medieval *Liber*

---

[12]   For an overall view of papal historiography see Fuhrmann, 'Papstgeschichtsschreibung'. On Protestant collections of lives of popes, which I do not examine here, see D. Solfaroli Camillocci, 'Dévoiler le Mal dans l'histoire: les recueils de vies des papes dans la Genève de Calvin', in F. Alazard and F. La Brasca (eds), *La papauté à la Renaissance* (Paris, 2007), 511–32. For a previous version of the following section see S. Bauer, 'Humanisten und Klienten: Grundlinien der Papstbiographik im 16. und 17. Jahrhundert', in M. Völkel and A. Strohmeyer (eds), *Historiographie an europäischen Höfen (16.–18. Jahrhundert)* (Berlin, 2009), 247–53.

[13]   A. Dihle, 'Antike Grundlagen', in W. Berschin (ed.), *Biographie zwischen Renaissance und Barock* (Heidelberg, 1993), 1–22; M. von Albrecht, 'Nochmals antike Grundlagen: Sueton', ibid. 311–32, at p. 316.

pontificalis, they ensured that all popes of the sixteenth century and beyond received biographies.[14]

The Italian humanist Platina published his collection, consisting of biographies from Christ to his own time, under Pope Sixtus IV in 1479. The short, schematic lives in the medieval *Liber pontificalis* had limited themselves to contents best described as *gesta* (principal public deeds).[15] Platina led papal biography back closer to classical models of the *vita*. In a liberal spirit, he showed the questionable character of certain popes, as well as the papacy's morally dubious sides. He also criticized worldliness and corruption at a time when the legitimacy of the papacy as an institution had not yet become a major bone of contention. The uninhibitedness which Platina displayed remained unparalleled among Catholics for centuries. Platina had brought to light the 'unvarnished truth' ('incorrupta veritas') about the deeds of the popes, as the historian Paolo Giovio—himself a biographer of popes—judged in 1546.[16] This notion of truth was, of course, problematic. Giovio, a historiographical survival artist, was aware that one could not simply describe the facts in a straightforward manner: one had to flatter the sensibilities of patrons in a rhetorically skilful way, though without saying untrue things.[17] We will see below how Platina's work, and Panvinio's editions of it, were censored in the sixteenth century.[18]

We turn now to the—rarer—biographies of individual popes. In the fifteenth century, there were such works about Nicholas V (by Giannozzo Manetti), Pius II (by Giovanni Antonio Campano), and Paul II (by Michele

---

[14] Latin editions of Platina's *Lives of the Popes* with continuations were produced until 1626, Italian ones until 1765. On Platina see Bauer, *Censorship*; id., 'Platina e le "res gestae" di Pio II', in A. Antoniutti and M. Sodi (eds), *Enea Silvio Piccolomini: Pius Secundus, poeta laureatus, pontifex maximus* (Rome; Vatican City, 2007), 17–32; id., 'Sacchi, Bartolomeo, detto il Platina', in *DBI*, lxxxix. 472–5; id., '*Liber pontificalis* in the Renaissance'; C. Märtl, 'Papstgeschichtsschreibung im Quattrocento: vom "Liber pontificalis" zu Platinas "Liber de vita Christi ac omnium pontificum"', in U. Friedrich, L. Grenzmann, and F. Rexroth (eds), *Geschichtsentwürfe und Identitätsbildung am Übergang zur Neuzeit*, 2 vols (Berlin; Boston, 2018), ii. 242–56.

[15] H. Schmidinger, 'Das Papstbild in der Geschichtsschreibung des späteren Mittelalters', *Römische historische Mitteilungen*, 1 (1956/57), 106–29, at pp. 109–12; F.-J. Schmale, *Funktion und Formen mittelalterlicher Geschichtsschreibung* (Darmstadt, 1985), 112–17; W. Berschin, *Biographie und Epochenstil im lateinischen Mittelalter*, 5 vols (Stuttgart, 1986–2004), i. 270–7.

[16] Paolo Giovio, *Elogia virorum literis illustrium* (first publ. 1546), in id., *Opera*, ed. Società Storica Comense (Rome, 1956–), viii, ed. R. Meregazzi, 31–225, at p. 53: 'Sacrati praesertim ordinis bonique mortales plurimum Platinae manibus debent, quando eius ingenuo labore ad exoptatam obscuri saeculi nec ideo perituram lucem pontificii principatus actionum incorrupta veritas nunciatur, quae procul eloquentiae illecebris uti pura et incompta fidem praefert...'

[17] M. Völkel, *Die Wahrheit zeigt viele Gesichter: der Historiker, Sammler und Satiriker Paolo Giovio (1486–1552) und sein Porträt Roms in der Hochrenaissance* (Basel, 1999), 50–3.

[18] See below, 162–166.

Canensi and Gaspare da Verona).[19] After these new humanist beginnings, a gap opened and no further individual biographies were published for more than five pontificates, from 1471 to 1503. Sixtus IV, Innocent VIII, Alexander VI, and Pius III were not described for posterity by contemporary authors in any detailed biography. Some minor attempts were made for Julius II (r. 1503–13),[20] but it was only Paolo Giovio who ended the biographical lull with his famous life of Leo X Medici (r. 1513–21), commissioned by Cardinal Ippolito de' Medici and Pope Clement VII Medici and composed around 1533.[21] Over fifty years had passed since the individual biographies of Paul II. Clearly, it was not obvious or obligatory for a pope to have a biographer. The recording of papal deeds was characterized by discontinuity, so it was up to every papal family to ensure that the memory of its pontifex remained for posterity. Though Giovio focused on the bright sunlight of Leo's pontificate, he included subtle criticisms of other popes. We can see this in his biography of the pope from Utrecht, Hadrian VI (r. 1522–3), which Giovio composed shortly afterwards. Hadrian had fallen out with the Roman court, and his short pontificate was the subject of widespread Italian ridicule. Giovio described how the cardinals sometimes had to ride on mules behind the impatient pope, and how Hadrian nearly made a fool of himself when he wanted to have the head of Pasquino, a symbol of Roman mockery, thrown into the Tiber.[22]

Neither Clement VII Medici (r. 1523–34), during whose pontificate the city of Rome suffered the Sack of 1527, nor Paul III Farnese (r. 1534–49) received contemporary individual biographies. Around this time, Panvinio started researching his serial biographies of the sixteenth-century popes, which were published as an appendix to his critical editions of Platina's *Lives*

---

[19] M. Miglio, *Storiografia pontificia del Quattrocento* (Bologna, 1975).

[20] J. F. D'Amico, 'Papal History and Curial Reform in the Renaissance: Raffaele Maffei's *Breuis Historia* of Julius II and Leo X', *Archivum historiae pontificiae*, 18 (1980), 157–210; J. Britnell and C. Shaw, 'A French Life of Pope Julius II, 1519: Jean Beaufils and his Translation of Platina', *Bibliothèque d'humanisme et Renaissance*, 62 (2000), 103–18.

[21] P. Giovio, *Vita Leonis X*, in id., *Opera*, vi, pt 1, ed. M. Cataudella, 5–106. For the date of composition see T. C. P. Zimmermann, *Paolo Giovio: The Historian and the Crisis of Sixteenth-Century Italy* (Princeton, NJ, 1995), 222. On Giovio's knowledge of classical models of biography see id., 'Paolo Giovio and the Rhetoric of Individuality', in T. F. Mayer and D. R. Woolf (eds), *The Rhetorics of Life-Writing in Early Modern Europe* (Ann Arbor, MI, 1995), 39–62.

[22] P. Giovio, *Vita Hadriani VI*, in id., *Opera*, vi, pt 1, pp. 107–40. See also J. Burckhardt, *Die Cultur der Renaissance in Italien: ein Versuch*, ed. M. Mangold (Munich; Basel, 2018), 114; Völkel, *Die Wahrheit*, 16–21. Panvinio collected records of consistories that took place during Hadrian's pontificate; these were published in Mercati, *Dall'Archivio Vaticano*, 83–113. See also above, 82.

of the Popes. Two editions of Platina came out in 1562: (1) *Opus de vitis ac gestis summorum pontificum ad sua usque tempora deductum* (Cologne: Maternus Cholinus), which contained Panvinio's five lives from Paul III to Pius IV as well as a short chronicle of popes by him (but since this edition carried no foreword by Panvinio, we can assume that he did not fully authorize it); (2) *Historia de vitis pontificum Romanorum a Domino Nostro Iesu Christo usque ad Paulum Papam II* (Venice: Michele Tramezzino), which contained Panvinio's dedication to Pius IV (dated 1 October 1561), Panvinio's thirteen lives from Sixtus IV to Pius IV (with a preface explaining his sources), critical annotations appended by Panvinio to over sixty of Platina's biographies, and a chronological index of popes. An expanded and revised edition came out in 1568 (Cologne: Cholinus), which contained Panvinio's lives from Sixtus IV to Pius V.[23]

In 1566, Panvinio produced a papal history in six manuscript volumes (*Pontificum Romanorum imagines*), consisting mainly of portraits of the popes from Christ to Pius V, with their coats of arms and those of the cardinals.[24] This work contained very short lives of the popes similar to those of the *Romani pontifices et cardinales* (1557); it also included epitaphs of popes and cardinals. Even so, the main interest of this work was the images. It has been considered the first attempt at an iconography of popes. Among other aspects, Panvinio paid attention to the varying shapes of the papal tiara and papal vestments.[25] This work was closely connected to a small book by Panvinio, the *XXVII pontificum maximorum elogia et imagines*, a series of papal portraits with short biographies from Urban VI (d. 1389) to Pius V, published by Antoine Lafréry in Rome in 1568.[26] As regards the

---

[23] On the editions of Platina's *Lives* see Bauer, *Censorship.* For a critical edition (without Panvinio's additions) see Platina, *Liber de vita Christi ac omnium pontificum*, ed. G. Gaida (Città di Castello, 1913–32). For Panvinio's remarks about these popes' artistic commissions, with which I do not deal here, see Occhipinti, *Ligorio*, pp. XL–XLVI and *passim*.

[24] Panvinio, *Pontificum Romanorum imagines eorundem et cardinalium Sanctae Romanae Ecclesiae insignia*, MSS Clm 155–60.

[25] See Hartig, 'Sammlung', 286: 'der erste Versuch einer Ikonographie der Päpste'; G. B. Ladner, *Die Papstbildnisse des Altertums und des Mittelalters*, 3 vols (Vatican City, 1941–84), iii. 186–93; H. J. Meier, 'Das Bildnis in der Reproduktionsgraphik des 16. Jahrhunderts', *Zeitschrift für Kunstgeschichte*, 58 (1995), 449–77, at pp. 459–64; Herklotz, '*Historia sacra*', 32–9. The relationship between this work and MS Barb. lat. 2738 (a collection of material on popes and cardinals) requires further study; see G. B. Ladner, 'I mosaici e gli affreschi ecclesiastico-politici nell'antico Palazzo Lateranense', in id., *Images and Ideas in the Middle Ages*, 2 vols (Rome, 1983), i. 347–66.

[26] Panvinio, *XXVII pontificum maximorum elogia et imagines*, with a dedication to Alberico Cibo, dated 6 January 1568 (Rome: Lafréry, 1568). On this work see Hartig, 'Sammlung', 299–300; D. Redig de Campos, 'Notizia critico-bibliografica intorno alla iconografia pontificia del Panvinio (1568)', *La rinascita*, 2 (1939), 794–800; id., 'Un ritratto ideale di Gregorio XII,

coats of arms, the *Pontificum Romanorum imagines* was a new and emended version of the collection of coats of arms that Jacopo Strada had produced for Fugger in c.1550–5, which has been mentioned above; they bore a striking similarity in that the first coat of arms contained in both was that of Pope Felix III (r. 483–92).[27]

In his editions of Platina's *Lives*, Panvinio portrayed the popes of the late fifteenth and sixteenth century in retrospect, devoting especially detailed attention to Pope Hadrian VI. He described Hadrian's reforming intentions and was impressed by his abolition of many venal offices at the Curia, though the papal treasury was becoming visibly emptier and he made enemies among those who lost their positions:

So that his promise to reform the churchmen would also be followed up in practice, and not only in words, he immediately turned many things in Rome upside down. He gradually abolished the new offices which Leo had instituted for the regular income of the Holy See and through which, because they had been allocated by payment, great gains had entered the treasury of the Holy See. He also allocated offices which became available free of charge, though he himself at the time suffered from a severe shortage of money. He was aware that these offices were a burden to the Holy See and that, allocated in this way, they often caused offence and envy. He also took away from some persons such offices which had been given to them without payment, as he thought it should suffice that they had gained no small benefit for many years without any cost or efforts. Although he ran into many difficulties in this cause and also suffered injury from many who saw their gains being greatly reduced, he regarded

---

attribuito a Girolamo Muziano, nuovamente collocato nella Pinacoteca vaticana', *Rivista d'arte*, ser. ii, 11 (1939), 166–75; B. Rubach, *'Ant. Lafreri formis Romae': der Verleger Antonio Lafreri und seine Druckgraphikproduktion* (Berlin, 2016), 114–24.

[27] M. Reuter, *'Insignia quantum haberi potuerunt*: papi, cardinali e nobili di tutta Italia in un armoriale commissionato da un umanista tedesco', *Strenna dei romanisti*, 71 (2010), 615–30. The relationship to Massarelli's collection of papal coats of arms in Vat. lat. 3755 should also be verified; see Bouyé, 'Les armoiries imaginaires'. The entire question of papal portraits in volumes of lives of the popes of the sixteenth century, such as can be found in the works of Platina, Panvinio, Giovanni Battista Cavalieri, Antonio Ciccarelli, Alfonso Chacón, and others, has so far been insufficiently investigated. See M. Pelc, *Illustrium imagines: das Porträtbuch der Renaissance* (Leiden, 2002); Herklotz, 'Alfonso Chacón e le gallerie'; R. Rusconi, *Santo Padre: la santità del papa da San Pietro a Giovanni Paolo II* (Rome, 2010), 215–20; Bauer, *Censorship*, 188–9 (with further references).

this as a small thing, as the morals of the time and the present state of events urged him to act in this way.[28]

Hadrian was met by a wave of indignation from the worldly Curia. Yet if the pious pope, who was unfamiliar with the Roman court, did not always act skilfully, Panvinio argued for leniency towards him:

> Whoever finds something lacking in him can be sure that it is divine rather than human to always watch over everything in such a way that nothing escapes you, especially with so many worries and among such cunning men who put forward their requests under a thousand false pretences and colourful accounts, so that they can place their affairs in a better light, and who attach no importance to the question of whether what follows is just or unjust, pious or impious, if only it is attained in some way by them. Let him, finally, believe that the execution of the business of the Holy See is more laborious than it may seem at first to the inexperienced and to those who act with leisure and in peace; here it is appropriate to cite a verse of the comic playwright: 'If you were in my place, you would think differently' [Terence, Andria, 310].[29]

By contrast, Panvinio presented Clement VII as a detested and disastrous pope, emphasizing his stinginess. Clement's 'uncommon avarice' ('inusitata avaritia') made him so unpopular, no one assisted him when the Colonna

---

[28] Panvinio, 'Hadrianus VI', in Platina, *Historia de vitis pontificum* (1568), 374–83, at p. 378: 'Atque ut promissum de corrigendis ecclesiasticis etiam re, non verbis praestaturus videretur, multa protinus Romae in statum alium vertit, nova officia super ordinariis sacrosanctae sedis proventibus a Leone instituta, ex quibus pretio datis plurimum quaestus fisco eius accesserat, paulatim abolebat et, quotquot eius generis deinde vacassent, nulli pretio dabat, etiamsi ipse id temporis graviter re nummaria laboraret. Sciebat quippe quantum illa sedi apostolicae onerosa essent et sic data amplissimam passim materiam offendiculis et obtrectationibus praeberent. Abrogabat quoque ea nonnullis, qui gratis nacti fuerant, ratus satis eis esse debere, quod inde annis plurimis sine ullo sumptu onereque commoda non exigua accepissent. Quanquam ea in re plurimum difficultatis passus est, multorum quoque offensam subiit, qui quaestui suo per hoc plurimum decedere videbant, quod tamen ipse minimi fecit, quia mores temporum statusque rerum praesens sic facere commoneret.'

[29] Ibid. 381: 'Ut, ut est, certum habeat, quisquis in eo nonnulla desideravit, divinum potius quam humanum esse ita ad omnia perpetuo vigilare, ut non alicubi tibi excidas, praesertim in tantis occupationibus et apud homines tam astutos, qui mille praestigias, mille colores quaerunt, sub quibus res suas meliores faciant, nihil interim pensi habentes, aequum sit an iniquum, pium an impium quod sequuntur, dummodo via aliqua assequantur. Credat denique functionem sedis apostolicae operosiorem esse, quam imperitis rerum et in otio quieteque agentibus prima specie videantur: ubi non intempestive quis illud Comici produxerit: "Tu si hic sis, aliter sentias."'

clan raided and plundered the papal palace, St Peter's Basilica, and large parts of the Borgo in September 1526.[30] On the other hand, Paul III Farnese appeared as a model pope: peace-loving, generous, equipped with a great ability to judge human nature, and well-disposed towards the learned. On the negative side, he excessively favoured his own relatives, to the point that he advanced them to the highest honours and positions of authority.[31] No doubt Panvinio received some information from Cardinal Alessandro Farnese. Panvinio rebuked Julius III (r. 1550–5) as pleasure-seeking and careless, while portraying the learned pope Marcellus II (1555), with whom Panvinio had been in close contact, as a frugal saint who, nonetheless, could have been a little more generous.[32]

With the pontificate of Paul IV Carafa (r. 1555–9), the stricter dogmatic climate of the Catholic Reformation was reflected in the demands made on papal biography. Paul polarized public opinion, and Panvinio had to revise his work several times.[33] The Carafa pope's harsh reform measures and anti-Spanish attitude created difficulties for Panvinio, who, as we have seen, awaited the end of his pontificate in Parma and Venice. Thus, it is hardly surprising that the first biography of Paul IV, which Panvinio published in 1562, was critical. It is surprising, however, that he initially gave only lukewarm approval to the government of Paul's successor, Pius IV Medici (r. 1559–65). Commenting on the spectacular trial during which the nephews of Pius's predecessor were sentenced to death, Panvinio described it as a 'horrid and memorable spectacle' ('horrendum et memorabile spectaculum'). His attitude changed suddenly in the same year, 1562, perhaps because Pius not only gave Panvinio money to support his studies but promised him a position in the Vatican Library. Panvinio went on to

---

[30] Ibid., 'Clemens VII', 383–90, at pp. 386–7: 'Clemens rebus desperatis trepidus in arcem fugit, frustra auxilium opemque quaerens, qui inusitata avaritia usque adeo omnium hominum odia in se concitarat, ut nemo esset, qui vicem eius...doleret. Nam sacratos viros novis decimis onerarat, officiorum collegiis redditus averterat, gymnasii salaria doctoribus constituta subtraxerat; irata etiam maxime plebs erat, quod certis horreorum monopoliis, magno fisci quaestu, annonae tum in urbe summa charitas esset....Nemine igitur in tanto pontificis periculo, qui omnium odio flagrabat, repugnante Columnenses...in urbem Leonianam irruperunt et Palatio Vaticano omni supellectile sacra et profana direpto in omnium quoque augustissimam basilicam Sancti Petri nefarias manus iniecere.' On Clement's stinginess see also T. C. P. Zimmermann, 'Guicciardini, Giovio, and the Character of Clement VII', in K. Gouwens and S. E. Reiss (eds), *The Pontificate of Clement VII: History, Politics, Culture* (Aldershot, 2005), 19–27.

[31] Panvinio, 'Paulus III', in Platina, *Historia de vitis pontificum* (1568), 390–414, at pp. 413–14: 'Doctos et eruditos viros amavit, erga suos vero sanguinis propinquitate sibi coniunctos adeo indulgens, ut et intemperanter eis faveret et ad summos honores aut ad summum auctoritatis locum stabilesque divitias eosdem proveheret.'

[32] Ibid., 'Iulius III', 414–[425]; 'Marcellus II', [425]–430.

[33] For what follows see Pastor, *Geschichte der Päpste*, vi. 693–4; Aubert, *Paolo IV*, 163–86.

produce two modified biographies, strongly differentiating between the two popes and justifying the death sentences of the Carafa nephews.[34]

Shortly before the end of his own life, Panvinio was again forced to revise his judgements of Paul IV and Pius IV. Under Pius V, the former Dominican inquisitor, it was again necessary to hide any criticism of Paul IV. Panvinio accordingly modified his lives of the popes for the 1568 edition. As we have seen, Panvinio had been caught between two different reforming movements inside the Catholic Church of the 1560s; the contrast between the fanatical Paul IV and the milder Pius IV was simply too strong for a balanced treatment. Thus ended the final attempts at critical papal biography in sixteenth-century Rome.[35]

Early Modern Censorship Seen From a Roman Perspective

I shall now present examples of interventions of the Catholic Church into works of historiography. Time and again for the Roman Church, the question arose of which negative aspects of its history were to be admitted before both Catholics and Protestants.[36] Censorship was exercised in the early modern period by both State and Church, since each felt the need to control thought. It was an obvious recourse in early modern Europe; freedom from censorship was only the exception.[37] After the invention of the printing press, the call for censorship was not long in coming. There were various possible motives for intervention. A humanist such as Niccolò Perotti

[34] For a detailed analysis see the section 'Panvinio as biographer of Pius IV' in Pastor, *Geschichte der Päpste*, vii. 676–87; English trans., *The History of the Popes from the Close of the Middle Ages*, 40 vols (London, 1891–1953), xv. 415–29. See also Panvinio's letters to Carlo Borromeo, 16 August and 4 October 1567, BAM, F 39 inf., fos 97ʳ–98ᵛ, and F 78 inf., fos 239ʳ–240ᵛ. Further material pertaining to Panvinio's revisions of his lives (particularly those of the sixteenth century) is contained in Vat. lat. 12121 and 12181.
[35] I pass over the hagiographical presentations of Pius V as well as the lives of Sixtus V (r. 1585–90) which in part were corrected by Sixtus himself. See Pastor, *Geschichte der Päpste*, x. 619–40; M. Gotor, 'Le vite di San Pio V dal 1572 al 1712 tra censura, agiografia e storia', in M. Guasco and A. Torre (eds), *Pio V nella società e nella politica del suo tempo* (Bologna, 2005), 207–49; M. Pattenden, 'Antonio de Fuenmayor's Life of Pius V: A Pope in Early Modern Spanish Historiography', *Renaissance Studies*, 32 (2018), 183–200.
[36] For a previous version of this section see S. Bauer, 'Wieviel Geschichte ist erlaubt? Frühmoderne Zensur aus römischer Perspektive', in S. Rau and B. Studt (eds), *Geschichte schreiben: ein Quellen- und Studienhandbuch zur Historiografie (ca. 1350–1750)* (Berlin, 2010), 334–47.
[37] For introductions see E. Tortarolo, 'Zensur als Institution und Praxis im Europa der Frühen Neuzeit: ein Überblick', in H. Zedelmaier and M. Mulsow (eds), *Die Praktiken der Gelehrsamkeit in der Frühen Neuzeit* (Tübingen, 2001), 277–94: M. Infelise, *I libri proibiti da Gutenberg all'Encyclopédie*, revised edn (Rome; Bari, 2013).

worried about the philological quality of the classics. If an edition of ancient literature was put on the market in hundreds of copies, this edition could quickly become a widespread point of reference and disseminate editorial mistakes. A manuscript, on the other hand, was unique; its circulation was limited and, thus, controllable. Perotti was horrified when, in 1470, he saw the flawed edition of Pliny by the German printers Sweynheym and Pannartz in Rome. He suggested in vain that a corrector, with papal authorization, should examine all future editions of classics and correct them if necessary before they went into print.[38]

Pre-publication censorship, motivated both politically and religiously, was first developed in German university towns such as Mainz and Cologne. Interventions remained sporadic, however. Only with the emergence of Protestantism were the authorities forced to make their control more systematic. In reaction to the well-organized book production in Calvin's Geneva, which infiltrated the French market, indexes of prohibited books were published in France from the 1540s onwards. Through tight control, the Spanish monarchy succeeded in halting any Protestant book production. In the Holy Roman Empire, which was confessionally divided, comprehensive surveillance of the book market would have been a hopeless endeavour: Luther himself witnessed the stunningly explosive diffusion of his writings. In Italy, a co-operation between local governments and the Roman Church developed; its purpose was to halt writings which were dangerous to both religion and State. In this process, the influence of the Church at first grew but later, towards the end of the early modern period, diminished.[39] The dominant centre of Italian book production, Venice, never completely gave up state control of this branch of the economy.[40]

The Protestant governments in Europe also exercised censorship; however, this has provoked less scholarly interest. According to one hypothesis, Protestant censorship—especially in Calvinism, in which Church and

---

[38] J. Monfasani, 'The First Call for Press Censorship: Niccolò Perotti, Giovanni Andrea Bussi, Antonio Moreto, and the Editing of Pliny's *Natural History*', *Renaissance Quarterly*, 41 (1988), 1–31. For papal attempts to control the printing press from 1487 onwards see J. Hasecker, *Quellen zur päpstlichen Pressekontrolle in der Neuzeit (1487–1966)* (Paderborn, 2017), 27–30.

[39] For the seventeenth century see M. Cavarzere, *La prassi della censura dell'Italia del Seicento: tra repressione e mediazione* (Rome, 2011). On censorship in the Enlightenment see W. Haefs and Y.-G. Mix (eds), *Zensur im Jahrhundert der Aufklärung* (Göttingen, 2007); R. Birn, *La censure royale des livres dans la France des Lumières* (Paris, 2007); P. Delpiano, *Il governo della lettura: Chiesa e libri nell'Italia del Settecento* (Bologna, 2007); E. Tortarolo, *The Invention of Free Press: Writers and Censorship in Eighteenth Century Europe* (Dordrecht, 2016).

[40] Grendler, *Roman Inquisition*.

State were closely intertwined—aimed for the comprehensive protection of certain modes of conduct in the community (*censura morum*), whereas Catholic censorship limited itself to the control of the contents of printed works. The validity of this thesis, however, has been called into question for Geneva.[41] In a comparison of Catholic and Protestant censorship, the most basic similarities prevail. Catholics and Protestants shared the basic goal of forming and maintaining orthodoxy through censorship.

In 1559 Pope Paul IV published the first Roman—that is, universal—Index of Prohibited Books.[42] Largely shaped by the Inquisition, this was the most severe Index ever promulgated. Through it, the Inquisition, whose central office was in Rome, tried to take from the local bishops in the periphery their role in allowing and prohibiting *any* kind of published expression of thought. The Index of the Council of Trent (1564) partly revised this centralization in favour of the bishops until, in 1571, Pius V created a congregation charged with centralizing and bureaucratizing the censorship of books in Rome: the Congregation of the Index of Prohibited Books.[43] Because of the complex disputes that arose between the organs of power at the centre and periphery (i.e., Index, Inquisition, bishops, and worldly authorities), only in 1596 was the publication of a new Roman Index achieved.

While the Index of 1559 emphasized prohibitions, the Index of the Council of Trent focused on the production of new editions of purged texts. Because the Congregation of the Index was overloaded with work, it was a stroke of luck for a book to be expurgated, as otherwise it simply remained forbidden. For this reason, the Dominican censor Girolamo Giovannini was justified in thinking that prohibited books (unless they were read illegally or by those rare individuals who had official licences to read) were, for all intents and purposes, dead; only the work of a censor could bring them back to life. Giovannini's understanding of his role as censor was exaggerated in one respect: he believed that the literary work he did was on the same level as that of the authors whom he corrected and that, therefore, he could properly consider censored books to be his own creations. In censoring the *Dialogi piacevoli* (Pleasant Dialogues) of Niccolò Franco of 1539,

---

[41] L. Bianchin, *Dove non arriva la legge: dottrine della censura nella prima età moderna* (Bologna, 2005), 53; I. Jostock, *La censure négociée: le contrôle du livre a Genève, 1560–1625* (Geneva, 2007).

[42] V. Frajese, *Nascita dell'Indice: la censura ecclesiastica dal Rinascimento alla Controriforma* (Brescia, 2006). See also above, 49–50.

[43] See below, 182.

after painstakingly removing all the Erasmian content, Giovannini changed the title to *Dialoghi piacevolissimi* (Very Pleasant Dialogues, 1590). Franco had been sentenced to death by the Inquisition twenty years earlier for another dialogue which dealt with Paul IV's deeds and morals.[44]

In general, historical writings received only modest attention from the Congregation of the Index. For example, in the three indexes with instructions for expurgation which were published in Antwerp (1571), Madrid (1584), and Rome (1607), we find 10 to 15 per cent of books with historical subject matter.[45] Franz Heinrich Reusch noted 'that in the selection of historical writings which were banned, one can no more recognize a plan than in the selection of theological writings'.[46]

Works on late antique and medieval history could come under particular scrutiny when their authors discussed the power of the Church. An example are the examinations of the works of Carlo Sigonio.[47] In 1571 Cardinals Sirleto and Ugo Boncompagni (who later became Pope Gregory XIII, r. 1572–85) made corrections to Sigonio's *History of Bologna* (*Historia Bononiensis*).[48] In this work, Sigonio proposed some doubts regarding the authenticity of the Donation of Constantine, which, according to him, was believed to be genuine 'by pious men' ('a piis hominibus'). The censors could not accept this statement. It would be better, they told Sigonio, if he wrote that 'many trustworthy authors' ('multi probatae fidei scriptores') had transmitted information about the Donation.[49] On the other hand, the censors conceded that the States of medieval Italy had parties which supported either the emperor or the pope—though only the papal side had *auctoritas*, whereas the imperial side was to be considered only a faction. Sigonio was not

---

[44] U. Rozzo, 'Erasmo espurgato dai *Dialogi piacevoli* di Nicolò Franco', in id., *La letteratura italiana negli 'Indici' del Cinquecento* (Udine, 2005), 245–310; Aubert, *Paolo IV*, 131–61.

[45] J. M. de Bujanda, 'La censure écclesiastique sur les œuvres historiques', in Firpo, *Nunc alia tempora*, 265–77, at pp. 270–1; Bujanda, *Index des livres interdits*.

[46] F. H. Reusch, *Der Index der verbotenen Bücher: ein Beitrag zur Kirchen- und Literaturgeschichte*, 2 vols (Bonn, 1883–5), ii. 188–205, at p. 188: 'daß in der Auswahl der geschichtlichen Schriften, die man verbot, ebenso wenig ein Plan zu erkennen ist wie in der Auswahl der theologischen'.

[47] For what follows see McCuaig, *Sigonio*, 251–90; G. Bartolucci, '*In falso veritas*: Carlo Sigonio's Forged Challenge to Ecclesiastical Censorship and Italian Jurisdictionalism', *Journal of the Warburg and Courtauld Institutes*, 81 (2018), 211–37.

[48] G. Manfrè, 'L'edizione bolognese della *Historia Bononiensis* di Carlo Sigonio', 2 pts, *Accademie e biblioteche d'Italia*, 61 (1993) no. 1, pp. 14–20, and 62 (1994) no. 2, pp. 16–35; Bastia, 'Vicende censorie'.

[49] Sigonio, *Opera*, iii, col. 334. On Sigonio and the Donation see also G. Bartolucci, 'Costantino nella storiografia della Controriforma: Sigonio e Baronio tra filologia, censura e apologetica', in A. Melloni et al. (eds), *Costantino I: Enciclopedia costantiniana*, 3 vols (Rome, 2013), iii. 99–114.

allowed to report that, around 1250, the town of Carpi was in the possession of Modena; Cardinal Sirleto insisted that Sigonio either say that the town had belonged to the Church or delete the passage.

A censorship of his Italian history (*De regno Italiae*) accused Sigonio of tracing the development of the Papal States throughout the course of history. The censors pointed out that, in his book, the popes captured more and more territories by means of a struggle with other powers. According to the Donation of Constantine, however, they were lords over the entire West; therefore—as the censor was convinced—the discussion about the growth of the Papal States not only was superfluous but also handed dangerous arguments to the Protestants.[50] Furthermore, there were objections to the classical Latin in Sigonio's *History of Bologna*. Where the Christian martyrs suffered *detrimentum* (damage), he should have written *calamitas* (disaster). Also, it was improper to write that a candidate *obtinuit* the office of the papacy (i.e., asserted himself in the election), as this looked more like career planning than divine providence.

In truth, Sigonio was not a particularly antipapal writer, as he only applied methods of source criticism to the history of the Italian Middle Ages. For instance, Sigonio's history of Italy (*De regno Italiae*) acknowledged the achievements of the reforming pope Gregory VII (r. 1073–85).[51] The censors' treatment of Sigonio shows that the Church did not tolerate doubts regarding the legitimacy of the temporal rule of the papacy. Even the Donation of Constantine, which had long been considered a fabrication among historians, could not be called into question. Against his better judgement, Sigonio was forced to defend it, especially in his *De occidentali imperio* (History of the Western Empire) of 1578. In the same year, thanks to support from Cardinal Gabriele Paleotti, Sigonio was officially commissioned by Gregory XIII to write an ample and ambitious *Church History* against the *Magdeburg Centuries*. However, his project stopped in its tracks in 1579, after Cardinal Sirleto had inspected the draft of the first books. Despite writing desperate letters, Sirleto never saw his draft again.[52]

---

[50] McCuaig, *Sigonio*, 278.

[51] C. Sigonio, *Historiarum de regno Italiae libri XV* (Venice, 1574), 353–75. See also McCuaig, *Sigonio*, 285.

[52] Sigonio's incomplete *Historia ecclesiastica* (up to AD 311) was published in the eighteenth century in his *Opera*, iv, separate pagination, cols 1–318. See McCuaig, *Sigonio*, 78–80; S. Zen, 'Cesare Baronio sulla Donazione di Costantino tra critica storica e autocensura', *Annali della Scuola Normale Superiore di Pisa, Classe di lettere e filosofia*, ser. 5, 2 (2010) no. 1, pp. 179–219, at pp. 200–5.

Another prominent, but posthumous, victim of censorial activity was Niccolò Machiavelli (1469–1527). Although his *Istorie fiorentine* were to be censored and purged by the Congregation of the Index, Gregory XIII blocked any authorized new edition and in 1579 prohibited all Machiavelli's works.[53] The prohibition was total; even on the official licences for reading prohibited books, Machiavelli was singled out as an exception. To cite another example, the only autobiography of a Renaissance pope, the *Commentarii* of Pius II (1458–64), came out in a heavily censored edition in 1584.[54] This masterpiece of Renaissance writing, containing the humanist pope's astute observations about his own times, was not published in its entirety until the critical edition of 1984.

Certain texts which were fundamental for the traditions and history of the Roman Church came out in new expurgated editions after the Council of Trent. One of these was the papal history of Platina. In this case, the Church saw itself confronted with a widely diffused work which concerned the core of its traditions. As we have seen, Platina criticized corrupt popes, greedy bishops, and clerics who could not read and write.[55] The book was a publishing success and was translated into five vernacular languages. For example, a German version was edited by the Strasbourg reformer Kaspar Hedio. The editions were always updated to the latest state of affairs by adding the biographies of the most recent popes. Panvinio's biographies were subjected to a sort of unofficial censorship for their Italian translation in 1563. Giovanni Tarcagnota (*alias* Lucio Fauno), their translator, had omitted what were considered inappropriate attacks on churchmen.[56] In 1587, when the Roman Church officially decided to act, eighteen Latin and eight Italian editions of Platina's *Lives* were already in circulation.[57] As we have seen, Panvinio had edited a definitive edition with his own commentaries and additions in 1562 and 1568. From 1587 to 1592, several censors dealt with the task of blunting Platina's criticisms and adapting his *Lives of the Popes* to the needs of the Church. Fortunately for historical research, their differences of

---

[53] P. Godman, *From Poliziano to Machiavelli: Florentine Humanism in the High Renaissance* (Princeton, NJ, 1998), 303–33.

[54] S. Honegger Chiari, 'L'edizione del 1584 dei "Commentarii" di Pio II e la duplice revisione di Francesco Bandini', *Archivio storico italiano*, 149 (1991), 585–612; A. Prosperi, 'Varia fortuna di Pio II nel '500', in id., *Eresie e devozioni: la religione italiana in età moderna*, 3 vols (Rome, 2010), i. 247–60.

[55] See above, 151.

[56] Platina, *La historia delle vite de' pontefici*, ed. Panvinio, trans. Lucio Fauno (pseudonym of Giovanni Tarcagnota) (Venice: Michele Tramezzino, 1563).

[57] See the list of editions in Bauer, *Censorship*, 325–6.

opinion can be traced, allowing us to formulate conclusions regarding the censors' conceptions of their task, the view of the Roman Church towards its own history, and the functioning of the organs of censorship in the centre and periphery. The censors were William Allen, Robert Bellarmine, and Pietro Galesini; their efforts concentrated on Platina's biographies.[58] In Venice, Girolamo Giovannini, mentioned above, also made recommendations for the censorship of Panvinio's added biographies, from Hadrian VI to Pius IV.[59] Giovannini sought to suppress passages concerning the vices of popes, cardinals, and other churchmen. In spite of that, however, the political intrigues, sale of cardinalates, military exploits of spiritual leaders, and various other kinds of moral turpitude that Panvinio described remained mostly unaltered in the 1592 Italian edition. Also, Panvinio's allegations in this edition—for example, that Clement VII sold cardinalates and that Paul III was habitually deceitful in all matters—were kept intact.[60]

Two areas in particular caused offence to the censors: church traditions and attacks on the moral behaviour of clerics. The censors, however, did not all agree on how the censorship should be carried out, since if they simply deleted the pope's reprehensible deeds, they could discredit themselves in front of the Protestants as falsifiers of the Catholic Church's own history.[61] In the case of Platina's *Lives of the Popes*, corrections were eventually applied only to the Italian version, not the original Latin one. At any rate, the arms of censorship would not have reached very effectively to Northern Europe, where the Latin version was printed.[62] Moreover, the Latin edition was intended for a learned audience and was, therefore, considered less dangerous than books intended for a popular readership. To understand the relevance of the problem of Latin and vernacular, a side glance at the question of the translation of the Bible can help: While Holy Scripture was always accessible to the Italian public in Latin, translations were prohibited and disappeared from the market completely after the Council of Trent. This prohibition remained in force until 1758.[63]

---

[58] The complete proposals for censoring Platina by Allen, Galesini, and Bellarmin are published ibid. 253–322.

[59] For an edition of Giovannini's recommendations from 1590 see ibid. 198–207.

[60] See ibid. 187, 189–90; Platina, *Historia delle vite dei sommi pontefici*, ed. Panvinio (Venice: Bernardo Basa; Barezzo Barezzi, 1592).

[61] Bauer, *Censorship*, 254.

[62] On censorship in the Holy Roman Empire see M. Cavarzere, 'Das alte Reich und die römische Zensur in der Frühen Neuzeit: ein Überblick', in A. Burkardt and G. Schwerhoff (eds), *Tribunal der Barbaren? Deutschland und die Inquisition in der Frühen Neuzeit* (Konstanz, 2012), 307–34.

[63] G. Fragnito, *Proibito capire: la Chiesa e il volgare nella prima età moderna* (Bologna, 2005).

In the 1570s, a censor suggested 'cleaning' the beginning of Panvinio's own history of the popes and cardinals (*Romani pontifices et cardinales*, 1557):

Notes on the Lives of the Popes by Onofrio

Page 9: 'Novatianus, a Roman' etc. Some do not like the fact that he includes the antipopes in the catalogue of popes. It would be better to list the schisms and antipopes in a separate little book or, if one wants to retain the order, Onofrio's antipopes should be printed in a different font.[64]

Page 14: Felix II. Onofrio makes him an antipope. Others, however, count him among the series of rightful popes.[65]

Page 15: 'The holy Damasus', 'elected in the schism by the party of Antipope Felix'. This sounds bad, and other historians do not talk about it.[66]

On the same page. He [the holy Ursicinus] was not holy, but an Arian, which is proved by the letter of St Jerome to Damasus beginning with the words *Quoniam vetusto*: 'And if this is true', he says, 'why are we separated by walls from Arius, when in dishonesty we are one with him? Let Ursicinus be made the colleague of your blessedness; let Auxentius be associated with Ambrose.'[67]

Page 23, line 6: 'his corpse was transferred to Rome and buried in St Peter's Basilica'. In a manner which is unusual in other authors, he refers to the bodies of dead popes as corpses.[68]

---

[64] 'Annotata in Vitas pontificum Honufrii', ACDF, Index, Prot., F, fo. 20ᵛ, secretarial hand: 'Pag. 9: "Novatianus Romanus" etc. Quibusdam non placet quod in Indice pontificum collocat antipapas. Separato libello melius et schismata et antipapae recenserentur vel, si placet retinere ordinem, Onuphrii antipapae alio charactere impressi esse deberent.' See also Panvinio, *Romani pontifices et cardinales*, 9, on Antipope Novatian (r. 251–8): 'Novatianus Romanus, Sanctae Romanae Ecclesiae Presbyter, in schismate contra Cornelium Papam legitimis suffragiis creatum XIIII Cal. Aprilis renunciatus sedit. Verum in haeresim lapsus, sacerdotio iniuste assumpto, et ecclesia exactus est.' In the margin: 'Primus antipapa'.

[65] 'Annotata in Vitas': 'Pag. 14: Foelix II. Hunc facit Onuphrius antipapam. Tamen alii in numero legitimorum pontificum reponunt.' See Panvinio, *Romani pontifices et cardinales*, 14, on Antipope Felix (II) (r. 355–65).

[66] 'Annotata in Vitas': 'Pag. 15: "Sanctus Damasus", "creatus in schismate a factione Foelicis Antipapae". Hoc male sonat, et alii historiographi nihil dicunt hac de re.' See Panvinio, *Romani pontifices et cardinales*, 15, on Damasus I (r. 366–84).

[67] 'Annotata in Vitas': 'Eadem pagina: Hic [Sanctus Ursicinus] sanctus non fuit, sed arianus, quod probat Epistola Beati Hieronymi ad Damasum, quae incipit *Quoniam vetusto*: "Et si ita est", inquit, "cur ab Ario parietibus separamur, perfidia copulati? Iungatur cum Beatitudine tua Ursicinus, cum Ambrosio societur Auxentius."' Ursinus (also referred to as Ursicinus) was an antipope during the time of Damasus; Auxentius, as bishop of Milan, was a main supporter of Arianism in the West. On Jerome's *Epistola XV ad Damasum*, which was cited by the censor, see F. Cavallera, *Le schisme d'Antioche (IVᵉ–Vᵉ siècle)* (Paris, 1905), 199–203.

[68] Ibid.: 'Pag. 23, linea 6: "cadaver Romam translatum ad Sanctum Petrum sepultum est". Inusitato caeteris scriptoribus more corpora pontificum mortuorum vocat cadavera.' See

The censor found fault with Panvinio's inclusion of the antipopes in his list of popes. He doubted that Felix (II) (r. 355–6) was an antipope. Felix had been styled as a rightful pope in legends of the early Middle Ages, which found their way into the *Liber pontificalis*.[69] Using the *Gesta inter Liberium et Felicem episcopos* from the *Collectio Avellana*, Panvinio proved that Felix was an antipope.[70] The *Avellana*, a collection of papal and imperial documents from the fourth to sixth centuries, was rediscovered by Panvinio's mentor, Pope Marcellus II.[71] From 1580 to 1583 the case of Felix was analysed by a commission which had been charged by Gregory XIII with reforming the previous martyrologies (calendars of saints) and creating the universally valid *Martyrologium Romanum*. After long discussions, the commission—of which Cesare Baronio was a member—confirmed Felix as a saint and martyr in the *Martyrologium Romanum* of 1583.[72] The censorships of Carlo Sigonio of *c*.1582 also dealt with Felix and accused Sigonio of having followed Panvinio in this point; this might have been a possible reference to the present document.[73]

Furthermore, the censor of the present document cast doubt on the sanctity of Antipope Ursinus (r. 366–7), in whose re-evaluation as a saint Panvinio again seems to have followed the *Collectio Avellana*. Finally, the censor remarked that Panvinio did not give enough respect to deceased popes. Since the censor's name is unknown, it is only from its archival context that the censorship can be assigned to the 1570s.[74] There is no indication

Panvinio, *Romani pontifices et cardinales*, 23, on Agapitus I (r. 535–6). A more common term was *corpus*: see, for example, the *Liber pontificalis* and Platina.

---

[69] *Liber pontificalis*, ed. L. Duchesne, 3 vols (Paris, 1886–1957), i. 211; J. J. I. von Döllinger, *Die Papst-Fabeln des Mittelalters*, 2nd edn (Stuttgart, 1890), 126–45.

[70] See *Quae gesta sunt inter Liberium et Felicem episcopos*, in *Epistulae imperatorum, pontificum... Avellana quae dicitur Collectio*, ed. O. Günther, 2 pts (Prague; Vienna; Leipzig, 1895), i. 1–4.

[71] See above, 38.

[72] B. de Gaiffier, 'Les notices des papes Félix dans le martyrologe romain', *Analecta Bollandiana*, 81 (1963), 333–50.

[73] See the censorship of Sigonio's *De occidentali imperio* (Sigonio, *Opera*, vi, col. 1096; McCuaig, *Sigonio*, 273 n. 55): '... de Liberio secutus est Honuphrium, qui scribit Liberium sanctum contra Divum Hieronymum et Foelicem appellat antipapam, qui semper in ecclesia Romana habitus est sanctus et in antiquo et reformato Breviario; et diligens scriptor debuit recensere varias opiniones et potius assentiri ecclesiae, quae veneratur Foelicem sicut ceteros sanctos.' By mentioning the reformed *Breviarium* the censor referred to *Breviarium Romanum ex decreto sacrosancti Concilii Tridentini restitutum, Pii V... iussu editum* (Rome, 1568).

[74] The archival volume Index, Protocolli, F, documents the expurgatory activity of the Congregation of the Index in the 1570s. See C. Arnold, *Die römische Zensur der Werke Cajetans und Contarinis (1558–1601): Grenzen der theologischen Konfessionalisierung* (Paderborn, 2008), 210–11, as well as the scattered dates in Protocolli, F. For another version of the same censorship

that the Congregation of the Index of Prohibited Books dealt with the book any further, and a censored version was never published. However, as Pius V had prohibited reprints of Panvinio's works in 1569, no uncensored reprint could be produced either. Without being on the Index, Panvinio's *Romani pontifices et cardinals* thus disappeared from the market.

Panvinio's *Church History*

Panvinio's unpublished *Church History* (*Historia ecclesiastica*) developed out of his papal biographies. It was an ongoing project during the 1560s. One of Panvinio's goals was to receive the sponsorship and endorsement of the Spanish king Philip II. In 1558 he had already dedicated his book on emperors (*Romani imperatores*), including his treatise on imperial elections (*De comitiis*), to Philip.[75] Having received no reply, Panvinio nevertheless kept writing to the king and eventually sent him an enlarged version of *De comitiis* in 1562. Finally, in 1563 Philip responded with thanks and the explicit encouragement to finish and send him his *Church History*, which 'in these times will be very necessary and helpful'.[76]

The dedicatory preface to Philip II in the first volume (covering the period to AD 401) outlined Panvinio's motivations.[77] In this manuscript Panvinio used the title *Ecclesiastica historia pontificum Romanorum* (Church History of the Roman Pontiffs).[78] As he said in the preface, he thought it

---

document, also without a date, see 'Annotationes in pontifices Onuphrii', ACDF, Index, Prot., C, fo. 115[r–v]; this volume contains mainly documents from the 1570s and 1580s.

[75] See Gersbach, '*De comitiis*'; and above, 49–50, 138–141.
[76] Philip II to Panvinio, March 1563, ed. in Gersbach, '*De comitiis*', 436, and in J. I. Tellechea Idígoras, 'La mesa de Felipe II', *Ciudad de Dios*, 215 (2002), 181–215, at p. 213: 'para estos tiempos será muy necessaria y provechosa'. For the other letters see Tellechea Idígoras, 'La mesa', 198 (Panvinio to Philip II, 8 March 1560), 212 (Panvinio to Philip II, 6 July 1562); Gersbach, '*De comitiis*', 431–2. See also the letter by Gonzalo Pérez (secretary to the king) to Panvinio, 5 May 1563, ibid. 433, as well as further letters from 1563–4, ibid. 436–48.
[77] Panvinio, *Ecclesiastica historia pontificum Romanorum* (up to AD 401), MS Madrid, Biblioteca del Monasterio de El Escorial, f-I-16, dedicatory preface to Philip II, fos I[r]–III[r]. The manuscript includes portraits of popes and emperors, which were glued in, as well as autograph corrections.
[78] In other manuscript versions, which remained in Rome, he used the title *Romanorum pontificum et cardinalium Sanctae Romanae Ecclesiae (quorum memoria extat) vitae* (Vat. lat. 12116, fo. 1[r], 12118, fo. 1[r]), so that the title of the work would not have been *Church History* but *Lives of the Popes and Cardinals*. Related material includes Vat. lat. 6102–6, 6113–14, 12113–24, 12535–6, Barb. lat. 2524 and 2738–9.

advisable to write a church history along the lines of the lives of the popes ('occasione sumpta ex pontificum Romanorum vitis') to reveal the divine order underpinning the development of the Church. True Catholic doctrine had always been utterly constant ('constantissime'). Apostolic succession had remained uninterrupted over the centuries despite the many reforms and the modifications of ceremonies and rites which had been carried out for good reasons ('ratione temporum ita postulante'). Though not every pope had been a perfect model of virtue, none had deviated from true doctrine.[79]

The authors of the *Magdeburg Centuries* had pounced on such variations and tales of moral turpitude and, according to Panvinio, had thrown their readers into confusion by attacking the foundations of the Catholic Church. They had inserted poisonous lies into church history and obscured the truth. Panvinio intended to set the record straight. He hoped that his work would serve as 'medicine'; he would employ and present the most reliable historical testimonies to refute the Protestants' fables.[80] Because Philip bore the title 'Catholic King', he was, in Panvinio's view, obliged to give universal protection to the orthodox faith. The work dedicated to him also helped protect this orthodoxy. In the Italian draft versions of the preface, Panvinio referred to his subject matter as 'the greatest and most important history that we Catholics have as a foundation for our faith'; however, this phrase was modified in the Latin version he sent to the king, perhaps because it seemed too boastful, as it appeared to refer to both the importance of the contents and the greatness of Panvinio's own achievement.[81] In the Latin version, Panvinio was at once more modest and more specific, writing about his subject matter: 'Catholics may truly acknowledge that nothing is more important than this and nothing is more useful for nourishing Christian piety and strengthening our faith.'[82]

---

[79] Panvinio, *Ecclesiastica historia pontificum Romanorum*, dedicatory preface to Philip II, fo. II[r]: 'At pontifices non omnes aeque boni, vel etiam improbi nonnulli. Quis negat? Omnes tamen sic animati, ut a veteribus institutis ad novarum sectarum opiniones nemo unquam deflexerit.' Other drafts of this preface (Vat. lat. 6113, fos 1[r]–14[v]) were dated 1 October 1565.

[80] Panvinio, *Ecclesiastica historia pontificum Romanorum*, dedicatory preface to Philip II, fo. II[v]: 'Quibus malis utinam hic labor meus medicinam afferat. Equidem id sum conatus, ut perditis istorum consiliis occurrem, fictas eorum fabulas nulla illorum blasphemia recitata verissimis certissimisque historiae testimoniis refellerem, dubios confirmarem, lapsos erigerem.'

[81] For the Italian draft versions see Vat. lat. 6113, fos 24[r]–32[v]; for the citation, fo. 25[v]: 'la maggior historia et più importante che habbino i catholici per fondamento della fede nostra'.

[82] Panvinio, *Ecclesiastica historia pontificum Romanorum*, dedication to Philip II, fo. III[r]: 'historiam illam conficerem, qua nihil gravius, nihil ad alendam Christianam pietatem firmandamque fidem nostram utilius esse catholici homines vere confitentur'.

On 10 July 1565 Panvinio wrote to the king's secretary, Gonzalo Pérez, reminding him that the king had encouraged Panvinio to complete his *Church History*. It was now nearly finished. Panvinio had shown the sections covering the first 800 years to Luis de Torres, a cleric of the Apostolic Chamber and friend of Pérez. He wondered whether Pérez wished to see the first 800 to 1000 years and sought his opinion about the book before it went into print. Panvinio's plan was to have the work printed in Venice in four volumes of 500 leaves each.[83] The text would cover the entire period from Christ to Panvinio's own time.[84] Pérez responded that Panvinio should show the text to various learned men and let them approve its doctrinal correctness—but not in Spain, where the theologians were at present too busy with their involvement in provincial councils. Pérez then said that after receiving such learned advice, Panvinio should print part of the work and send it to Spain.[85]

On 17 July Panvinio requested money from Cardinal Farnese, so that he could feed the five mouths he employed to finish his *Church History*: three scribes, an illustrator, and even a cook.[86] On 1 October 1565 Panvinio wrote to Pérez again, saying that the work was 'nearly finished' ('quasi finita'); but he crossed out the word 'nearly' in the draft, presumably to make his letter sound more convincing.[87] He wrote that he had already shown his manuscripts to theologians in Rome for corrections and that he would do so again. Panvinio added that Pérez had misunderstood him on this point: He had not been asking for the advice of Spanish theologians. He did not want to send to Philip a manuscript but only the printed version, the whole of which should be printed in one go. Panvinio planned to include 2,000 illustrations. The work would be lavish and costly, so he needed the king's help even more. In a postscript to this letter, Panvinio described in great detail the title-page he envisioned. It would contain allegorical figures as

---

[83] In a draft letter to an uncertain addressee of 1567 (MS BAM, P 244 sup., fasc. 6, fo. 141^r), Panvinio mentioned that the four volumes should be made in a similar format as the edition of the councils ('quelli di Concilii'). This clearly referred to the folio edition of the *Concilia omnia tum generalia tum provincialia atque particularia*, ed. Laurentius Surius (4 vols, Cologne, 1567), the dedication of which to Philip II carried the date 30 January 1567.

[84] Panvinio to an unnamed addressee (i.e., Gonzalo Pérez), 10 July 1565, Vat. lat. 6412, fo. 184^{r-v}.

[85] G. Pérez to Panvinio, 22 August 1565, Vat. lat. 6412, fo. 180^r.

[86] Panvinio to Farnese (Caprarola), 17 July 1565, in Ronchini, 'Panvinio', 220–1: 'tre scrittori, un pittore e un cuoco'. In a letter of 1563, Panvinio wrote that he had 'quattro e sei scrittori a mie spese' (Gersbach, 'De comitiis', 443).

[87] Panvinio to an unnamed addressee (Gonzalo Pérez), 1 October 1565, Vat. lat. 6113, fos 16^r–20^v (two drafts), at fo. 16^r.

well as Philip's coat of arms. Another page would contain a recent engraved portrait of the king. Since, however, no such image was available in Rome, Panvinio asked his Spanish connection to obtain a drawing for him.[88] Panvinio asked numerous intermediaries to intercede with King Philip and seek his help with the publication.[89] This now included both financial help and the granting of a printing privilege, so that he would not be defrauded of his labour. Panvinio now planned to produce seven volumes; but at Christmas 1567, printing had still not begun. He at last resolved to send the first volume of the manuscript to the Spanish king.[90] The presentation manuscript might have arrived in Spain shortly before or during Panvinio's fateful journey to Sicily.

For the first centuries, his text combined church historical sources (such as the *Liber pontificalis*, Jerome, Socrates, Sozomen, and Theodoret) with information from his own *Fasti* of 1558. He also included documents such as papal letters, canons of synods, and imperial edicts. Key theologians such as St Augustine were given separate and detailed sections.[91] For later centuries, Panvinio included papal bulls as well as material on cardinals.[92] The structure was chronological—Panvinio frequently provided the years in the margins—which may have foreshadowed Baronio's annalistic principle. His longer digressions (such as that on Augustine's life), however, broke up this strict chronological framework, as these spanned several decades.

Contemporary observations on his text, as usual, are valuable for determining what was regarded as important. In order to look at these observations,

---

[88] Ibid., fos 17^r–19^r, partly published in Robertson, *Farnese*, 297–8.

[89] See the letters on behalf of Panvinio: Cardinal Giovanni Morone to Fernando Álvarez de Toledo, Duke of Alba, 17 July 1566; Morone to Juan Manrique de Lara, former ambassador to the Holy See, same date; Cardinal Clemente Dolera to Bishop Bernardo de Fresneda, Philip's confessor, 16 July 1566, in Vat. lat. 6113, fos 22^r–23^r, ed. Perini, *Panvinio*, 245–8; Luis de Requesens, Spanish ambassador in Rome, to Philip II, 21 July 1566, in J. I. Tellechea Idígoras, 'La mesa de Felipe II', *Ciudad de Dios*, 215 (2002), 605–39, at pp. 638–9 (copy in MS BAM, P 244 sup., fasc. 6. fo. 142^r) (he mentioned 'three very large books' that were to be printed); Cardinal Farnese to Philip II, undated, ed. Perini, *Panvinio*, 242; Farnese to Philip's minister Ruy Gómez de Silva, Prince of Eboli, undated, ibid. 243.

[90] A. Farnese to Francesco Maria II della Rovere, at the Spanish court, 25 December 1567, ed. Perini, *Panvinio*, 244–5. The dispatch of the manuscript was connected in some way to the imminent return of the Spanish ambassador, Luis de Requesens, to Madrid in December 1567 ('l'occasione della venuta del Signor Commendador maggior di Castiglia'). See also the letter by Farnese to Ruy Gómez, 25 December 1567, ibid. 243–4. On Requesens's return see L. Serrano (ed.), *Correspondencia diplomática entre España y la Santa Sede durante el pontificado de San Pío V*, 4 vols (Madrid, 1914), ii. 278–84.

[91] Panvinio, *Ecclesiastica historia pontificum Romanorum*, fos 409^r–413^r.

[92] See Kehr, 'Diplomatische Miszellen, iv: Die Scheden des Panvinius' (who describes the material collected in Vat. lat. 12117, 12535–6); and Mai, *SR*, ix. 532–3. See also above, 96.

we need to consider question of the posthumous fate of Panvinio's text. In 1575 Cardinal Farnese sought to enlist the Jesuits' help in examining the *Church History* and presumably preparing it for publication. The Jesuit general answered that his brethren were unable to provide assistance, as they were too busy hearing confessions during the Holy Year.[93] At last, there was an examination of the *Historia ecclesiastica* in 1584, thanks to Paolo Panvinio's urging. In a consistory, Cardinal Colonna proposed to Gregory XIII an assessment of this work; together with Cardinals Antonio Carafa and Sirleto, he sent the pope a list of possible scholars who could revise Panvinio's *Church History*. The names put forward were (in this order): Giulio Ruggieri, Latino Latini, Antonio Caracciolo, Silvio Antoniano, Flaminio Nobili, Antonio d'Aquino, Gerard Vossius, Alfonso Chacón, José Esteve, and Lelio Landi.[94]

Cardinal Savelli, the keeper of Panvinio's manuscripts, chose Silvio Antoniano for this task. Antoniano had a special interest in Panvinio's work; he had planned to publish a continuation of Panvinio's *Romani pontifices et cardinales* in 1571. In that year he had written to Cardinal Antonio Carafa with details of his plan (which was never carried out). Antoniano had wanted to follow Panvinio 'in the entire form of his writing' ('in tutta la forma di scrivere'), extending Panvinio's work to cover cardinals created after 1557; the only new elements he had wanted to insert were more epitaphs of cardinals.[95] In 1584 Cardinal Savelli ordered Antoniano to inspect Volumes 4–6 of Panvinio's *Church History*. This referred to material which is now bound together in one manuscript volume, Vat. lat. 6105, covering the popes from Benedict IX (elected 1032) to Pius V (1566).[96]

Antoniano wrote to Savelli and explained his views on Panvinio's work. In the cardinal's rooms, he had looked at the fourth volume with particular

---

[93] Everard Mercurian to A. Farnese, 31 August 1575, in Ronchini, 'Panvinio', 224. Mercurian promised to assign a Jesuit to this task the following year, but it is not clear what became of this initiative.

[94] M. Colonna to Gregory XIII, 22 February 1584, ASV, A.A., Arm. I–XVIII, 6464, fos 20ʳ, 23ʳ.

[95] S. Antoniano to A. Carafa, 7 July 1571, MS BAV, Barb. lat. 5728, fos 15ʳ–16ᵛ, ed. E. Patrizi, *Silvio Antoniano*, 3 vols (Macerata, 2010), ii. 727–30. For books by Panvinio in Antoniano's possession by the end of the 1580s (*Romani pontifices et cardinales*, 1557; Platina, *Historia de vitis pontificum*, ed. Panvinio, 1568; *Fasti*, Heidelberg or Geneva, 1588; *De primatu*, 1589) see E. Patrizi, '*Del congiungere le gemme de' gentili con la sapientia de' Christiani*': la biblioteca del cardinal Silvio Antoniano... (Florence, 2011), *ad indicem*. For another plan to update Panvinio, by Alfonso Chacón, see above, 144.

[96] The commission in 1592 noted that the work was divided into six volumes, but the extent to which such a division was made by Panvinio himself remains to be established.

attention.[97] The first thing that struck him was that the *Church History* was an expansion of Panvinio's *Romani pontifices et cardinales* of 1557. In that book, Panvinio had noted the dates of popes and cardinals but had provided little additional historical material. To elaborate on this basic information, Panvinio provided three sections for each pontificate: (1) the pope's actions before his pontificate; (2) his actions during his reign; (3) additional details about temporal rulers, cardinals, and learned men who flourished at the time. Much of this structure was inherited from previous church historians such as Eusebius and Platina. There were also features which Antoniano thought were less important but curious: papal portraits, coats of arms of popes and cardinals, as well as seals of papal bulls. According to Antoniano, these features were added primarily in the hope of boosting the work's commercial success. He doubted the historical accuracy of most papal portraits but realized that many readers would take great pleasure in seeing them. Comparing the work to Platina's *Lives of the Popes*, his judgement of Panvinio was favourable:

Concerning what is most important, I take it as certain that this *Papal History* is much more complete and correct than the one by Platina, who wrote at a time when there was very little knowledge of church history and when the Church Fathers and the councils were not in sight. Apart from that, Friar Onofrio worked hard and was very diligent. He looked at both the Vatican Registers and the archives of the noblest cities of Italy and of monasteries and churches, where many papal bulls are scattered. Furthermore, Platina wrote in great haste and, as they say, lumped everything together, which is why he was corrected by Friar Onofrio on many points, such as the story of the female pope and that of Silvester II, reputed to be a magician, who was a most holy man, and similar things. Those annotations have already been printed. And without doubt, no small gain will be derived from the abundance and propriety of the *History*, as is shown moreover by its vast size.[98]

Thus, Antoniano considered Panvinio's work to be diligent, especially because of its reliance on many previously unused primary sources. Antoniano recognized that the book had been left unfinished at Panvinio's death. He

[97] For what follows see the letter by S. Antoniano to G. Savelli, 3 September 1584, Vat. lat. 6105, fos 5ʳ–6ᵛ, ed. Perini, *Panvinio*, 238–41.
[98] Antoniano to Savelli, 3 September 1584, 239–40. See also Bauer, *Censorship*, 111–12.

found numerous corrections, annotations, deletions, and blank spaces in the manuscripts; in addition, he noted that a number of popes were missing at the beginning of the fourth volume.[99]

Antoniano drew attention to Platina's presentation of Pope Silvester II (r. 999–1003). Citing medieval legends, Platina recounted that Silvester had made a pact with the devil and used magical arts in order to obtain the papacy. Just before his death, Silvester repented and warned his flock about the dangers of Satan. After his death, the bones in his tomb rattled to foretell the death of other popes. Platina used this story as a moral warning and commented sarcastically, 'let those popes whom it concerns see if this is true or not'.[100] In his annotation to Platina's life of Silvester, Panvinio debunked the myth of the pope-magician, arguing that it was a figment of the popular imagination. He explained that Silvester was very learned in mathematics and philosophy, which was so rare in the medieval West that the ignorant populace could not help but regard him as a diabolical sorcerer. Antoniano, who was pleased with Panvinio's rehabilitation of this pope, must have been aware that Platina's story provided potent ammunition for Protestant attacks on the papacy. Examples of this are the accounts of Silvester's pontificate in the *Magdeburg Centuries* and in Robert Barnes's *Lives of the Popes* (published, with a preface by Luther, in 1536).[101]

Antoniano was surprised that Panvinio's life of Pope Gregory VII was so short, because Panvinio, in an annotation to Platina, had announced that he had written a life of Gregory in five books.[102] Perhaps, as Antoniano surmised, Panvinio had saved this longer version for a separate publication. This interest by Antoniano can be seen in the context of a recent insertion of Gregory VII's name into the *Roman Martyrology*, which constituted a confirmation of a local cult in Salerno and marked the first step on the way to

[99] According to Antoniano, thirteen popes were missing; today, fifty-four popes are lacking between the end of Vat. lat. 6104 and the beginning of Vat. lat. 6105—that is, between Leo VIII (98th pope, d. 816) and Benedict IX (149th pope, elected 1032). See also the note in Vat. lat. 6105, fo. 2ʳ.

[100] Platina, *Historia de vitis pontificum* (1562), fo. 122ᵛ: 'Verum ne sit an secus ipsi pontifices viderint ad quos pertinet.' For what follows see Panvinio's annotation ibid., fos 122ᵛ–123ʳ. See also Bauer, *Censorship*, 315–16; id., 'Quod adhuc extat', 227.

[101] R. Barnes, *Vitae Romanorum pontificum, quos papas vocamus* (Wittenberg, 1536), sigs O2ʳ–O3ᵛ; Flacius et al., *Ecclesiastica historia*, Centuria X (1567), cols 547–8. On Barnes's *Vitae* see K. D. Maas, *The Reformation and Robert Barnes: History, Theology and Polemic in Early Modern England* (Woodbridge, 2010), 107–36. For other Reformation accounts of Silvester II see H. L. Parish, *Monks, Miracles and Magic: Reformation Representations of the Medieval Church* (London, 2005), 129–34.

[102] Panvinio, Vat. lat. 6105, fos 57ʳ–60ʳ (Gregory VII); Panvinio's annotation to Gregorius VII, in Platina, *Historia de vitis pontificum* (1562), fo. 135ᵛ; (1568), 177.

his canonization.[103] Overall, Antoniano advised that many fundamental questions about Panvinio's text were still to be considered: Was it a prudent work overall? Were there useless digressions, as there had been in Platina's *Lives*? Did this history always express the truth? What could be said appropriately and what should be passed over in silence, considering the current climate ('rispetto ai tempi che corrono')? According to Antoniano, the work should be discussed at length by a competent scholar such as Cesare Baronio.[104]

Also by Cardinal Savelli's order, the Jesuit Robert Bellarmine prepared a censorship of Volume 1 (that is, Vat. lat. 6102) in *c*.1584–7. When Savelli promised Paolo Panvinio that his brother's 'perfected' works ('quelle che saranno in perfettione') would be printed, this was to include the *Historia ecclesiastica* in six volumes.[105] On 23 November 1587, a few days before Cardinal Savelli's death, Panvinio's *Church History*, by order of Sixtus V, was transferred to the Apostolic Palace. This was part of Sixtus's initiative to have Panvinio's works on ecclesiastical matters printed.[106] (As we will see in the next section, only *De primatu Petri* eventually appeared in print.)

By comparison to Antoniano's report, Bellarmine's censorship was much more concerned with details.[107] Some of the points which he thought in need of correction concerned questions of chronology and historical details such as names. Bellarmine dedicated much attention to the chronology of

---

[103] G. Miccoli, 'Gregorio VII', in *Bibliotheca sanctorum*, 13 vols (Rome, 1961–70), vii, cols 294–379, at cols 367–70. The insertion was made by order of Gregory XIII in 1584. See also below, 200–201.

[104] Antoniano to Savelli, 3 September 1584, 240–1. Three years later, Antoniano censored Papire Masson's Gallican history of the popes (*De episcopis Urbis*, Paris, 1586). See J.-L. Quantin, 'Érudition gallicane et censure romaine au tournant des XVIᵉ e XVIIᵉ siècles: Papire Masson devant l'Index', in G. Fragnito and A. Tallon (eds), *Hétérodoxies croisées: catholicismes pluriels entre France et Italie, XVIᵉ–XVIIᵉ siècles* (Rome, 2015), Web, http://books.openedition.org/efr/2849.

[105] Paolo Panvinio, 'Lectori' (draft preface to *De primatu*), fo. 67ʳ, ed. Maffei, *Verona illustrata*, ii. 350.

[106] Orbaan, 'La Roma di Sisto V', 302. See also above, 86.

[107] R. Bellarmine, 'Censura in primum tomum *Historiae ecclesiasticae* Fratris Onuphrii Panvinii, facta mandato bonae memoriae Jacobi Cardinalis Savelli', Vat. lat. 6105, fos 8ʳ-19ʳ (autograph), ed. X. M. Le Bachelet, *Auctarium Bellarminianum: supplément aux œuvres du Cardinal Bellarmin* (Paris, 1913), 554–64. See also P. Godman, *The Saint as Censor: Robert Bellarmine between Inquisition and Index* (Leiden, 2000), 127–8; Baumgarten, *Neue Kunde*, i. 341 (with a negative judgement on the quality of this censorship: 'Diese sehr mäßige Arbeit trägt nicht gerade zur Vermehrung des literarischen Ruhmes Bellarminos bei'). On Bellarmine's work for the Inquisition and the Index see also F. Motta, 'Roberto Bellarmino', in A. Prosperi (ed.), *Dizionario storico dell'Inquisizione*, 4 vols (Pisa, 2010), iii. 1334–5; Schwedt, *Anfänge der römischen Inquisition*, 72–4; id., *Die römische Inquisition*, 84–5.

Christ, St Peter, and the first popes.[108] Other points not only concerned historical facts but also had consequences for the confessional struggle. For example, like Platina before him, Panvinio had noted that the commemoration of the dead in the mass was introduced by Pope Pelagius (r. 556–61).[109] Bellarmine remarked that this tradition was much older, as the Church Fathers (although he did not say which ones) had recorded. According to Bellarmine, the tradition dated back to apostolic times. He added that Panvinio's stance was dangerous: 'Certainly in our time, in which heretics ridicule purgatory and say that it was invented by the popes, this cannot be tolerated in any way.'[110] A similar remark concerned the institution of the ember days—that is, the days of fasting at the beginning of each of the four seasons ('ieiunium quatuor temporum'). Panvinio followed Platina and the *Liber pontificalis* in stating that these days were introduced by Pope Calixtus I (r. 217–22). Bellarmine was adamant that the tradition went back to apostolic times, as Pope Leo I (r. 440–61) had affirmed in his sermons. According to Bellarmine, Leo's affirmation took precedence over the *Liber pontificalis*.[111]

Bellarmine recommended that exact references to the Church Fathers be added wherever possible. When Panvinio listed the errors of Arianism, he should have detailed where these errors appeared in the writings of the Fathers.[112] Bellarmine found it dangerous to refer to canons of the ancient church councils. Citing the example of Pope Silvester I's 'Roman synod', Bellarmine warned that these canons were often difficult to interpret. Some of them had been superseded, and it would be best to avoid inserting any canons into the text. Neither Bellarmine nor Panvinio, however, seem to have been aware that this Roman synod of 315 was apocryphal and had never taken place. Its 'acts' were part of the forgeries emanating from the Curia of Pope Symmachus (r. 498–514).[113]

---

[108] Bellarmine, 'Censura in primum tomum *Historiae ecclesiasticae*', 555–6 (on Panvinio's life of Christ). See also id., 'De successione primorum pontificum Romanorum', ed. Le Bachelet, *Auctarium Bellarminianum*, 549–52, referring to Panvinio's annotations to Platina.

[109] Platina, 'Xystus I', in id., *Historia de vitis pontificum* (1568), 18; Panvinio, Vat. lat. 6102, fo. 107ᵛ. See also Bellarmine's censorship from 1587 of Platina's *Lives*, in Bauer, *Censorship*, 267.

[110] Bellarmine, 'Censura in primum tomum *Historiae ecclesiasticae*', 560, ad 'fo. 107' (life of Xystus I): 'Certe hoc tempore, quo haeretici purgatorium irrident et a pontificibus confictum esse dicunt, id nullo modo est tolerandum.'

[111] Ibid. 561, ad 'fo. 168' (Callistus I). See Platina, *Historia de vitis pontificum* (1568), 27; Panvinio, Vat. lat. 6102, fo. 168ʳ; and, for Bellarmine's comments on Platina, Bauer, *Censorship*, 274.

[112] Bellarmine, 'Censura in primum tomum *Historiae ecclesiasticae*', 562, ad 'fo. 307' (Silvester I).

[113] Ibid. 561–2, ad 'fo. 287' (Silvester I): 'Praestaret fortasse nullos canones historiae inserere, praesertim cum multi iam sint antiquati.' For an edition of the forged canons of the 'Roman

In the field of ecclesiastical politics, Panvinio had given too much autonomy to Emperor Constantine. Bellarmine disliked his statement that Constantine had convoked the Council of Nicaea (AD 325) on his own initiative, after having consulted with some bishops. It would have been worthwhile to add that he merely followed the decision of bishops. Councils, as Bellarmine noted, could never be convened without the consent of bishops and the Apostolic See. Therefore, Panvinio should have given prominence to Pope Silvester's role in the convocation of the Council of Nicaea.[114] Regarding Felix II, Bellarmine, like the censor of Panvinio's *Roman Pontiffs*, objected to Panvinio's decision to make Felix an antipope.[115]

To sum up, Bellarmine's censorship included elements of philological, historical, and theological criticism. Many of these criticisms would today be considered justified, but others would not, especially those in which Bellarmine pushed certain points for reasons of confessional polemic, such that theological concerns overrode historical considerations. For instance, the notion that it was Constantine's own initiative to convoke the Council of Nicaea is now accepted by historians.[116] Bellarmine's effort to trace church traditions back to apostolic times was also motivated by polemical necessity. Panvinio did not feel so strongly bound to this need, and neither did he show any hesitation in citing canons of the ecumenical councils which may have been superseded by those of the Council of Trent published in 1564. It is well known that the importance of the Council of Trent loomed much larger in the 1580s than it did in the 1560s, when its implementation was not fully enforced and when many contemporaries—among them Panvinio— had not yet recognized its secular significance for the Church.[117]

---

synod' see E. Wirbelauer, *Zwei Päpste in Rom: der Konflikt zwischen Laurentius und Symmachus (498–514)* (Munich, 1993), 228–46.

[114] Bellarmine, 'Censura in primum tomum *Historiae ecclesiasticae*', 562, ad 'fo. 306' and 'fo. 308' (Silvester I). In his *Annales*, Baronio alluded to Silvester's role in persuading Constantine; see E. Norelli, 'L'autorità della Chiesa antica nelle Centurie di Magdeburgo e negli *Annales* del Baronio', in De Maio et al., *Baronio storico e la Controriforma*, 253–307, at p. 298.

[115] Bellarmine, 'Censura in primum tomum *Historiae ecclesiasticae*', 562–3, ad 'fo. 432' (Felix II), 'fo. 486', 'fo. 493' (Ursicinus). See also Bellarmine, 'An Felix Secundus sit verus papa et martyr', ed. Le Bachelet, *Auctarium Bellarminianum*, 547–8; Bauer, *Censorship*, 289; and above, 165.

[116] See, e.g., C. Luibhéid, *The Council of Nicaea* (Galway, 1982), 68.

[117] See Jedin, *Das Konzil von Trient*, 47: Panvinio 'lässt … jedes Gespür für die Tragweite des Konzils, wie man es bei einem so guten Kenner der Papstgeschichte am ehesten erwarten sollte, vollständig vermissen'. On the implementation of the conciliar decrees see A. Koller, 'The Definition of a New Ecclesiastical Policy by the Papal Curia after the Council of Trent and its Reception *in partibus*', in P. Tusor and M. Sanfilippo (eds), *Il papato e le chiese locali/The Papacy and the Local Churches* (Viterbo, 2014), 33–54; François and Soen, *The Council of Trent*.

Bellarmine's censorship notes contained no general statements about the value of Panvinio's work. In his 1587 censorship of Panvinio's edition of Platina's *Lives*, Bellarmine was more critical of Panvinio than he was of Platina, whom he regarded as an author from a bygone era. A new church history had to be a state-of-the-art display of the Roman Church's view of history, with polemical aims in mind. Where theological considerations were in conflict with historical ones, the former often had to prevail. However, Bellarmine was not consistent in his approach to Platina and Panvinio. In 1610, much like Antoniano had done in 1584, he declared that he appreciated the rigorous research which Panvinio had carried out, whereas Platina had neglected the Roman archives. When discussing the conflict between Pope Gregory II (r. 715–31) and Byzantine Emperor Leo III, in his work *On the Temporal Power of the Pope*, Bellarmine also noted that Platina was less trustworthy. He observed that Platina had wrongly claimed that Gregory II had protected the iconoclast Leo from an uprising in the Italian provinces:

> I say that if Platina contradicts the other historians, one must believe the other historians rather than him, for these historians are many and are more ancient and diligent, and they write the history of the period, not the life of one pontiff only, as Platina does. And how little diligence Platina showed in examining the documents of the Roman archives can be understood from the fact that Onofrio Panvinio, in his additions to Platina, shows many things that were either omitted or wrong in Platina. For instance, in his addition preceding the biography of Gregory II, Panvinio declares that the Roman pontiff, Gregory II, rightfully deprived the heretical emperor Leo III of his empire in Italy.[118]

In this case, Bellarmine's scolding of Platina seems rather opportunistic, because he simply preferred to not believe that the pope protected the iconoclast emperor and accepted his institutional authority. In fact, this is what Gregory did, so Platina was right.[119] Panvinio, too, recognized and corrected his error in his unpublished *Church History* in the 1560s. He

---

[118] R. Bellarmine, *Tractatus de potestate summi pontificis in rebus temporalibus, adversus Gulielmum Barclaium* (Rome, 1610), 269–70. The translation is taken from id., *On Temporal and Spiritual Authority*, trans. S. Tutino (Indianapolis, IN, 2012), 397. See also Platina, *Historia de vitis pontificum* (1568), 109; for Panvinio's annotation, ibid. 107: 'iure eripuit'.

[119] See P. Delogu, 'Gregorio II', in *Enciclopedia dei papi*, i. 647–51; C. Gantner, *Freunde Roms und Völker der Finsternis: die päpstliche Konstruktion von Anderen im 8. und 9. Jahrhundert* (Vienna, 2014), 84–5 and *ad indicem* s.v. Leon III.

followed the *Liber pontificalis* and Platina, writing that the pope did protect the emperor during the rebellion.[120]

Regarding the legendary ninth-century Pope Joan, Bellarmine stated in his 1586 *Controversies* that Panvinio had refuted the fable 'accurately enough'.[121] In his catalogue of ecclesiastical writers of 1613, Bellarmine judged that Panvinio's annotations to Platina's *Lives* were 'not to be disregarded'.[122] The appendix to this catalogue listed Panvinio, along with Gerhard Mercator (d. 1594) and Gilbert Génébrard (d. 1597), as one of the four most important scholars of chronology in the second half of the sixteenth century. The fourth and last scholar in the list was Bellarmine himself, who had added his own name as an expert on chronology from the creation of the world to AD 1612.[123] It is telling that in another list, a directory of church historians, Bellarmine named only a single representative of that genre for his time ('nostro tempore'): Cesare Baronio.[124] Catholic readers were to rely only on this official historian of the Church. For those who did consult Panvinio's manuscripts in the Vatican Library, advice was made readily available. Both Antoniano's letter and Bellarmine's censorship of Panvinio's *Church History* were bound with the Vatican manuscripts. They illustrated the work's benefits and dangers, much like medical information leaflets today.

Another reason why the *Church History* was never published was that Panvinio had bet on the wrong horse: Spain. Though efforts were made to find answers to the *Magdeburg Centuries* in Spain, these were never fully carried through, partly because of bureaucratic sluggishness, partly because no concerted, sustained, and efficient team effort existed on the Spanish side to produce and/or revise such a work.[125] In Rome, Panvinio's principal problem was ecclesiastical censorship. This was surely the reason why he looked elsewhere for the necessary patronage to print his works, up to the moment of his unexpected death.

---

[120] Panvinio, *Historia ecclesiastica*, Vat. lat. 6104, fo. 1067ʳ: 'Compescuit pontifex eam deligendi imperatoris Italicorum voluntatem, principis penitentiam sperans'.

[121] Bellarmine, *Disputationes de controversiis Christianae fidei*, i, 3rd gen. controversy, III.24, col. 964: 'fabulam...satis accurate refellit Onuphrius in additione ad Platinam'. See also above, 148–149.

[122] Bellarmine, *De scriptoribus ecclesiasticis*, 245: 'notae non contemnendae'.

[123] Ibid., Appendix, 'Index chronologorum' (not paginated).

[124] Ibid., 'Index historicorum ecclesiasticorum' (not paginated).

[125] 'Red tape nennts der Engländer, *rond de cuire* nennts der Franzose und *Amtsschimmel* der Deutsche, wenn er gefragt wird, wer denn diesen Plan umgebracht habe'—this is how Baumgarten (*Hispanica IV*, 4) explained why the plan by Panvinio and others to refute *Magdeburg Centuries* had not been brought to a conclusion. On the constraints placed upon historical research in Spain see also C. Esteve (ed.), *Disciplining History: Censorship, Theory and Historical Discourse in Early Modern Spain* (London; New York, 2018).

In addition, the rise of Baronio as the Church's new preferred historian compromised Panvinio's posthumous success. It became less likely that Panvinio's works could be printed after Baronio began publishing his *Annales ecclesiastici* (twelve volumes from 1588 to 1607). Baronio, as an author, believed—or at least claimed to believe—that he was on a divinely inspired mission. This type of motivation for his work allowed him to avoid agonizing too much about the scholarly competition of Panvinio. At the same time, this was a traditional *topos* of modesty, reminiscent of the attitude, for example, of those popes who claimed they had been elected to the papacy against their own will.[126] Baronio recounted that one night, in the late 1550s or early 1560s, he had a dream about a conversation with Panvinio, in which he urged Panvinio to finish his *Church History*. In this dream, Baronio suddenly perceived a voice, informing him that he himself had to take up this task (Fig. 4.1). Baronio assumed he had heard the voice of Filippo Neri, who revealed to him God's will concerning the writing of ecclesiastical histories. Baronio related this episode during Neri's canonization process in 1607 (when the episode was used to demonstrate Neri's prophetic powers):

At first when I started to join in discussions at the Oratory [of Filippo Neri], I always spoke about dreadful things, such as death, hell, and the last judgement. After I had done this for a while, the blessed father [Neri] asked me to stop speaking about such matters and instead to take up the narration of church history. Several times and on different occasions, he repeated this command to me. Though all this seemed to me rather hard and contrary to my talents, one night Our Lord let me know that this was his will. It seemed to me that I was speaking to Onofrio Panvinio, who at the time was writing some histories of the Church; and, discussing the matter with him, I urged him to bring the *Church History* (*Historia ecclesiastica*) to completion. But when I said this, it seemed to me that Onofrio was not listening to me; and when I was about to continue speaking, I heard a perceptible and clear voice which said: 'Calm yourself, Baronio, and do not tire yourself further with these discussions, because you are the one who has to produce the church histories.' And this seemed to me the voice of the blessed father, and I have always thought so.[127]

---

[126] On this *topos* see Hack, 'Papst wider Willen'.

[127] Deposition by Cesare Baronio, 22 May 1607, in G. Incisa della Rocchetta and N. Vian (eds), *Il primo processo per San Filippo Neri*, 4 vols (Vatican City, 1957–63), ii. 292–3: 'Nel principio che cominciai a ragionare nell'Oratorio, parlava sempre di cose spaventose come di morte, inferno et giuditio. Il che dopo haver fatto per qualche tempo, mi disse il beato padre

Fig. 4.1 Baronio's dream. From Pietro Giacomo Bacci, *Vita di San Filippo Neri fiorentino, fondatore della Congregazione dell'Oratorio*, ed. G. Ricci (Rome, 1745). Courtesy of the Getty Research Institute, Los Angeles (3016–866, after p. 42).

Rumour had it that the greatest part of Baronio's first volume consisted, with few changes, of material that Panvinio had collected—which is, of course, unlikely.[128] At any rate, it is clear that, for Baronio, Panvinio was the elephant in the room. We do not know if an actual conversation between Baronio and Panvinio ever took place; yet Neri's Oratory (in the church of San Girolamo della Carità) was practically next door to Palazzo Farnese, which made casual encounters between the two scholars in the 1560s likely.[129] Baronio was only eight years younger than Panvinio, so there was no generational difference between the two men. However, as Baronio died in 1607, he lived long enough to see the full shape of the post-Tridentine Church.

The last time that Panvinio's *Church History* was examined was in 1592, when a commission dealt with Panvinio's manuscripts.[130] On 25 September 1592, Volumes 2 and 3 of the *Church History* were given to Alfonso Chacón for review. On 29 September, the same volumes were handed over to Bellarmine, while Volume 1 was given to Chacón.[131] Neither Chacón nor Bellarmine seem to have produced any suggestions for censorship on this final occasion. However, Bellarmine showed the censorship originally made

---

che non ragionasse più di simile materia, ma che pigliassi a raccontare l'historia ecclesiastica: il che più volte in diversi tempi mi replicò et comandò. Con tutto ciò, parendomi un poco duro et cosa contraria al mio genio, il Signore una notte mi fece sapere che questa era sua volontà. Mi pareva ragionare con Onophrio Panvinio, il quale all'hora componeva alcune istorie ecclesiastiche, et, ragionando insieme, io lo pregavo che volesse seguitare a dare compimento all'*Historia ecclesiastica*. Et mentre dicevo questo mi pareva detto Onophrio non mi volesse ascoltare e, volendo io seguitare il mio ragionamento, sentii sensibilmente et distintamente una voce che disse: "Quietatevi, Baronio, e non vi affatigate più in questo vostro ragionamento, perché l'historie ecclesiastiche l'havete da far voi." E questa mi parve la voce del beato padre et così ho sempre tenuto...' See also ibid., i. 136–7; S. Bertelli, *Ribelli, libertini e ortodossi nella storiografia barocca* (Florence, 1973), 64–5; Zen, *Baronio storico*, 117–18; G. A. Guazzelli, 'Riflessioni conclusive', in Guazzelli et al., *Baronio*, 503–16, at pp. 503–5. An up-to-date biography of Baronio is still missing.

---

[128] For this claim see, e.g., Nicolaus Crusenius, *Monasticon Augustinianum* (Munich, 1623), 207. For examples of Baronio's actual use of Panvinio's *Church History* (Vat. lat. 6104) see J. Gretser, 'Ad lectorem', in id. (ed.), *Volumen epistolarum quas Romani pontifices...miserunt ad principes et reges Francorum* [i.e., *Codex Carolinus*] (Ingolstadt, 1613), 1–8; G. Cenni, *Monumenta dominationis pontificiae*, 2 vols (Rome, 1760–1), i. 115–21. From 1597, when Baronio succeeded Marcantonio Colonna as cardinal-librarian, he surely had easy access to Panvinio's manuscripts.

[129] On Panvinio's rooms see above, 50–51.

[130] For the work of the commission see below, 187–200.

[131] See the notes in Vat. lat. 6103, fo. I^r, 6104, fo. III^r, 6105, fo. 1^r; and C. M. Grafinger, *Die Ausleihe vatikanischer Handschriften und Druckwerke (1563–1700)* (Vatican City, 1993), 352–3. See also above, 144.

for Savelli to the 1592 commission.[132] We can assume that this did not help to bring Panvinio's *Church History* closer to publication.

Panvinio's *De primatu Petri*

In his *De primatu Petri*, Panvinio aimed to counter the arguments of the Centuriators of Magdeburg by collecting and ordering testimonies, starting from the Bible, which proved that Christ gave the primacy to St Peter, that Peter exerted it during his lifetime (Book I) and that all the succeeding popes did so as well (Book II).[133] Peter and Paul, according to Eusebius, had been executed in Rome under Nero. The Centuriators cited him as a source but pointed out that the dates of their stays and deaths were far from clear—and indeed that, despite Eusebius's affirmation, it could not be proved with certainty that Peter had ever been in Rome. They relied on some of the arguments advanced by the Bohemian scholar Ulrichus Velenus, who had emphatically denied the Petrine tradition in 1520, and also on the considerations of Luther, who had been more reserved and who recognized that the questions about the chronological details could not be easily settled.[134] Of course, this lingering uncertainty alone was enough to unsettle the Roman side; for if Peter's stay in Rome was in doubt, so, too, was the claim to primacy of the Bishop of Rome. Panvinio took pride in answering the Centuriators' polemical and insulting language, as well as their mixture of truth and lies, with a factual and orderly presentation of testimonies from authors who wrote primarily before the time of Charlemagne.[135] Book I contained two

---

[132] Vat. lat. 6105, fo. 8ʳ: 'ab auctore nobis exhibita, die 29 Septembris, feria 3, 1592'.

[133] See Panvinio's dedication to Pius V, dated 1 March 1566, in id., *De primatu Petri et Apostolicae Sedis potestate libri tres contra Centuriarum auctores* (1589), sigs †3ᵛ–††1ᵛ; and his preface to Book I, ibid., sigs A1ʳ–A4ʳ. For a table of contents of the three books see ibid., sigs ††2ʳ–†††4ᵛ; for a detailed summary see Orella y Unzué, *Respuestas católicas*, 284–95. MSS of *De primatu*: Vat. lat. 6883 (the 1553 version, partly autograph); Vat. lat. 6773, 6774, 6782 (partly autograph); Vat. lat. 12092; Ottob. lat. 2344; Rome, Biblioteca Angelica, Ang. lat. 1251 (18th c.). On the historical development of the papal primacy see also K. Schatz, *Papal Primacy: From Its Origins to the Present*, trans. J. Otto and L. M. Maloney (Collegeville, MN, 1996).

[134] Flacius et al., *Ecclesiastica historia*, Centuria I, Book II, cols 524–30 ('Argumenta contra primatum Petri'), 562; U. Velenus, *In hoc libello…probatur Apostolum Petrum Romam non venisse* (s.l., c.1520). See also A. J. Lamping, *Ulrichus Velenus (Oldřich Velenský) and his Treatise against the Papacy* (Leiden, 1976), 139–42, 180–4. Whether Peter was martyred in Rome is still being discussed today; see S. Heid (ed.), *Petrus und Paulus in Rom: eine interdisziplinäre Debatte* (Freiburg im Breisgau, 2011).

[135] Panvinio, *De primatu*, dedication to Pius V and preface to Book I, esp. sig. A1ᵛ: 'conviciis et maledictis a quibus ego vehementer abhorreo'.

chapters dealing with the arguments of the *Magdeburg Centuries* against the primacy, as well as a long chapter in which Panvinio picked apart the entire treatise of Ulrich Velenus, citing it in its entirety and seeking to refute it passage by passage.[136] Book III (yet to be written at the time of Panvinio's death) would have dealt entirely with the arguments of the Protestants.

Panvinio became a member of a commission which was instituted by the Holy Office in August 1565 to refute the *Centuries*. The commission members received an official license from the Holy Office to read prohibited books freely so as to prepare an answer to the Lutherans. Panvinio and Aquiles Estaço—a Portuguese philologist and poet—were referred to as the two 'historians' (*historici*) in this commission.[137] Estaço was acquainted with antiquarians in Rome but had, in fact, little interest in history writing. Apart from Cardinal Colonna, all other members of the commission came from religious orders; these were the Dominicans Tomás Manrique (master of the Sacred Palace), Eustachio Locatelli, and Giovanni Matteo Valdina, the Franciscan Felice Peretti (who later became Pope Sixtus V) as well as the Jesuit theologians Alfonso Salmerón, Diego de Ledesma, Miguel de Torres, and Juan de Mariana. In 1571, the Congregation of the Index was founded by Pius V for 'the revision and censorship of the *Centuries* and other books of the Augsburg Confession as well as the revision and creation of an Index of books'; however, the first task was soon left out of its work.[138]

Around the same time, several writers tried to refute the *Centuries*; but the Catholic hierarchy in Rome did not seem to be willing or able to put together an orchestrated effort to counter the Lutheran work. Initiatives in Rome tended to centre around Cardinals Colonna and Sirleto.[139] In Germany, Konrad Braun issued a criticism of the *Centuries'* historical method in 1565.[140] Wilhelm Eisengrein published the first volume of his refutation of

---

[136] Panvinio, *De primatu*, 121–37, 157–76 (on the *Magdeburg Centuries*), 206–320 (on Velenus). Panvinio had received the first six volumes of the *Centuries* (published 1559–62) from Cardinal Rodolfo Pio da Carpi (a member of the Holy Office and the dean of the College of Cardinals from 1562; d. 1564); see *De primatu*, preface to Book I, sig. A2ʳ. Later volumes were sent to him by Fugger and Otto von Waldburg.

[137] ACDF, Sanctum Officium, Decreta 1565–7, fo. 5ʳ, and Stanza storica, Q-1-a ('Extensorum S.O.'), fo. 100ʳ⁻ᵛ. See also Hasecker, *Quellen*, 59.

[138] Diary entry by Cardinal Santoro, reporting the foundation of the Congregation of the Index on 5 March 1571: 'Sanctissimus [Pius V] vocavit cardinales...quibus commisit *Centuriarum* et librorum confessionis Augustanae revisionem seu censuram, et Indicis librorum revisionem seu confectionem'; cited by Hasecker, *Quellen*, 58 n. 99.

[139] See Orella y Unzué, *Respuestas católicas*.

[140] K. Braun, *Adversus novam Historiam ecclesiasticam...admonitio catholica* (Dillingen, 1565). See also S. Benz, *Zwischen Tradition und Kritik: katholische Geschichtsschreibung im barocken Heiligen Römischen Reich* (Husum, 2003), 28–37.

the *Centuries* (which has been judged 'a mediocre compilation') in Ingolstadt in 1566.[141] Other isolated initiatives were Francesco Giovannetti's *Pontificum Romanorum liber* (Bologna, 1570), a history of the papacy based on medieval German sources, as well as Girolamo Muzio's *Della historia sacra* (Venice, 1570), up to c.AD 250, which was based more on religious fervour than on penetrating historical research.

Panvinio's *De primatu* was originally to be dedicated to Pius V in 1566. However, it remained stuck with the ecclesiastical authorities. Until his death, Panvinio was unable to retrieve the manuscript from Cardinal Marcantonio Colonna, who held on to it. Panvinio asked Otto von Waldburg to intervene on his behalf in this matter. Otto obliged and wrote to Cardinal Michele Bonelli in Rome (a Dominican and a relative of Pius V), asking him to ensure that the Procurator of the Dominicans had the work revised as soon as possible, so that it could be printed. In addition, Otto wrote to Colonna. Otto was extremely keen on getting his hands on this work, as he underlined repeatedly in his letters to Panvinio. Otto's plan was to publish *De primatu* in Germany.[142]

In 1567, the Jesuit Peter Canisius was told that the pope wished for his order in Germany to refute the *Magdeburg Centuries*, or at least to discredit them, by providing examples of their contradictions, errors, and distortions. Canisius was expected to put together such a book quickly with the help of his brethren in Dillingen, Ingolstadt, Munich, Cologne, and other places.[143] Canisius's letter to Francis Borgia, Superior General of the Jesuits, is noteworthy for its praise of Panvinio's *De primatu*:[144]

> As for what is requested from us [i.e., a short refutation of the *Centuries*], Father Onofrio has practically carried this through, having written against the authors of the *Church History* from Magdeburg 'three books which

---

[141] W. Eisengrein, *Centenarii XVI...adversus novam Historiam ecclesiasticam*, i, dedicated to Pius V (Ingolstadt, 1566). Sixteen volumes were planned; but after vol. ii (Munich, 1568) no more were published, although Eisengrein moved to Rome in 1568, where he received some half-hearted support from Pius V and Gregory XIII until his death in 1584. For the quotation see L. Pfleger, 'Wilhelm Eisengrein, ein Gegner des Flacius Illyrius', *Historisches Jahrbuch*, 25 (1904), 774–92, at p. 786: 'eine recht mittelmäßige Kompilation'; Eisengrein was 'naïve' and uncritical towards his sources (ibid.). See also J. Schmid, Review of J. Janssen, *Geschichte des deutschen Volkes*, *Historisches Jahrbuch*, 17 (1896), 73–100, at pp. 79–82.

[142] See Otto's letter to Panvinio, 28 November 1566, Vat. lat. 6412, fos 222^r–223^v. Otto mentioned that he wrote to Colonna in his letter to Panvinio, 13 February 1567, ibid., fo. 253^{r-v}.

[143] F. Borgia (Rome) to Canisius (Dillingen), 31 May 1567, in Canisius, *Epistulae et acta*, v. 480–3.

[144] Canisius to Borgia, 24 July 1567, ibid., v. 522–3; translation adapted from J. Brodrick, *Saint Peter Canisius, S.J., 1521–1597* (London, 1939), 682.

display clear and authentic knowledge of nearly all matters pertaining to ecclesiastical history from the time of Christ Our Lord to Pope Gregory, especially regarding the office and power of the Roman pontiffs'. This work, which is completed but not yet in print, runs to '150 folio pages'.[145] I should not have known about it but for the letters sent recently to our cardinal [i.e., Otto von Waldburg] by the author, who is the only man absolutely competent to carry out this task successfully. He might well be encouraged in every way, as he has hardly an equal nowadays in knowledge of history, which requires the whole of a man's attention if he is to expound it properly to others, especially in opposition to learned and contentious people.

This praise should be taken with a grain of salt because it is obvious that Canisius himself was hoping to avoid doing the work on the book; it was, nevertheless, a strong appreciation of both Panvinio's capabilities and reputation (though it is unlikely that Canisius had actually seen *De primatu*). The other interesting point is that Pius V, if he had so desired, could easily have given this task to Panvinio, who lived in Rome; but he chose to ask the German Jesuits as, evidently, he had reservations about Panvinio. This was also, of course, the reason why Panvinio tried to publish his works in Germany and not in Italy in the last years before his death.

After Panvinio's death, a congregation of cardinals, charged with finding replies to the *Magdeburg Centuries*, may have considered publishing *De primatu* in 1570–2; but if so, the plan was aborted.[146] After 1583, Paolo Panvinio succeeded in obtaining Cardinal Colonna's permission for the publication of the two books of *De primatu*; but the work was now held back by the Inquisition. In 1585 Popes Gregory XIII and Sixtus V granted Paolo Panvinio and Marco Antonio Lanfranchi the privilege to publish *De primatu* as soon

---

[145] Canisius quoted here *verbatim* from Panvinio's list of books to be printed ('Index librorum imprimendorum'), which Panvinio had sent to Otto von Waldburg on 9 November 1566. See BAM, P 244 sup., fasc. 6, fos 129ʳ–131ʳ, at fo. 129ʳ: 'Tres libri contra auctores *Historiae ecclesiasticae* Magdeburgensium in centurias distributae, in quibus est cognitio distincta et authentica omnium fere rerum ad historiam ecclesiasticam pertinentium a Christo usque ad Sanctum Gregorium Papam, et praesertim de officio et potestate Romani pontificis. Huius operis capita mitto. Folia 150 in folio'. Otto mentioned this list in his letter to Panvinio of 28 November 1566, Vat. lat. 6412, fos 222ʳ–223ᵛ.

[146] Canisius wrote to Otto von Waldburg in *c*.1570–2 that *De primatu* would finally be published soon: 'Onophrii opus tamdiu desideratum brevi edendum esse gaudeo et cupio sane videre, quid contra Centuriatores non solum ipse, sed et alii sive historiographi sive theologi in lucem edent post diuturnam expecationem': fragment of a letter, published in id., *Epistulae et acta*, vii. 2, and in J. A. F. Orbaan and G. J. Hoogewerff, *Bescheiden in Italië omtrent Nederlandsche kunstenaars en geleerden*, 3 vols (The Hague, 1911–17), i. 46–50. On the congregation see Orella y Unzué, *Respuestas católicas*, 162–70.

as the Inquisition had examined it.[147] Sixtus told his inquisitors in 1586 that although Panvinio had shown poor judgement on some issues, *De primatu* was valuable and therefore should be revised.[148]

Paolo Panvinio created his will in October 1586 and likely died soon after.[149] In the 1589 edition of the first book of *De primatu* (the only book published), Cardinal Colonna (the head of the Congregation of the Index) did not mention Paolo or the Inquisition. He stated that after Panvinio's death, his literary executors had approached him because Panvinio, on his deathbed, had uttered the wish that this work should be printed. Latino Latini had made editorial revisions (checking, in particular, Panvinio's references to Church Fathers), while some theologians, including Cardinal Sirleto, had been consulted to confirm that the book was fit for publication.[150]

As archival documents show, in 1586 Latino Latini had also been asked to comment on Panvinio's sections regarding St Peter's stays in Antioch and Rome, because Sixtus V had ordered an inquiry into Panvinio's opinion on this matter. Panvinio thought that Peter had not been bishop of Antioch before he arrived in Rome. Latini concluded that he did not see why some accused Panvinio of an opinion that was 'absurd or alien to Sacred Scripture' ('absurda aut sacrae scripturae aliena').[151] Here, Latini was probably referring to Cesare Baronio's edition of the *Martyrologium Romanum* (1586), which criticized Panvinio's opinion as 'unheard of' and its implications as 'absurd'.[152]

---

[147] Baumgarten, *Hispanica IV*, 32; Gersbach, 'Brother', 252–3, 261–2.

[148] ASV, Arm. LII, 19 (Santoro's diary), fo. 7[r–v]: 'Con Nostro Signore nella congregatione del Santo Officio a' 2 di gennaro 1586.... Del libro *De primatu Petri* di Frate Onofrio Panvinio che si stampa in Verona, ritenuto per ordine del Santo Officio [added:] et che si rivegga qui. Disse del poco giudicio di Frate Onofrio et ch'era ben fatto et che si vedesse.' See also Baumgarten, *Neue Kunde*, i. 340–1; Gersbach, 'Brother', 253.

[149] Will of Paolo Panvinio, in Campagnola, 'Materiali', fos 25[r]–25b[r].

[150] Panvinio, *De primatu*, dedication by M. Colonna to Sixtus V, 15 July 1589, sigs †2[r]–†3[r]. *De primatu* was reprinted in Venice in 1591; in Rome in 1698, in J. T. de Rocaberti (ed.), *Bibliotheca maxima pontificia*, 21 vols (1695–9), xvii. 536–645; and in Venice again in 1762, in F. A. Zaccaria (ed.), *Thesaurus theologicus*, 13 vols (1762–3), vii. 1001–1186.

[151] See Latino Latini's judgement, 12 May 1586, ACDF, Index, Prot., C, fos 199[r]–200[r].

[152] *Martyrologium Romanum*, ed. C. Baronio (Rome, 1586), 22 February, pp. 94–5 n. a: 'Miratus sum vehementer Reverendum Patrem Onufrium Panvinium, virum alioqui eruditum, sed cito nimis ex humanis praereptum, ut non potuerit suas lucubrationes emendare, novam quandam, hactenus inauditam, nec ab aliquo excogitatam opinionem de Cathedra Antiochena astruere conatum esse, dum in suis ad Platinam additionibus absque ullius antiquorum vel recentiorum testimonio affirmat Petrum Romae primum ac demum sedisse Antiochiae. Quae quidem opinio quam sit falsa, quam adversa syncerae veritati, quam denique faveat novantibus qualemcunque occasionem captantibus, quotque ex ea sequantur absurda vix credi potest.' Baronio referred to Panvinio's annotation to Platina's life of St Peter, in *Historia de vitis pontificum* (1568), 10–11. See also Guazzelli, 'Baronio and the Roman Catholic Vision', 58–9. On Baronio's *Martyrologium* see id., 'Baronio attraverso il *Martyrologium Romanum*', in Guazzelli et al., *Baronio*, 67–110.

In addition, Latini might have been referring to Baronio's source—that is, a short commentary or treatise written by Silvio Antoniano explicitly against Panvinio's opinion.[153]

The thorny question concerning St Peter came up also in Panvinio's annotations to Platina and in his *Fasti*; both of these were consulted by Bellarmine. In 1588, Bellarmine presented his opinion on the question during a meeting of the Congregation of the Index at Cardinal Colonna's residence. In his statement, he concluded that Panvinio's opinion was both false and imprudent ('non solum falsa, sed etiam temeraria') because it went against the beliefs of most ancient authorities.[154] Bellarmine flagged up Panvinio's view only very briefly in the first two editions of his *Controversies*, stating that it was 'not likely' to be correct. In the 1596 edition of his *Controversies*, however, Bellarmine included the full text of his opinion on Peter's stay in Antioch; he denounced Panvinio's opinion as 'new' ('nova')—that is, not founded on tradition.[155]

As regards *De primatu*, due surely to backing from Cardinal Colonna, Latino Latini's recommendation got the upper hand. Thus, despite Baronio's and Bellarmine's broadsides, Panvinio's text was not changed on this point. However, a note was placed in the margin of the 1589 text, stating that the opinion of other authors (namely that Peter came to Rome after having been bishop of Antioch for seven years) was 'held to be more common and closer to the truth' than that of Panvinio and some other scholars from the past.[156] Wisely, perhaps, Panvinio himself had inserted a remark into his discussion of the dates of Christ's passion in his *Fasti* of 1558, saying that the Church had not determined anything officially about these dates. If this

---

[153] See *Martyrologium*, ed. Baronio, 95, where Baronio cited Antoniano's unpublished 'commentariolus' (which now seems to be lost): 'Legi adversus huiuscemodi novam opinionem eruditissimum commentariolum Reverendi Domini Silvii Antoniani, pientissimi ac disertissimi viri, cuius censurae scriptiones meas subiicere consuevi: expectamus si aliquando ab invito poterimus extorquere eius editionem.' For notes by Panvinio on the chronology of St Peter see also Vat. lat. 6160, fos 1ʳ–5ᵛ.

[154] ACDF, Index, Diari, 1, fo. 30ʳ⁻ᵛ; Prot., B., fos 70ʳ, 72ʳ: 'de Onufrio audiendus Belarminius' (7 January 1588); 'Bellarminius retulit aliqua de opinione Honuphrii de adventu Petri ad Urbem' (21 January 1588). See also Panvinio, *Fastorum libri V, Commentarii*, 306–12 (on the passion of Christ, correlated to Peter's dates); C. P. E. Nothaft, *Dating the Passion: The Life of Jesus and the Emergence of Scientific Chronology (200–1600)* (Leiden, 2012), 254–9.

[155] Bellarmine, *Disputationes de controversiis Christianae fidei*, i (1586), 3rd general controversy: 'De summo pontifice', II.6, col. 741; 2nd edn, 3 vols (Ingolstadt, 1588–93), i, col. 736; 3 vols (Lyon, 1596), i, cols 550–4. See also id., 'An Beatus Petrus Antiochiae sederit antequam Romam venerit; ubi etiam de annis vitae Christi', ed. Le Bachelet, *Auctarium Bellarminianum*, 544–7.

[156] Panvinio, *De primatu Petri*, 188: 'Haec est Onuphrii, immo aliquorum etiam veterum doctorum opinio. Veruntamen altera sententia...ut communior et veritati proximior tenetur'.

ever happened, Panvinio continued, he would humbly submit to its ruling and correct his writings.[157]

The marginal note was not everything, however. A long censorship by an unnamed censor was also used to prepare the 1589 edition of Book I of *De primatu*. This censorship carried the inscription 'IHS Maria' and ended with 'Laus Deo', pointing perhaps to a Jesuit author.[158] It had a special status as it was kept, together with a manuscript of *De primatu*, in the *guardarobba* of Pope Clement VIII. The censor's name was already unknown to the member of the commission charged with ordering and revising Panvinio's works, who drew up a list of Panvinio's manuscripts in 1592. In the course of the work of this commission, both pieces were transferred to Cardinal Santoro's residence.[159] The author of this censorship was concerned about Panvinio's language, which he thought should be more reverential, and about Panvinio's open discussion of contradictory ancient sources about St Peter. He also suggested adding more precise references to the Church Fathers, deleting phrases he found offensive (e.g., passages containing critical statements about saints or, for that matter, any Catholic authors, past or present) and adding information about further relevant sources.[160] Some—but not all—of these suggestions were implemented. Thus, the tortuous travels of *De primatu* through the Church's governmental machinery ended in a partial, censored edition.

Censorships of *De varia creatione*

Francisco Peña's Censorship

The way the Church dealt with Panvinio's history of papal elections in 1592 provides another example of ecclesiastical censorship. Panvinio's *De varia*

---

[157] Id., *Fastorum libri V, Commentarii*, 311: 'Ceterum quum de his quae dixi nihil adhuc a catholica Romana ecclesia, quod sciam, determinatum sit, ego, si quandoque occurrerit ut de his rebus aliter statuerit, me meaque omnia scripta in omnibus eiusdem ministrorumque eius examini et decretis humiliter subiicio atque omnia quae attuli ad eius praescriptum redigi curabo.'

[158] 'Observationes in librum primum *De potestate Divi Petri et eius usu*', Vat. lat. 6782, fos 1r–23r.

[159] 'Incerti authoris': Vat. lat. 7030, fo. 3v. For the transferral see Vat. lat. 7762, fo. 555r; Bertolotti, 'Varietà archivistiche', 33; Baumgarten, *Neue Kunde*, i. 341. On Panvinio manuscripts held by several popes see also above, 85–86. For the work of the 1592 commission see my next section.

[160] 'Observationes in librum primum *De potestate Divi Petri*', fos 2r–3v.

creatione was possibly singled out at that time for a particular reason: The work might have been considered useful in connection with an attempted reform of the conclave under Pope Clement VIII (r. 1592–1605). Four conclaves taking place in rapid succession (1590–2) had created uncertainty and confusion about the legitimate role, in these elections, of the Spanish monarchy, which had used a combination of pressure and presents to win over cardinals and gain their votes for its preferred candidates. In particular, during the election of Gregory XIV in 1590, Ambassador Enrique de Guzmán, Count of Olivares, had played out Philip II's power.[161] A commission for a reform of the conclave met from 1591, and a draft reform bull was sent to all cardinals in September 1592. In these reform plans, reference was made to the previous reform bull of Pius IV, *In eligendis*. In connection with these efforts, Clement VIII provoked a dispute about the Spanish ambassador's political interventions in the conclave that had led to his own election in 1592. A legal opinion, commissioned by the pope in 1593, criticized such behaviour. The conclave reform was abandoned, however, because the Spanish faction in the college of cardinals did not yield.[162]

On 23 September 1592 a papal commission, created by Pope Clement, met to decide what should be done with all Panvinio's manuscripts. Members of the commission were Cardinal Santoro, prefect of the Congregation of the Inquisition;[163] Bartolomé de Miranda, master of the Sacred Palace;[164] Robert Bellarmine; Francisco Peña, a canonist and consultant to the Index; and Federico Mezio, a translator of Greek texts for Baronio and member of the household of Santoro.[165] The commission decided that Federico Mezio should create a list of all Panvinio's unpublished works. Francisco Peña suggested sorting them by subject matter.[166] Furthermore, Peña recommended transferring those manuscripts by Panvinio which were 'complete and useful'

---

[161] M. Pattenden, 'The Conclaves of 1590 to 1592: An Electoral Crisis of the Early Modern Papacy?', *Sixteenth Century Journal*, 44 (2013), 391–410.

[162] P. Herre, *Papsttum und Papstwahl im Zeitalter Philipps II.* (Leipzig, 1907), 635–42; M. T. Fattori, *Clemente VIII e il Sacro Collegio, 1592–1605* (Stuttgart, 2004), 64–6; Wassilowsky, *Konklavereform*, 154–65. Members of the commission for the reform of the conclave were Cardinals Federico Borromeo, Antonio Carafa, Agostino Cusani, Scipione Lancelotti, Gabriele Paleotti, and Agostino Valier.

[163] On Santoro see S. Ricci, 'Santoro, Giulio Antonio', in Prosperi, *Dizionario storico dell'Inquisizione*, iii. 1370–7; Schwedt, *Anfänge der römischen Inquisition*, 226–7.

[164] E. Marchetti, 'Miranda, Bartolomé de', in Prosperi, *Dizionario storico dell'Inquisizione*, ii. 1048.

[165] On Peña see below. On Mezio see M. Ceresa, 'Mezio, Federico', in *DBI*, lxxiv. 56–8. Marcantonio Colonna, cardinal-librarian 1591–7, is a conspicuous absence from this list.

[166] See the minutes of the commission meeting presided over by Cardinal Santoro, at the cardinal's palace, 23 September 1592 (autograph by Francisco Peña), Vat. lat. 7030, fo. 1a^(r–v), ed.

to the Vatican Library, then preparing them for publication by purging them if they contained any 'false or dangerous dogmas'. Those which were incomplete could be neglected if they did not have any benefit for the 'common good'.[167] Mezio (possibly together with Peña) divided the manuscripts into ten categories, seven of which related to ecclesiastical topics (i.e., the primacy of Peter, the history of the popes and of the Church, papal elections, matters pertaining to popes and cardinals, the lives of cardinals, churches in Rome, and liturgy). Three belonged to 'other' subjects (Roman history, elections of emperors, and 'useless things').[168] There was a total of eighty-seven items (which included some texts which were not by Panvinio).

A censorship of *De varia creatione* followed this list. The censorship consisted, firstly, of a description of the work's contents ('Aeconomia'); the second part bore the specific title 'Censura'.[169] The style adopted in both was so similar that one must assume that they were written by the same person. Not only was the introduction to each text similar, but certain expressions were also repeated.

None of the members of the commission can be entirely excluded from consideration as the author of the censorship. Its belligerent approach is not at all characteristic of Bellarmine, although he was named as the author by Perini and others who followed him.[170] Bellarmine's censorship of Panvinio's *Church History*, which we have seen above, was more circumspect and displayed a wider knowledge of ecclesiastical sources than this censorship. Federico Mezio was more active as a translator than as an expert on questions of church history. It also unlikely that Santoro or Miranda took the time to occupy themselves with this text, as they rarely intervened personally by writing censorships.

Francisco Peña (*c*.1540–1612) was the most likely censor. He was born in Spain and studied arts and theology at the University of Valencia, from

---

Perini, *Panvinio*, 55 n. 1. For a copy of the minutes see Vat. lat. 7298, fo. 134^{r-v}; for a summary in Italian: Vat. lat. 6105, fo. 1^r.

[167] Vat. lat. 7030, fo. 1a^v.
[168] 'Onuphrii Panvinii scripta mandato Illustrissimi Domini in suas classes digesta et suis fasciculis litera, numero et ordine singula collocata', ibid., fos 2^r–10^r.
[169] 'Aeconomia quatuor librorum (quarti, quinti, sexti et septimi) Fratris Onophrii Panvinii *De varia Romani pontificis creatione*, item libri Fratris Bernardi monachi et abbatis Farfensis de donatione Constantini, item *Epitomes decem librorum de pontificis Romani varia electione* eiusdem Onophrii', ibid., fos 11^r–19^v; 'Censura in libros Honophrii Panvini *De varia Romani pontificis creatione*', ibid., fos 20^r–26^r.
[170] Perini, *Panvinio*, 148.

which he graduated in 1570–1.[171] He then left Spain in 1571 and continued his studies in Bologna. It seems that there he received the title of doctor of canon and civil law (*iuris utriusque doctor*), which he began using in 1575. From about 1577 Peña lived in Rome. His arrival there coincided with the completion of the trial of Bartolomé de Carranza, Archbishop of Toledo, who had been arrested by the Spanish Inquisition in 1559. The result of this trial—the most famous case tried by the Spanish Inquisition in the sixteenth century—was that Carranza was acquitted of the charges of heresy in Rome in 1576. The trial provoked a conflict between the Spanish and the Roman Inquisitions, which, in turn, stimulated research into the history and rules of these sacred tribunals. This research was carried out primarily by two Spanish legal scholars: Diego de Simancas (Carranza's judge) and Peña. When Diego de Simancas updated his inquisitorial manual *Institutiones catholicae* (Catholic Institutes) for the third edition of 1575, he highlighted the differences between the two Inquisitions.[172]

From then on, Peña devoted most of his life to studying the history of the Inquisitions, starting with his first major study, *De poenis haereticorum* (On the Punishments of Heretics), begun in 1575.[173] His best-known work in this field was his 1578 edition of the *Directorium inquisitorum* (Manual of Inquisitors) by Nicholas Eymerich (d. 1399); Peña included a commentary which was so extensive that it has been labelled 'a manual within a manual'.[174] He produced several revised editions of this work and also wrote a detailed treatise on the procedure adopted in Inquisition trials, published posthumously.[175]

Peña's career in Rome was facilitated by letters of recommendation from Cardinal Gabriele Paleotti, archbishop of Bologna, to Cardinal Sirleto. In 1577 he wrote a treatise on censoring law books (*De expurgandis iurisconsultorum*

---

[171] On Peña's life see H. Kaufhold, *Franciscus Peña und der Inquisitionsprozeß nach seiner 'Introductio seu Praxis Inquisitorum'* (Sankt Ottilien, 2014), 1–115; V. Lavenia, 'Peña, Francisco', in Prosperi, *Dizionario storico dell'Inquisizione*, iii. 1186–9.

[172] Diego de Simancas, *De catholicis institutionibus* (Rome, 1575). See also S. Pastore, 'Simancas, Diego de', in Prosperi, *Dizionario storico dell'Inquisizione*, iii. 1430–1; Lavenia, 'Peña', 1186; K. Lynn, *Between Court and Confessional: The Politics of Spanish Inquisitors* (Cambridge, 2013), *ad indicem*.

[173] F. Peña, *De poenis haereticorum*, Vat. lat. 6982.

[174] Lavenia, 'Peña', 1187. See also J. K. Wickersham, *Rituals of Prosecution: The Roman Inquisition and the Prosecution of Philo-Protestants in Sixteenth-Century Italy* (Toronto, 2012), *ad indicem*; T. F. Mayer, *The Roman Inquisition: A Papal Bureaucracy and Its Laws in the Age of Galileo* (Philadelphia, PA, 2013), 152–205; Kaufhold, *Peña*, 30–9, 131.

[175] F. Peña, *Instructio seu praxis Inquisitorum* (c.1605), in C. Carena, *Tractatus de officio sanctissimae Inquisitionis* (Bologna, 1668), 348–434.

libris), which carried a dedication to Sirleto.[176] In 1584 Peña became a consultant to the Congregation of the Index. In this capacity, he voted in 1587 that Erasmus should not be considered a heretic and that the Bible should be made available in Italian. He also made recommendations for a new edition of the works of Thomas Aquinas.[177] In 1599 Peña expressed his opinion that Jean Bodin's *Démonomanie des sorciers* (Demonomania of Sorcerers) should be prohibited.[178]

A particular interest of Peña was the history of canon law, which he saw in constant evolution; he believed it could be brought up to date through the knowledge of the juridical sources. He contributed to the new edition of the Decretals of Gregory IX (*Liber extra*, 1234), published in 1582.[179] As we learn from a remark by Panvinio's friend, the leading canonist Antonio Agustín, Peña's additions to the Decretals were printed without his name because he had 'set fire to the temple of Diana'—surely an allusion to Peña's excessive ambition.[180] From 1589 Peña was also involved in the preparation of a canonical collection entitled *Liber septimus*, containing more recent decrees from the fourteenth century onwards. As part of this project, which remained unfinished, he carried out preparatory work on decrees from Gregory VII to Pius II and delivered a lecture to the other commission members on the decrees of Gregory VII.[181] In 1588 Peña was named one of the twelve auditors (judges) of the papal tribunal known as the Roman Rota. In this capacity, he played an influential role in canonization trials, beginning in 1588 with that of Diego of Alcalá, the first saint declared for the whole Church after the Reformation (the last canonization before this

---

[176] R. Savelli, 'The Censoring of Law Books', in G. Fragnito (ed.), *Church, Censorship and Culture in Early Modern Italy* (Cambridge, 2001), 223–53, at pp. 243–5; id., *Censori e giuristi: storie di libri, di idee e di costumi (secoli XVI–XVII)* (Milan, 2011), 32–4; Kaufhold, *Peña*, 15.

[177] Godman, *Saint as Censor*, 113–14, 404–5, 431–2; P. Godman and J. Brandt, *Weltliteratur auf dem Index: die geheimen Gutachten des Vatikans* (Berlin, 2001), 30; Frajese, *Nascita dell'Indice*, 109, 113–15; Arnold, *Die römische Zensur*, 163–4, 398–400. My thanks to Jyri Hasecker for his help.

[178] M. Valente, 'The Works of Bodin under the Lens of Roman Theologians and Inquisitors', in H. A. Lloyd (ed.), *The Reception of Bodin* (Leiden, 2013), 219–35, at p. 229.

[179] *Decretales Domini Gregorii Papae IX suae integritati una cum glossis restitutae* (Rome, 1582).

[180] A. Agustín, *De emendatione Gratiani dialogorum libri duo* (Tarragona, 1587), 214: 'Franciscus Pegna Hispanus, cuius sunt additiones Decretalium sine nomine, quia templum Dianae incendisse visus est'. The burning down of the Temple of Artemis (Diana), one of the Seven Wonders of the World, by Herostratus in 356 BC was emblematic of those who desired to achieve fame at any cost. See also Kaufhold, *Peña*, 62–3.

[181] E. Dickerhof-Borello, *Ein Liber Septimus für das Corpus Iuris Canonici: der Versuch einer nachtridentinischen Kompilation* (Cologne, 2002), 50, 57, 117, 119, 182, 256.

had taken place in 1523). Peña assembled the documentation and wrote this saint's life.[182] In 1606 Peña became a consultant to the Holy Office.[183]

A key exponent of Spanish political interests in Rome, Peña became involved in numerous affairs regarding church politics. After Philip II had pushed through the election of Gregory XIV at the conclave of 1590, Francisco Peña celebrated this success in a confidential memorandum.[184] In 1594 Peña was one of three experts whom Philip II called upon after Clement VIII had criticized the Spanish ambassador's interventions in the conclave of 1592. Peña, the Jesuit José de Acosta, and the Dominican Juan Vincente duly justified such political interventions.[185] Another politically sensitive issue was the conversion of Henry IV of France to Catholicism in 1593. Peña rejected the idea that Henry should receive papal absolution; consequently, Peña fell into disfavour with Clement VIII. This stance likely cost him a cardinal's hat, despite Spanish pressure for him to receive it. Under Paul V (r. 1605–21), Peña regained papal favour when he defended the fullness of papal authority, *plenitudo potestatis*, in temporal affairs during the Venetian Interdict crisis (1606–7). On several accounts he attacked Cardinal Bellarmine, whom he described, in a letter to Pope Paul of 1610, as a 'christianello' ('little Christian'). In particular, according to Peña, Bellarmine's theory of *potestas indirecta* (which held that the pope had only indirect authority in temporal matters) had furnished weapons to those (such as the Venetians) who were in revolt against papal temporal authority throughout Europe.[186]

---

[182] F. Peña, *De vita, miraculis et actis canonizationis Sancti Didaci* (Rome, 1589). See also L. J. A. Villalon, 'San Diego de Alcalá and the Politics of Saint-Making in Counter-Reformation Europe', *Catholic Historical Review*, 83 (1997), 691–715; T. J. Dandelet, *Spanish Rome, 1500–1700* (New Haven, CT, 2001), 171–9.

[183] Schwedt, *Die römische Inquisition*, 468.

[184] Peña's autograph memorandum of 1590 is in London, British Library, Add. MS 28463, fos 141ʳ–146ʳ. He warned on this occasion that Italians should never be trusted to keep any secrets ('el italiano está inhabilitado para esta virtud del guardar el secreto', fo. 144ᵛ). See also Herre, *Papsttum und Papstwahl*, 532, 539–42.

[185] Herre, *Papsttum und Papstwahl*, 638–42; Wassilowsky, *Konklavereform*, 162–3; M. A. Visceglia, 'Factions in the Sacred College in the Sixteenth and Seventeenth Centuries', in M. A. Visceglia and G. Signorotto (eds), *Court and Politics in Papal Rome, 1492–1700* (Cambridge, 2002), 99–131, at pp. 107–8. For Peña's dependence on Spain see also Dandelet, *Spanish Rome*, 92–3, 139, 143–4.

[186] S. Tutino, *Empire of Souls: Robert Bellarmine and the Christian Commonwealth* (Oxford, 2010), 83–4, 99–101, 106, 126–7, 153, 156 ('christianello'), 321 n. 48; ead., 'A Spanish Canonist in Rome: Notes on the Career of Francisco Peña', *California Italian Studies*, 5 (2014) no. 1, Web, https://escholarship.org/uc/item/6jz907xp. See also V. Frajese, 'Regno ecclesiastico e Stato moderno: la polemica tra Francisco Peña e Roberto Bellarmino sull'esenzione dei chierici', *Annali dell'Istituto storico italo-germanico di Trento/Jahrbuch des italienisch-deutschen historischen Instituts in Trient*, 14 (1988), 273–339, at p. 330.

Peña's interest in the *Liber pontificalis* (Book of Pontiffs) has so far received little attention. In 1593 a twelfth-century manuscript of the *Liber* (Vat. lat. 3764) was brought to Rome from the Benedictine abbey of La Trinità della Cava near Salerno. Antonio d'Aquino had discovered it, and Cesare Baronio had convinced the Cardinal-Protector of the Benedictines to have it transferred to Rome. Peña obtained the manuscript and decided to transcribe it and collate it with other copies.[187] It may be that his interest in the *Liber* was sparked or increased by his reading of Panvinio's work on papal elections in late 1592.

Peña's private library betrayed a marked interest in Panvinio's works. According to a catalogue most likely drawn up at his death, he possessed an extensive collection of Panvinio's printed works, with no fewer than eleven editions. Thus, Peña owned most of Panvinio's works. In his rooms sat the *Epitome pontificum Romanorum* (1557); the *Fasti et triumphi* (1557) and *Fastorum libri V* (1558); *Reipublicae Romanae commentarii* (1558); *Romani principes* (with *De comitiis*, 1558); *Chronicon ecclesiasticum* (1568); *Le sette chiese romane* (1570); both a Cologne (1568) and a Leuven (1572) printing of Panvinio's edition of Platina's *Vitae pontificum*; *De primatu Petri* (1589); and *De ludis circensibus* (1600).[188]

Peña's attitudes have been labelled 'rigorous and thrusting, learned and arrogant' (Godman); 'hard-core pro-Papalist', 'ultrapapalist', 'militant', 'muscular', and 'aggressive' (Tutino); 'frank almost to the point of being violent', 'radicalizing and demonizing' (Frajese); and 'intransigent' (Arnold).[189] In 1588 Peña himself reportedly referred to moderate cardinals in the Congregation of the Index as 'reeds shaken by the wind' ('arundines vento agitatae', Matthew 11:7)—that is, as fickle and wavering.[190] Nevertheless, Hubert Kaufhold has argued, in the first ever monograph devoted to Peña, that the most negative assessments of him are exaggerated and should be

[187] See Peña's account in Anastasius Bibliothecarius, *De vitis Romanorum pontificum*, ed. F. Bianchini, 4 vols (Rome, 1718–35), i. 3. See also *Libri di Monsignor Peña già Auditor di Rota*, MS BAV, Barb. lat. 3115, fos 1ʳ–91ʳ, at fo. 7ᵛ; Kaufhold, *Peña*, 101–3. For the idea that a large part of the *Liber pontificalis* was composed by Anastasius Bibliothecarius see G. Arnaldi, *Come nacque la attribuzione ad Anastasio del* Liber Pontificalis (Rome, 2001).
[188] *Libri di Monsignor Peña*, fos 13ʳ, 20ᵛ, 43ʳ, 44ʳ, 45ʳ, 66ᵛ, 67ʳ, 68ᵛ, 71ᵛ, 72ʳ, 73ʳ⁻ᵛ, 88ᵛ. On Peña's library see also Kaufhold, *Peña*, 105–7. Peña acquired parts of Alfonso Chacón's library (d. 1599), which may have contained some of Panvinio's works. On Chacón see above, 143–145.
[189] Godman, *Saint as Censor*, 90; Tutino, *Empire of Souls*, 99, 126, 156; V. Frajese, 'La revoca dell'*Index* sistino e la Curia romana (1588–1596)', *Nouvelles de la République des Lettres*, 6 (1986), 15–49, at p. 21 ('franco fin quasi alla violenza'); id., *Nascita dell'Indice*, 164 ('radicalizzante e demonizzatrice'); Arnold, *Die römische Zensur*, 163, 304 n. 683.
[190] A. Chacón to Peña, 19 January 1588, in F. A. Zaccaria, *Storia polemica delle proibizioni de' libri* (Rome, 1777), 164. See also Frajese 'La revoca', 21.

qualified. According to Kaufhold, Peña often simply supported Spanish views or majority opinions; his philological work was diligent, and he employed humanist methods in his work with sources. His judgements were often measured and based on facts.[191]

Some elements typical of Peña's style suggest that he was the censor in the case of Panvinio. These were, first, the inquisitorial language and mind-set; second, a certain bellicosity; and third, expressions which he favoured and often used. Some phrases, such as 'ingenue fateor' ('I candidly admit' or 'confess'), which were characteristic of Peña, were repeated in various forms four times in the censorship document. These could also be found in Peña's published works, including his commentary on the inquisitorial handbook by Nicholas Eymerich.[192] Although the expression was fairly common in Latin, it may, because of the frequency of its use here, provide evidence for identifying the author.

For the censorship of Panvinio, Peña (whom I shall treat as the presumed author) used MS Vat. lat. 6107, which contained Books IV to VII of *De varia creatione*, followed by the epitome of the ten books.[193] Peña began by reconstructing, from the epitome, the content of the first three books. Regarding Book I in the epitome, he was satisfied with what Panvinio had written about the institution of the Church by Christ and the primacy conferred on St Peter. In Book II, regarding the fourth mode of election, where Panvinio described the schism between Liberius and Felix II, and the following popes up to Vigilius (d. 555), the censor stated that Panvinio had appended a wealth of material, which was worth knowing, about events that had happened in the Church.[194] He then supplied a neutral summary of Panvinio's description of the modes until the end of Book III.

Books IV–VII received more attention, as full versions of them were contained in the manuscript. In Book IV, where Panvinio described the Investiture Controversy from Henry IV onwards, the censor made a clear judgement:

[191] Kaufhold, *Peña*, 23–4, 37–9.

[192] Examples: 'ingenue fateor' ('Aeconomia' on Book IV, 12th mode, fo. 15ʳ), 'ingenue fatetur' (ibid. on Book V, 18th mode, fo. 17ᵛ), 'ingenue fateatur' ('Censura', Introduction, fo. 21ᵛ), 'ingenue fatetur' ('Censura' on Epitome, Preface to Book VIII, fo. 26ʳ). Compare N. Eymerich, *Directorium inquisitorum*, ed. with a commentary by F. Peña (first publ. 1578) (Venice, 1595), 64, 76, 358, 512, 594, 617. There are more examples in this book and in other works by Peña.

[193] Vat. lat. 6107 had been kept in the archives of the Apostolic Chamber and was loaned to Cardinal Santoro on 9 November 1592; see the note in Vat. lat. 6105, fo. 1ᵛ. On Vat. lat. 6107 see also below, n. 212.

[194] Peña, 'Aeconomia', fo. 13ʳ⁻ᵛ: 'Adiiciuntur praeterea complura scitu digna, quae in ecclesia Dei contigerent, et huiusmodi argumento pro serie historiae intelligenda lucem et opem afferunt non mediocrem'.

I frankly confess that where Panvinio describes these things, I would desire him to be more pious, for he seems so attached to the Empire that he cares little about the Church of God, having been badly duped by some German political heretic and atheist. This is something which he also quite openly declares in his book 'On the Elections of Emperors'. But for these things, see the censorship.[195]

This characteristically strong stand against 'heretics' supports my hypothesis that Peña was the author. In addition, the cross-reference to the censorship proper suggests that both texts—the 'Aeconomia' and the 'Censura'—were written by the same author.

Going through Book V, Peña referred to the dispute between Pope Alexander III and Emperor Frederick Barbarossa. He thought that Panvinio had described this power struggle 'in such in a way that he gives the pious reader strong cause to doubt his integrity and piety'.[196] At the end of Book V, Peña noted that this book greatly annoyed not only the pious reader but also the author himself, as Panvinio had candidly confessed.[197] Book VI again contained events which were too much for Peña's ideal 'pious reader' to take; they certainly 'cannot be passed over without great disturbance of the soul'.[198] He referred in particular to the schism of three antipopes from 1159 onwards, the struggle of Boniface VIII with Philip IV of France (and Boniface's captivity), as well as Celestine V's renunciation of the papacy. Again, Peña noted Panvinio's lack of 'faith' and 'piety'.[199] In the seventh Book, in which Panvinio dealt with the elections from Clement V to Antipope Clement (VIII) under Louis the Bavarian and the succeeding rulers, Panvinio excerpted many passages from Giovanni Villani's *Florentine Chronicle*— passages which, according to Peña, 'instil misery in us'.[200]

---

[195] Ibid., fo. 15^v: 'Quibus recensendis (ingenue fateor) maiorem Honophrii desidera[re]m pietatem, ita enim imperio addictus videtur ut ecclesia Dei curare videatur parum, ab aliquo germano politico haeretico et atheo male lactatus. Quod etiam libro *De comitiis imperat(orum)* satis aperte declaravit. Sed de his in censura.'

[196] Ibid., fos 16^v–17^r: 'usque ad Alexandrum III tempore Friderici Aenobarbi, quando aliae graviores ortae sunt turbae et controversiae, iis fortasse perniciosores quae sub Henricis contingerant, quas Honophrius ita recenset ut pio lectori de sui integritate et pietate non mediocriter dubitandi prebeat occasionem'.

[197] Ibid., fo. 17^v: 'Et ita quintus tandem terminatur liber, non sine magna pii lectoris, sed etiam ipsius authoris (quod ingenue fatetur) molestia.' See also above, 119–120.

[198] Peña, 'Aeconomia', fo. 17^v: 'quae sine animi perturbatione praeteriri non possunt'.

[199] Ibid.: 'Quapropter aliquando nil mirum fortasse, si Onophrii fidem vel pietatem in aliquibus desideres.'

[200] Ibid., fo. 18^r: 'pleraque ex Joanne Villano Florentino historico illorum temporum, ut etiam praecedenti libro fecit, Onophrius excerpta adiecit, quae miserias illas nobis insinuarent'.

Peña then found the *Liber Beraldi*, a treatise which Panvinio thought was by Frater Berardus, the abbot of Farfa who took the side of Henry IV in the Investiture Controversy against Pope Gregory VII.[201] In a struggle between the monastery of Farfa and the papacy over possessions in the Sabina territory, Berardus interpreted the Donation of Constantine as relevant solely to spiritual dominion (that is, churches, and what was necessary for the upkeep and the promotion of the faith).[202] 'Bernardaccius' (Peña's derogatory name for him) cited many examples of historical instances which demonstrated that the emperors had maintained their territorial dominion over Italy, punishing popes and confirming newly elected ones before they could be consecrated. Thus, Berardus, in Peña's opinion, not only misinterpreted the Donation but also claimed that papal primacy had been instituted by Constantine rather than by Christ.[203] Peña failed to distinguish between the author of *De varia creatione* and his source, transferring part of the blame from the Abbot of Farfa to Panvinio: 'From these things we see not only Berardus's bad heart and bad designs', noted Peña, 'but also Friar Onofrio cannot be easily considered innocent'.[204] In his introductory remarks to the *Liber Beraldi*, Panvinio had promised to also append Cardinal Deusdedit's treatise in defence of Gregory VII. Peña was displeased to see that Panvinio, despite his promise, had failed to include this treatise; for Peña, this omission showed to which side Panvinio inclined.[205] To finish this first part of his censorship ('Aeconomia'), Peña gave a quick summary of the contents of Books VIII–X from the epitome, noting the contents in just a few sentences

---

[201] This treatise was actually written by Gregory of Catino at the time of Abbot Beraldus III. On the *Liber Beraldi* and for what follows (i.e., the discussion about the Donation of Constantine) see my Appendix, below, 213–220. For the fact that the *Liber Beraldi* came at the end of Book VII in this MS see below, n. 207.

[202] *Fratris Berardi monachi et abbatis monasterii Farfensis liber*, Clm 148, fos 186ʳ–196ᵛ, ed. K. Heinzelmann, *Die Farfenser Streitschriften: ein Beitrag zur Geschichte des Investiturstreites* (Strasbourg, 1904), 40–64, at p. 41: 'Tum Berardus enucleatius diligentiusque ipsum perspiciens edictum ita locutus est: "Res sic non habet, quia Constantinus non iura privatorum nec ex toto terreni imperii dominium beato Silvestro concessit, sed, sicut ibi legitur, ut principatum teneat super omnes in universo terrarum orbe Dei ecclesias, et eius iudicio, quaecumque ad cultum Dei et fidei christianae stabilitatem procuranda fuerint, disponantur."'

[203] Peña, 'Aeconomia', fo. 19ʳ: 'non solum Constantini donatio irrita vel simulata hoc pacto dignoscatur, verum etiam ecclesiae Romanae primatus a Deo institutus ab homine Constantino, scilicet imperatore, ortum habuisse insinuetur'.

[204] Ibid.: 'Quibus non solum Fratris Bernardi mala mens et malus animus perspicitur, verum etiam Frater Onophrius a culpa immunis non ita facile tuetur'.

[205] Ibid., fo. 18ᵛ: 'ut hinc utrius partes foveret Onophrius aperte videatur'. The pages where Deusdedit's treatise was to appear were left empty in the MS. See also below, 217.

and remarking that the conclaves and councils described in Book VIII were 'worth knowing'.[206]

As has been said, Peña's censorship proper, which came next in the manuscript, bore the actual title 'Censura'. Here, he followed closely the sequence of the material in the manuscript.[207] In his opening observations, Peña mentioned Panvinio's infamous appendix to Book IV, the *Liber Beraldi*, 'in which Bernardus tries to do away with the Donation of Constantine'.[208] He then offered a devastating general judgement of Panvinio's *De varia creatione*:

We certainly wondered at Onofrio's relentless toil, how it could come about that a little friar ('fraterculus') was able to stitch together so many things; for this reason, it is no wonder that everything is imperfect, most things are jumbled, many confused, some useless and several dangerous.[209] This causes no small pain because there is some guilt and at least strong suspicion;[210] for Onofrio everywhere declares that he is very attached to the Empire and wants to diminish the majesty of the Holy Church, to reprehend its rule, to gnaw at the reputation of the popes and to criticize the morals of prelates, as he himself acknowledges and openly admits that what he wrote will not please the pious and Christian reader. Not to mention that, although he purports to be a theologian, one finds that he perhaps pays his respects to theology only from the doorstep. If only he had not erred in what is evident enough even to shallow theologians of mediocre erudition,[211] such as the things which he states on fo. 1 verso, line 16, about the mystical body of the Church which, as he teaches, was conceived from the Holy Spirit and born from the Virgin.[212]

---

[206] Peña, 'Aeconomia', fo. 19ᵛ: 'scitu digna censentur'.

[207] He first ran through Books IV to VII, then discussed the *Liber Beraldi*, which in this MS was appended to the end of Book VII, even though it belonged to the end of Book IV (where it was correctly placed in Clm 148); finally, he went through the epitome included at the end of the Vatican manuscript.

[208] Peña, 'Censura', fo. 21ʳ: 'adiectus est libellus quidam nescio cuius Fratris Bernardi monachi et abbatis Farfensis, quo bonus ille frater Constantini donationem nititur e medio tollere'.

[209] For a similar construction see Peña, 'Praefatio', in Eymerich, *Directorium*, sig. †4ʳ: 'multa incognita...multa obscura...nonnulla immutata'.

[210] Peña explained the idea of a 'vehemens suspicio' (of heresy) in his edition of the *Directorium*, 439–40.

[211] Peña used the expression 'mediocriter eruditus' elsewhere to describe theologians and inquisitors. See the *Directorium*, 389, 439, 482, 592.

[212] Peña, 'Censura', fo. 21ʳ⁻ᵛ: 'Et admirati certe sumus Onuphrii improbum laborem, qui fieri potuerit ut fraterculus tot tantaque consarcinare quiverit, ut nihil mirum propterea si omnia imperfecta, indigesta pleraque, multa confusa, inutilia quedam et nonnulla perniciosa, quod

Peña justly highlighted the sheer size and disorderly state of Panvinio's manuscript, Panvinio's criticism of the papacy's worldly powers, and his account of the worrisome sides of church history.[213] His disparagement of Panvinio's theological knowledge, however, failed to hit its target, because the passage cited here regarding the mystical body of the Church, from the preface to Book IV, had in fact been taken from Otto of Freising.[214]

After these remarks came Peña's list of censorship points. These points can be divided into four main categories: (1) Panvinio believed that for many centuries emperors exerted power over the popes (and sided with them); (2) according to Panvinio, from the time of Gregory VII onwards, this relationship was inverted, so that popes gained power over emperors, which was not beneficial to the Church; (3) Panvinio used unreliable and unorthodox sources; and (4) he was critical of members of the clergy.

Examples of the first category were: Henry III's deposition of Pope Gregory VI (1046);[215] the outbreak of the schism under Henry IV because the emperor's customary power was not respected;[216] Panvinio's declaration that the imperial version of the 1059 decree on elections was authentic and that the papal version of Nicholas II was 'corrupt' ('corruptum');[217] his denial of the validity of the Donation of Constantine;[218] his belief that Hadrian I had granted the right to elect the popes to Charlemagne and

---

non mediocriter dolendum cum non vacet culpa vel saltem vehementi suspicione, ita enim Imperio se addictum Onophrius ubique manifeste declarat, et Ecclesie sancte maiestati velle detrahere, ipsius regimen reprehendere, pontifices carpere, prelatorum mores arguere, ut ipsemet id agnoscat et ingenue fateatur que scripsit pio et Christiano lectori non placitura. Omitto quod, licet se theologum vendicet, a limine tamen theologiam forsan salutare cognoscitur. Utinam non erraret in iis que mediocriter eruditis theologastris sunt satis aperta, qualia sunt ea que ponit: fo. p.o pag. 2.a [= DVC-X, Preface to Book IV, Vat. lat. 6107.i, fo. 1aᵛ] vers. 16 de corpore mystico ecclesie, quod de *spiritu sancto conceptum et natum ex virgine* docet.' For this passage see also Le Bachelet, *Auctarium Bellarminianum*, 564 n. 1; Gersbach, 'De comitiis', 420 n. 34. The page references by the censor are to Vat. lat. 6107, which is now bound in 3 separate parts: pt i, fos 1ʳ–189ᵛ (Book IV; part of Book V); pt ii, fos 190ʳ–388ᵛ (rest of Book V; Book VI); pt iii, fos 389ʳ–604ᵛ (Book VII; Epitome).

---

[213] On possible models for Panvinio's criticism of the Church's temporal power see above, 94–95.

[214] Peña, 'Censura', fo. 21ᵛ (on DVC-X, Preface to Book IV, Vat. lat. 6107.i, fo. 1aᵛ). See *Chronica sive Historia de duabus civitatibus*, VI.36, p. 305, and the edition of the works of Otto and Rahewin owned by Panvinio (*Rerum ab origine mundi…*, 1515), fos 73ᵛ–74ʳ.

[215] Peña, 'Censura', fo. 22ʳ (on Book IV, Vat. lat. 6107.i, fo. 4ᵛ/Clm 148, fo. 87ʳ).

[216] Ibid. (on Book IV, Vat. lat. 6107.i, fo. 14ʳ/Clm 148, fo. 94ᵛ).

[217] Ibid., fo. 22ʳ⁻ᵛ (on Book IV, Vat. lat. 6107.i, fos 21ʳ⁻ᵛ, 22ᵛ/Clm 148, fos 99ᵛ–100ᵛ).

[218] Ibid., fo. 22ᵛ (on Book IV, Vat. lat. 6107.i, fo. 52ʳ/Clm 148, fo. 100ᵛ); fo. 24ʳ (on Book V, Vat. lat. 6107.i, fo. 160ʳ/Clm 148, fo. 222ᵛ); fo. 24ᵛ (on *Liber Beraldi*, Vat. lat. 6107.iii, fo. 472ʳ/Clm 148, fo. 186ʳ).

that Leo VIII had confirmed this right for Otto I;[219] and his opinion that the agreement by which Louis the Pious assured free papal elections was a forgery.[220]

The second category, regarding passages where Panvinio argued that the Church had gained too much worldly power, included the following points: the Church appeared to break under its own weight;[221] it treated the emperors like the lowest slaves;[222] it was God's will that priestly power almost annihilated imperial authority;[223] and Gregory VII 'spewed out' ('evomuit') his plans against the emperors, then systematically went to work to destroy their authority.[224]

Peña's criticism of Panvinio's use of sources—the third category of censorial remarks—consisted of points where the censor suspected that Panvinio availed himself of unreliable texts. These included the comparison of the schisms under Gregory VII to the deepest darkness of Egypt (which was actually taken from Otto of Freising);[225] Panvinio's note that he had read fables about Gregory VII written by a 'story-teller' ('fabulator');[226] and his statement that he cited an unidentified ('incertus') author of papal biographies, where Peña suspected him of concealing the name of a heretic.[227]

The fourth type of criticism dealt with Panvinio's attacks on the clergy. At the beginning of his preface to Book IV, Panvinio noted that the great changes which happened in the following period would show that the Church was ruled by divine government. As Peña saw it, Panvinio downplayed the role of the popes and the church hierarchy and, perhaps, even held fatalistic

---

[219] Ibid., fo. 22ᵛ (on Book IV, Vat. lat. 6107.i, fos 52ʳ, 53ʳ/*Gregorii Papae VII electio*, cols 254, 256).
[220] Ibid., fo. 25ᵛ (on the Epitome, Book III, Vat. lat. 6107.iii, fo. 532ʳ/DVC-X-Epitome, Book III, BNF, Lat. 4244B, fo. 45ᵛ).
[221] Ibid., fo. 21ᵛ (on the Preface to Book IV, Vat. lat. 6107.i, fo. 1aᵛ/Clm 148, fo. 84ʳ); fo. 24ᵛ (on the Preface to Book VI, Vat. lat. 6107.ii, fo. 258ʳ⁻ᵛ/Clm 149, fo. 1ʳ⁻ᵛ); fo. 25ᵛ (on the Epitome, Preface to Book IV, Vat. lat. 6107.iii, fo. 540ᵛ). See also above, 107.
[222] Peña, 'Censura', fo. 22ʳ (on the Preface to Book IV, Vat. lat. 6107.i, fo. 1aᵛ/Clm 148, fo. 84ʳ⁻ᵛ).
[223] Ibid., fo. 22ᵛ (on Book IV, Vat. lat. 6107.i, fo. 47ʳ/*Gregorii Papae VII electio*, col. 247). Here Panvinio had inserted a phrase of his own ('cum imperium Romanum a sacerdotali potestate minuendum esset et ad nihilum fere redigendum') into a passage quoted from Lampert of Hersfeld's *Annales*. See Panvinio's printed copy, Lampert, *Germanorum res praeclarae olim gestae* (1533), ad AD 1073, fo. 106ʳ⁻ᵛ; id., *Annales*, ed. Holder-Egger, 145–6.
[224] Peña, 'Censura', fo. 23ʳ (on Book IV, Vat. lat. 6107.i, fo. 56ʳ/*Gregorii Papae VII electio*, cols 260–1). See also ibid., fo. 23ʳ⁻ᵛ (on Vat. lat. 6107.i, fos 54ʳ, 57ᵛ, 59ʳ, 60ʳ/*Gregorii Papae VII electio*, cols 257, 262, 265, 266); fo. 25ᵛ (on the Epitome, Book IV, Vat. lat. 6107.iii, fo. 544ᵛ). See also above, 114; below, 204.
[225] Peña, 'Censura', fo. 22ʳ (on the Preface to Book IV, Vat. lat. 6107.i, fo. 2ʳ/Clm 148, fo. 84ᵛ). See Otto of Freising, *Rerum ab origine mundi...* (1515), VI.36, fo. 74ʳ; id., *Chronica*, 306.
[226] Peña, 'Censura', fo. 22ᵛ (on Book IV, Vat. lat. 6107.i, fo. 37ʳ/*Gregorii Papae VII electio*, col. [235]–[236]). See also above, 110.
[227] Peña, 'Censura', fo. 23ᵛ (on Book IV, Vat. lat. 6107.i, fo. 90ᵛ/Clm 148, fo. 156ʳ).

beliefs.[228] Commenting on a passage taken from Johannes Aventinus, Peña assumed that Panvinio shared his source's negative view of prelates.[229] The fact that Panvinio asked his pious readers to forgive him for narrating troublesome events was construed by Peña as plain evidence of his guilt.[230] Moreover, the censorship ended with the observation that Panvinio had asked his readers for patience if his writings did not always correspond to the teachings of the Church. Peña interpreted this as Panvinio's frank admission that he had consciously departed from those teachings.[231] Thereby, our censor read the worst possible intentions into Panvinio's statements—when in fact, Panvinio had only wanted to supply his readers with trigger warnings for the distressing historical sources that they encountered in his works.

Jakob Gretser on Gregory VII

In 1609, Pope Paul V authorized the commemoration of Gregory VII through a special local office at Salerno, which was a further step towards his canonization.[232] In the same year, the German Jesuit Jakob Gretser (1562–1625) wrote an *Apologia pro Gregorio VII* (Defence of Gregory VII). Gretser was known for his uncompromising stance against Protestants and deviant Catholics. He was variously referred to as the 'great tamer of Lutherans' ('magnus Lutheranorum domitor') and 'terror of the heretics and of the slanderers of Jesuits' ('haereticorum et calumniatorem Societas Iesu terror').[233] In his *Apologia*, Gretser listed fifty sources championing Gregory

---

[228] Ibid., fo. 21ᵛ (on the Preface to Book IV, Vat. lat. 6107.i, fo. 1aʳ/Clm 148, fo. 84ʳ): 'cum mundum omnem, tum precipue ecclesiam sanctam solo divinitatis moderamine gubernari etc. His verbis vel fati necessitas ponitur, vel ecclesiastica aeconomia improbatur.'

[229] Ibid., fo. 22ᵛ (on Book IV, Vat. lat. 6107.i, fo. 31ʳ⁻ᵛ/Clm 148, fo. 107ʳ⁻ᵛ). This passage on the schism between Alexander II (r. 1061–73) and Antipope Honorius II was taken from Johannes Aventinus; see his *Annales Boiorum* (1554), 548–9; *Annales ducum Boiariae*, ed. Riezler, ii. 86–7.

[230] Peña, 'Censura', fo. 24ᵛ (on the Preface to Book VI, Vat. lat. 6107.ii, fo. 258ʳ/Clm 149, fo. 1ʳ); fo. 25ᵛ (on the Epitome, Preface to Book VI, Vat. lat. 6107.iii, fo. 558ʳ).

[231] Ibid., fo. 26ʳ (on the Epitome, Preface to Book VIII, Vat. lat. 6107.iii, fo. 572ᵛ/Clm 150, fo. 1ᵛ/BNF, Lat. 4244B, fo. 81ʳ⁻ᵛ).

[232] In 1728, Benedict XIII ordered that his feast day be observed throughout the Church. This confirmation of universal cult was an 'equipollent' (i.e., equivalent) canonization since it did not involve the usual judicial process. See Benedict XIV, *De servorum Dei beatificatione et beatorum canonizatione*, 4 vols (Bologna, 1734–8), i. 373; Miccoli, 'Gregorio VII', cols 367–70. My thanks to Simon Ditchfield for his help.

[233] 'De vita, virtute et doctrina venerabilis Patris Jacobi Gretseri S.I.', in J. Gretser, *Opera omnia*, 17 vols (Regensburg, 1734–41), i, pp. I–XV, at p. XIV; H. Fitz-Simon, *Britannomachia*

VII, beginning with Anselm of Lucca (d. 1086) and ending with Sigonio's *De regno Italiae* and Panvinio's annotation to Platina.[234] By including Panvinio's annotation in this list, Gretser gave it his mark of approval. In his annotation, Panvinio praised Gregory as a matchless protector of the Church's liberty ('totius ecclesiasticae libertatis unicus assertor'). Panvinio related that although Gregory had been a most holy man, he had also been accused of holding foolish opinions. Some had called him a necromancer, others a simoniac—charges which Panvinio denied. Panvinio noted that these accusations had been fabricated to support the emperor.

As an appendix to his *Apologia*, Gretser published Panvinio's account of Gregory VII from *De varia creatione*.[235] In this case, however, Gretser injected a stark warning into his introductory remarks. He cautioned readers that Panvinio had relied too much on authors such as Sigebert of Gembloux, the 'Abbot of Ursberg', and Johannes Aventinus. By following schismatics such as Sigebert and others lacking in sound faith and doctrine ('parum sanae fidei et doctrinae scriptores'), Panvinio—according to Gretser—had sometimes strayed from the right path.[236] The source authors mentioned by Gretser were controversial among Catholics but were held in esteem by Protestants. Sigebert of Gembloux (*c*.1030–1112) was known not only for his World Chronicle but also for his strenuous defence of Emperor Henry IV in the Investiture Controversy. Some of his works were placed on the Roman

---

ministrorum (Douai, 1614), 99. See also U. Herzog, 'Jacob Gretsers Leben und Werk', *Literaturwissenschaftliches Jahrbuch*, n. s. 11 (1970), 1–36; Benz, *Zwischen Tradition und Kritik*, 85–6 and *ad indicem*.

[234] Gretser, *Apologia pro Gregorio VII*, cols 1–34 (for full reference see above, 110 n. 71). See also H. Zimmermann, 'Von der Faszination der Papstgeschichte besonders bei Protestanten: Gregor VII. und J. F. Gaab', in W. Hartmann and K. Herbers (eds), *Die Faszination der Papstgeschichte* (Cologne, 2008), 11–27, at pp. 16–18.

[235] Panvinio, *Gregorii Papae VII electio; Clementis III Antipapae electio*, in Gretser, *Apologia pro Gregorio VII*, cols [235]–273, 273–8, sig. O3ᵛ ('Errata'). The corresponding sections in the manuscript are: DVC-X, Book IV, Clm 148, fos 111ʳ–134ʳ, 134ʳ–136ʳ. Gretser left out some of the documents cited by Panvinio. For a shortened reprint of Gretser's edition see *Patrologia Latina*, ed. J.-P. Migne, 221 vols (Paris, 1844–64), cxlviii, cols 151–84.

[236] Gretser, 'Lectori' (preface to his edition of Panvinio's section on Gregory VII), in his *Apologia pro Gregorio VII*, cols [229]–[234], at cols [229]–[230]: 'Paucis te, Christiane lector, monitum volo, Onuphrium, dum Sigeberti, Urspergensis et Aventini vestigia nimis propere sequitur, a recta linea aliquando excidisse, ut contingere solet iis qui duces schismaticos, qualis fuit Sigebertus, vel alioqui parum sanae fidei et doctrinae scriptores, qualis Aventinus, absque accurato singulorum quae adferunt examine sibi deligunt.' See also Gretser, *Controversiarum…defensio*, ii, col. 767: 'Onuphrius…secutus vestigia schismaticorum et Aventini, a quibus non semel circumventus et in fraudem inductus est.'

Indexes of 1559 and 1564, as well as other indexes.[237] The Chronicle of the 'Abbot of Ursberg' was published in a Protestant edition with a continuation by Kaspar Hedio and a preface by Philipp Melanchthon.[238] Johannes Aventinus was an author known for his unabashed criticism of the contemporary Church and his pro-imperial polemic against the papacy, although he never became a Protestant. Gretser was not alone in thinking that Aventinus was a dangerous writer; both Baronio and Gretser's fellow Jesuit Canisius issued warnings about him. Aventinus's works were placed on various indexes of prohibited books, including the Roman Index of 1564.[239]

Accordingly, Gretser felt the need to set many points in Panvinio's text straight. He did so by adding marginal notes, which he based on Baronio's *Annales*.[240] Gretser's use of Baronio had two functions: not only did he draw on the *Annales* to correct and contradict Panvinio, but his heavy reliance on this work was also part of a larger initiative by Gretser to defend Baronio against attacks from Protestant scholars. An example of Gretser's corrections is his discussion of Hadrian's privilege of 785 for Charlemagne, in which the pope seemed to give the emperor the right to elect the popes and invest bishops and abbots. In his marginal notes, Gretser was careful to point out that this privilege had never existed. As Baronio had shown, the story was based on false information from Gratian's *Decretum*. Gratian, in turn, had taken it, according to Baronio, from Sigebert's chronicle.[241]

Gretser was misled, however, by another mistake made by Panvinio, who had cited Gratian's own statement that he received the information from a 'Historia ecclesiastica'.[242] Panvinio took this to refer to Anastasius Bibliothecarius's *Historia ecclesiastica*. In his marginal note, Gretser wrote that he did not believe that Anastasius could have written such a thing. The question vexed him so much, he returned to it when he was able to consult a

[237] Bujanda, *Index des livres interdits*, viii. 678, x. 367. On Sigebert and the Investiture Controversy see M. Chazan, *L'Empire et l'histoire universelle: de Sigebert de Gembloux à Jean de Saint-Victor (XIIᵉ–XIVᵉ siècle)* (Paris, 1999), 269–80.

[238] See above, 116.

[239] Bujanda, *Index des livres interdits*, viii. 519; x. 67–8. See also A. Schmid, 'Die historische Methode des Johannes Aventinus', *Blätter für deutsche Landesgeschichte*, 113 (1977), 338–95, at pp. 338–9; and above, 116–117, 139.

[240] Gretser, 'Lectori', cols [229]–[230].

[241] Gretser, marginal note, in Panvinio, *Gregorii Papae VII electio*, col. 254: 'Nihil de hac synodo hoc anno celebrata in legitimis et genuinis ecclesiasticis monumentis occurrit. Totum hoc commentum refellit Baronius'; ibid.: 'Gratianus in errorem inductus est a Sigeberto, cuius verba verbatim exscripsit.' See also Baronio, *Annales*, ix (1600), ad AD 774, pp. 323–5 (ed. Pagi, xiii. 102–5).

[242] Gratian, *Decretum*, D. 63 c. 22 (ed. Friedberg, col. 241): 'ex Historia ecclesiastica'.

manuscript of Anastasius to prove that this work did not contain the story. He added a new note 'To the reader' ('Lectori') after his 'Errata' at the end of the book, confirming that no traces of Hadrian's privilege appeared in Anastasius.[243]

The *Historia ecclesiastica* to which Gratian had referred was actually not Anastasius's work but an addition to Sigebert of Gembloux's Chronicle. Either Panvinio had not verified his inaccurate assumption that Gratian had referred to Anastasius or he intentionally provided a misleading reference. The second possibility is likely because Panvinio could rely on the fact that not many readers would have access to a manuscript of Anastasius's work; as we have seen, it took Gretser quite a while to check the reference. This seems reminiscent of the small but decisive falsifications which Panvinio inserted into several of his histories of Roman families. Had he so desired, Panvinio could easily have cited Sigebert, since he owned a printed edition of his Chronicle with the passage about the privilege (and he did quote Sigebert frequently in other parts of *De varia creatione*).[244] However, by adding the name of the papal librarian Anastasius to that of the compiler of canon law Gratian, Panvinio likely hoped to lend even more authority to the document.

Where Panvinio quoted Gratian, again, to show that Pope Leo VIII renewed Hadrian's privilege in 962, Gretser pointed out that Leo had been an antipope and that this privilege, too, was fictitious. Moreover, Baronio, in his discussion of the year 964, had refuted Gratian. While Baronio maintained that Gratian had dealt with the matter too carelessly ('inconsiderate nimis'), Gretser, adopting a somewhat more pejorative tone, claimed that Gratian's mind had wandered (i.e., his canon was a 'hallucinatio').[245]

---

[243] Gretser, 'Lectori', in Panvinio, *Gregorii Papae VII electio*, sig. O3ᵛ (after the 'Errata'). The *Historia ecclesiastica* or *Chronographia tripertita* was a compilation from Nicephoros, Syncellus, and Theophanes, made by Anastasius Bibliothecarius in *c.*871–4. It was not printed until 1649. On Anastasius (whom Panvinio believed to have been also the author of a large part of the *Liber pontificalis*) see Arnaldi, *Come nacque la attribuzione*.

[244] Sigebert of Gembloux, *Chronicon ab anno 381 ad 1113 cum insertionibus...*, ed. Antonius Rufus (Paris, 1513), ad AD 773, fo. 56ᵛ. See also ILS, fo. 27ʳ; and above, 112–114. Both Baronio and Gretser, who were misled by the 1513 edition and its reprints, believed that Sigebert had written the passage about the privilege. When Aubert Miraeus established the original text of the *Chronicon* in his Antwerp edition of 1608, it emerged (p. 90) that the passage was an addition and, as such, was not part of Sigebert's work.

[245] Baronio, *Annales*, x (1602), ad AD 964, pp. 783–8 (ed. Pagi, xvi. 148–54); Gratian, *Decretum*, D. 63 c. 23 ('Electio Romani pontificis ad ius pertinet imperatoris'), ed. Friedberg, col. 241; Gretser, marginal note, in *Gregorii Papae VII electio*, col. 255.

Lastly, some of Panvinio's criticisms of Gregory VII were harshly rebuked by Gretser. Using deliberately provocative language, Panvinio had written that, at the Lateran Synod of 1080, the pope had 'openly spewed out what he had long designed and what he had gradually indicated in other decrees'. Gretser remarked that this manner of speaking 'befitted a schismatic, not a Catholic'.[246] When, however, Panvinio praised Gregory in the last sections of his account, Gretser clearly took satisfaction in drawing attention to this fact in his marginal notes.[247]

It is noteworthy that the Jesuit Gretser thought it advisable to publish a text as problematic as Panvinio's account of Gregory VII. Gretser's introduction and notes functioned in some ways like an *Index expurgatorius*—that is, they highlighted passages of a text that were dangerous to faith and morals.[248] Panvinio's piece could be read safely only if the reader was aware of the errors contained in it. Yet unlike an *Index expurgatorius*, Gretser did not explicitly recommend deleting any passages. Perhaps the publication of Panvinio's work was made possible by a new approach in the seventeenth century to historical texts. Several Jesuit scholars, such as Heribert Rosweyde (d. 1629), began editing medieval historical sources using a new principle which has been labelled 'the untouchability of the historical'.[249] Panvinio's description of Gregory's life may have received a treatment similar to that of medieval sources: it was published as it was, although Gretser found some details to be highly disagreeable and drew attention to them.

Baronio, Gretser's guiding star, was especially resented by Protestants who worked on the constitutional history of the Empire. Baronio had treated questions such as the *translatio imperii*, the birth of the electoral college, and the role of Gregory VII in the Investiture Controversy from such a vigorously papal standpoint that he was perceived as an enemy of the Empire's constitution.[250] Therefore, Protestants were astonished to see how different

[246] Panvinio, *Gregorii Papae VII electio*, col. 260; Gretser, marginal note, ibid.: 'Schismaticum haec locutio decet, non catholicum'. For the citation from Panvinio see also above, 114, 199.

[247] Gretser, marginal notes, in Panvinio, *Gregorii Papae VII electio*, cols 270–1: 'Encomia Gregorii VII'; 'Laus Gregorii VII'.

[248] For an example of an *Index expurgatorius* see Bujanda, *Index des livres interdits*, vii (Index of Antwerp, 1571).

[249] M. C. Ferrari, '*Mutare non lubuit*: die mediävistische Philologie der Jesuiten im frühen 17. Jahrhundert', *Filologia Mediolatina*, 8 (2001), 225–48; J. M. Sawilla, *Antiquarianismus, Hagiographie und Historie im 17. Jahrhundert: zum Werk der Bollandisten* (Tübingen, 2009), 764: 'neuartiger Primat des Intangibilität des Historischen'.

[250] M. Völkel, 'Caesar Baronius in Deutschland im 17. Jahrhundert', in Firpo, *Nunc alia tempora*, 517–43.

Panvinio's work was from that of Baronio. In 1611 the Calvinist Melchior Goldast wrote a reply to Gretser's *Apologia* of Gregory VII, presenting an array of authors who were critical of Gregory. Goldast thought that Panvinio was all the more credible because he had been 'the chief literary courtier of the popes'.[251] After citing several passages from Panvinio's account of Gregory VII's life and election, Goldast judged that no one was more diligent and trustworthy than Panvinio when it came to medieval texts.[252] He praised Panvinio's 'unrestrained voice, constant spirit, truthful pen and bold style'.[253] The Lutheran Hermann Conring, author of a work which became decisive for the history of the constitution of the Empire (*De Germanorum imperio Romano*), quoted Panvinio at length for information about the privilege given to the emperors by Leo VIII.[254] The jurist and philosopher Hugo Grotius also cited several long passages from Panvinio's account of Gregory VII's deeds. In his *De imperio summarum potestatum circa sacra* (The Authority of the Supreme Powers in Matters of Religion, 1647), Grotius noted with admiration that Panvinio 'in the city of Rome was not afraid to write the truth', which was that Gregory VII was the first pontiff to disdain the emperors' supreme authority and to rob them of their right to elect popes.[255]

The Protestant church historian Johann Matthias Schröckh (1733–1808) searched for balanced accounts of Gregory. Among the published biographies of this pope, Schröckh found either hagiographical works or outright attacks. He believed that the most moderate and best work of all was Panvinio's. Schröckh gave a lucid assessment of Panvinio's achievement. Although Panvinio had been a Catholic, he had been able to assess and describe the

---

[251] M. Goldast, *Replicatio pro sacra Caesarea et regia Francorum maiestate illustrissimisque Imperii ordinibus adversus Jacobi Gretseri…crimina laesae maiestatis, rebellionis et falsi* (Hannover, 1611), 132–3: 'pontificum Romanorum primus ac summus satelles literarius fuit'. See also ibid. 95: 'Et quia Onuphrius fuit strenuissimus Romanae ecclesiae ac fidissimus athleta, non pigebit plures eius sententias adscribere, quas veritate coactus supprimere cum ingenuo animo suo non cogitavit.' On the Gretser-Goldast polemic see M. Mulsow, *Die unanständige Gelehrtenrepublik: Wissen, Libertinage und Kommunikation in der Frühen Neuzeit* (Stuttgart, 2007), 146–76. On Goldast see also I. Maclean, *Scholarship, Commerce, Religion: The Learned Book in the Age of Confessions, 1560–1630* (Cambridge, MA, 2012), *ad indicem*.

[252] Goldast, *Replicatio*, 136: 'Onuphrius, quo nemo diligentius et maiori cum fide in veterum scriptis versatus est'.

[253] Ibid. 194: 'Denique Onuphrius Panvinus, voce libera, animo constanti, calamo veraci et licenti stilo in ipsa urbe Roma adversus Hildebrandi et successorum eius tyrannidem pro legis regiae senatusconsulto nihil dubitavit perorare.' Panvinio's style was 'non inelegans'.

[254] H. Conring, *De Germanorum imperio Romano* (Helmstedt, 1644), 74–6. See also Panvinio, *Gregorii Papae VII electio*, cols 255–7.

[255] H. Grotius, *De imperio summarum potestatum circa sacra*, ed. and trans. H.-J. van Dam, 2 vols (Leiden, 2001), i. 434–5, 488–91, 500–5. For the citation, ibid., i. 488: 'Onufrius, qui in ipsa urbe Roma non dubitavit haec verissima scribere'.

novelty of Gregory's actions in relation to the Empire within the historical context of the pope's own time, and he did this without leaning towards the radical views of either side.[256]

Moreover, Panvinio was appreciated by scholars who had no particular interest in religious controversy. For example, the French antiquarian Nicolas-Claude Fabri de Peiresc (1580–1637) wrote that he did not normally collect books on religious controversy such as Gretser's heavy tome; however, he made an exception because this book contained Panvinio's life of Gregory. Peiresc's love for all Panvinio's works swayed him to break his own rule.[257]

[256] J. M. Schröckh, *Christliche Kirchengeschichte*, 45 pts (Frankfurt; Leipzig, 1768–1812), xxv. 533: 'Unerwartet aber ist es vermuthlich vielen Lesern, daß die Lebensbeschreibung Gregors von dem berühmten Augustiner-Mönch Onufrio Panvini die gemäßigteste von allen und, so weit nur ein Mönch und geistlicher Unterthan der Päpste, deren Hoheit er allerdings verehrt, die Wahrheit sagen konnte, die beste von allen ist.'

[257] Peiresc to Dupuy, 16 May 1627, in P. Tamizey de Larroque (ed.), *Lettres de Peiresc aux frères Dupuy*, 7 vols (Paris, 1888–98), i. 218–19: 'je vous diray que bien que je ne fasse pas de recueil de cez libvres de controverses, toutefoys je me condamne à ce volume de Gretserus pour l'amour de la *Vie de Gregoire VII* d'Onufrius, dont j'ayme toutes les oeuvres avec inclination particulière.'

Epilogue

The epilogue provides some thoughts on the development of ecclesiastical historiography after *c*.1580. Catholics published relatively few works on church history during this period. This was largely because Catholic universities neglected the teaching of church history. The influential *ratio studiorum* ('plan of studies') of the Jesuits (1599) compounded this negative tendency, because it did not include church history. While the moral uses of classical history remained fundamental to the Jesuit teaching of rhetoric and preaching, a chair of ecclesiastical history was introduced at the Jesuit Collegio Romano only in 1742.[1] As Hubert Jedin noted, church history in Rome was studied in private circles. Pontianus Polman succinctly summarized this tendency when he observed that Catholics were 'neither prepared for nor especially attracted to the study of history'.[2]

After the Magdeburg Centuriators had successfully created a new Protestant church history, historical criticism in the Lutheran camp remained subdued in the shadow of their great achievement. While Lutherans in Germany tended to focus on the study of Scripture, Calvinist polemics in France concentrated more on patristics and church traditions. Calvinists continued the humanist-inspired approach of Oecolampadius and Bullinger. For example, they produced editions of Church Fathers, a continuation of Flacius's *Catalogus* (edited by Simon Goulart, 1597–1608), and discussions of the Eucharist.[3] In the first half of the seventeenth century, great Calvinist

---

[1] P. Nelles, '*Historia magistra antiquitatis*: Cicero and Jesuit History Teaching', *Renaissance Studies*, 13 (1999), 130–72; F. Neumann, *Geschichtsschreibung als Kunst: Famiano Strada S.I. (1572–1649) und die ars historica in Italien* (Berlin, 2013), 80–100.

[2] Polman, *L'élément historique*, 500: 'les catholiques n'étaient ni préparés ni spécialement attirés à l'étude de l'histoire'; H. Jedin, 'General Introduction to Church History', in H. Jedin and J. Dolan (eds), *History of the Church*, 10 vols (London, 1980–1), i. 1–56, at p. 31. See also P. Prodi, 'La storia umana come luogo teologico', in id., *Profezia vs. utopia* (Bologna, 2013), 217–42, at pp. 228–9.

[3] I. Backus, 'Quels témoins de quelle vérité? Le *Catalogus testium veritatis* de Matthias Flacius Illyricus revu par Goulart', in O. Pot (ed.), *Simon Goulart: un pasteur aux intérêts vastes comme le monde* (Geneva, 2013), 125–39; M. P. Holt, 'Divisions within French Calvinism: Philippe Duplessis-Mornay and the Eucharist', in id. (ed.), *Adaptations of Calvinism in Reformation Europe* (Aldershot, 2007), 165–77; Polman, *L'élément historique*, 248–77.

The Invention of Papal History: Onofrio Panvinio between Renaissance and Catholic Reform. Stefan Bauer, Oxford University Press (2020). © Stefan Bauer.
DOI: 10.1093/oso/9780198807001.001.0001

controversialists such as Philippe Duplessis-Mornay (d. 1623) dominated the international debates on the Protestant side, setting themselves apart from Lutherans because of their enmity towards the Lutherans and frequently also because of their strong humanist education.

In the Catholic Church, the censorship of historical authors remained a widespread practice. After Panvinio, additional historians, from Francesco Guicciardini, Jacques-Auguste De Thou, and Edward Gibbon to Leopold von Ranke and Ferdinand Gregorovius, shared the fate of being included on the Index or being censored.[4] Similarities in censorship methods stemmed from a fundamental problem: The Roman Church's censorship of historical books was placed mostly in the hands of theologians who had a religious view of history combined with polemical and political aims, and who therefore intervened in historical works, even if this meant neglecting or contradicting the factual evidence of sources.[5]

Very few biographies appeared in print as individual publications directly after a pope's death. Towards the end of the century, in the 1580s and 1590s, papal biographers sought to forestall censorship by resorting to empirical methods. For example, the natural son of Pope Gregory XIII, Duke Giacomo Boncompagni (1548–1612), sent a questionnaire to important persons who had known the pope.[6] Addressees included Cardinal Tolomeo Gallio, who had been responsible for foreign policy under Gregory XIII; Cesare Speciano, who had been an official at the Apostolic Signatura; and Lodovico Taverna, who under Gregory had held the significant offices of nuncio and papal collector in Spain. Dozens of questions were intended to shed light on the most important details of Gregory's pontificate. These concerned the pope's character, political achievements, calendar reform, private devoutness, and, unsurprisingly, his demonstrations of goodwill towards Giacomo Boncompagni himself. The resulting biography was composed by the

---

[4] A. Esch, 'Aus den Akten der Indexkongregation: verurteilte Schriften von Ferdinand Gregorovius', in A. Esch and J. Petersen (eds), *Ferdinand Gregorovius und Italien* (Tübingen, 1993), 240–52; D. Burkard, U. Muhlack, and H. Wolf, *Rankes 'Päpste' auf dem Index: Dogma und Historie im Widerstreit* (Paderborn, 2003); Reusch, *Index*, i. 388–9; Godman and Brandt, *Weltliteratur auf dem Index*, 284–303.

[5] On the problem of church history as theology see H. Jedin, 'Kirchengeschichte als Heilsgeschichte?', in id., *Kirche des Glaubens, Kirche der Geschichte*, 2 vols (Freiburg im Breisgam, 1966), i. 37–48; R. Kottje (ed.), *Kirchengeschichte heute: Geschichtswissenschaft oder Theologie?* (Trier, 1970).

[6] For what follows see P. Blastenbrei, '*Clemenza* und *equità*: zur Justizpolitik Papst Gregors XIII. (1572–1585)', *QFIAB*, 80 (2000), 360–452, at pp. 360–5; S. Andretta, 'Le biografie papali e l'informazione politica tra Cinque e Seicento', in E. Fasano Guarini and M. Rosa (eds), *L'informazione politica in Italia (secoli XVI–XVIII)* (Pisa, 2001), 239–79.

Jesuit Giovanni Pietro Maffei in the 1590s but was printed, despite all the precautions, only in the eighteenth century.[7]

Papal biography was a minefield also because frequently a successor was not well-disposed towards the preceding pope, as he did not belong to the same family dynasty. It was often desirable that manuscripts of biographies circulated only among a select group of readers. Probably the most interesting case of a papal biography of the seventeenth century was that of Urban VIII Barberini (r. 1623–44), written by Andrea Nicoletti, a canon of San Lorenzo in Damaso. The nine manuscript volumes, which are kept in the Vatican Library, were apparently never destined for publication.[8] For their composition, Nicoletti used extensive archival sources, such as letters to and from the nuncios, which enabled him to take a broader view of the Holy See's European relations. Nicoletti's biography showed, on the one hand, the methodical progress of a more complete utilization of sources and, on the other hand, the intensification of panegyrical tendencies, which were characteristic of papal biography in the seventeenth century. This episode shows that the tone changed and that papal biography assumed a resolutely propagandistic role. The Church did not tolerate criticism from within, and it sought to triumph over attacks from outside. Popes and their historians had to serve the struggle against Protestantism and heterodoxy. Historiography began to fabricate propaganda in harmony with the official self-interpretation of the Church.[9]

The official Catholic answers to the *Magdeburg Centuries* are well known. After the individual and—ultimately—unsuccessful efforts by Catholic authors such as Panvinio, large-scale projects of synthesis were required to refute the *Centuries*. In the field of doctrine, one such project was Robert Bellarmine's *Disputations concerning the Controversies of the Christian Faith against the Heretics of this Age* (1586–93). This work grew out of his lectures on controversial theology at the Collegio Romano and was divided into thematic parts. The first dealt with Scripture, Christ, the pope, councils, clergy, saints, images, and relics; another part was devoted to the sacraments. Lastly, a section on the forgiveness of sins discussed issues such as grace, predestination, and justification. Bellarmine systematically upheld the role of tradition and the teaching authority (*magisterium*) of the Church. For his

[7] G. P. Maffei, *Annali di Gregorio XIII*, ed. C. Cocquelines, 2 vols (Rome, 1742).
[8] Andrea Nicoletti, *Vita di Papa Urbano VIII: storia del suo pontificato*, MSS BAV, Barb. lat. 4730–8. See also Andretta, 'Le biografie', 268–73.
[9] See also V. Reinhardt, 'Vergangenheit als Wahrheitsbeweis: Rom und die Geschichte im Konfessionellen Zeitalter', in L. Grenzmann et al. (eds), *Die Präsenz der Antike im Übergang vom Mittelalter zur Frühen Neuzeit* (Göttingen, 2004), 143–60.

arguments, he used a wide range of historical sources, and he accepted, alongside Scripture, the body of tradition constituted by the Church Fathers. Bellarmine thus provided a doctrinal handbook for polemicists, which became the manual par excellence of the late sixteenth century and the seventeenth century.

The *Ecclesiastical Annals* (1588–1607) of Cesare Baronio provided the official Catholic answer to the *Magdeburg Centuries* on the historical side. The members of Baronio's Oratory would have favoured the title *Historia ecclesiastica controversa* (Controversial Church History) for his work, but Baronio preferred to be less openly polemical.[10] In this comprehensive history of the Church, which went down to the year 1198, Baronio aimed to show that church institutions and doctrine from apostolic times had always been the same. He adopted a strictly chronological framework and attempted to establish precise dates for all events. This led him to correct Eusebius and many other writers on numerous details. The *Annales* were not a systematic treatise of theological doctrine; but since they postulated that the Church's doctrine had never changed, they offered an image of what the Church should be.[11] Baronio recognized the authority of the Roman Church and presented its doctrinal traditions—which, he argued, had already been fixed in the first centuries.[12] In particular, Baronio strove to demonstrate the origins of the primacy of the bishop of Rome. He also paid much attention to heresies as a means of demonstrating, through historical narration, how these were always defeated by the true Church. Baronio built on previous catalogues of heretics published by Catholics, such as those of Bernard of Luxembourg (1522) and Gabriel du Préau (1568), who had compared ancient heresies to the Protestant movement.[13] Because there was a 'symbiotic relationship between Catholic history and Catholic orthodoxy', it is difficult to establish Baronio's personal positions.[14] Nonetheless, one such position was his denial of the authenticity of the Donation of Constantine. Yet, for Baronio this did not mean that the legitimacy of the Church was damaged, as its privileges had been transferred

---

[10] Jedin, *Baronius*, 37.

[11] On the devotional and edifying character of Baronio's *Annales*—historiography as prayer—see S. Ditchfield, 'Baronio storico nel suo tempo', in Guazzelli et al., *Baronio*, 3–21.

[12] See Francesco Panigarola, *Il Compendio degli Annali ecclesiastici del padre Cesare Baronio* (Rome, 1590), 1: 'La Chiesa di Dio...è sempre stata la medesima' ('the Church of God has always been the same'). See also H. Zimmermann, *Ecclesia als Objekt der Historiographie: Studien zur Kirchengeschichtsschreibung im Mittelalter und in der Frühen Neuzeit* (Vienna, 1960), 72–5; Cochrane, *Historians*, 461.

[13] Backus, *Historical Method*, 382–90.

[14] Guazzelli, 'Baronio and the Roman Catholic Vision', 61.

to it directly from Christ; the Church did not require a secular ruler such as Constantine to confer power on it.[15]

Two competing historical works dealt with the Council of Trent. In 1619, the Servite friar Paolo Sarpi argued that the popes, keen to avoid reforms, had used this council selfishly to strengthen their own power. In 1656–7 the Jesuit Sforza Pallavicino published a new history of the council to refute Sarpi and defend the papacy. Pallavicino openly admitted that his history was 'mixed' with apologetics.[16] Ecclesiastical erudition in the seventeenth century was principally carried forward by the two large-scale projects of the Bollandists and Maurists.[17] Seeking to publish the sources for the lives of the saints, the Jesuits Jean Bolland (1596–1665), Godefroid Henskens (1601–81), and Daniel Papebroch (1628–1714) in Antwerp set out to find the oldest versions of each hagiographical text and publish them in their original form. Publication of the *Acta sanctorum* (Acts of the Saints) began in 1643 with two volumes for the saints who had their feast-days in January. Next to Baronio's *Annales*, the *Acta* were the second great pillar of Catholic *historia sacra* in the early modern period. By compiling the lives of saints, the editors demonstrated the presence of God in the Church through the centuries. Their daunting chore of sorting through countless texts to find the most authentic versions led to an ever-more-conscious employment of philological techniques. The Bollandists' work was also a stimulus for researchers in the Benedictine Order, the history of which reached back into the early Middle Ages. A member of the Benedictine Congregation of Saint-Maur, Jean Mabillon (1632–1707), elevated the auxiliary sciences of history to a new level. In his *De re diplomatica* (On Diplomatics, 1681), Mabillon established the principles for determining the authenticity of medieval manuscripts. The Maurists published a vast array of historical material, including histories of their own order, editions of Latin and Greek Church Fathers, studies on liturgy, as well as regional and civic histories.

[15] Baronio, *Annales*, xii (1607), ad AD 1191, p. 845. See also Fubini, *Storiografia dell'umanesimo*, 363–6; Zen, 'Baronio sulla Donazione'.

[16] S. Bauer, 'Writing the History of the Council of Trent', in M. Delbeke (ed.), *Sforza Pallavicino: A Jesuit Life in Baroque Rome* (Leiden, forthcoming).

[17] For what follows see Sawilla, *Antiquarianismus*; J.-L. Quantin, 'Document, histoire, critique dans l'érudition ecclésiastique des temps modernes', *Recherches de science religieuse*, 92 (2004), 597–635; S. Ditchfield, ' "Historia magistra sanctitatis?" The Relationship between Historiography and Hagiography in Italy after the Council of Trent (1564–1742 ca.)', in Firpo, *Nunc alia tempora*, 3–23; id, 'What Was Sacred History? (Mostly Roman) Catholic Uses of the Christian Past after Trent', in Van Liere et al., *Sacred History*, 72–97; M. Dorna, 'Von der Hagiographie zur Diplomatik: Daniel Papebrochs Lehre zur Erkennung von frühmittelalterlichen Urkundenfälschungen', *Archiv für Diplomatik*, 60 (2014), 165–89.

To sum up, both Catholics and Protestants had many reasons to appeal to and invoke history. In the beginning, Catholic attacks involving history concentrated on Martin Luther. After his death, several orthodoxies and systems emerged, so that a battle of individuals turned into a battle of systems. There was a continuation of Renaissance humanist working methods on both sides because, as Polman remarked, 'polemical passion stimulated research.'[18] Polemicists, however, naturally preferred the solutions which were closest to their own interests; and, depending on these interests, they accepted or rejected the results of the humanist scholarship.

Through the example of Panvinio, it has been a central concern of this study to analyse the origin and use of historiographical texts, not only in the context of the confessional struggle but also under the changing conditions of patronage. I have provided insights into the writing process, the use of sources, and the authorial intentions of a sixteenth-century historian; in short, I have sought to open the doors to his laboratory, at an important moment in time, and observe him at work. History-writing was an endeavour that was not yet tied to professional institutions such as universities but relied on financial resources made available by patrons. These patrons— together with censorship by the authorities—exerted a pervasive influence on the contents of historiography. Judged against the background of such obstacles, Panvinio's achievement becomes all the more noteworthy. In his research, he found numerous historical sources that shed an uncomfortable light on the Catholic Church, within which he himself operated; and his willingness to follow where the documents led caused some of his works to suppressed. Exploring the limits of what could be said and written, Panvinio at times overstepped the perilously fine line which he attempted to tread.

He nevertheless remains an outstanding example of the type of research that was possible in the late Renaissance and the Catholic Reformation. His works belonged to the open and imaginative phase of history-writing before Baronio. Yet, Panvinio lived in a transitional period full of contradictions. Historical method had started to become more and more sophisticated, but the confessional struggle made increasingly pressing demands on historians to write religious propaganda. In this book I have examined these complex issues by interweaving three stories: Panvinio and his personal fortunes; the invention of a critical, source-based papal history; and the confessionalization and dogmatization of church history.

---

[18] Polman, L'élément historique, 542: 'la passion polémique a stimulé les recherches'. See also S. Bauer (ed.), *The Uses of History in Religious Controversies from Erasmus to Baronio*, special issue of *Renaissance Studies* (forthcoming).

The Papal Election Decree of 1059

Book IV of Panvinio's *De varia creatione Romani pontificis* included, notably, the discussion of Pope Nicholas II's decree on papal elections of 1059. This decree was of crucial importance for two reasons: first, because it was the first time that a precise instruction concerning the order of a canonical election of the pope was published, and second, because the right of election was restricted to cardinals—a fundamental feature that has remained in existence until today. Two versions of this decree circulated: an authentic and a falsified version. Still today, historians argue about the meaning of those two versions.[1]

The authentic version (the so-called 'papal' version) mentioned the emperor's role in the election, but the scope of his participation remained unclear. The decree stated that the pope was to be elected primarily by the cardinal-bishops and that after them the other cardinals, as well as the clergy and people of Rome, were also to be consulted. It specified that the cardinal-bishops were to choose a pope but also that due respect was to be given to King Henry IV ('salvo debito honore et reverentia dilecti filii nostri Henrici').[2] Some scholars have argued that emperor's right was severely limited here to a mere confirmation ex-post of an election that had already taken place; the decree was revolutionary in that it deprived the emperor expressly of his rights of intervention. Others have maintained that, to the contrary, the formula *salvo debito honore* meant that the emperor was still assured a leading role in the electoral process.[3] The original draft, or even a contemporary copy of this version, has not been found; the decree was transmitted through French copies from the late eleventh century onwards.[4]

The meaning of the false ('imperial') version was easier to understand. The 'imperial' version openly gave a leading role to the emperor. Here it was clearly stated that the pope was to be chosen by the emperor together with the cardinals.

---

[1] A parallel edition of the two versions is published in D. Jasper, *Das Papstwahldekret von 1059: Überlieferung und Textgestalt* (Sigmaringen, 1986), 98–119. On the importance of this decree see also D. Hägermann, *Das Papsttum am Vorabend des Investiturstreits: Stephan IX. (1057–1058), Benedikt X. (1058) und Nikolaus II. (1058–1061)* (Stuttgart, 2008), 102–27.

[2] Jasper, *Papstwahldekret*, 104–5. The full wording is: 'Eligant...salvo debito honore et reverentia dilecti filii nostri Henrici, qui inpraesentiarum rex habetur et futurus imperator Deo concedente speratur, sicut iam sibi concessimus, et successorum illius, qui ab hac apostolica sede personaliter hoc ius impetraverint'.

[3] These scholarly positions are summarized ibid. 5–6.

[4] On the manuscript traditions see Jasper, *Papstwahldekret*; H.-G. Krause, 'Die Bedeutung der neuentdeckten handschriftlichen Überlieferungen des Papstwahldekrets von 1059', *Zeitschrift der Savigny-Stiftung für Rechtsgeschichte*, 107, *Kanonistische Abteilung*, 76 (1990), 89–134.

Scholars have not agreed on the precise date of the falsification; it has usually been assigned to the period between 1076 (when the German bishops at Worms withdrew their obedience from Gregory VII) and the 1080s. While it certainly represented the general lines of Henry IV's ideas about his rights in papal elections, it differed in some respects from these ideas and was, therefore, probably not created by a member of his inner entourage.[5] This version was transmitted through copies in Germany and Italy, of which the version deriving from the imperial Abbey of Farfa in Latium—used by Panvinio—was possibly the earliest example.[6]

Panvinio attached the two versions of the decree to his discussion, so that his readers could see the evidence for themselves.[7] He believed that the 'papal' version was too revolutionary to be a historically authentic document. For him, only the 'imperial' version could have been authentic because it aligned with historical practice at the time. Panvinio began his argument by offering assurance that his own copy of the 'imperial' version had been drawn from a contemporary medieval source. He stated:

I have extracted the true and non-corrupt copy of this decree from a very old book in parchment with nearly majuscule and Lombardic letters written about five hundred years ago—that is, during that time [of Nicholas II]. This book deals with all those things which pertain to the Abbey and Monastery of Farfa, such as the numbers of abbots of that monastery, all the privileges both imperial and papal, the abbey's movable goods, and numerous similar matters.[8]

Panvinio's argument for the authenticity of this 'imperial' version was twofold. His first point was that he had found a contemporary source—although it must be said that his evidence was not very precise. The best he could do was assume that the manuscript had been written about the same time as Nicholas's decree of 1059. This manuscript was, in fact, most likely a slightly later compilation by Gregory of Catino (that is, the *Chronicon Farfense*, the *Regestum*, or the *Liber largitorius*). Gregory of Catino was not born until 1060, and only from the 1090s did he start organizing the

---

[5] Jasper, *Papstwahldekret*, 69–88; W. Stürner, 'Das Papstwahldekret von 1059 und seine Verfälschung: Gedanken zu einem neuen Buch', in *Fälschungen im Mittelalter*, 6 vols (Hannover, 1988–90), ii. 157–90, at pp. 182–90.

[6] H.-G. Krause, *Das Papstwahldekret von 1059 und seine Rolle im Investiturstreit* (Rome, 1960), 220, 240.

[7] Panvinio, DVC-X, Book IV, Clm 148, fos 100ᵛ–103ʳ, 103ᵛ–104ᵛ. In a previous work, *De cardinalium origine*, Panvinio had seemed to believe that the 'papal' version was authentic. See Grauert, 'Dekret', 591–2; Stroll, *Farfa*, 154–7; and above, 97.

[8] DVC-X, Book IV, Clm 148, fo. 99ᵛ, cited by Grauert, 'Dekret', 592–3: 'cuius decreti exemplum verum et non corruptum exc[er]psi ex vetustissimo libro in membranis litteris pene maiusculis et Longobardis, ante quingentos fere annos, hoc videlicet tempore scripto, in quo tractantur omnia quae ad abbatiam et monasterium Farfense pertinent, ut abbatum illius monasterii numerus, privilegia omnia tam pontificalia quam imperialia, bonaque mobilia et eiusmodi complura.' See also Panvinio, 'Auctores quibus tum in hoc Chronico sive Fasteis, tum in Historia ecclesiastica conscribenda usi sumus' (1568), sig. *4ʳ: 'Libri quattuor grandes registrorum scripti in membranis monasterii Farfensis, quibus multa scitu digna continentur ab anno 700 usque ad 1100'.

APPENDIX: THE PAPAL ELECTION DECREE OF 1059   215

documents relating to the abbey's privileges.[9] The most likely source for Panvinio was the *Chronicon Farfense*.[10] Panvinio's second point was that this version was authentic because it was consistent with the historical facts of the time; it gave Henry (who was then king) the authority to elect the pope—or, rather, it confirmed what had been conceded to his father. It then added a few safety clauses to prevent future schisms.[11]

Consequently, Panvinio believed that the other version (which scholars have referred to as the 'papal' version), transmitted by Gratian, was corrupt for the opposite reason: It did not give Henry IV the authority to elect the pope but, instead, took it away from him and gave it to the cardinals. Panvinio was certain that Gregory VII or Victor III had brought this version into circulation. His reason for this attribution was that Gregory VII, in his synodal constitutions, had taken from the emperor the power to elect a pope.[12] If Gregory or Victor had not fabricated this version, it had been made up by another person who was 'ignorant of history' ('historiae imperitus').[13] Panvinio hit out more broadly at Gratian here, stating that he had included, apart from this decree, many other false documents. It is worth bearing in mind that, by Panvinio's time, Gratian's *Decretum* had already been printed on many occasions.[14] Although Panvinio came to a wrong conclusion here, his point that the 'true' version of the decree must have been consistent with historical practice at the time was perceptive. Medieval normative texts were usually not keen on setting new norms; they were intended to reflect and put into writing what was already standard practice.[15]

Panvinio aimed to consolidate his argument by adducing a historiographical text: the Chronicle of Montecassino by Leo Marsicanus (d. 1115/17) with the continuation most likely written by Guido of Montecassino.[16] The passage paraphrased from the

---

[9] The *Correctores Romani* seem to have used the same manuscript as Panvinio in preparing their edition of Gratian's *Decretum*, on which they worked from 1566 to 1582. See P. Scheffer-Boichorst, *Die Neuordnung der Papstwahl durch Nikolaus II.* (Strasbourg, 1879), 19 n. 7; Gratian, *Decretum*, D. 23 c. 1 (ed. Friedberg, col. 77), under 'Notationes correctorum': 'Huius decreti integrum exemplum est in vetustissimo libro abbatiae monasterii Farfensis literis Longobardicis ante annos pene quingentos scripto'. On the *Correctores* see also M. E. Sommar, *The Correctores Romani: Gratian's* Decretum *and the Counter-Reformation Humanists* (Berlin, 2009).

[10] Krause, *Papstwahldekret*, 240. Scheffer-Boichorst (*Neuordnung*, 20) maintained that a copy of the decree was included in the registers (dating to *c*.1092–9), but this copy has not been found.

[11] DVC-X, Book IV, Clm 148, fo. 99ᵛ; Grauert, 'Dekret', 593.

[12] See above, 110–117.

[13] DVC-X, Book IV, Clm 148, fo. 99ᵛ; Stroll, *Farfa*, 160 nn. 23–4.

[14] DVC-X, Book IV, Clm 148, fo. 100ᵛ: 'Haec autem ut facilius intelligantur utriusque decreti exemplum subiiciam, et primum germani et veri, deinde adulterini et corrupti atque in *Decretis* perverse, ut pleraque alia, a Gratiano registrati'. See also Jasper, *Papstwahldekret*, 15, 92: 'wiederholt den Druck aus Grat. D. 23 c. 1'. The 'imperial' version, on the other hand, was not available in print until Muratori's edition of the *Chronicon Farfense* in 1726 (although Muratori rendered the text to some degree useless by integrating emendations from Gratian); see ibid. 14 nn. 52, 96.

[15] R. Schieffer, 'Rechtstexte des Reformpapsttums und ihre zeitgenössische Resonanz', in H. Mordek (ed.), *Überlieferung und Geltung normativer Texte des frühen und hohen Mittelalters* (Sigmaringen, 1986), 51–69, at p. 68.

[16] Panvinio indicated the Montecassino Chronicle as one of his sources: DVC-X, Book IV, Clm 148, fo. 95ʳ. He owned a copy of the first printed edition, *Chronica sacri Casinensis coenobii* (Venice, 1513); see ILS, fo. 23ᵛ.

Chronicle concerned a disputation allegedly held in 1082 at Albano. The debate was said to have taken place in the presence of Henry IV and was between Desiderius, abbot of Montecassino and legate of Gregory VII (who later became Pope Victor III, r. 1086–7), and Cardinal Odo of Ostia (who later became Pope Urban II, r. 1088–99).[17] According to Panvinio, Cardinal Odo made the point that Nicholas II, in the election decree, had confirmed that the pope should not be elected without the emperor's authority; if he was, he would not be recognized. Hildebrand (who became Gregory VII) himself had signed the decree. Abbot Desiderius 'never denied this, but he replied that neither Nicholas II nor any other pope was allowed to damage the Church's liberty'. Panvinio's argument here was that Desiderius, although he found himself in disagreement with Nicholas's decree, did not deny its content and, thus, accepted the validity of Odo's description of it.[18]

Guido's continuation of the Montecassino Chronicle, which contained the disputation, was probably written in the 1120s. It was the last of the contemporary sources to provide an overall discussion of the struggles related to the decree. By now, the Investiture Controversy had ended through the Concordat of Worms (1122), and papal elections had been removed from the emperor's influence. The disputation in Albano was most likely not a historical event. Therefore, Panvinio's source was doubtful.[19] Still, his argument was ingenious: If contemporaries referred to the content of the decree as to a document favouring the emperor's rights, and if they did not question its authenticity, then this must have been the 'true' version. Panvinio may have been misled in particular by the remark in the Chronicle that Odo had explicitly 'exhibited' ('proferret') a copy of the decree to Desiderius to prove his point that the pope could not be elected without the emperor's consent.[20] Scholars now think that Guido invented this dialogue to illustrate the debates occurring in the schism between Gregory VII and Clement III and, in general, to create a colourful impression of the discussions about *regnum* and *sacerdotum*.[21]

Slightly later in his text, in the appendix to Book IV, Panvinio again included what he considered to be the 'true' ('imperial') version. This appendix consisted of the *Liber Fratris Beraldi*. The *Liber* was a text composed, according to the modern scholarly consensus, by Gregory of Catino around 1105 and inserted into his *Chronicon Farfensis* sometime before his death in 1119.[22] The separate version of the *Liber* has

---

[17] DVC-X, Book IV, Clm 148, fo. 100[r]; Grauert, 'Dekret', 593–4. See also *Chronica sacri Casinensis coenobii*, III.49, fo. 111[v]. This printed version owned by Panvinio contains the text edited by Ambrogio Traversari and differs substantially from the critical edition, *Chronica monasterii Casinensis*, ed. H. Hoffmann (Hannover, 1980), III.50, p. 433.

[18] DVC-X, Book IV, Clm 148, fo. 100[r–v]; Grauert, 'Dekret', 594.

[19] Two reasons have been given by modern scholars for this conclusion. The first is that Desiderius himself had signed the election decree, a fact of which Guido was evidently not aware and which proves that he had never seen it; Desiderius would not have disputed in this way a document that he himself had signed. The second reason is that Odo defended the emperor here when, in fact, he was known to be a zealous supporter of Gregory VII.

[20] See Panvinio's printed copy, *Chronica sacri Casinensis coenobii*, fo. 111[v]. The critical edition, *Chronica monasterii Casinensis*, 433, has 'ostendisset'.

[21] Krause, *Papstwahldekret*, 223–7. See also Scheffer-Boichorst, *Neuordnung*, 92–3.

[22] Gregory of Catino, *Chronicon Farfense*, ed. U. Balzani, 2 vols (Rome, 1903), ii. 233–55. For what follows see Heinzelmann, *Farfenser Streitschriften*; Stroll, *Farfa*, 7–12, 105–32, 163–5.

been transmitted only by Panvinio, who claimed that he had taken it from a 'very old book of the monastery of Farfa written four hundred years ago, in which the deeds of all the abbots of this monastery are recorded chronologically'.[23] Panvinio gave the following title for the treatise: *Fratris Bernardi monachi et abbatis monasterii Farfensis liber* (The Book of Brother Bernardus, Monk and Abbot of Farfa). In the text itself, Panvinio used the spelling 'Berardus'. Although it is now thought that the text referred to Beraldus III (abbot from 1099 to 1119), Panvinio may have believed that it referred to Berardus I (d. 1089).[24]

Panvinio wrote a short introduction to this text, from which it became clear that his objective was to provide examples of the two positions—favouring Empire and papacy, respectively—in the schism begun by Gregory VII and ended by Calixtus II. In particular, Panvinio wanted to mention one supporter of each side.[25] One was Deusdedit, a cardinal-presbyter who, according to Panvinio, under Victor III published a book to defend Gregory VII. The other was Berardus, abbot of Farfa, who, as Panvinio believed, was the author of the *Liber Beraldi*; he wrote 'shortly before Deusdedit' against Gregory VII and in favour of Clement III and Emperor Henry.

However, the text by Deusdedit, which Panvinio promised to append, is missing from Panvinio's manuscript, where some pages were left empty. One may assume that what Panvinio intended to include were sections of Deusdedit's *Collectio canonum* (Collection of Canons), where, in the dedicatory epistle to Victor III, Deusdedit sharply criticized Nicholas II's election decree, which he thought had no legal validity. Deusdedit claimed that Nicholas had had no authority to publish a new decree because the principles of elections had been established by the highest authority of ecumenical councils and could not be modified by a pope. For Deusdedit, it was not the king and not primarily the cardinal-bishops but the entire clergy, together with people of Rome, who traditionally held the right to elect the pope.[26] Another possibility was that Panvinio aimed to include Deusdedit's *Libellus contra invasores et symoniacos*, which proposed similar theses; however, this text was not composed under Victor III but rather about ten years after this pope's death. Deusdedit was one of the chief defenders of Gregorian reforms and of the Church's liberty from temporal powers, so he was a useful author for Panvinio to include here.[27]

---

[23] DVC-X, Book IV, Clm 148, fo. 185ʳ: 'Hunc vero tractatum excepi ex antiquissimo et ante CCCC annos scripto libro monasterii Farfensis, in quo omnium eius monasterii abbatum res gestae per singulas aetates referuntur.' This seems to imply that the MS from which Panvinio copied the *Liber* was a hundred years younger than the one from which he took the first copy of the decree; see above, 214–215.

[24] *Fratris Berardi monachi et abbatis monasterii Farfensis liber*, ed. Heinzelmann, 40–1. It can be hypothesized that Panvinio falsified the original text by changing 'Beraldus' to 'Berardus'. If this is true, Panvinio may have done this for a specific purpose: He may have wanted to date the text back from the early twelfth century to the 1080s. See also Heinzelmann, *Farfenser Streitschriften*, 10–25.

[25] DVC-X, Book IV, Clm 148, fos 184ᵛ–185ʳ. See Heinzelmann, *Farfenser Streitschriften*, 8–9 n. 1.

[26] In the inventory of his personal library (ILS, fo. 8ᵛ), Panvinio referred to this text by Deusdedit as 'de ratione eligendi papam et alios episcopos'.

[27] On Deusdedit's writings see U.-R. Blumenthal, 'Rom in der Kanonistik', in B. Schimmelpfennig and L. Schmugge (eds), *Rom im hohen Mittelalter* (Sigmaringen, 1992),

Beraldus's position becomes clear from a legal dispute between the abbey and the Ottaviani family regarding possessions in the Sabina territory.[28] In the course of this dispute, momentous issues of political theory were adduced. The Ottaviani, evoking the Donation of Constantine, claimed that the Church had possessed the land in question on account of the Donation; the Church had then rightfully given it to the Ottaviani. What was more, they took the implied meaning of the Donation to the extreme, arguing that all of Italy was papal property and no other property could exist there except that of the Curia. This has been referred to as 'perhaps the most outrageous conclusion ever drawn from the Donation of Constantine'.[29] Beraldus and the other Benedictine monks from Farfa interpreted the Donation differently. They accepted only the religious dominion of the popes. They pointed out that the emperors had never given up their own secular dominion over Italy. Over the course of the centuries, the popes had received donations from the emperors; such acts would have been pointless if the entire territory had already been theirs. The abbey of Farfa rightfully held their possessions, which had been received through privileges from the emperors. Also, these privileges, according to the monks, had perpetual validity (a point that Farfa's opponents doubted).[30]

In connection to this argument, the *Liber* also contained a discussion of the imperial rights contained in the papal election decree. The author of the *Liber*, Gregory of Catino, looked back into history and included a considerable number of historical references to demonstrate that the emperor, up to the time of Gregory VII, had possessed the privilege of confirming a newly elected candidate as pope. References went back to the Byzantine and Frankish periods and led up to the decree of 1059.[31] In the election decree, too, Nicholas had merely confirmed what had been ancient practice. In his text, Gregory of Catino probably made reference to polemical writings on the imperial privilege in papal elections from the 1080s and 1090s. Gregory also reproduced the election decree. This was a copy of the 'imperial' version, so that Panvinio, by including Gregory's *Liber*, provided this version of the decree for a second time here.[32]

---

[28] For what follows see I. Schuster, *L'imperiale abbazia di Farfa* (Rome, 1921), 249–50; Heinzelmann, *Farfenser Streitschriften*, 89–100. See also Peña's censorship, above, 196–197.

[29] G. Laehr, *Die Konstantinische Schenkung in der abendländischen Literatur des Mittelalters bis zur Mitte des 14. Jahrhunderts* (Berlin, 1926), 42: 'vielleicht die ungeheuerlichste Folgerung, die jemals aus der Konstantinischen Schenkung gezogen ist'. For what follows see ibid. 41–3.

[30] T. Kölzer, 'Prolegomena', in id. (ed.), *Collectio canonum Regesto Farfensi inserta* (Vatican City, 1982), 1–123, at pp. 108–11.

[31] Krause, *Papstwahldekret*, 219–23.

[32] In Heinzelmann's edition (*Fratris Berardi monachi et abbatis monasterii Farfensis liber*, 55), the election decree was left out; in Clm 148, however, it is found on fos 191ᵛ–193ʳ. See also Jasper, *Papstwahldekret*, 14–15. Minor differences existed between the copy in Book IV and the copy from the *Liber Beraldi* in the appendix to Book IV. While Stroll argued that Panvinio had copied from two different source manuscripts, Krause and Jasper showed that the variants were not important enough to warrant this hypothesis. See Stroll, *Farfa*, 163–5; Jasper, Review of Stroll, *Farfa*; Krause, 'Bedeutung', 98 n. 36.

Panvinio's conclusion about the genuineness of the 'imperial' version was not only wrong, it also contrasted with beliefs at the time. As the 'papal' version was included in Gratian's *Decretum* and was generally considered authentic, Panvinio's scholarly sensibility about the question of authenticity remained unheard in the centuries that followed. However, his judgement received confirmation from an eminent historian in the nineteenth century, at a time when German scholars began conducting research on the election decree and recognized with certainty that there were two version of it. In 1837 Georg Heinrich Pertz, who produced the first critical edition of the decree in the *Monumenta Germaniae Historica* (of which he was a director), chose for publication only the 'imperial' version, which he considered authentic. Because Pertz's authority carried much weight in scholarship, the question was wide open again.[33] Only since Paul Scheffer-Boichorst's detailed study of 1879 has the general scholarly consensus been that the 'papal' version alone was authentic.[34] Nonetheless, several scholars continued to argue, at least until 1939, that both versions were false.[35] Recently, Mary Stroll defended Panvinio's argument that the Farfa 'imperial' version was the oldest existing version and, therefore, the 'authentic' draft of the decree; but her reasoning did not stand up against scholarly examination.[36]

In the late nineteenth century, Panvinio received high praise. His treatment of the election decree led the German canonist Johannes Baptist Sägmüller to refer to him, in 1896, as 'a model of erudition' and to describe his *De varia creatione* as a work which was 'composed with a brand of historical knowledge that still commands respect today'.[37] Sägmüller and other nineteenth-century historians arrived at such judgements because they recognized that Panvinio not only collected sources, but also subjected them to careful scrutiny. A significant example of this was the way in which he dealt with the 1059 decree. Panvinio was the first scholar to identify the differences between the two versions of the decree and to discuss them in a scholarly fashion. In 1880 the German historian Hermann Grauert, after citing the discussion by Panvinio analysed above, maintained that these passages 'probably contain the first attempt made since the birth of a modern historical science, which genuinely engages in research, to reach an informed opinion about the different versions of the papal election decree of 1059, based on their critical examination'.[38]

---

[33] *Monumenta Germaniae Historica*, Leges, ii.2, 176–80. See also Grauert, 'Dekret', 590–1. In 1869 Paul Hinschius discussed this situation of scholarship; see his *Kirchenrecht*, i. 251.

[34] Scheffer-Boichorst, *Neuordnung*.

[35] Among these were Wilhelm von Giesebrecht (1866), Julius von Pflugk-Harttung (1906), and Anton Michel (1939); see Jasper, *Papstwahldekret*, 3 n. 9.

[36] Stroll, *Farfa*, 154–69; ead., *Popes and Antipopes: The Politics of Eleventh Century Church Reform* (Leiden, 2012), 96–103. See also the reviews of her *Farfa* book by G. A. Loud, *English Historical Review*, 114 (1999), 940–1; K. Pennington, *American Historical Review*, 105 (2000), 262–3; and D. Jasper, *Deutsches Archiv für Erforschung des Mittelalters*, 56 (2000), 366–7.

[37] Sägmüller, 'Ein angebliches Dekret', 423–4: 'dieses für jene Zeit hochgelehrte, mit heute noch Achtung gebietenden historischen Kenntnissen abgefasste Werk'; ibid.: 'Onuphrius Panvinius, ein Muster von Gelehrsamkeit'.

[38] Grauert, 'Dekret', 594: 'Die mitgetheilte Stelle dürfte den ersten Versuch enthalten, der seit dem Erwachen einer modernen, wirklich forschenden Geschichtswissenschaft gemacht worden ist, um auf Grund einer kritischen Prüfung zu einem sicheren Urtheil über die verschiedenen Fassungen des Papstwahldekretes von 1059 zu gelangen.'

Panvinio's preference for the 'imperial' version of the decree led Grauert to regard him as loyal to the Empire. We have seen that the same assumption about Panvinio's political leanings played a key role in the censorship of *De varia creatione* in 1592.[39] We have also seen, however, that, rather than an imperialist, Panvinio was papalist who was prepared to criticize greed and ambition in the Church. He evaluated medieval documents based on what he perceived as historical practice at the time they were produced.

---

[39] Ibid. 594–5 n. 1: 'entschiedener Imperialist'. See also above, 194–200.

Bibliography

Primary Sources

(i) Manuscripts and archival sources

Bologna, Biblioteca arcivescovile
4915 (Panvinio, DVC-III).

Bologna, Biblioteca universitaria
1117, vol. vi (*Modus eligendi pontifices*).
1173 (Panvinio, DVC-III).

Copenhagen, Det Kongelige Bibliotek
GKS 539 2° (Panvinio, DVC-III).

Fano, Biblioteca comunale Federiciana
Amiani 80 (Chacón's plan for a history of popes and cardinals).

Florence, Biblioteca nazionale
II III 391 (Panvinio, DVC-X-Epitome).
II V 38 (Panvinio, DVC-III).

Madrid, Biblioteca del Monasterio de El Escorial
f-I-16 (Panvinio, *Ecclesiastica historia pontificum Romanorum*).

Milan, Biblioteca Ambrosiana (BAM)
A 68 inf. (Panvinio, DVC-X-Epitome).
B 238 suss. (Rancati's epitome of DVC-III).
D 357 inf. (*Modus eligendi pontifices*).
D 422–3 inf. (Orsini's letters to Pinelli).
D 501 inf. (collection of letters sent to Panvinio by Pantagato, Agustín, Sigonio, et al.).
F 39 inf. and F 78 inf. (Panvinio's letters to Borromeo).
F 40 inf. (Galesini's letter to Borromeo).
G 31 inf. (Panvinio, *Vita* and *Registrum* of Gregory VII).
G 41 inf. (Panvinio, *De cardinalium origine*).
H 142 inf. (Panvinio, *Vetusti aliquot rituales libri*).
I 129 inf. and P 189 sup. (Panvinio's library catalogue).
P 244 sup., fasc. 6 (on Panvinio's last publication projects).
Q 115 sup. (Paolo Panvinio, *Vita* of Onofrio Panvinio and preface to *De primatu Petri*).

Munich, Bayerische Staatsbibliothek
Clm 132–45 (Panvinio, *Vetusti aliquot rituales libri*; *Diaria caeremoniarum magistrorum*).
Clm 147–52 (Panvinio, DVC-X).
Clm 153 (Panvinio, *De comitiis imperatoris libri V*).
Clm 154 (Panvinio, DVC-X-Epitome).
Clm 155–60 (Panvinio, *Pontificum Romanorum imagines*).

London, British Library
Add. MS 12107 (Manuzio's letter to Panvinio).
Add. MS 28463 (memorandum by Peña).
Add. MS 48073 (*Modus eligendi pontifices*).

Naples, Archivio di Stato
Archivio Farnesiano, busta 283.I, fasc. 1 (report from Rome, 1568).

Naples, Biblioteca nazionale
I D 2 (Panvinio, *Vetusti aliquot rituales libri* and DVC-X-Epitome).
XIII AA 53 (Panvinio's letter to Seripando).
XIII AA 60 (Seripando's letter to Torres).

Padua, Biblioteca universitaria
263 (Panvinio, *De gente nobili Matthaeia liber*).

Paris, Bibliothèque Sainte-Geneviève
149 (Panvinio, DVC-X-Epitome).

Paris, Bibliothèque nationale de France (BNF)
Lat. 939 (Panvinio, *Vetusti aliquot rituales libri* and DVC-X-Epitome).
Lat. 4244B (Panvinio, DVC-X-Epitome).

Perugia, Biblioteca comunale Augusta
2895 (continuation of Martin of Troppau's Chronicle).

Rome, Archivio di Stato
Agostiniani in Sant'Agostino, buste 99 and 303 (payment to Sibilla).
Archivio Sforza Cesarini, Iª parte, 33 (AA XXI, 1) (Panvinio, *Gentis Sabellae monumenta*).

Rome, Biblioteca Angelica
Ang. lat. 64 (Panvinio, *Antiquitates Veronenses*).
Ang. lat. 83 (Panvinio, DVC-III).
Ang. lat. 293 (Panvinio, DVC-III).
Ang. lat. 1112 (Panvinio, DVC-X-Epitome).
Ang. lat. 1251 (Panvinio, *De primatu Petri*).
Ang. lat. 2581 (Panvinio, *De gente Maxima libri duo*).

Rome, Biblioteca Casanatense
401 (*Epitome librorum V de varia creatione Romani pontificis*).
829 (annotated copy of Panvinio, *Romani pontifices et cardinales*).
1347 (Panvinio, *De gente Sabella liber*).

Rome, Biblioteca dell'Accademia dei Lincei e Corsiniana
Corsin. 671 (inventories of Panvinio's manuscripts and Gregory XIII's books).

Rome, Biblioteca nazionale
Sess. 236 (Panvinio, DVC-III).
Sess. 268 (Rancati's epitome of DVC-III).

Rome, Biblioteca Vallicelliana
Allacci 96 (Holste's letter to Barberini).
G 87 (Panvinio, *Vetusti aliquot rituales libri*).

Rome, Deutsches Historisches Institut
Minucciani, 16 (*Epitome librorum V de varia creatione Romani pontificis*).
Minucciani, 17 (Panvinio, DVC-X-Epitome).

Vatican City, Archivio della Congregazione per la dottrina della fede (ACDF)
Index, Diari, 1, and Prot., B (Chacón on Panvinio's *De praecipuis urbis Romae basilicis*; Bellarmine on Panvinio).
Index, Prot., C (censorship of Panvinio's *Romani pontifices et cardinales*; Latini on Panvinio's *De primatu Petri*).
Index, Prot., F (censorship of Panvinio's *Romani pontifices et cardinales*).
Sanctum Officium, Decreta 1565–7, and Stanza storica, Q-1-a ('Extensorum S.O.') (on the commission charged with refuting the *Magdeburg Centuries*).

Vatican City, Archivio dell'Ufficio delle celebrazioni liturgiche del Sommo Pontefice
Vol. 137 (Panvinio, *Vetusti aliquot rituales libri*).

Vatican City, Archivio Segreto Vaticano (ASV)
A.A., Arm. I–XVIII, 6464 (list of scholars who could revise Panvinio's *Historia ecclesiastica*).
Arch. Concist., Acta Misc., 54 and 70 (Panvinio's collection of material on consistories and conclaves).
Arm. XLIV, 11 (Pius IV's letter of recommendation for Panvinio).
Arm. LII, 1 (Pius IV on the tasks of a *corrector* and *revisor*).
Arm. LII, 3 (Pius IV employs Panvinio in the Vatican Library).
Arm. LII, 19 (Santoro's diary).
Fondo Borghese, ser. ii, 461 (Farnese's journey to Sicily).

Vatican City, Biblioteca Apostolica Vaticana (BAV)
Barb. lat. 724 (Panvinio, *Vetusti aliquot rituales libri*).
Barb. lat. 2481 (Panvinio, *De gente Fregepania libri IV*).
Barb. lat. 2487 (Panvinio, DVC-X-Epitome).
Barb. lat. 2524 (Panvinio, lives of popes and cardinals).
Barb. lat. 2604 (Panvinio, DVC-X-Epitome).
Barb. lat. 2738–9 (Panvinio et al., collection of material on popes and cardinals).
Barb. lat. 2754 (Panvinio, *Epitome pontificum Romanorum*).
Barb. lat. 3115 (inventory of Peña's books).
Barb. lat. 4730–8 (Nicoletti, *Vita di Urbano VIII*).
Barb. lat. 5728 (Antoniano's plan for a continuation of Panvinio's *Romani pontifices et cardinales*).
Barb. lat. 6490 (Holste's letters to Barberini).
Barb. lat. 6492 (Barberini's letters to Holste).
Boncompagni-Ludovisi, C.8 (Panvinio, DVC-III).
Chig. H II 24 (Panvinio, *De vicecancellario*).
Chig. S V 15 (Visconti's letter; notes about Panvinio's works).
Ottob. lat. 764 (Panvinio, *Vita* and *Registrum* of Gregory VII).
Ottob. lat. 2344 (Panvinio, *De primatu Petri*).
Ottob. lat. 2961 (Panvinio, *De cardinalium origine*).
Urb. lat. 1055 (*Avvisi di Roma*).

Vat. lat. 3393 (Panvinio, *De ludis*).

Vat. lat. 3439 (material concerning Roman antiquity collected by Panvinio et al.; so-called *Codex Ursinianus*).

Vat. lat. 3451.i–ii (Panvinio, *Fasti* and ILS).

Vat. lat. 3554 (Panvinio, DVC-X-Epitome).

Vat. lat. 3755 (Massarelli's collection of papal coats of arms).

Vat. lat. 4103 (Matal's letter to Orsini).

Vat. lat. 4973 (Panvinio, *Vetusti aliquot rituales libri*).

Vat. lat. 6102–6 (Panvinio, material for *Historia ecclesiastica*).

Vat. lat. 6105 (notes by the commission charged with revising Panvinio's works; Antoniano's letter to Savelli; Bellarmine's censorship of Panvinio's *Historia ecclesiastica*).

Vat. lat. 6107.i–iii (Panvinio, material for DVC-X and DVC-X-Epitome).

Vat. lat. 6111 (Panvinio, DVC-X-Epitome; *De cardinalium origine*).

Vat. lat. 6112 (Panvinio, *Vetusti aliquot rituales libri*).

Vat. lat. 6113–14 (Panvinio, material for *Historia ecclesiastica*).

Vat. lat. 6115 (Panvinio, *De rebus antiquis basilicae Sancti Petri*).

Vat. lat. 6160 (Panvinio on the chronology of St Peter and St Paul).

Vat. lat. 6168 (Panvinio, *De gente Maxima libri duo*).

Vat. lat. 6185 (Gambardelli's letter to Sirleto).

Vat. lat. 6189.iii (Panvinio's letter to Sirleto).

Vat. lat. 6206 (Panvinio's title page for the *Collectio Avellana*).

Vat. lat. 6277 (Panvinio's letters to Fugger).

Vat. lat. 6412 (collection of letters, mostly sent to, or concerning, Panvinio).

Vat. lat. 6773–4 (Panvinio, *De primatu Petri*).

Vat. lat. 6775, 6777–8 (Panvinio, material for DVC-X).

Vat. lat. 6779 (Panvinio, material for DVC-III).

Vat. lat. 6780–1 (Panvinio, material on Roman churches).

Vat. lat. 6782 (Panvinio, *De primatu Petri*, preceded by a censorship).

Vat. lat. 6883 (Panvinio, *De primatu Petri* and *De sacrorum cleri ordinum origine*).

Vat. lat. 6982 (Peña, *De poenis haereticorum*).

Vat. lat. 7030 (documents of the commission charged with revising Panvinio's works).

Vat. lat. 7205 (inventory of Panvinio's books and belongings).

Vat. lat. 7298 (minutes of a commission meeting, 1592).

Vat. lat. 7762 (list of Panvinio's works; inventories of his manuscripts).

Vat. lat. 12092 (formerly ASV, Misc., Arm. XI, 5) (Panvinio, *De primatu Petri*).

Vat. lat. 12113–24 (Misc., Arm. XI, 30–34, 36–42) (Panvinio, material for *Historia ecclesiastica/Vitae Romanorum pontificum et cardinalium*).

Vat. lat. 12120 (*Modus eligendi pontifices*, here entitled *Modus servatus in electione pontificum*).

Vat. lat. 12121 (Panvinio, material for DVC-X).

Vat. lat. 12123 (Jean de Puydenoix's report on the election of Martin V).

Vat. lat. 12125–7 (Misc., Arm. XI, 43–5) (Massarelli's collection of material on popes and cardinals).

Vat. lat. 12125 (Panvinio, *De cardinalium origine*; Massarelli, *Modi seu formae observatae diversis temporibus in electione pontificum*).

Vat. lat. 12181 (Misc., Arm. XI, 122) (Panvinio, material for DVC-X).

Vat. lat. 12535–6 (Misc., Arm. XV, 128–128bis) (Panvinio, collection of material on popes).

Venice, Biblioteca Marciana

Marc. lat. IX 83 (3724) (annotated copy of Panvinio, *Romani pontifices and cardinales*).

Verona, Biblioteca civica

2852 (Campagnola's collection of material on Panvinio).

(ii) Printed works by Panvinio[*]

(Panvinio et al.), *Commentarium rerum Ordinis Fratrum Eremitarum Sancti Augustini*, in *Constitutiones Ordinis Fratrum Eremitarum Sancti Augustini nuper recognitae* (Rome: Antonio Blado, 1551), separate page numbering, fos 25^r–58^r.

Omnium Francorum ducum et regum quorum apud veteres auctores memoria est epilogus a Priamo duce usque ad Regem Heinricum II Valesium (Rome: Antonio Blado, 1553).

Epitome pontificum Romanorum a Sancto Petro usque ad Paulum IV, gestorum videlicet electionisque singulorum et conclavium compendiaria narratio; cardinalium item nomina, dignitatum tituli, insignia legationes, patria et obitus (Venice: Jacopo Strada, 1557).

Romani pontifices et cardinales Sanctae Romanae Ecclesiae ab eisdem a Leone IX ad Paulum Papam IV per quingentos posteriores a Christi natali annos creati (Venice: Michele Tramezzino, 1557). Also contains *De episcopatibus, titulis et diaconiis cardinalium*, Appendix, 51–75.

Fasti et triumphi Romanorum a Romulo rege usque ad Carolum V (Venice: Jacopo Strada, 1557).

Fastorum libri V a Romulo rege usque ad Imperatorem Caesarem Carolum V Austrium Augustum; In Fastorum libros commentarii; Commentariorum in Fastos consulares Appendix (Venice: Vincenzo Valgrisi, 1558). Also contains (with separate page numbering): *De ludis saecularibus*, 1–25; *De sibyllis et carminibus sibyllinis*, 26–35; *De antiquis Romanorum nominibus*, 37–82. Reprints: Heidelberg: Hieronymus Commelinus; Geneva: Pierre de Saint-André, 1588.

Reipublicae Romanae commentariorum libri tres (Venice: Vincenzo Valgrisi, 1558).

Romanorum principum et eorum quorum maxima in Italia imperia fuerunt libri IV; De comitiis imperatoriis liber, in quo praeter caetera septem imperii electorum origo demonstrata est atque communis quae adhuc obtinuit fama refutata (Basel: Heinrich Petri, 1558).

De baptismate paschali, origine et ritu consecrandi Agnus Dei liber ex commentariis Onuphrii Panvinii . . . in historiam ecclesiasticam excerptus (Rome: Antonio Blado, 1560; repr. Rome: Angelo Bernabò, 1656).

(ed.), Platina, Bartolomeo, *Opus de vitis ac gestis summorum pontificum ad sua usque tempora deductum*; contains lives by Panvinio (Paul III–Pius IV); Panvinio,

---

[*] Reprints are included only if they have been mentioned in the text.

Breve…omnium Romanorum pontificum et schismatum chronicon (Cologne: Maternus Cholinus, 1562).

(ed.), Platina, *Historia de vitis pontificum Romanorum a Domino Nostro Iesu Christo usque ad Paulum Papam II*; contains lives by Panvinio (Sixtus IV–Pius IV); *Variae annotationes* (Venice: Michele Tramezzino, 1562).

(ed.), Platina, *La historia delle vite de' pontefici*, trans. Lucio Fauno (pseudonym of Giovanni Tarcagnota) (Venice: Michele Tramezzino, 1563); revised edn, *Historia delle vite dei sommi pontefici* (Venice: Bernardo Basa; Barezzo Barezzi, 1592).

(ed.), Platina, *Historia de vitis pontificum Romanorum; Annotationes Onuphrii Panvinii*; contains lives by Panvinio (Sixtus IV–Pius IV); Panvinio, *Interpraetatio multarum vocum ecclesiasticarum quae obscurae vel barbarae videntur; De stationibus urbis Romae; De ritu sepeliendi mortuos apud veteres Christianos et eorum coemeteriis* (Cologne: Maternus Cholinus, 1568).

Chronicon ecclesiasticum a C. Iulii Caesaris dictatoris imperio usque ad Imperatorem Caesarem Maximilianum II (Cologne: Maternus Cholinus, 1568).

XXVII pontificum maximorum elogia et imagines (Rome: Antoine Lafréry, 1568).

De praecipuis urbis Romae sanctioribusque basilicis, quas septem ecclesias vulgo vocant, liber (Rome: heirs of Antonio Blado, 1570).

Le sette chiese romane, trans. Marco Antonio Lanfranchi (Rome: heirs of Antonio Blado, 1570).

De triumpho commentarius (Venice: Michele Tramezzino, 1571).

De Bibliotheca Vaticana, in Juan Bautista Cardona, *De regia Sancti Laurentii Bibliotheca, De Pontificia Vaticana, De expungendis haereticorum propriis nominibus, De dyptichis* (Tarragona: Felipe Mey, 1587), 37–49.

De primatu Petri et Apostolicae Sedis potestate libri tres contra Centuriarum auctores (Verona: Girolamo Discepolo, 1589). Reprints: Venice: Francesco de' Franceschi, 1591; in J. T. de Rocaberti (ed.), *Bibliotheca maxima pontificia*, 21 vols (Rome: Giovanni Francesco Buagni, 1695–99), xvii. 536–645; in F. A. Zaccaria (ed.), *Thesaurus theologicus*, 13 vols (Venice, 1762–3), vii. 1001–1186.

Sommario di capitoli et leggi che si osservano nell'elettione del sommo pontefice, trans. Cornelio Massimini (Venice: Domenico Imberti, 1590).

De ludis circensibus; De triumphis (Venice: Giovanni Battista Ciotti, 1600).

De urbis Veronae viris doctrina et bellica virtute illustribus (Verona: Angelo Tamo, 1621).

Antiquitatum Veronensium libri VIII, ed. Marco Antonio Clodio et al. (Padua: Paolo Frambotto, 1647), 2nd edn (1648).

De ecclesiis Christianorum liber, ed. A. Mai, in *Spicilegium Romanum*, 10 vols (Rome, 1839–44), ix. 141–80.

De rebus antiquis memorabilibus et praestantia basilicae Sancti Petri apostolorum principis libri VII (long extract), ibid. 192–382.

De cardinalium origine liber, ibid. 469–511.

De Fabiorum familia, De Maximorum familia, ibid. 549–91.

De gente Sabella, ed. E. Celani, '"De gente Sabella": manoscritto inedito di Onofrio Panvinio', *Studi e documenti di storia e diritto*, 12 (1891), 271–309; 13 (1892), 187–206. The offprint of this article (Rome, 1892) additionally contains an index of names (81–8).

Gregorii Papae VII vita, in *Appendix ad opera edita ab Angelo Maio*, ed. G. Cozza-Luzi (Rome, 1871), 78–94.

De gente Fregepania, partial ed. E. Celani, '"De gente Fregepania" di Onofrio Panvinio', *Nuovo archivio veneto*, 5 (1893), 479–86.

Creatio Pii IV Papae, ed. S. Merkle (under the title *De creatione Pii IV Papae*), *Concilium Tridentinum*, ii. 575–601.

De sacrosancta basilica, baptisterio et patriarchio Lateranensi libri IV, ed. P. Lauer, *Le Palais de Latran* (Paris, 1911), 410–90.

(iii) Other printed primary sources (up to *c*.1700)

Agustín, Antonio: *De emendatione Gratiani dialogorum libri duo* (Tarragona, 1587).

Agustín, Antonio: *Epistolae Latinae et Italicae*, ed. J. Andrés (Parma, 1804).

Agustín, Antonio: *Epistolario*, ed. C. Flores Sellés (Salamanca, 1980).

Amaseo, Romolo: *Oratio habita in funere Pauli III Pontificis Maximi* (Bologna, 1563).

Ammannati Piccolomini, Jacopo: *Epistolae et commentarii* (Milan, 1506).

Anastasius Bibliothecarius: *De vitis Romanorum pontificum*, ed. F. Bianchini, 4 vols (Rome, 1718–35).

Antoninus of Florence: *Chronica*, 3 vols (Lyon, 1543).

Arámburu Cendoya, I. (ed.): *Las primitivas Constituciones de los Agustinos* (Valladolid, 1966).

Aventinus, Johannes: *Annales Boiorum* (Ingolstadt, 1554).

Aventinus, Johannes: *Annales ducum Boiariae*, ed. S. Riezler, 2 vols (Munich, 1882–4).

Bacci, Pietro Giacomo: *Vita di San Filippo Neri fiorentino, fondatore della Congregazione dell'Oratorio*, ed. G. Ricci (Rome, 1745).

Baldo degli Ubaldi: *In sextum Codicis librum Commentaria*, ed. Alessandro Tartagni, Andrea Barbazza, and Filippo Decio (Venice, 1577).

Barnes, Robert: *Vitae Romanorum pontificum, quos papas vocamus*, with a preface by Martin Luther (Wittenberg, 1536).

Baronio, Cesare: *Annales ecclesiastici*, 12 vols (Rome, 1588–1607).

Baronio, Cesare: *Annales ecclesiastici*, ed. Antoine Pagi, 19 vols (Lucca, 1738–46).

Baronio, Cesare: *Annales ecclesiastici*, with continuations by Odorico Rinaldi, Giacomo Laderchi, and Augustin Theiner, 37 vols (Bar-le-Duc, 1864–83).

Bellarmine, Robert: *Disputationes de controversiis Christianae fidei adversus huius temporibus haereticos*, 3 vols (Ingolstadt, 1586–93); 2nd edn, 3 vols (Ingolstadt, 1588–93); 3 vols (Lyon, 1596).

Bellarmine, Robert: *De translatione Imperii Romani a Graecis ad Francos, adversus Matthiam Flaccium Illyricum* (Antwerp, 1589).

Bellarmine, Robert: *Tractatus de potestate summi pontificis in rebus temporalibus, adversus Gulielmum Barclaium* (Rome, 1610); trans. S. Tutino, *On Temporal and Spiritual Authority* (Indianapolis, IN, 2012).

Bellarmine, Robert: *De scriptoribus ecclesiasticis* (Rome, 1613).

Bellarmine, Robert: 'An Beatus Petrus Antiochiae sederit antequam Romam venerit; ubi etiam de annis vitae Christi', in X.-M. Le Bachelet (ed.), *Auctarium Bellarminianum: supplément aux œuvres du Cardinal Bellarmin* (Paris, 1913), 544–7.

Bellarmine, Robert: 'An Felix Secundus sit verus papa et martyr', ibid. 547–8.

Bellarmine, Robert: 'Censura in primum tomum *Historiae ecclesiasticae* Fratris Onuphrii Panvinii, facta mandato bonae memoriae Jacobi Cardinalis Savelli', ibid. 554–64.

Beno: *Vita et gesta Hildebrandi*, in Ortwin Gratius (ed.), *Fasciculus rerum expetendarum et fugiendarum* (Cologne, 1535), fos 39^v–43^v.

Biondo Flavio: *Opera* (Basel, 1531).

The Book of Daniel, trans. L. F. Hartmann (Garden City, NY, 1978).

Borghini, Vincenzio: *Il carteggio*, ed. D. Francalanci, F. Pellegrini, and E. Carrara (Florence, 2001–).

Braun, Konrad: *Adversus novam Historiam ecclesiasticam...admonitio catholica* (Dillingen, 1565).

Breviarium Romanum ex decreto sacrosancti Concilii Tridentini restitutum, Pii V...iussu editum (Rome, 1568).

Bujanda, J. M. de (ed.): *Index des livres interdits*, 12 vols (Sherbrooke, Quebec; Geneva; Madrid, 1984–2016).

Bullarum, diplomatum et privilegiorum Sanctorum Romanorum pontificum Taurinensis editio, 25 vols (Turin; Naples, 1857–85).

Burchard of Ursberg: *Chronicon*, 2nd edn by O. Holder-Egger and B. von Simson (Hannover; Leipzig, 1916).

Burckard, Johannes: *Diarium*, ed. L. Thuasne, 3 vols (Paris, 1883–5).

Canisius, Peter: *Epistulae et acta*, ed. O. Braunsberger, 8 vols (Freiburg im Breisgau, 1896–1923).

Carafa, Antonio and Antonio d'Aquino (eds): *Epistolae decretales summorum pontificum*, 3 vols (Rome, 1591).

Caro, Annibale: *Lettere familiari*, ed. A. Greco, 3 vols (Florence, 1957–61).

Cassander, Georg: *Liturgica de ritu et ordine dominicae coenae celebrandae* (Cologne, 1558).

Cassander, Georg: *Ordo Romanus de officio missae* (Cologne, 1561).

Chacón, Alfonso: *Vitae et gesta summorum pontificum a Christo domino usque ad Clementem VIII necnon Sanctae Romanae Ecclesiae cardinalium cum eorundem insignibus*, 2 vols (Rome, 1601).

Christophori Patavini O.S.A. Registra generalatus, 1551–1567, ed. A. Hartmann (Rome, 1985–).

Chronica monasterii Casinensis, ed. H. Hoffmann (Hannover, 1980).

Chronica sacri Casinensis coenobii (Venice, 1513).

Chronicum abbatis Urspergensis, with a continuation by Kaspar Hedio and a preface by Philipp Melanchthon (Strasbourg, 1537 and 1540).

Concilia omnia tam generalia quam particularia, ed. Petrus Crabbe, 2 vols (Cologne, 1538).

Concilia omnia tum generalia tum provincialia atque particularia, ed. Laurentius Surius, 4 vols (Cologne, 1567).

Conciliorum oecumenicorum generaliumque decreta: editio critica (Turnhout, 2006–).

Conring, Hermann: *De Germanorum imperio Romano* (Helmstedt, 1644).

Corpus inscriptionum Latinarum (Berlin, 1862–).

Cortesi, Paolo: *De cardinalatu* (San Gimignano, 1510).

Crusenius, Nicolaus: *Monasticon Augustinianum* (Munich, 1623).

Curtius, Cornelius: *Virorum illustrium ex Ordine Eremitarum Divi Augustini elogia cum singulorum expressis ad vivum iconibus* (Antwerp, 1636).

Decretales Domini Gregorii Papae IX suae integritati una cum glossis restitutae (Rome, 1582).

Diego de Simancas: *De catholicis institutionibus* (Rome, 1575).

Dietrich of Niem: *De schismate... libri III* (Nuremberg, 1536).

Dietrich of Niem: *De scismate libri III*, ed. G. Erler (Leipzig, 1890).

Du Moulin, Charles: *Commentarius ad edictum Henrici II Regis Galliarum contra parvas datas et abusus curiae Romanae* (Basel, 1552).

Ebers, G. J. (ed.): *Der Papst und die römische Kurie*, i (no more publ.) (Paderborn, 1916).

Eck, Johann: *De primatu Petri adversus Ludderum* (Paris, 1521).

Egnazio, Giovanni Battista: *De Caesaribus libri III...*; Aelius Spartianus, Iulius Capitolinus..., ed. id. (Venice, 1516), again published in Florence (1519).

Eisengrein, Wilhelm: *Centenarii XVI...adversus novam Historiam ecclesiasticam*, 2 vols (no more publ.) (Ingolstadt; Munich, 1566–8).

Epistulae imperatorum, pontificum... Avellana quae dicitur Collectio, ed. O. Günther, 2 pts (Prague; Vienna; Leipzig, 1895–8).

Eymerich, Nicholas: *Directorium inquisitorum*, ed. with a commentary by Francisco Peña (first publ. 1578) (Venice, 1595).

Fitz-Simon, Henry: *Britannomachia ministrorum* (Douai, 1614).

Flacius Illyricus, Matthias: *Catalogus testium veritatis qui ante nostram aetatem reclamarunt papae* (Basel, 1556).

Flacius Illyricus, Matthias: *De translatione Imperii Romani ad Germanos* (Basel, 1566).

Flacius Illyricus, Matthias et al.: *Ecclesiastica historia* [i.e., *Magdeburg Centuries*], 13 vols (Basel, 1559–74).

Foresti, Giacomo Filippo: *Sopplimento delle croniche universali del mondo*, ed. Francesco Sansovino (Venice, 1575).

Frutolfi et Ekkehardi Chronica necnon anonymi Chronica imperatorum, ed. F.-J. Schmale and I. Schmale-Otte (Darmstadt, 1972).

Gaeta, F. et al. (eds): *Nunziature di Venezia* (Rome, 1958–).

Garimberti, Girolamo: *La prima parte delle vite overo fatti memorabili d'alcuni papi et di tutti i cardinali passati* (Venice, 1567).

Giovannetti, Francesco: *Pontificum Romanorum liber ex veteribus Germanis desumptus authoribus* (Bologna, 1570).

Giovio, Paolo: *Vita Leonis X Pontificis Maximi; Hadriani VI Pontificis Maximi et Pompeii Columnae Cardinalis vitae* (Florence, 1548).

Giovio, Paolo: *Historiae sui temporis*, 2 vols (Florence, 1550–2).

Giovio, Paolo: *Elogia virorum literis illustrium* (first publ. 1546), in id., *Opera*, ed. Società Storica Comense (Rome, 1956–), viii, ed. R. Meregazzi, 31–225.

Giovio, Paolo: *Vita Leonis X*, in id., *Opera*, vi, pt 1, ed. M. Cataudella, 5–106.

Giovio, Paolo: *Vita Hadriani VI*, ibid. 107–40.

Görres-Gesellschaft (ed.): *Concilium Tridentinum: diariorum, actorum, epistularum, tractatuum nova collectio*, 13 vols (Freiburg im Breisgau, 1901–2001).

Goldast, Melchior: *Replicatio pro sacra Caesarea et regia Francorum maiestate illustrissimisque Imperii ordinibus adversus Jacobi Gretseri...crimina laesae maiestatis, rebellionis et falsi* (Hannover, 1611).

Gratian: *Decretum Divi Gratiani* (Lyon, 1554; reprint 1559).

Gratian: *Decretum*, in *Corpus iuris canonici*, 2nd edn, ed. E. Friedberg, 2 vols (Leipzig, 1879), i.

Gregory of Catino: *Chronicon Farfense*, ed. U. Balzani, 2 vols (Rome, 1903).

Gretser, Jakob: *Controversiarum Roberti Bellarmini Sanctae Romanae Ecclesiae Cardinalis amplissimi defensio*, 2 vols (Ingolstadt, 1607–9).

Gretser, Jakob: *Apologia pro Gregorio VII*, ibid., ii, separate numbering, cols [235]–273.

Gretser, Jakob: *Opera omnia*, 17 vols (Regensburg, 1734–41).

Gretser, Jakob (ed.): *Volumen epistolarum quas Romani pontifices...miserunt ad principes et reges Francorum* [i.e., *Codex Carolinus*] (Ingolstadt, 1613).

Grotius, Hugo: *De imperio summarum potestatum circa sacra*, ed. and trans. H.-J. van Dam, 2 vols (Leiden, 2001).

Guicciardini, Francesco: *La historia di Italia* (Florence, 1561); trans. S. Alexander, *The History of Italy* (New York, 1969).

Incisa della Rocchetta, G. and N. Vian (eds): *Il primo processo per San Filippo Neri*, 4 vols (Vatican City, 1957–63).

Kölzer, T. et al. (eds): *Die Urkunden Ludwigs des Frommen*, 3 pts (Wiesbaden, 2016).

Lampert of Hersfeld: *Germanorum res praeclare olim gestae*, ed. Ludwig Schradin, with a foreword by Philipp Melanchthon (Tübingen, 1533).

Lampert of Hersfeld: *Annales*, in his *Opera*, ed. O. Holder-Egger (Hannover; Leipzig, 1894), 3–304; trans. I. S. Robinson, *The Annals* (Manchester, 2015).

Latini, Latino: *Epistolae*, 2 vols (Rome; Viterbo, 1659–67).

Liber pontificalis, ed. L. Duchesne, 3 vols (Paris, 1886–1957).

Linck, Wenzeslaus: *Bapsts gepreng, ausz dem Cerimonien Buch* (Strasbourg, 1539).

Lipsius, Justus: *Dissertatiuncula apud principes; item C. Plini Panegyricus* (Antwerp, 1600).

Liutprand of Cremona: *Rerum ab Europae imperatoribus ac regibus gestarum libri VI*, in Widukind of Corvey, *Rerum ab Henrico et Ottone I imperatoribus gestarum libri III...*, ed. Martin Frecht (Basel, 1532), 219–314.

Liutprand of Cremona: *Historia Ottonis*, in id., *Opera*, 3rd edn, ed. J. Becker (Hannover, 1915), 159–75.

Mabillon, Jean: *Museum italicum*, 2 vols (Paris, 1687–9).

Märtl, C. (ed.): *Die falschen Investiturprivilegien* (Hannover, 1986).

Maffei, Giovanni Pietro: *Annali di Gregorio XIII*, ed. C. Cocquelines, 2 vols (Rome, 1742).

Mai, A. (ed.): *Spicilegium Romanum*, 10 vols (Rome, 1839–44).

Martin of Troppau: Marianus Scotus, *Chronica*; Martinus Polonus, *Historia* (Basel, 1559).

Martin, Gregory: *Roma sancta*, ed. G. B. Parks (Rome, 1969).

Martinelli, Fioravante: *Roma ex ethnica sacra Sanctorum Petri et Pauli apostolica praedicatione profuso sanguine publicae venerationi exposita* (Rome, 1653).

Martyrologium Romanum, ed. Cesare Baronio (Rome, 1586).

Massarelli, Angelo: *De modis seu formis per diversa tempora observatis in electione pontificum maximorum a Divo Petro usque ad Iulium III*, in *SR*, ix. 518–30.

Massarelli, Angelo: *Diarium V: de conclavi post obitum Pauli III (1549–50)*, ed. S. Merkle, in *Concilium Tridentinum*, ii. 1–145.

Massarelli, Angelo: *Diarium VII: a Marcello II usque ad Pium IV (1555–61)*, ibid. 245–362.

Masson, Papire: *De episcopis Urbis* (Paris, 1586).

Mittarelli, G. B. and A. Costadoni (eds): *Annales Camaldulenses Ordinis Sancti Benedicti*, 9 vols (Venice, 1755–73).

Monumenta Germaniae Historica, Leges, ii, ed. G. H. Pertz (Hannover, 1837).

Muratori, Lodovico Antonio: *Epistolario*, ed. M. Càmpori, 14 vols (Modena, 1901–22).

Muzio, Girolamo: *Della historia sacra*, 2 vols (Venice, 1570).

Otto and Rahewin of Freising: *Gesta Friderici I imperatoris*, 3rd edn, ed. G. Waitz and B. von Simson (Hannover; Leipzig, 1912).

Otto of Freising: *Rerum ab origine mundi ad ipsius usque tempora gestarum libri octo*; Otto and Rahewin of Freising, *De gestis Friderici*, ed. Johannes Cuspinianus (Strasbourg, 1515).

Otto of Freising: *Chronica sive Historia de duabus civitatibus*, 2nd edn, ed. A. Hofmeister (Hannover; Leipzig, 1912).

Panfilo, Giuseppe: *Chronica Ordinis Fratrum Eremitarum Sancti Augustini* (Rome, 1581).

Panigarola, Francesco: *Il Compendio degli Annali ecclesiastici del padre Cesare Baronio* (Rome, 1590).

Pantagato, Ottavio: 'La correspondència d'Ottavio Pantagato (1494–1567)', ed. A. Soler i Nicolau, 2 vols (doctoral thesis, Universitat Autònoma de Barcelona, 2000).

Patrologia Latina, ed. J.-P. Migne, 221 vols (Paris, 1844–64).

Peiresc, Nicolas-Claude Fabri de: *Lettres de Peiresc aux frères Dupuy*, ed. P. Tamizey de Larroque, 7 vols (Paris, 1888–98).

Peña, Francisco: *De vita, miraculis et actis canonizationis Sancti Didaci* (Rome, 1589).

Peña, Francisco: *Instructio seu praxis Inquisitorum*, in C. Carena, *Tractatus de officio sanctissimae Inquisitionis* (Bologna, 1668), 348–434.

Petramellari, Giovanni Antonio: *Ad librum Onuphrii Panvinii De summis pontificibus et Sanctae Romanae Ecclesiae cardinalibus a Paulo IV ad Clementis VIII annum pontificatus octavum continuatio* (Bologna, 1599).

Petrus de Herenthals: *Secunda Vita Clementis VII*, in É. Baluze and G. Mollat (eds), *Vitae paparum Avenionensium*, 4 vols (Paris, 1914–22), i. 519–35.

Pirri, Rocco: *Notitiae Siciliensium ecclesiarum* (Palermo, 1630).

Platina, Bartolomeo: *Liber de vita Christi ac omnium pontificum*, ed. G. Gaida (Città di Castello, 1913–32).

Platina, Bartolomeo: *Historia delle vite dei sommi pontefici*, see under Panvinio.

Platina, Bartolomeo: *Historia de vitis pontificum Romanorum*, see under Panvinio.

Platina, Bartolomeo: *La historia delle vite de' pontefici*, see under Panvinio.

Platina, Bartolomeo: *Opus de vitis ac gestis summorum pontificum*, see under Panvinio.

Poggiani, Giulio: *Epistolae et orationes*, ed. G. Lagomarsini, 4 vols (Rome, 1756–62).

Pole, Reginald: *De summo pontifice Christi in terris vicario eiusque officio et potestate* (Leuven, 1569).

Rahewin of Freising *see* Otto of Freising.

Robortello, Francesco: *In librum Aristotelis De arte poetica explicationes* (Florence, 1548).

Rocca, Angelo: *Bibliotheca Apostolica Vaticana* (Rome, 1591).

Ruscelli, Girolamo: *Le imprese illustri* (Venice, 1566).

Ruscelli, Girolamo: *Lettere*, ed. C. Gizzi and P. Procaccioli (Manziana, 2010).

Scaliger, Joseph Justus: *De emendatione temporum* (Paris, 1583).

Scaliger, Joseph Justus: *Confutatio fabulae Burdonum*, in Daniel Heinsius, *Hercules tuam fidem* (Leiden, 1608), 365–7.

Schard, Simon: *De principum, quibus electio imperatoris in Germania commendata est, origine seu institutione*, in id. (ed.), *De iurisdictione, autoritate et praeeminentia imperiali ac potestate ecclesiastica...variorum authorum...scripta* (Basel, 1566), 861–914.

Seripando, Girolamo: *Hieronymi Seripando O.S.A. Registra generalatus, 1538–1551*, ed. D. Gutiérrez, 7 vols (Rome, 1982–96).

Serrano, L. (ed.): *Correspondencia diplomática entre España y la Santa Sede durante el pontificado de San Pio V*, 4 vols (Madrid, 1914).

Sigebert of Gembloux: *Chronicon ab anno 381 ad 1113 cum insertionibus...*, ed. Antonius Rufus (Paris, 1513).

Sigebert of Gembloux: *Chronicon*, in *Rerum toto orbe gestarum chronica*, ed. Aubert Miraeus (Antwerp, 1608).

Sigebert of Gembloux: *Chronica cum continuationibus*, ed. L. C. Bethmann, in *Monumenta Germaniae Historica*, Scriptores, vi (Hannover, 1844), 300–474.

Sigonio, Carlo: *Historiarum de regno Italiae libri XV* (Venice, 1574).

Sigonio, Carlo: *Opera omnia edita et inedita*, ed. F. Argelati, 6 vols (Milan, 1732–7).

Steinherz, S. (ed.): *Nuntiaturberichte aus Deutschland*, 2. Abtheilung, iii: *Nuntius Delfino 1562–1563* (Vienna, 1903).

Suetonius: *C. Suetonius Tranquillus, Dion Cassius Nicaeus, Aelius Spartianus...*, ed. Desiderius Erasmus (Basel, 1518), again published in Cologne (1527).

Suetonius: *XII Caesares...*; G. B. Egnazio, *De Romanis principibus* (Lyon, 1532; and reprints).

Torelli, P. (ed.): *Regesto mantovano* (Rome, 1914).

Valla, Lorenzo: *On the Donation of Constantine*, ed. and trans. G. W. Bowersock (Cambridge, MA, 2007).

Van Durme, M. (ed.): *Supplément à la Correspondance de Christophe Plantin* (Antwerp, 1955).

Vasari, Giorgio: *Le vite de' più eccellenti pittori, scultori ed architettori*, ed. G. Milanesi, 9 vols (Florence, 1878–85).

Velenus, Ulrichus: *In hoc libello...probatur Apostolum Petrum Romam non venisse* (s.l., *c*.1520).

Vergerio, Pier Paolo: *Ordo eligendi pontificis et ratio* (Tübingen, 1556).

Villani, Giovanni: *La prima [-seconda] parte delle historie universali de' suoi tempi*, 2 vols (Venice, 1559).

Secondary Sources

Albrecht, M. von: 'Nochmals antike Grundlagen: Sueton', in W. Berschin (ed.), *Biographie zwischen Renaissance und Barock* (Heidelberg, 1993), 311–32.

Andretta, S.: 'Le biografie papali e l'informazione politica tra Cinque e Seicento', in E. Fasano Guarini and M. Rosa (eds), *L'informazione politica in Italia (secoli XVI–XVIII)* (Pisa, 2001), 239–79.

Andrieu, M.: 'Note sur quelques manuscrits et sur une édition de l'"Ordo romanus primus"', *Revue des sciences religieuses*, 2 (1922), 319–30.

Andrieu, M.: *Les 'Ordines Romani' du Haut Moyen Age*, 5 vols (Leuven, 1931–61).

Aretin, J. C. von: *Beyträge zur Geschichte und Literatur*, 9 vols (Munich, 1803–7).

Arnaldi, G.: *Come nacque la attribuzione ad Anastasio del Liber Pontificalis* (Rome, 2001).

Arnold, B.: 'Frangipani', in V. Reinhardt (ed.), *Die großen Familien Italiens* (Stuttgart, 1992), 277–86.

Arnold, C.: *Die römische Zensur der Werke Cajetans und Contarinis (1558–1601): Grenzen der theologischen Konfessionalisierung* (Paderborn, 2008).

Aubert, A.: *Paolo IV: politica, Inquisizione e storiografia* (Florence, 1999).

Augenti, A.: *Il Palatino nel Medioevo: archeologia e topografia (secoli VI–XIII)* (Rome, 1996).

Backus, I.: *Historical Method and Confessional Identity in the Era of the Reformation (1378–1615)* (Leiden, 2003).

Backus, I.: 'Quels témoins de quelle vérité? Le *Catalogus testium veritatis* de Matthias Flacius Illyricus revu par Goulart', in O. Pot (ed.), *Simon Goulart: un pasteur aux intérêts vastes comme le monde* (Geneva, 2013), 125–39.

Badea, A.: 'Geschichte schreiben über die Renaissancepäpste: römische Zensur und Historiographie in der ersten Hälfte des 18. Jahrhunderts', in H. Wolf (ed.), *Inquisition und Buchzensur im Zeitalter der Aufklärung* (Paderborn, 2011), 278–303.

Barberi, F.: *Paolo Manuzio e la Stamperia del popolo romano (1561–1570)* (Rome, 1942).

Bartòla, A.: 'Onofrio Panvinio e il Regesto del monastero dei Santi Andrea e Gregorio al Celio', *Nuovi annali della Scuola speciale per archivisti e bibliotecari*, 6 (1992), 101–12.

Bartòla, A.: 'Introduzione', in id (ed.), *Il Regesto del monastero dei Santi Andrea e Gregorio ad Clivum Scauri*, 2 vols (Rome, 2003), i, pp. VII–LXIX.

Bartolucci, G.: 'Costantino nella storiografia della Controriforma: Sigonio e Baronio tra filologia, censura e apologetica', in A. Melloni et al. (eds), *Costantino I: Enciclopedia costantiniana*, 3 vols (Rome, 2013), iii. 99–114.

Bartolucci, G.: '*In falso veritas*: Carlo Sigonio's Forged Challenge to Ecclesiastical Censorship and Italian Jurisdictionalism', *Journal of the Warburg and Courtauld Institutes*, 81 (2018), 211–37.

Bastia, C.: 'Per una ricostruzione della genesi e delle vicende censorie dell'*Historia Bononiensis* di Carlo Sigonio', *Schede umanistiche*, n. s. 3 (1993) no. 2, pp. 99–113.

Bauer, S.: *The Censorship and Fortuna of Platina's Lives of the Popes in the Sixteenth Century* (Turnhout, 2006).

Bauer, S.: 'Platina e le "res gestae" di Pio II', in A. Antoniutti and M. Sodi (eds), *Enea Silvio Piccolomini: Pius Secundus, poeta laureatus, pontifex maximus* (Rome; Vatican City, 2007), 17–32.

Bauer, S.: 'Humanisten und Klienten: Grundlinien der Papstbiographik im 16. und 17. Jahrhundert', in M. Völkel and A. Strohmeyer (eds), *Historiographie an europäischen Höfen (16.–18. Jahrhundert)* (Berlin, 2009), 247–53.

Bauer, S.: 'Wieviel Geschichte ist erlaubt? Frühmoderne Zensur aus römischer Perspektive', in S. Rau and B. Studt (eds), *Geschichte schreiben: ein Quellen- und Studienhandbuch zur Historiografie (ca. 1350–1750)* (Berlin, 2010), 334–47.

Bauer, S.: '*Quod adhuc extat*: le relazioni tra testo e monumento nella biografia papale del Rinascimento', *QFIAB*, 91 (2011), 217–48.

Bauer, S.: 'Enea Silvio Piccolomini', in G. Galasso et al. (eds), *Il contributo italiano alla storia del pensiero: storia e politica*, Enciclopedia italiana, Appendix viii (Rome, 2013), 137–43; German trans. with illustrations: 'Enea Silvio Piccolomini als Geschichtsschreiber', in M. Dall'Asta (ed.), *Anwälte der Freiheit! Humanisten und Reformatoren im Dialog* (Heidelberg, 2015), 91–103.

Bauer, S.: 'Panvinio, Onofrio', in *DBI*, lxxxi (2014), 36–9.

Bauer, S.: 'Sacchi, Bartolomeo, detto il Platina', in *DBI*, lxxxix (2017), 472–5.

Bauer, S.: 'History for Hire in Sixteenth-Century Italy: Onofrio Panvinio's Histories of Roman Families', *Erudition and the Republic of Letters*, 4 (2019), 397–438.

Bauer, S.: 'Pontianus Polman Re-imagined: How (Not) to Write a History of Religious Polemics', *Renaissance Studies* (forthcoming).

Bauer, S.: 'The *Liber pontificalis* in the Renaissance', *Journal of the Warburg and Courtauld Institutes* (forthcoming).

Bauer, S.: 'Theology and History', in K. G. Appold and N. H. Minnich (eds), *The Cambridge History of Reformation Era Theology, c. 1500–1675* (forthcoming).

Bauer, S.: 'Writing the History of the Council of Trent', in M. Delbeke (ed.), *Sforza Pallavicino: A Jesuit Life in Baroque Rome* (Leiden, forthcoming).

Bauer, S. (ed.): *The Uses of History in Religious Controversies from Erasmus to Baronio*, special issue of *Renaissance Studies* (forthcoming).

Baumgarten, P. M.: *Neue Kunde von alten Bibeln*, 2 vols (Rome; Krumbach, 1922–7).

Baumgarten, P. M.: *Von den Kardinälen des sechzehnten Jahrhunderts* (Krumbach, 1926).

Baumgarten, P. M.: *Hispanica IV: spanische Versuche der Widerlegung der Centuriae Magdeburgenses* (Krumbach, 1927).

Baumgärtner, I.: 'Savelli', in V. Reinhardt (ed.), *Die großen Familien Italiens* (Stuttgart, 1992), 480–4.

Beard, M.: *The Roman Triumph* (Cambridge, MA, 2007).

Bedouelle, G.: *The Reform of Catholicism, 1480–1620*, trans. J. K. Farge (Toronto, 2008).

Begert, A.: *Die Entstehung und Entwicklung des Kurkollegs* (Berlin, 2010).

Benedict XIV: *De servorum Dei beatificatione et beatorum canonizatione*, 4 vols (Bologna, 1734–8).

Benz, S.: *Zwischen Tradition und Kritik: katholische Geschichtsschreibung im barocken Heiligen Römischen Reich* (Husum, 2003).

Berschin, W.: *Biographie und Epochenstil im lateinischen Mittelalter*, 5 vols (Stuttgart, 1986–2004).

Bertelli, S.: *Ribelli, libertini e ortodossi nella storiografia barocca* (Florence, 1973).

Bertolotti, A.: 'Varietà archivistiche e bibliografiche', *Il bibliofilo*, 3 (1882), 33–5.

Bianchin, L.: *Dove non arriva la legge: dottrine della censura nella prima età moderna* (Bologna, 2005).

Biancolini, G. B.: *Notizie storiche delle chiese di Verona*, 8 vols (Verona, 1749–71).

Bignami Odier, J.: *La Bibliothèque Vaticane de Sixte IV à Pie XI: recherches sur l'histoire des collections de manuscrits* (Vatican City, 1973).

Biondi, A.: 'La storiografia apologetica e controversistica', in N. Tranfaglia and M. Firpo (eds), *La storia: i grandi problemi dal Medioevo all'età contemporanea*, 10 vols (Turin, 1986–8), iv. 315–33.

Birn, R.: *La censure royale des livres dans la France des Lumières* (Paris, 2007).

Biscardi, L. A.: 'Lettera intorno al giorno della morte di Frate Onofrio Panvinio all'Illustrissimo Signore...Girolamo Tiraboschi', *Nuovo giornale de' letterati d'Italia*, 39 (1788), 107–30.

Bizzocchi, R.: 'Familiae Romanae antiche e moderne', *Rivista storica italiana*, 103 (1991), 355–97.

Bizzocchi, R.: *Genealogie incredibili: scritti di storia nell'Europa moderna*, 2nd edn (Bologna, 2009).

Blastenbrei, P.: '*Clemenza* und *equità*: zur Justizpolitik Papst Gregors XIII. (1572–1585)', QFIAB, 80 (2000), 360–452.

Blumenthal, U.-R.: 'Rom in der Kanonistik', in B. Schimmelpfennig and L. Schmugge (eds), *Rom im hohen Mittelalter* (Sigmaringen, 1992).

Bollbuck, H.: 'Testimony of True Faith and the Ruler's Mission: The Middle Ages in the *Magdeburg Centuries* and the Melanchthon School', *Archiv für Reformationsgeschichte/Archive for Reformation History*, 101 (2010), 238–62.

Bollbuck, H.: *Wahrheitszeugnis, Gottes Auftrag und Zeitkritik: die Kirchengeschichte der Magdeburger Zenturien und ihre Arbeitstechniken* (Wiesbaden, 2014).

Bölling, J.: 'Römisches Zeremoniell in Bayern: Herzog Albrecht V., Kardinal Otto Truchseß von Waldburg und die Fugger', in R. Becker and D. J. Weiß (eds), *Bayerische Römer, römische Bayern: Lebensgeschichten aus Vor- und Frühmoderne* (Sankt Ottilien, 2016), 167–98.

Bölling, J.: 'Bereinigte Geschichte? Umstrittene Päpste in der Historiografie des 15. Jahrhunderts', in *Der Verlust der Eindeutigkeit: zur Krise päpstlicher Autorität im Kampf um die Cathedra Petri*, ed. H. Müller (Berlin; Boston, 2017), 187–213.

Boshof, E.: *Ludwig der Fromme* (Darmstadt, 1996).

Boureau, A.: *The Myth of Pope Joan*, trans. L. G. Cochrane (Chicago, IL, 2001).

Bouyé, É.: 'Les armoiries imaginaires des papes: archéologie et apologétique romaines à la fin du XVIᵉ siècle', in F. Alazard and F. La Brasca (eds), *La papauté à la Renaissance* (Paris, 2007), 589–618.

Britnell, J. and C. Shaw: 'A French Life of Pope Julius II, 1519: Jean Beaufils and his Translation of Platina', *Bibliothèque d'humanisme et Renaissance*, 62 (2000), 103–18.

Brockmann, T. and D. J. Weiß: 'Einleitung', in iid. (eds), *Das Konfessionalisierungsparadigma: Leistungen, Probleme, Grenzen* (Münster, 2013), 1–22.

Brodrick, J.: *Saint Peter Canisius, S.J., 1521–1597* (London, 1939).

Buchner, M.: 'Die Entstehung und Ausbildung der Kurfürstenfabel: eine historiographische Studie', *Historisches Jahrbuch*, 33 (1912), 54–100, 255–322.

Bujanda, J. M. de: 'La censure écclesiastique sur les œuvres historiques', in Firpo, *Nunc alia tempora*, 265–77.

Buonocore, M.: 'Onuphrius Panvinius et Antonius Augustinus: de codicibus Vaticanis Latinis 6035–6 adnotationes nonnullae', in M. H. Crawford (ed.), *Antonio Agustín between Renaissance and Counter-Reform* (London, 1993), 155–71.

Burckhardt, A.: *Johannes Basilius Herold: Kaiser und Reich im protestantischen Schrifttum des Basler Buchdrucks um die Mitte des 16. Jahrhunderts* (Basel, 1967).

Burckhardt, J.: *Die Cultur der Renaissance in Italien: ein Versuch*, ed. M. Mangold (Munich; Basel, 2018).

Burkard, D., U. Muhlack, and H. Wolf: *Rankes 'Päpste' auf dem Index: Dogma und Historie im Widerstreit* (Paderborn, 2003).

Busch, R. von: 'Studien zu deutschen Antikensammlungen des 16. Jahrhunderts' (doctoral thesis, Universität Tübingen, 1973).

Cameron, E.: *Interpreting Christian History: The Challenge of the Churches' Past* (Oxford, 2005).

Cameron, E.: 'Primitivism, Patristics, and Polemic in Protestant Visions of Early Christianity', in Van Liere et al., *Sacred History*, 27–51.

Cameron, E.: 'The Bible and the Early Modern Sense of History', in id. (ed.), *The New Cambridge History of the Bible*, iii (Cambridge, 2016), 657–85.

Camporeale, S. I.: *Christianity, Latinity, and Culture: Two Studies on Lorenzo Valla*, ed. P. Baker and C. S. Celenza (Leiden, 2014).

Carbonell i Manils, J.: 'Epigrafia i numismàtica a l'epistolari d'Antonio Agustín (1551–1563) (vol. 1)' (doctoral thesis, Universitat Autònoma de Barcelona, 1991).

Carocci, S.: *Baroni di Roma: dominazioni signorili e lignaggi aristocratici nel Duecento e nel primo Trecento* (Rome, 1993).

Cassio, A.: *Memorie istoriche della vita di Santa Silvia* (Rome, 1755).

'Catalogus codicum hagiographicorum Latinorum Bibliothecae Ambrosianae Mediolanensis', *Analecta Bollandiana*, 11 (1892), 205–368.

Catalogus codicum manu scriptorum Bibliothecae Regiae Monacensis, iii.1, 2nd edn (Munich, 1892).

Cavallera, F.: *Le schisme d'Antioche (IVᵉ–Vᵉ siècle)* (Paris, 1905).

Cavarzere, M.: *La prassi della censura dell'Italia del Seicento: tra repressione e mediazione* (Rome, 2011).

Cavarzere, M.: 'Das alte Reich und die römische Zensur in der Frühen Neuzeit: ein Überblick', in A. Burkardt and G. Schwerhoff (eds), *Tribunal der Barbaren? Deutschland und die Inquisition in der Frühen Neuzeit* (Konstanz, 2012), 307–34.

Cenni, G.: *Monumenta dominationis pontificiae*, 2 vols (Rome, 1760–1).

Ceretti, L.: 'Gabriele Faerno filologo in otto lettere inedite al Panvinio', *Aevum*, 27 (1953), 307–31.

Chazan, M.: *L'Empire et l'histoire universelle: de Sigebert de Gembloux à Jean de Saint-Victor (XIIᵉ–XIVᵉ siècle)* (Paris, 1999).

La chiesa, la Biblioteca Angelica, l'Avvocatura generale dello Stato: il complesso di Sant'Agostino in Campo Marzio (Rome, 2009).

Chilese, V.: *Una città nel Seicento veneto: Verona attraverso le fonti fiscali del 1653* (Verona, 2002).

Chmel, J.: *Die Handschriften der k.k. Hofbibliothek in Wien*, 2 vols (Vienna, 1840–1).

Clausi B. and S. Lucà (eds): *Il 'sapientissimo calabro' Guglielmo Sirleto nel V centenario della nascita (1514–2014)* (Rome, 2018).

Claussen, P. C.: *Die Kirchen der Stadt Rom im Mittelalter 1050–1300*, 3 vols (Stuttgart, 2002–10).

Cochrane, E.: *Historians and Historiography in the Italian Renaissance* (Chicago, IL, 1981).

Collins, A.: 'Renaissance Epigraphy and Its Legitimating Potential: Annius of Viterbo, Etruscan Inscriptions, and the Origins of Civilization', in A. E. Cooley (ed.), *The Afterlife of Inscriptions* (London, 2000), 57–76.

Collins, J. C.: *Daniel: a Commentary on the Book of Daniel* (Minneapolis, MN, 1993).

Cooley, A. E.: *The Cambridge Manual of Latin Epigraphy* (Cambridge, 2012).

Cowdrey, H. E. J.: *Pope Gregory VII, 1073–1085* (Oxford, 1998).

Crawford, M. H.: 'Benedetto Egio and the Development of Greek Epigraphy', in id. (ed.), *Antonio Agustín between Renaissance and Counter-Reform* (London, 1993), 133–54.

Cugnoni, G.: 'Documenti chigiani concernenti Felice Peretti, Sisto V, come privato e come pontefice', *Archivio della Società romana di storia patria*, 5 (1882), 1–32, 210–304, 542–89.

D'Amico, J. F.: 'Papal History and Curial Reform in the Renaissance: Raffaele Maffei's *Breuis Historia* of Julius II and Leo X', *Archivum historiae pontificiae*, 18 (1980), 157–210.

D'Onofrio, C.: *Scalinate di Roma* (Rome, 1974).

Dandelet, T. J.: *Spanish Rome, 1500–1700* (New Haven, CT, 2001).

Decot, R., G. Walther, and R. Kanz: 'Catholic Reformation', in F. Jaeger and G. Dunphy (eds), *Encyclopedia of Early Modern History* (Leiden, 2016–), ii. 447–57.

De Maio, R.: 'La Biblioteca Vaticana sotto Paolo IV e Pio IV (1555–1565)', in *Collectanea Vaticana in honorem Anselmi M. Cardinalis Albareda*, 2 vols (Vatican City, 1962), i. 265–313.

De Maio, R.: 'Introduzione: Baronio storico', in R. De Maio, L. Gulia, and A. Mazzacane (eds), *Baronio storico e la Controriforma* (Sora, 1982), pp. XVII–XXIV.

De Nolhac, P.: *La bibliothèque de Fulvio Orsini* (Paris, 1887).

De Rossi, G. B.: 'Delle sillogi epigrafiche dello Smezio e del Panvinio', *Annali dell'Istituto di corrispondenza archeologica*, 34 (1862), 220–44.

De Rossi, G. B.: *La Roma sotterranea cristiana*, 3 vols (Rome, 1864–77).

Defrenne, B.: 'Les "Diaria" et les "Acta" du Concile de Trente', *Revue bénédictine*, 30 (1913), 346–53.

Degrassi, A.: 'Fasti consulares et triumphales Capitolini', in id. (ed.), *Fasti consulares et triumphales* (Rome, 1947), 1–142.

Del Forno, F.: *Case e palazzi di Verona* (Verona, 1973).

Del Re, N.: 'Il "Consilium pro Urbano VI" di Bartolomeo da Saliceto', in *Collectanea Vaticana in honorem Anselmi M. Cardinalis Albareda*, 2 vols (Vatican City, 1962), i. 213–63.

Delogu, P.: 'Gregorio II', in *Enciclopedia dei papi*, 3 vols (Rome, 2000), i. 647–51.

Delpiano, P.: *Il governo della lettura: Chiesa e libri nell'Italia del Settecento* (Bologna, 2007).

Dickerhof-Borello, E.: *Ein Liber Septimus für das Corpus Iuris Canonici: der Versuch einer nachtridentinischen Kompilation* (Cologne, 2002).

Dihle, A.: 'Antike Grundlagen', in W. Berschin (ed.), *Biographie zwischen Renaissance und Barock* (Heidelberg, 1993), 1–22.

Dingel, I., J. Hund, and L. Ilić (eds): *Matthias Flacius Illyricus: biographische Kontexte, theologische Wirkungen, historische Rezeption* (Göttingen, 2019).

Ditchfield, S.: *Liturgy, Sanctity and History in Tridentine Italy: Pietro Maria Campi and the Preservation of the Particular* (Cambridge, 1995).

Ditchfield, S.: 'Of Dancing Cardinals and Mestizo Madonnas: Reconfiguring the History of Roman Catholicism in the Early Modern Period', *Journal of Early Modern History*, 8 (2004), 386–408.

Ditchfield, S.: '"Historia magistra sanctitatis?" The Relationship between Historiography and Hagiography in Italy after the Council of Trent (1564–1742 ca.)', in Firpo, *Nunc alia tempora*, 3–23.

Ditchfield, S.: 'Baronio storico nel suo tempo', in Guazzelli et al., *Baronio*, 3–21.

Ditchfield, S.: 'What Was Sacred History? (Mostly Roman) Catholic Uses of the Christian Past after Trent', in Van Liere et al., *Sacred History*, 72–97.

Dizionario biografico degli italiani (Rome, 1960–).

Döllinger, J. J. I. von: *Beiträge zur politischen, kirchlichen und Culturgeschichte der sechs letzten Jahrhunderte*, 3 vols (Regensburg; Vienna, 1862–82).

Döllinger, J. J. I. von: *Die Papst-Fabeln des Mittelalters*, 2nd edn (Stuttgart, 1890).

Donati, U.: 'Gli architetti del convento di Sant'Agostino a Roma', *L'Urbe: rivista romana*, 5 (1940) no. 8, pp. 20–6.

Dorez, L.: 'Le cardinal Marcello Cervini et l'imprimerie à Rome (1539–1550)', *Mélanges d'archéologie e d'histoire*, 12 (1892), 289–313.

Dorna, M.: 'Von der Hagiographie zur Diplomatik: Daniel Papebrochs Lehre zur Erkennung von frühmittelalterlichen Urkundenfälschungen', *Archiv für Diplomatik*, 60 (2014), 165–89.

Drei, G.: *I Farnese*, ed. G. Allegri Tassoni (Rome, 1954).

Dürrwächter, A.: *Christoph Gewold* (Freiburg im Breisgau, 1904).

Dykmans, M.: 'La troisième élection du pape Urbain VI', *Archivum historiae pontificiae*, 15 (1977), 217–64.

Esch, A.: 'Aus den Akten der Indexkongregation: verurteilte Schriften von Ferdinand Gregorovius', in A. Esch and J. Petersen (eds), *Ferdinand Gregorovius und Italien* (Tübingen, 1993), 240–52.

Esteban, E.: 'De antiquarum constitutionum Ordinis praecipuis editionibus', *AAug*, 2 (1907–8), 35–41, 84–94, 109–14.

Esteban, E.: 'Excerpta e regestis Reverendissimi Seripandi circa Constitutiones Ordinis ab ipso in lucem editas', *AAug*, 2 (1907–8), 58–62, 79–84.

Esteban, E.: 'De capitulo generali Veronae celebrato anno 1538', *AAug*, 9 (1921–2), 263–71.

Esteve, C. (ed.): *Disciplining History: Censorship, Theory and Historical Discourse in Early Modern Spain* (London; New York, 2018).

Fattori, M. T.: *Clemente VIII e il Sacro Collegio, 1592–1605* (Stuttgart, 2004).

Ferrari, M. C.: '*Mutare non lubuit*: die mediävistische Philologie der Jesuiten im frühen 17. Jahrhundert', *Filologia Mediolatina*, 8 (2001), 225–48.

Ferrary, J.-L.: *Onofrio Panvinio et les antiquités romaines* (Rome, 1996).

Ferrary, J.-L.: 'Panvinio (Onofrio)', in C. Nativel (ed.), *Centuriae Latinae* (Geneva, 1997), 595–9.

Ferretto, G.: *Note storico-bibliografiche di archeologia cristiana* (Vatican City, 1942).

Fiocchi Nicolai, V. 'San Filippo Neri, le catacombe di San Sebastiano e le origini dell'archeologia cristiana', in M. T. Bonadonna Russo and N. Del Re (eds), *San Filippo Neri nella realtà romana del XVI secolo* (Rome, 2000), 105–30.

Firpo, M.: 'Rethinking "Catholic Reform" and "Counter-Reformation": What Happened in Early Modern Catholicism—a View from Italy', *Journal of Early Modern History*, 20 (2016), 293–312.

Firpo, M. (ed.): '*Nunc alia tempora, alii mores*': storici e storia in età postridentina (Florence, 2005).

Firpo, M. and F. Biferali: '*Navicula Petri*': l'arte dei papi nel Cinquecento, 1527–1571 (Bari, 2009).

Fragnito, G.: *Proibito capire: la Chiesa e il volgare nella prima età moderna* (Bologna, 2005).

Frajese, V.: 'La revoca dell'*Index* sistino e la Curia romana (1588–1596)', *Nouvelles de la République des Lettres*, 6 (1986), 15–49.

Frajese, V.: 'Regno ecclesiastico e Stato moderno: la polemica tra Francisco Peña e Roberto Bellarmino sull'esenzione dei chierici', *Annali dell'Istituto storico italo-germanico di Trento/Jahrbuch des italienisch-deutschen historischen Instituts in Trient*, 14 (1988), 273–339.

Frajese, V.: *Nascita dell'Indice: la censura ecclesiastica dal Rinascimento alla Controriforma* (Brescia, 2006).

François W. and V. Soen (eds): *The Council of Trent: Reform and Controversy in Europe and Beyond (1545–1700)*, 3 vols (Göttingen, 2018).

Frenken, A.: *Das Konstanzer Konzil* (Stuttgart, 2015).

Fritze, W. H.: *Papst und Frankenkönig: Studien zu den päpstlich-fränkischen Rechtsbeziehungen zwischen 754 und 824* (Sigmaringen, 1973).

Fubini, R.: 'Onofrio Panvinio: alle origini del mito di Varrone come fondatore della scienza antiquaria', in id., *Storiografia dell'umanesimo in Italia da Leonardo Bruni ad Annio da Viterbo* (Rome, 2003), 83–9.

Fuhrmann, H.: 'Die Wahl des Papstes: ein historischer Überblick', *Geschichte in Wissenschaft und Unterricht*, 9 (1958), 762–80.

Fuhrmann, H.: 'Papstgeschichtsschreibung: Grundlinien und Etappen', in A. Esch and J. Petersen (eds), *Geschichte und Geschichtswissenschaft in der Kultur Italiens und Deutschlands* (Tübingen, 1989), 141–83.

Fulin, R.: 'Onofrio Panvinio', *Archivio veneto*, 4 (1872), 158.

Fumi, L. and A. Cerlini: 'Una continuazione orvietana della Cronaca di Martino Polono', *Archivio Muratoriano*, 14 (1914), 97–139.

Gaiffier, B. de: 'Les notices des papes Félix dans le martyrologe romain', *Analecta Bollandiana*, 81 (1963), 333–50.

Gamrath, H.: *The Farnese: Pomp, Power and Politics in Renaissance Italy* (Rome, 2007).

Gandolfo, D. A.: *Dissertatio historica de ducentis celeberrimis Augustinianis scriptoribus* (Rome, 1704).

Gantner, C.: *Freunde Roms und Völker der Finsternis: die päpstliche Konstruktion von Anderen im 8. und 9. Jahrhundert* (Vienna, 2014).

Gersbach, K. A.: 'The Books and Personal Effects of Young Onofrio Panvinio, O.S.A., in Vat. Lat. 7205', *AAug*, 52 (1989), 51–76.

Gersbach, K. A.: 'Onofrio Panvinio's De comitiis imperatoriis and its Successive Revisions: Biographical Background and Manuscripts', *AAug*, 53 (1990), 409–52.

Gersbach, K. A.: 'Onofrio Panvinio and Cybo Family Pride in his Treatment of Innocent VIII and in the *XXVII pontificum maximorum elogia et imagines*', *AAug*, 54 (1991), 115–41.

Gersbach, K. A.: 'A History of Biblioteca Angelica Latin Manuscript 64: Onofrio Panvinio's "Antiquitatum Veronensium libri VIII" ', *AAug*, 55 (1992), 207–20.

Gersbach, K. A.: 'A Letter of Ambrogio of Verona, O.S.A.', *Augustiniana*, 42 (1992), 207–12.

Gersbach, K. A.: 'Onofrio Panvinio's Brother, Paolo, and his Role in the Posthumous Edition of the *De primatu Petri et Apostolicae Sedis potestate* and the Purchase of Onofrio's Manuscripts for the Vatican Library', *AAug*, 56 (1993), 241–64.

Gersbach, K. A.: 'Giuseppe Panfilo, OSA, Papal Sacristan and Bishop of Segni: Biography, Literary Activity, and Relationship to Onofrio Panvinio, OSA', *AAug*, 58 (1995), 45–83.

Gersbach, K. A.: 'Onofrio Panvinio, OSA, and his Florentine Correspondents Vincenzio Borghini, OSB, Pietro Vettori, Francesco de' Medici', *AAug*, 60 (1997), 207–80.

Giombi, S.: 'Lo studio umanistico dell'antichità cristiana nella riforma cattolica', *Rivista di storia e letteratura religiosa*, 28 (1992), 143–62.

Giordano, N.: 'Alessandro Farnese (con documenti inediti)', *Archivio storico siciliano*, ser. iii, 16 (1965–6), 191–227.

Girgensohn, D.: 'Berichte über Konklave und Papstwahl auf dem Konstanzer Konzil', *Annuarium historiae conciliorum*, 19 (1987), 351–91.

Godman, P.: *From Poliziano to Machiavelli: Florentine Humanism in the High Renaissance* (Princeton, NJ, 1998).

Godman, P.: *The Saint as Censor: Robert Bellarmine between Inquisition and Index* (Leiden, 2000).

Godman, P. and J. Brandt: *Weltliteratur auf dem Index: die geheimen Gutachten des Vatikans* (Berlin, 2001).

Goetz, H.-W.: *Das Geschichtsbild Ottos von Freising* (Cologne; Vienna, 1984).

Goez, W.: *Translatio imperii: ein Beitrag zur Geschichte des Geschichtsdenkens und der politischen Ideen im Mittelalter und in der frühen Neuzeit* (Tübingen, 1958).

Gotor, M.: 'Le vite di San Pio V dal 1572 al 1712 tra censura, agiografia e storia', in M. Guasco and A. Torre (eds), *Pio V nella società e nella politica del suo tempo* (Bologna, 2005), 207–49.

Grafinger, C. M.: *Die Ausleihe vatikanischer Handschriften und Druckwerke (1563–1700)* (Vatican City, 1993).

Grafinger, C. M.: *Die Ausleihe vatikanischer Handschriften und Druckwerke im 18. Jahrhundert*, 2 pts (Vatican City, 2002).

Grafinger, C. M.: 'Servizi al pubblico e personale', in *Storia della Biblioteca Apostolica Vaticana* (Vatican City, 2010–), ii, ed. M. Ceresa, 217–36.

Grafton, A.: *Joseph Scaliger: A Study in the History of Classical Scholarship*, 2 vols (Oxford, 1983–93).

Grafton, A.: *Forgers and Critics: Creativity and Duplicity in Western Scholarship* (Princeton, NJ, 1990).

Grafton, A.: Review of W. Stenhouse, *Reading Inscriptions*, *Sixteenth Century Journal*, 39 (2008), 911–13.

Grafton, A.: 'Church History in Early Modern Europe: Tradition and Innovation', in Van Liere et al., *Sacred History*, 3–26.

Grafton, A.: 'Past Belief: The Fall and Rise of Ecclesiastical History in Early Modern Europe', in P. Nord, K. Guenther, and M. Weiss (eds), *Formations of Belief: Historical Approaches to Religion and the Secular* (Princeton, NJ, 2019), 13–40.

Grauert, H.: 'Das Dekret Nikolaus II. von 1059', *Historisches Jahrbuch*, 1 (1880), 502–602.

Grauert, H.: Review of F. X. Kraus, *Über das Studium der Theologie sonst und jetzt*, *Historisches Jahrbuch*, 11 (1890), 816–17.

Gregorovius, F.: *Geschichte der Stadt Rom im Mittelalter*, 8 vols (Stuttgart, 1859–72).

Grendler, P. F.: *The Roman Inquisition and the Venetian Press, 1540–1605* (Princeton, NJ, 1977).

Grendler, P. F.: *The Universities of the Italian Renaissance* (Baltimore, MD, 2002).

Groll, T. (ed.): *Kardinal Otto Truchseß von Waldburg (1514–1573)* (Augsburg, 2015).

Grotefend, C. L.: 'Zur Literaturgeschichte', *Anzeiger für Kunde der deutschen Vorzeit*, n. s. 19 (1872), cols 4–9, 38–43.

Gryson, R.: *Répertoire général des auteurs ecclésiastiques latins de l'antiquité et du haut Moyen Âge* (Freiburg im Breisgau, 2007).

Guazzelli, G. A.: 'Cesare Baronio and the Roman Catholic Vision of the Early Church', in Van Liere et al., *Sacred History*, 52–71.

Guazzelli, G. A.: 'Baronio attraverso il *Martyrologium Romanum*', in Guazzelli et al., *Baronio*, 67–110.

Guazzelli, G. A.: 'Riflessioni conclusive', ibid. 503–16.

Guazzelli, G. A.: 'Roman Antiquities and Christian Archaeology', in P. M. Jones, B. Wisch, and S. Ditchfield (eds), *A Companion to Early Modern Rome, 1492–1692* (Leiden, 2019), 530–45.

Guazzelli, G. A., R. Michetti, and F. Scorza Barcellona (eds): *Cesare Baronio tra santità e scrittura storica* (Rome, 2012).

Guerrieri, G.: 'Il mecenatismo dei Farnesi', *Archivio storico per le provincie parmensi*, ser. iii, 6 (1941), 95–130; 7–8 (1942–3), 127–67; ser. iv, 1 (1945–8), 59–119.

Guerrini, R.: 'Plutarco e l'iconografia umanistica a Roma nel Cinquecento', in M. Fagiolo (ed.), *Roma e l'antico nell'arte e nella cultura del Cinquecento* (Rome, 1985), 87–108.

Gutiérrez, D.: 'Patres ac theologi augustiniani qui concilio Tridentino interfuerunt', *AAug*, 21 (1947–50), 55–177.

Gutiérrez, D.: 'Hieronymi Seripandi "Diarium de vita sua" (1513–1562)', *AAug*, 26 (1963), 5–193.

Gutiérrez, D.: 'Los estudios en la Orden agustiniana desde la edad media hasta la contemporánea', *AAug*, 33 (1970), 75–149.

Gutiérrez, D.: *The Augustinians from the Protestant Reformation to the Peace of Westphalia 1518–1648*, trans. J. J. Kelly (Villanova, PA, 1979).

Gutiérrez, D.: *The Augustinians in the Middle Ages 1357–1517*, with contributions by R. Arbesmann and A. Zumkeller, trans. T. Martin (Villanova, PA, 1983).

Gutiérrez, D.: *The Augustinians in the Middle Ages 1256–1356*, trans. A. J. Ennis (Villanova, PA, 1984).

Hack, A. T.: 'Papst wider Willen: zur Geschichte eines Motivs', *QFIAB*, 96 (2016), 3–34.

Häberlein, M.: *Die Fugger: Geschichte einer Augsburger Familie (1367–1650)* (Stuttgart, 2006).

Haefs, W. and Y.-G. Mix (eds): *Zensur im Jahrhundert der Aufklärung* (Göttingen, 2007).

Hägermann, D.: *Das Papsttum am Vorabend des Investiturstreits: Stephan IX. (1057–1058), Benedikt X. (1058) und Nikolaus II. (1058–1061)* (Stuttgart, 2008).

Hahn, A.: 'Das Hludowicianum: die Urkunde Ludwig des Frommen für die römische Kirche von 817', *Archiv für Diplomatik*, 21 (1975), 15–135.

Hardy, N. and D. Levitin (eds): *Confessionalisation and Erudition in Early Modern Europe: An Episode in the History of the Humanities* (Oxford, forthcoming).

Hartig, O.: 'Des Onuphrius Panvinius Sammlung von Papstbildnissen in der Bibliothek Johann Jakob Fuggers (Codd. lat. monac. 155–160)', *Historisches Jahrbuch*, 38 (1917), 284–314.

Hartig, O.: *Die Gründung der Münchener Hofbibliothek durch Albrecht V. und Johann Jakob Fugger* (Munich, 1917).

Hartmann, M.: *Humanismus und Kirchenkritik: Matthias Flacius Illyricus als Erforscher des Mittelalters* (Stuttgart, 2001).

Hasecker, J.: *Quellen zur päpstlichen Pressekontrolle in der Neuzeit (1487–1966)* (Paderborn, 2017).

Hasecker, J. and J. Schepers: *Römische Inquisition und Indexkongregation, Grundlagenforschung 1542–1700: Personen und Profile* (Paderborn, forthcoming).

Heid, S. (ed.): *Petrus und Paulus in Rom: eine interdisziplinäre Debatte* (Freiburg im Breisgau, 2011).

Heinzelmann, K.: *Die Farfenser Streitschriften: ein Beitrag zur Geschichte des Investiturstreites* (Strasbourg, 1904).

Herde, P.: 'Die Entwicklung der Papstwahl im dreizehnten Jahrhundert: Praxis und kanonistische Grundlagen', *Österreichisches Archiv für Kirchenrecht*, 32 (1981), 11–41.

Herklotz, I.: 'Historia sacra und mittelalterliche Kunst während der zweiten Hälfte des 16. Jahrhunderts in Rom', in R. De Maio et al. (eds), Baronio e l'arte (Sora, 1985), 21–74.

Herklotz, I.: Review of J.-L. Ferrary, Onofrio Panvinio, Wolfenbütteler Renaissance-Mitteilungen, 22 (1998), 19–22.

Herklotz, I.: Cassiano Dal Pozzo und die Archäologie des 17. Jahrhunderts (Munich, 1999).

Herklotz, I.: 'Christliche und klassische Archäologie im sechzehnten Jahrhundert', in D. Kuhn and H. Stahl (eds), Die Gegenwart des Altertums (Heidelberg, 2002), 291–307.

Herklotz, I.: 'Arnaldo Momigliano's "Ancient History and the Antiquarian": A Critical Review', in P. N. Miller (ed.), Momigliano and Antiquarianism: Foundations of the Modern Cultural Sciences (Toronto, 2007), 127–53.

Herklotz, I.: 'Alfonso Chacón e le gallerie dei ritratti nell'età della Controriforma', in P. Tosini (ed.), Arte e committenza nel Lazio nell'età di Cesare Baronio (Rome, 2009), 111–42.

Herklotz, I.: 'Basilica e edificio a pianta centrale: continuità ed esclusione nella storiografia architettonica all'epoca del Baronio', in L. Gulia (ed.), Baronio e le sue fonti (Sora, 2009), 549–78.

Herklotz, I.: 'Chi era Priscilla? Baronio e le ricerche sulla Roma sotterranea', in Guazzelli et al., Baronio, 425–44.

Herklotz, I.: 'Antike Denkmäler Roms in Streit der Konfessionen', in C. Stiegemann (ed.), Wunder Roms im Blick des Nordens von der Antike bis zur Gegenwart (Petersberg, 2017), 212–25.

Herre, P.: Papsttum und Papstwahl im Zeitalter Philipps II. (Leipzig, 1907).

Herzog, U.: 'Jacob Gretsers Leben und Werk', Literaturwissenschaftliches Jahrbuch, n. s. 11 (1970), 1–36.

Hillgarth, J. N.: 'The Image of Alexander VI and Cesare Borgia in the Sixteenth and Seventeenth Centuries', Journal of the Warburg and Courtauld Institutes, 59 (1996), 119–29.

Hinschius, P.: Das Kirchenrecht der Katholiken und Protestanten in Deutschland, 6 vols (Berlin, 1869–97).

Hirst, M.: 'The Artist in Rome, 1496–1501', in Making and Meaning: The Young Michelangelo (London, 1994), 13–81.

Holt, M. P.: 'Divisions within French Calvinism: Philippe Duplessis-Mornay and the Eucharist', in id. (ed.), Adaptations of Calvinism in Reformation Europe (Aldershot, 2007), 165–77.

Honegger Chiari, S.: 'L'edizione del 1584 dei "Commentarii" di Pio II e la duplice revisione di Francesco Bandini', Archivio storico italiano, 149 (1991), 585–612.

Horsch, N.: Ad astra gradus: Scala Santa und Sancta Sanctorum in Rom unter Sixtus V. (1585–1590) (Munich, 2014).

Hudon, W. V.: Marcello Cervini and Ecclesiastical Government in Tridentine Italy (DeKalb, IL, 1992).

Hülsen, C.: Le chiese di Roma nel medio evo (Florence, 1927).

Hurter H.: Nomenclator literarius theologiae catholicae, 3rd edn, 5 vols (Innsbruck, 1903–13).

Ianziti, G.: *Writing History in Renaissance Italy: Leonardo Bruni and the Uses of the Past* (Cambridge, MA, 2012).

Infelise, M.: *I libri proibiti da Gutenberg all'Encyclopédie*, revised edn (Rome; Bari, 2013).

Jansen, D. J.: *Jacopo Strada and Cultural Patronage at the Imperial Court: The Antique as Innovation*, 2 vols (Leiden, 2019).

Jasper, D.: *Das Papstwahldekret von 1059: Überlieferung und Textgestalt* (Sigmaringen, 1986).

Jasper, D.: Review of M. Stroll, *The Medieval Abbey of Farfa*, *Deutsches Archiv für Erforschung des Mittelalters*, 56 (2000), 366–7.

Jedin, H.: Review of P. Polman, *L'élément historique*, *Theologische Revue*, 8 (1933), cols 305–11.

Jedin, H.: *Girolamo Seripando: sein Leben und Denken im Geisteskampf des 16. Jahrhunderts*, 2 vols (Würzburg, 1937).

Jedin, H.: *Katholische Reformation oder Gegenreformation?* (Lucerne, 1946); partial English trans., 'Catholic Reformation or Counter-Reformation?', in D. M. Luebke (ed.), *The Counter-Reformation: The Essential Readings* (Oxford, 1999), 21–45.

Jedin, H.: *Papal Legate at the Council of Trent: Cardinal Seripando* (St Louis, MO; London, 1947).

Jedin, H.: *Das Konzil von Trient: ein Überblick über die Erforschung seiner Geschichte* (Rome, 1948).

Jedin, H.: *A History of the Council of Trent*, trans. E. Graf, 2 vols (no more publ.) (London, 1957–61).

Jedin, H.: 'Kirchengeschichte als Heilsgeschichte?', in id., *Kirche des Glaubens, Kirche der Geschichte*, 2 vols (Freiburg im Breisgau, 1966), i. 37–48.

Jedin, H.: *Kardinal Caesar Baronius: der Anfang der katholischen Kirchengeschichtsschreibung im 16. Jahrhundert* (Münster, 1978).

Jedin, H.: 'General Introduction to Church History', in H. Jedin and J. Dolan (eds), *History of the Church*, 10 vols (London, 1980–1), i. 1–56.

Jobst, C.: 'La basilica di San Pietro e il dibattito sui tipi edili: Onofrio Panvinio e Tiberio Alfarano', in G. Spagnesi (ed.), *L'architettura della Basilica di San Pietro* (Rome, 1997), 243–6.

Jong, J. L. de: *The Power and the Glorification: Papal Pretensions and the Art of Propaganda in the Fifteenth and Sixteenth Centuries* (University Park, PA, 2013).

Jostock, I.: *La censure négociée: le contrôle du livre a Genève, 1560–1625* (Geneva, 2007).

Kaufhold, H.: *Franciscus Peña und der Inquisitionsprozeß nach seiner 'Introductio seu Praxis Inquisitorum'* (Sankt Ottilien, 2014).

Kaufmann, T.: 'Confessionalization', in F. Jaeger and G. Dunphy (eds), *Encyclopedia of Early Modern History* (Leiden, 2016–), iii. 362–74.

Kehr, P. F.: 'Diplomatische Miszellen, iv: Die Scheden des Panvinius' (first publ. 1901), in id., *Papsturkunden in Italien: Reiseberichte zur Italia Pontificia*, 6 vols (Vatican City, 1977), iii. 1–26.

Kellenbenz, H.: 'Hans Jakob Fugger', in *Lebensbilder aus dem Bayerischen Schwaben* (Munich etc., 1952–), xii, ed. A. Layer, 48–104.

Kelley, D. R.: *Foundations of Modern Historical Scholarship: Language, Law, and History in the French Renaissance* (New York, 1970).

Kelly, J. N. D.: *The Oxford Dictionary of Popes* (Oxford, 1986).

Kess, A.: *Johann Sleidan and the Protestant Vision of History* (Aldershot, 2008).

Klapczynski, G.: *Katholischer Historismus? Zum historischen Denken in der deutschsprachigen Kirchengeschichte um 1900* (Stuttgart, 2013).

Kölzer, T.: 'Prolegomena', in id. (ed.), *Collectio canonum Regesto Farfensi inserta* (Vatican City, 1982), 1–123.

Koller, A.: 'The Definition of a New Ecclesiastical Policy by the Papal Curia after the Council of Trent and its Reception *in partibus*', in P. Tusor and M. Sanfilippo (eds), *Il papato e le chiese locali/The Papacy and the Local Churches* (Viterbo, 2014), 33–54.

Kottje, R. (ed.): *Kirchengeschichte heute: Geschichtswissenschaft oder Theologie?* (Trier, 1970).

Krause, H.-G.: *Das Papstwahldekret von 1059 und seine Rolle im Investiturstreit* (Rome, 1960).

Krause, H.-G.: 'Die Bedeutung der neuentdeckten handschriftlichen Überlieferungen des Papstwahldekrets von 1059', *Zeitschrift der Savigny-Stiftung für Rechtsgeschichte*, 107, *Kanonistische Abteilung*, 76 (1990), 89–134.

Ladner, G. B.: *Die Papstbildnisse des Altertums und des Mittelalters*, 3 vols (Vatican City, 1941–84).

Ladner, G. B.: 'I mosaici e gli affreschi ecclesiastico-politici nell'antico Palazzo Lateranense', in id., *Images and Ideas in the Middle Ages*, 2 vols (Rome, 1983), i. 347–66.

Laehr, G.: *Die Konstantinische Schenkung in der abendländischen Literatur des Mittelalters bis zur Mitte des 14. Jahrhunderts* (Berlin, 1926).

Lamping, A. J.: *Ulrichus Velenus (Oldřich Velenský) and his Treatise against the Papacy* (Leiden, 1976).

Lauer, P.: *Le Palais de Latran* (Paris, 1911).

Lavenia, V.: 'Peña, Francisco', in Prosperi, *Dizionario storico dell'Inquisizione*, iii. 1186–9.

Leuschner, E.: 'Otium und Virtus: Kontemplation als Tugendübung in der Stanza della Solitudine von Caprarola', in T. Weigel and J. Poeschke (eds), *Leitbild Tugend: die Virtus-Darstellungen in italienischen Kommunalpalästen und Fürstenresidenzen des 14. bis 16. Jahrhunderts* (Münster, 2013), 229–53.

Lezowski, M.: *L'Abrégé du monde: une histoire sociale de la bibliothèque Ambrosienne (v. 1590–v. 1660)* (Paris, 2015).

Litta, P.: *Famiglie celebri di Italia*, 184 fascs. (Milan, 1819–83).

Loffredo, F. and G. Vagenheim (eds): *Pirro Ligorio's Worlds: Antiquarianism, Classical Erudition and the Visual Arts in the Renaissance* (Leiden, 2019).

Lohse, B.: *Martin Luther's Theology*, trans. R. A. Harrisville (Edinburgh, 1999).

Lotz-Heumann, U.: 'Confessionalization', in A. Bamji, G. H. Janssen, and M. Laven (eds), *The Ashgate Research Companion to the Counter-Reformation* (Farnham, 2013), 33–53.

Loud, G. A.: Review of M. Stroll, *The Medieval Abbey of Farfa*, *English Historical Review*, 114 (1999), 940–1.

Luibhéid, C.: *The Council of Nicaea* (Galway, 1982).

Lurin, E.: 'Étienne Dupérac, graveur, peintre et architecte (vers 1535?–1604): un artiste-antiquaire entre l'Italie et la France' (doctoral thesis, Université Paris-Sorbonne, 2006).

Lurin, E.: 'Les restitutions de scènes antiques: Onofrio Panvinio iconographe et inventeur d'images', in M. Hochmann et al. (eds), *Programme et invention dans l'art de la Renaissance* (Paris, 2008), 153–73.

Lynn, K.: *Between Court and Confessional: The Politics of Spanish Inquisitors* (Cambridge, 2013).

Maas, K. D.: *The Reformation and Robert Barnes: History, Theology and Polemic in Early Modern England* (Woodbridge, 2010).

Maasen, W.: *Hans Jakob Fugger (1516–1575)*, ed. P. Ruf (Munich, 1922).

Maclean, I.: *Scholarship, Commerce, Religion: The Learned Book in the Age of Confessions, 1560–1630* (Cambridge, MA, 2012).

Märtl, C.: 'Papstgeschichtsschreibung im Quattrocento: vom "Liber pontificalis" zu Platinas "Liber de vita Christi ac omnium pontificum"', in U. Friedrich, L. Grenzmann, and F. Rexroth (eds), *Geschichtsentwürfe und Identitätsbildung am Übergang zur Neuzeit*, 2 vols (Berlin; Boston, 2018), ii. 242–56.

Maffei, S.: *Verona illustrata*, 4 vols (Verona, 1731–2).

Manfrè, G.: 'L'edizione bolognese della *Historia Bononiensis* di Carlo Sigonio', 2 pts, *Accademie e biblioteche d'Italia*, 61 (1993) no. 1, pp. 14–20, and 62 (1994) no. 2, pp. 16–35.

Marini, G.: *Degli archiatri pontifici*, 2 vols (Rome, 1784).

Masetti Zannini, G. L.: 'Biblioteche bolognesi a Roma', *L'archiginnasio*, 63–5 (1968–70), 489–511.

Mayer i Olivé, M.: 'El canon de los humanistas de su tiempo interesados en la epigrafía y las antigüedades clásicas según el criterio de Onofrio Panvinio', *Sylloge Epigraphica Barcinonensis*, 8 (2010), 29–65.

Mayer, T. F.: 'Il fallimento di una candidatura: il partito della riforma, Reginald Pole e il conclave di Giulio III', *Annali dell'Istituto storico italo-germanico in Trento/Jahrbuch des italienisch-deutschen historischen Instituts in Trient*, 21 (1995), 41–67.

Mayer, T. F.: *The Roman Inquisition: A Papal Bureaucracy and Its Laws in the Age of Galileo* (Philadelphia, PA, 2013).

Mazza, M.: 'La metodologia storica nella *Praefatio* degli *Annales ecclesiastici*', in Guazzelli et al., *Baronio*, 23–45.

McCarthy, T. J. H.: 'Introduction', in id. (ed.), *Chronicles of the Investiture Contest: Frutolf of Michelsberg and his Continuators* (Manchester, 2014), 1–83.

McCuaig, W.: 'Andreas Patricius, Carlo Sigonio, Onofrio Panvinio, and the Polish Nation of the University of Padua', *History of Universities*, 3 (1983), 87–100.

McCuaig, W.: *Carlo Sigonio: The Changing World of the Late Renaissance* (Princeton, NJ, 1989).

McCuaig, W.: 'The *Fasti Capitolini* and the Study of Roman Chronology in the Sixteenth Century', *Athenaeum*, 69 (1991), 141–59.

Meier, H. J.: 'Das Bildnis in der Reproduktionsgraphik des 16. Jahrhunderts', *Zeitschrift für Kunstgeschichte*, 58 (1995), 449–77.

Menke-Glückert, E.: *Die Geschichtsschreibung der Reformation und Gegenreformation* (Leipzig, 1912).

Mercati, A.: *Dall'Archivio Vaticano* (Vatican City, 1951).

Merkle, S.: 'Das Concilium Tridentinum der Görresgesellschaft', *Zeitschrift der Savigny-Stiftung für Rechtsgeschichte*, 33, Kanonistische Abteilung, 2 (1912), 345–60.

Miccoli, G.: 'Gregorio VII', in *Bibliotheca sanctorum*, 13 vols (Rome, 1961–70), vii, cols 294–379.

Miglio, M.: *Storiografia pontificia del Quattrocento* (Bologna, 1975).

Momigliano, A.: *The Classical Foundations of Modern Historiography* (Berkeley, CA, 1990).

Monfasani, J.: 'The First Call for Press Censorship: Niccolò Perotti, Giovanni Andrea Bussi, Antonio Moreto, and the Editing of Pliny's *Natural History*', *Renaissance Quarterly*, 41 (1988), 1–31.

Moroni, G.: 'Savelli, famiglia', in id., *Dizionario di erudizione storico-ecclesiastica*, 109 vols (Venice, 1840–79), lxi. 294–304.

Mouren, R.: 'La bibliothèque du palais Farnèse avant Fulvio Orsini', *Mélanges de l'Ecole française de Rome: Italie et Méditerranée*, 107 (1995), 7–14.

Mulsow, M.: *Die unanständige Gelehrtenrepublik: Wissen, Libertinage und Kommunikation in der Frühen Neuzeit* (Stuttgart, 2007).

Neel, C. L.: 'The Historical Work of Burchard of Ursberg, V: The Historian, the Emperor and the Pope', *Analecta Praemonstratensia*, 60 (1984), 224–55.

Nelles, P.: '*Historia magistra antiquitatis*: Cicero and Jesuit History Teaching', *Renaissance Studies*, 13 (1999), 130–72.

Nelles, P.: 'The Renaissance Ancient Library Tradition and Christian Antiquity', in R. De Smet (ed.), *Les humanistes et leur bibliothèque/Humanists and their Libraries* (Leuven, 2002), 159–73.

Nerini, F. M.: *De templo et coenobio Sanctorum Bonifacii et Alexii historica monumenta* (Rome, 1752).

Neumann, F.: *Geschichtsschreibung als Kunst: Famiano Strada S.I. (1572–1649) und die ars historica in Italien* (Berlin, 2013).

Noble, T. F. X.: *The Republic of St. Peter: The Birth of the Papal State, 680–825* (Philadelphia, PA, 1984).

Norelli, E.: 'L'autorità della Chiesa antica nelle Centurie di Magdeburgo e negli *Annales* del Baronio', in R. De Maio, L. Gulia, and A. Mazzacane (eds), *Baronio storico e la Controriforma* (Sora, 1982), 253–307.

Nothaft, C. P. E.: *Dating the Passion: The Life of Jesus and the Emergence of Scientific Chronology (200–1600)* (Leiden, 2012).

Occhipinti, C.: *Pirro Ligorio e la storia cristiana di Roma da Costantino all'Umanesimo* (Pisa, 2007).

O'Malley, J. W.: *Giles of Viterbo on Church and Reform: A Study in Renaissance Thought* (Leiden, 1968).

O'Malley, J. W.: *Trent and All That: Renaming Catholicism in the Early Modern Era* (Cambridge, MA, 2000).

Orbaan, J. A. F.: 'La Roma di Sisto V negli *Avvisi*', *Archivio della Società romana di storia patria*, 33 (1910), 277–312.

Orbaan, J. A. F. and G. J. Hoogewerff: *Bescheiden in Italië omtrent Nederlandsche kunstenaars en geleerden*, 3 vols (The Hague, 1911–17).

Orella y Unzué, J. L.: *Respuestas católicas a las Centurias de Magdeburgo (1559–1588)* (Madrid, 1976).

Orlandi, S., M. L. Caldelli, and G. L. Gregori: 'Forgeries and Fakes', in C. Bruun and J. Edmondson (eds), *The Oxford Handbook of Roman Epigraphy* (Oxford, 2015), 42–65.

Ott, M.: *Die Entdeckung des Altertums: der Umgang mit der römischen Vergangenheit Süddeutschlands im 16. Jahrhundert* (Kallmünz, 2002).

Paravicini Bagliani, A.: *Morte e elezione del papa: norme, riti e conflitti; il Medioevo* (Rome, 2013).

Parish, H. L.: *Monks, Miracles and Magic: Reformation Representations of the Medieval Church* (London, 2005).

Partridge, L. W.: 'Divinity and Dynasty at Caprarola: Perfect History in the Room of the Farnese Deeds', *Art Bulletin*, 60 (1978), 494–530.

Paschini, P.: 'Un cardinale editore: Marcello Cervini', in id., *Cinquecento romano e riforma cattolica* (Rome, 1958), 183–217.

Pastor, L. von: *Geschichte der Päpste seit dem Ausgang des Mittelalters*, 16 vols (Freiburg im Breisgau, 1886–1933); English trans., *The History of the Popes from the Close of the Middle Ages*, 40 vols (London, 1891–1953).

Patrizi, E.: *Silvio Antoniano*, 3 vols (Macerata, 2010).

Patrizi, E.: 'Del congiungere le gemme de' gentili con la sapientia de' Christiani': la biblioteca del cardinal Silvio Antoniano tra studia humanitatis e cultura ecclesiastica (Florence, 2011).

Pattenden, M.: 'The Conclaves of 1590 to 1592: An Electoral Crisis of the Early Modern Papacy?', *Sixteenth Century Journal*, 44 (2013), 391–410.

Pattenden, M.: *Electing the Pope in Early Modern Italy, 1450–1700* (Oxford, 2017).

Pattenden, M.: 'Antonio de Fuenmayor's Life of Pius V: A Pope in Early Modern Spanish Historiography', *Renaissance Studies*, 32 (2018), 183–200.

Pelc, M.: *Illustrium imagines: das Porträtbuch der Renaissance* (Leiden, 2002).

Pelissier, L.-G.: 'Catalogue des manuscrits de Panvini', *Revue des bibliothèques*, 1 (1891), 192–4.

Pennington, K.: Review of M. Stroll, *The Medieval Abbey of Farfa*, *American Historical Review*, 105 (2000), 262–3.

Perini, D. A.: *Onofrio Panvinio e le sue opere* (Rome, 1899).

Perini, D. A.: *Bibliographia Augustiniana*, 4 vols (Florence, 1929–38).

Pfleger, L.: 'Wilhelm Eisengrein, ein Gegner des Flacius Illyrius', *Historisches Jahrbuch*, 25 (1904), 774–92.

Piacentini, P.: 'Marcello Cervini (Marcello II): la Biblioteca Vaticana e la biblioteca personale', in *Storia della Biblioteca Apostolica Vaticana* (Vatican City, 2010–), ii, ed. M. Ceresa, 105–43.

Piergiovanni, P.: *Galleria Colonna in Roma: catalogo dei dipinti* (Rome, 2015).

Polman, P.: *L'élément historique dans la controverse religieuse du XVIe siècle* (Gembloux, 1932).

Prodi, P.: *Il sovrano pontefice. Un corpo e due anime: la monarchia papale nella prima età moderna*, new edn (Bologna, 2006); trans. S. Haskins, *The Papal*

Prince. *One Body and Two Souls: The Papal Monarchy in Early Modern Europe* (Cambridge, 1987).

Prodi, P.: 'La storia umana come luogo teologico', in id., *Profezia vs. utopia* (Bologna, 2013), 217–42.

Prosperi, A.: *Tra evangelismo e controriforma: G. M. Giberti, 1495–1543* (Rome, 1969).

Prosperi, A.: 'Varia fortuna di Pio II nel '500', in id., *Eresie e devozioni: la religione italiana in età moderna*, 3 vols (Rome, 2010), i. 247–60.

Prosperi, A. (ed.): *Dizionario storico dell'Inquisizione*, 4 vols (Pisa, 2010).

Pullapilly, C. K.: *Caesar Baronius: Counter-Reformation Historian* (Notre Dame, IN, 1975).

Quantin, J.-L.: 'Document, histoire, critique dans l'érudition ecclésiastique des temps modernes', *Recherches de science religieuse*, 92 (2004), 597–635.

Quantin, J.-L.: 'Érudition gallicane et censure romaine au tournant des XVIe e XVIIe siècles: Papire Masson devant l'Index', in G. Fragnito and A. Tallon (eds), *Hétérodoxies croisées: catholicismes pluriels entre France et Italie, XVIe–XVIIe siècles* (Rome, 2015), Web, http://books.openedition.org/efr/2849.

Quaranta, C.: *Marcello II Cervini (1501–1555): riforma della Chiesa, concilio, Inquisizione* (Bologna, 2010).

Rabe, H.: 'Aus Lucas Holstenius' Nachlass', *Centralblatt für Bibliothekswesen*, 12 (1895), 441–8.

Recio Veganzones, A.: 'Alfonso Chacón, O.P., hacia una primera Roma subterránea (1578–1599)', in M. D. Rincón González (ed.), *Doce calas en el Renacimiento y un epílogo* (Jaén, 2007), 349–95.

Redig de Campos, D.: 'Notizia critico-bibliografica intorno alla iconografia pontificia del Panvinio (1568)', *La rinascita*, 2 (1939), 794–800.

Redig de Campos, D.: 'Un ritratto ideale di Gregorio XII, attribuito a Girolamo Muziano, nuovamente collocato nella Pinacoteca vaticana', *Rivista d'arte*, ser. ii, 11 (1939), 166–75.

Rehberg, A.: 'Ein "Gegenpapst" wird kreiert: Fakten und Fiktionen in den Zeugenaussagen zur umstrittenen Wahl Urbans VI. (1378)', in H. Müller and B. Hotz (eds), *Gegenpäpste: ein unerwünschtes mittelalterliches Phänomen* (Vienna, 2012), 231–59.

Reinhard, W.: *Kleinere Schriften zur Rom-Forschung*, ed. B. Emich et al. (Rome, 2017), Web, http://dhi-roma.it/reinhard-kleinere-schriften.html.

Reinhardt, V.: *Rom: Kunst und Geschichte 1480–1650* (Freiburg im Breisgau, 1992).

Reinhardt, V.: 'Vergangenheit als Wahrheitsbeweis: Rom und die Geschichte im Konfessionellen Zeitalter', in L. Grenzmann et al. (eds), *Die Präsenz der Antike im Übergang vom Mittelalter zur Frühen Neuzeit* (Göttingen, 2004), 143–60.

Reinhardt, V.: *Der unheimliche Papst: Alexander VI. Borgia, 1431–1503* (Munich, 2005).

Reinhardt, V.: *Pontifex: die Geschichte der Päpste von Petrus bis Franziskus* (Munich, 2017).

Reumont, A. von: *Geschichte der Stadt Rom*, 3 vols in 4 pts (Berlin, 1867–70).

Reusch, F. H.: *Der Index der verbotenen Bücher: ein Beitrag zur Kirchen- und Literaturgeschichte*, 2 vols (Bonn, 1883–5).

Reuter, M.: 'Insignia quantum haberi potuerunt: papi, cardinali e nobili di tutta Italia in un armoriale commissionato da un umanista tedesco', *Strenna dei romanisti*, 71 (2010), 615–30.

Riebesell, C.: *Die Sammlung des Kardinal Alessandro Farnese: ein 'studio' für Künstler und Gelehrte* (Weinheim, 1989).

Rietbergen, P.: *Power and Religion in Baroque Rome: Barberini Cultural Politics* (Leiden, 2006).

Robertson, C.: *'Il Gran Cardinale': Alessandro Farnese, Patron of the Arts* (New Haven, CT, 1992).

Ronchini, A.: 'Onofrio Panvinio', *Atti e memorie delle RR. Deputazioni di storia patria per le provincie modenesi e parmensi*, ser. i, 6 (1872), 207–26.

Rozzo, U.: 'Erasmo espurgato dai *Dialogi piacevoli* di Nicolò Franco', in id., *La letteratura italiana negli 'Indici' del Cinquecento* (Udine, 2005), 245–310.

Rubach, B.: *'Ant. Lafreri formis Romae': der Verleger Antonio Lafreri und seine Druckgraphikproduktion* (Berlin, 2016).

Rurale, F.: 'Pio IV', in *Enciclopedia dei papi*, 3 vols (Rome, 2000), iii. 142–60.

Rusconi, R.: *Santo Padre: la santità del papa da San Pietro a Giovanni Paolo II* (Rome, 2010).

Russell, C.: 'Dangerous Friendships: Girolamo Seripando, Giulia Gonzaga and the Spirituali in Tridentine Italy', in François and Soen, *The Council of Trent*, i. 249–76.

Ruysschaert, J.: 'Recherche des deux bibliothèques romaines Maffei des XVᵉ et XVIᵉ siècles', *La bibliofilía*, 60 (1958), 306–55.

Saak, E. L.: *High Way to Heaven: The Augustinian Platform between Reform and Reformation 1292–1524* (Leiden, 2002).

Sachet, P.: 'Publishing for the Popes: The Cultural Policy of the Catholic Church towards Printing in Sixteenth-Century Rome' (doctoral thesis, Warburg Institute, University of London, 2015).

Sägmüller, J. B.: *Die Papstwahlbullen und das staatliche Recht der Exklusive* (Tübingen, 1892).

Sägmüller, J. B.: *Die Thätigkeit und Stellung der Cardinäle bis Papst Bonifaz VIII.* (Freiburg im Breisgau, 1896).

Sägmüller, J. B.: 'Ein angebliches Dekret Pius' IV. über die Designation des Nachfolgers durch den Papst', *Archiv für katholisches Kirchenrecht*, 75 (1896), 413–29.

Salmon, P.: *Les manuscrits liturgiques latins de la Bibliothèque Vaticane*, 5 vols (Vatican City, 1968–72).

Savelli, R.: 'The Censoring of Law Books', in G. Fragnito (ed.), *Church, Censorship and Culture in Early Modern Italy* (Cambridge, 2001), 223–53.

Savelli, R.: *Censori e giuristi: storie di libri, di idee e di costumi (secoli XVI–XVII)* (Milan, 2011).

Sawilla, J. M.: *Antiquarianismus, Hagiographie und Historie im 17. Jahrhundert: zum Werk der Bollandisten* (Tübingen, 2009).

Schatz, K.: *Papal Primacy: From Its Origins to the Present*, trans. J. Otto and L. M. Maloney (Collegeville, MN, 1996).

Schäufele, W.-F.: 'Theologie und Historie: zur Interferenz zweier Wissensgebiete in Reformationszeit und konfessionellem Zeitalter', in W.-F. Schäufele and I. Dingel (eds), *Kommunikation und Transfer im Christentum der Frühen Neuzeit* (Mainz, 2007), 129–56.

Scheffer-Boichorst, P.: *Die Neuordnung der Papstwahl durch Nikolaus II.* (Strasbourg, 1879).

Scheible, H.: 'Der Catalogus testium veritatis: Flacius als Schüler Melanchthons', in id., *Aufsätze zu Melanchthon* (Tübingen, 2010), 415–30.

Schieffer, R.: 'Rechtstexte des Reformpapsttums und ihre zeitgenössische Resonanz', in H. Mordek (ed.), *Überlieferung und Geltung normativer Texte des frühen und hohen Mittelalters* (Sigmaringen, 1986), 51–69.

Schirmer, E.: *Die Persönlichkeit Kaiser Heinrichs IV. im Urteil der deutschen Geschichtschreibung* (Jena, 1931).

Schludi, U.: *Die Entstehung des Kardinalkollegiums: Funktion, Selbstverständnis und Entwicklungsstufen* (Ostfildern, 2014).

Schmale, F.-J.: *Funktion und Formen mittelalterlicher Geschichtsschreibung* (Darmstadt, 1985).

Schmid, A.: 'Die historische Methode des Johannes Aventinus', *Blätter für deutsche Landesgeschichte*, 113 (1977), 338–95.

Schmid, J.: Review of J. Janssen, *Geschichte des deutschen Volkes*, *Historisches Jahrbuch*, 17 (1896), 73–100.

Schmidinger, H.: 'Das Papstbild in der Geschichtsschreibung des späteren Mittelalters', *Römische historische Mitteilungen*, 1 (1956/57), 106–29.

Scholz, S.: *Politik, Selbstverständnis, Selbstdarstellung: die Päpste in karolingischer und ottonischer Zeit* (Stuttgart, 2006).

Schreiner, S. E.: *Are you Alone Wise? The Search for Certainty in the Early Modern Era* (Oxford, 2011).

Schreurs, A.: *Antikenbild und Kunstanschauungen des neapolitanischen Malers, Architekten und Antiquars Pirro Ligorio (1513–1583)* (Cologne, 2000).

Schröckh, J. M.: *Christliche Kirchengeschichte*, 45 pts (Frankfurt; Leipzig, 1768–1812).

Schuster, I.: *L'imperiale abbazia di Farfa* (Rome, 1921).

Schwedt, H. H.: *Die Anfänge der römischen Inquisition: Kardinäle und Konsultoren 1542–1600* (Freiburg im Breisgau, 2013).

Schwedt, H. H.: *Die römische Inquisition: Kardinäle und Konsultoren 1601 bis 1700* (Freiburg im Breisgau, 2017).

Seifert, A.: *Der Rückzug der biblischen Prophetie von der neueren Geschichte* (Cologne, 1990).

Serrai, A.: *La biblioteca di Lucas Holstenius* (Udine, 2000).

Setton, K. M.: *The Papacy and the Levant (1204–1571)*, 4 vols (Philadelphia, PA, 1976–84).

Setz, W.: *Lorenzo Vallas Schrift gegen die Konstantinische Schenkung: De falsa credita et ementita Constantini donatione* (Tübingen, 1975).

Sickel, T.: *Zur Geschichte des Concils von Trient* (Vienna, 1872).

Sickel, T.: *Das Privilegium Otto I. für die römische Kirche vom Jahre 962* (Innsbruck, 1883).

Solfaroli Camillocci, D.: 'Dévoiler le Mal dans l'histoire: les recueils de vies des papes dans la Genève de Calvin', in F. Alazard and F. La Brasca (eds), *La papauté à la Renaissance* (Paris, 2007), 511–32.

Sommar, M. E.: *The Correctores Romani: Gratian's* Decretum *and the Counter-Reformation Humanists* (Berlin, 2009).

Souchon, M.: *Die Papstwahlen von Bonifaz VIII. bis Urban VI. und die Entstehung des Schismas 1378* (Braunschweig, 1888).

Souchon, M.: *Die Papstwahlen in der Zeit des großen Schismas*, 2 vols (Braunschweig, 1898–9).

Spagnolo, A.: 'Le scuole accolitali di grammatica e di musica in Verona', *Atti e memorie dell'Accademia d'agricoltura, scienze, lettere, arti e commercio di Verona*, ser. iv, 5 (1904) no. 1, pp. 97–330.

Staubach, N.: '"Honor Dei" oder "Bapsts Gespreng"? Die Reorganisation des Papstzeremoniells in der Renaissance', in id. (ed.), *Rom und das Reich vor der Reformation* (Frankfurt am Main, 2004), 91–136.

Stenhouse, W.: *Reading Inscriptions and Writing Ancient History: Historical Scholarship in the Late Renaissance* (London, 2005).

Stenhouse, W.: 'Panvinio and *descriptio*: Renditions of History and Antiquity in the Late Renaissance', *Papers of the British School at Rome*, 80 (2012), 233–56.

Stroll, M.: *The Medieval Abbey of Farfa: Target of Papal and Imperial Ambitions* (Leiden, 1997).

Stroll, M.: *Popes and Antipopes: The Politics of Eleventh Century Church Reform* (Leiden, 2012).

Stürner, W.: 'Das Papstwahldekret von 1059 und seine Verfälschung: Gedanken zu einem neuen Buch', in *Fälschungen im Mittelalter*, 6 vols (Hannover, 1988–90), ii. 157–90.

Šusta, J.: *Die römische Kurie und das Konzil von Trient*, 4 vols (Vienna, 1904–14).

Tacchella, L.: *Il processo agli eretici veronesi nel 1550: Sant'Ignazio di Loyola e Luigi Lippomano (carteggio)* (Brescia, 1979).

Tagliaferri, A.: *L'economia veronese secondo gli estimi dal 1409 al 1635* (Milan, 1966).

Tallon, A.: 'Les conclaves dans l'historiographie de la Contre-Réforme', in Firpo, *Nunc alia tempora*, 25–46.

Tellechea Idígoras, J. I.: 'La mesa de Felipe II', *Ciudad de Dios*, 215 (2002), 181–215, 605–39.

Thier, A.: *Hierarchie und Autonomie: Regelungstraditionen der Bischofsbestellung in der Geschichte des kirchlichen Wahlrechts bis 1140* (Frankfurt am Main, 2011).

Thompson, M.: 'Luther on God and History', in R. Kolb, I. Dingel, and L. Batka (eds), *The Oxford Handbook of Martin Luther's Theology* (Oxford, 2014), 127–42.

Thumser, M.: 'Die Frangipane: Abriß der Geschichte einer Adelsfamilie im hochmittelalterlichen Rom', *QFIAB*, 71 (1991), 106–63.

Tillmann, H.: 'Ricerche sull'origine dei membri del Collegio Cardinalizio nel XII secolo (II.2)', *Rivista di storia della Chiesa in Italia*, 29 (1975), 363–402.

Tomasi Velli, S.: 'Gli antiquari intorno al circo romano: riscoperta di una tipologia monumentale antica', *Annali della Scuola Normale Superiore di Pisa, Classe di lettere e filosofia*, ser. iii, 20 (1990) no. 1, pp. 61–168.

Tortarolo, E.: 'Zensur als Institution und Praxis im Europa der Frühen Neuzeit: ein Überblick', in H. Zedelmaier and M. Mulsow (eds), *Die Praktiken der Gelehrsamkeit in der Frühen Neuzeit* (Tübingen, 2001), 277–94.

Tortarolo, E.: *The Invention of Free Press: Writers and Censorship in Eighteenth Century Europe* (Dordrecht, 2016).

Tschudi, V. P.: *Baroque Antiquity: Archaeological Imagination in Early Modern Europe* (Cambridge, 2017).

Tutino, S.: *Empire of Souls: Robert Bellarmine and the Christian Commonwealth* (Oxford, 2010).

Tutino, S.: '"For the Sake of the Truth of History and of the Catholic Doctrines": History, Documents and Dogma in Cesare Baronio's *Annales Ecclesiastici*', *Journal of Early Modern History*, 17 (2013), 125–59.

Tutino, S.: 'A Spanish Canonist in Rome: Notes on the Career of Francisco Peña', *California Italian Studies*, 5 (2014) no. 1, Web, https://escholarship.org/uc/item/6jz907xp.

Vagenheim, G.: 'La critique épigraphique aus XVIᵉ siècle: Ottavio Pantagato, Paolo Manuzio, Onofrio Panvinio, Antonio Agustín et Pirro Ligorio: à propos des tribus romaines', *Aevum*, 86 (2012), 949–68.

Valente, M.: 'The Works of Bodin under the Lens of Roman Theologians and Inquisitors', in H. A. Lloyd (ed.), *The Reception of Bodin* (Leiden, 2013), 219–35.

Van Liere, K., S. Ditchfield, and H. Louthan (eds): *Sacred History: Uses of the Christian Past in the Renaissance World* (Oxford, 2012).

Vianello, C.: 'Introduzione', in *Edizione nazionale del carteggio di L. A. Muratori* (Florence, 1975–), iii, ed. ead., 1–12.

Villalon, L. J. A.: 'San Diego de Alcalá and the Politics of Saint-Making in Counter-Reformation Europe', *Catholic Historical Review*, 83 (1997), 691–715.

Visceglia, M. A.: 'Factions in the Sacred College in the Sixteenth and Seventeenth Centuries', in M. A. Visceglia and G. Signorotto (eds), *Court and Politics in Papal Rome, 1492-1700* (Cambridge, 2002), 99–131.

Visceglia, M. A.: *Morte e elezione del papa: norme, riti e conflitti; l'età moderna* (Rome, 2013).

Voci, A. M.: 'Giovanni I d'Angiò e l'inizio del grande scisma d'Occidente', *QFIAB*, 75 (1995), 178–255.

Völkel, M.: *Die Wahrheit zeigt viele Gesichter: der Historiker, Sammler und Satiriker Paolo Giovio (1486-1552) und sein Porträt Roms in der Hochrenaissance* (Basel, 1999).

Völkel, M.: 'Caesar Baronius in Deutschland im 17. Jahrhundert', in Firpo, *Nunc alia tempora*, 517–43.

Wassilowsky, G.: *Die Konklavereform Gregors XV. (1621/22): Wertekonflikte, symbolische Inszenierung und Verfahrenswandel im posttridentinischen Papsttum* (Stuttgart, 2010).

Wassilowsky, G.: 'Posttridentische Reform und päpstliche Zentralisierung: zur Rolle der Konzilskongregation', in A. Merkt, G. Wassilowsky, and G. Wurst (eds), *Reformen in der Kirche: historische Perspektiven* (Freiburg im Breisgau, 2014), 138–57.

Weber, C.: *Senatus Divinus: verborgene Strukturen im Kardinalskollegium der frühen Neuzeit (1500-1800)* (Frankfurt am Main, 1996).

Wesjohann, A.: *Mendikantische Gründungserzählungen im 13. und 14. Jahrhundert* (Berlin, 2012).

Wickersham, J. K.: *Rituals of Prosecution: The Roman Inquisition and the Prosecution of Philo-Protestants in Sixteenth-Century Italy* (Toronto, 2012).

Wirbelauer, E.: *Zwei Päpste in Rom: der Konflikt zwischen Laurentius und Symmachus (498–514)* (Munich, 1993).

Zaccaria, Francesco Antonio: *Storia polemica delle proibizioni de' libri* (Rome, 1777).

Zanolli Gemi, N.: *Sant'Eufemia: storia di una chiesa e del suo convento a Verona* (Verona, 1991).

Zeillinger, K.: 'Otto III. und die Konstantinische Schenkung: ein Beitrag zur Interpretation des Diploms Kaiser Ottos III. für Papst Silvester II. (DO III. 389)', in *Fälschungen im Mittelalter*, 6 vols (Hannover, 1988–90), ii. 509–36.

Zen, S.: *Baronio storico: Controriforma e crisi del metodo umanistico* (Naples, 1994).

Zen, S.: 'Cesare Baronio sulla Donazione di Costantino tra critica storica e autocensura', *Annali della Scuola Normale Superiore di Pisa, Classe di lettere e filosofia*, ser. 5, 2 (2010) no. 1, pp. 179–219.

Zimmermann, H.: *Ecclesia als Objekt der Historiographie: Studien zur Kirchengeschichtsschreibung im Mittelalter und in der Frühen Neuzeit* (Vienna, 1960).

Zimmermann, H.: 'Parteiungen und Papstwahlen in Rom zur Zeit Kaisers Ottos des Großen', in id. (ed.), *Otto der Große* (Darmstadt, 1976), 325–414.

Zimmermann, H.: 'Von der Faszination der Papstgeschichte besonders bei Protestanten: Gregor VII. und J. F. Gaab', in W. Hartmann and K. Herbers (eds), *Die Faszination der Papstgeschichte* (Cologne, 2008), 11–27.

Zimmermann, T. C. P.: *Paolo Giovio: The Historian and the Crisis of Sixteenth-Century Italy* (Princeton, NJ, 1995).

Zimmermann, T. C. P.: 'Paolo Giovio and the Rhetoric of Individuality', in T. F. Mayer and D. R. Woolf (eds), *The Rhetorics of Life-Writing in Early Modern Europe* (Ann Arbor, MI, 1995), 39–62.

Zimmermann, T. C. P.: 'Guicciardini, Giovio, and the Character of Clement VII', in K. Gouwens and S. E. Reiss (eds), *The Pontificate of Clement VII: History, Politics, Culture* (Aldershot, 2005), 19–27.

Zwierlein, C.: 'Fuggerzeitungen als Ergebnis von italienisch-deutschem Kulturtransfer 1552–1570', *QFIAB*, 90 (2010), 169–224.

Index